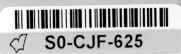

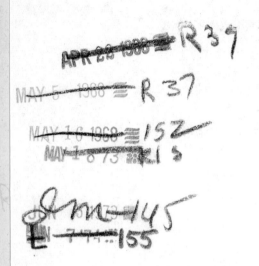

PORTRAIT OF
A CHINESE LADY
AND CERTAIN OF HER CONTEMPORARIES

By permission of T. Butler, Esq., F.R.G.S.

The Covered Way, Summer Palace, Peking

PORTRAIT OF A CHINESE LADY

AND CERTAIN OF HER CONTEMPORARIES

BY

LADY HOSIE

AUTHOR OF "TWO GENTLEMEN OF CHINA"

ILLUSTRATED

謝福芸

WILLIAM MORROW AND COMPANY
NEW YORK, 1930

PRINTED IN THE U. S. A.
BY NATIONAL PROCESS CO.

FOREWORD

My dear Li Cheng—Encourager of Sincerity,

Is it indeed five years since I wrote a book mainly about your family, with a Letter to you as a Foreword? It is your own fault that here is a second come knocking at your door. Do you remember the call we paid together, you and I, on Mrs. Sung that August day at Peitaiho on the yellow Gulf of Chihli? As we came away, you said, "Why do you not write another book about Chinese people?" I said, "How can I? I know so very little, and what I know I have already written down." You reasoned amiably with me, and said, "Oh well, it was right enough, that first book: but now you should write about us." "About us!" I echoed: "What can you mean by that?" "In the *Two Gentlemen of China*, you wrote about my father and his friends, the generation that was passing: and it was very commendable of you to write of the Elders. But now write about us who are the Chinese of to-day. Surely we are interesting!"

Thus you urged me: and undoubtedly I felt flattered that you could and did thus trust me. "But," I objected, "I have already written about yourself, Li Cheng. If I write any more about you, how conceited you will become!" You laughed. "It is obvious whom you must paint next," you answered; "you must write about our new Chinese ladies. Are they not very charming and very much alive? Take Mrs. Sung as your heroine: you know her well. Write about her and all the people who are making China so different from the past."

Here, then, is the book you commanded of me. It has taken two years to mature, and yet I am not satisfied. While I have been writing, my ideas of China have constantly been changing. As I have studied your lives, China has been teaching me many things. There is that grand word *li*, for instance—so short on Chinese lips, *lee*—over the translation of which Western scholars have disputed since first they sank into the seas of Chinese literature. The Reverence that leads to Good Manners, which it connotes, ought it not to enter into our thoughts as nations, when we look at each other? Perhaps the Apostle was meaning *li*, when he wrote that each should esteem other better than himself. What do you say, Li Cheng?

There is, moreover, this dream of friendship and co-operation between the nations, which stirs in hearts East and West; especially since an unforgettable War showed us of the Occident the anguished cost of national jealousies. You and I cannot contribute much to further the dream. Yet the sharing of a cup of tea, a joke, a walk on a seashore may make as warm and lasting a Pact of Peace as any signed by statesmen. A pinch of dried brown leaves, brought from your own hill-sides: a porcelain cup, whose fabrication we learned from your forbears—and friendship is cemented as firmly as by the most solemn League and Covenant.

Sometimes small things usher in the mighty. It may be that the great solutions of inter-racial problems will come of themselves—as is the manner of great things. In any case, incontrovertible bases always remain for our mutual compassion. Laughter and tears, pity and terror, family affections and friendship: such make the lot of our common humanity. Finally and perforce, all need physical sustenance. Then let us sit and talk together sometimes; and learn understanding through the creatures of sense and matter, of food and drink. It is when the Word becomes flesh that eyes of flesh can perceive its Illumination.

This book is supposed to be more particularly about China's women. Yet how shall we divide the sexes like that? Impossible to do it. Women can only be tender and generous where men are valiant and gentle.

Once more, then, I sign myself with the lovely name given me by your father. Many times have I used it in letters to you during these twenty years of our correspondence,

Your Sister,

FU YÜN—HAPPY GARDENER.

DOROTHEA HOSIE.

OXFORD, 1929.

CONTENTS

CONTENTS

AUTHOR'S ACKNOWLEDGMENT

THE author's thanks are due to the Editors and Proprietors of the *Contemporary Review*, *Daily Express*, *Evening News*, *The Observer*, and the *Windsor Magazine*, for permission to incorporate various incidents into this book; and to the following for the use of photographs: Thomas Butler, Esq., F.R.G.S.; Mrs. Calhoun, formerly of the American Legation, Peking; Camera Craft Co., Peking; Rev. A. Shorrock; G. V. Kitson, Esq., H.B.M. Consular Service, China; the *Windsor Magazine*; and the Rockefeller Foundation.

ILLUSTRATIONS

POEM BY THE LADY PAN

Translated from the Chinese for his Daughter, the Author of this Book, by W. E. Soothill, Professor of Chinese, Oxford University

NEEDLE AND THREAD

Forg'd of the pure spirit of steel from autumn's ore,[1]
Of form fine and subtle, straight and sharp,
By nature piercing and threading through all,
Uniting things divided into one :

Only by order'd steps do thread and needle
Prove their unlimited scope and power,
Backward, forward, around, amending flaws—
Till all is perfect as the silky floss of a lamb.

What peck or bushel can measure up their harvest?
Carved in stone, they should stand in the Hall of Fame.

1 *Autumn is under the rule of the metal element, as Spring is under wood, Summer fire, and Winter water.*

DRAMATIS PERSONAE

The Lady : Mrs. Sung of Shanghai.

Her family: Mr. Sung; and her two children Yün-Yün, a girl of five, and Nieh-Nieh, a boy of two, *i.e.* Little Cloud and Strong-as-a-Rock.

Miss Wu, a tutor in a Women's College.

Three Chinese gentlemen of intellect :

A director of a railway.

A professor of logic.

A gold medallist in geology.

Miss Way, the headmistress of a Girls' School, a Chinese.

Miss Scented Blossom Lo, her colleague, the daughter of a former Manchu Governor of Shansi.

Kung Li Cheng, scion of a scholarly stock, his wife and five small boys. His name means " Encourager of Sincerity." His wife's name, Shu Ying, means " Virtuous and Brave."

Others :

An English Viscount.

His wife.

Several missionaries, American, English and French.

A Doctor or Two.

A Chinese General and his son.

A Manchu Princess.

Nuns, Buddhist and Catholic.

Soldiers, rickshawmen, servants, amahs, lepers, bandits, etc.

Time : China To-day.

Scene : Shanghai, the Yangtsze, Nanking, Hangchow : Wenchow, a small Southern port : Peking, Tientsin, Peitaiho : Moukden and Manchuria.

CHAPTER I MOTHER CHINA

THE river steamer, with her comfortable breadth of beam and her white awnings, began to move her paddles, duck-like. Slowly she drew away from her sisters tied to the noisy dock. Away from the Shanghai Bund, out into the current of the Huangpu she turned. Higher up lay the craft of many nations. On the Pootung side a Soviet ship, sorely in need of a coat of paint, swung at anchor and, scorning ostracism, fluttered flags from stern to bow in remembrance of one of the recurrent Soviet fête days. An Italian gunboat, at the French Bund opposite, was dressing ship for some Italian occasion. British merchantmen were hasting to deliver cargo. The morning sun came out and shone on a curious hulk amid-stream, and glinted on the yellow hair of its crew.

" That is the submarine cable boat," said the First Officer, pausing for a minute beside me. " The Danes run the cables on this coast, and very efficiently, too."

A diminutive steamer came fussing to pass us.

" That is from Wenchow," said he, " a port where there are few white people, the real China, 300 miles or so south of Ningpo. They make oiled umbrellas there—kittysols, we call them. I 've been on that run a few times."

I smiled at him.

" I was born in Ningpo and bred in Wenchow," I told him. " Like Brer Rabbit in the briar-bush, if you threw me on board that ship I should feel at home, from the smell of the garlic and frying pork in the galley to the kind fat steward who had sweet potatoes cooked for me every meal because I once said I liked them. I could tell you the ship's cargo. There are baskets and baskets of big oranges, a trifle bitter in flavour and much prized for this by gourmets. Very good for fevers, they are supposed to be, and they sell for fabulous prices in Manchuria, I can tell you. Personally I prefer the small Mandarin oranges which the urchins on the lower deck will be peeling."

"There will also be vast quantities of succulent carrots of enormous size for the Shanghai market," he said.

"Yes, and other strange flat, wide baskets," I chorussed, "from which comes a perpetual twittering. Baby chicks. Their owner squats by, watching over their nurture and watering. If you speak politely to him, he will be delighted to show you the pretty balls of yellow fluff."

I looked longingly after the homely coasting vessel, picking its way amongst the leviathans like a small and unassuming hen, finding its living contentedly on the trifles disdained by those mighty devourers of coal and oil. A wave of homesickness took me—homesickness for the sweet countryside of Southern China. It takes a Kiangsu or a Chekiang man in Peking sometimes: till he rushes out and buys an oleander for his veranda, or a belated pumelo or a bundle of bamboo shoots for his next dinner—poor in quality and dear in price; but for a short space they take him back home.

With my mind's eye, as the First Officer and I looked, I saw the coolie swinging down from the hills with two flat baskets of cheeping chickens, one at each end of a pole over his shoulder. Newly hatched they are, from oven-incubators in some farmstead. Through the young spring rice, tenderly green and just planted out, his feet have come pattering, as he half runs, half walks on the narrow winding ways. Bamboo groves have waved and whispered above his head. Every now and again he has stopped to dip the entire basket, gingerly, carefully, into the pool of a shallow sun-warmed stream, wetting the feet of his nurselings. Gently he has uncovered them, lifting the basket-lid to watch that they do not harm each other as they weakly scramble and climb about in the shock of this experience, before they take their first hesitating sip of water with soft unaccustomed beaks.

The river steamer turned her nose and floated easily down the broad waters of the Huangpu. The First Officer passed on to his duties. The cupolas and domes of Shanghai's banks and newspaper offices, the façades of her magnificent palaces of commerce faded into the distance. They looked like pieces of London or Berlin, New York or Paris, come to rest—a stately flock of egrets on that low-lying marshy portion of Chinese soil. But I scarcely saw them. I was a girl again, and down in Wenchow, from which had come that steamer of no account. I was up amongst the homesteads whence those baskets of spring chickens had come: away from Wenchow city, up into the country by river-junk and then by foot and sedan-chair, to the quiet hills which would soon be flaming with azaleas from their summits to the crystal streams at their feet. I was a girl filling my arms with the delicate flowers. My father and mother were ahead, walking under the trees; happy with their Chinese friends and helpers, men who had faced much tribulation and to whom such company in such a place was delightful. I was nibbling doubtfully at a petal, at the insistence of a chair-bearer who assured me that an occasional azalea flower added flavour to the finest teas. Presently the chair-bearers had begun to call to each other, while they sought the best boughs of flowers for me, as is their engaging way with their foreign mistresses. Chattering, laughing at their own jokes, they were enjoying life while they could, simple hard-working bearers of many burdens. Then I discovered that one of them was addressing himself to me.

"Ku-nyie," he was reiterating, "Honoured young mistress!"

"What is it?" I queried, dimly aware that the word "pretty" had been flying between them, but connecting it with the azaleas.

"We were just chatting together, our words floating like duck-weed in a pond. But Ah Loa there, my mate, said he would be surprised if some of you foreigners did not think each other good-to-behold, pretty. He persists that this may be so. Will you think me lacking in correct manners if I ask you?"

I laughed.

"Some of us are pretty, we think: and others are not. Why? Don't you Chinese think any of us strangers from over the sea good-to-behold?"

Compassion was written on his honey-yellow face. He felt compunction at telling me the truth as he saw it.

"Well," he stammered, "not really pretty," shaking his head. "Very good and kind, as we know. But, then, nobody can help their looks, can they?"

"What is the matter with us, do you think?" I tormented him.

"Ah, yah!" he puzzled. There was so much wrong, he hardly knew how to begin. "To begin with, one rarely sees a foreign lady with a beautiful round moon face, as we call it: now does one? Your hair and eyes are every different shade of colour, rarely coal-black as eyes and hair ought to be. Also your noses are so big: they stand out so far from your faces. But do, pray, forgive me for putting things so plainly: still, you certainly asked me for the truth, did you not?" He was dismayed.

Mischief took me. The man must be taught a lesson.

"You encourage me to be bold also," I said with mock earnestness. "I too have often wondered: do any of you Chinese think each other pretty?"

He brightened. "Some of us are, and some of us——" he began. Then he saw the point and went into a shout of laughter that echoed across the valley and back. "I understand," he ended: and in every village we stopped at, he retailed this conversation to the assembled farmers, ending, "So it is possible, you will now perceive, that some of the foreigners may even be good-to-behold in their own strange way!"

A chair scraped behind me on the deck and I was brought back to the Huangpu and the receding stateliness of the Shanghai Bund. I realized that I was leaning over the deck smiling to myself, stupidly unconscious of all around me. I looked down and met the unwinking gaze of an old Chinese farmer, a passenger. He had come into the bows beneath our deck, was leaning against a capstan and was contemplating me. He was puffing leisurely at his slender long reed of a pipe with its thimble-bowl of tobacco, and, like myself, he was ruminating—on my strange looks, probably, thought I with a flicker of amusement. A large sea-going junk swished past us, driving before the wind: the crew, Cantonese or

Ningpoese no doubt—excellent mariners—keen and alert, hardly glancing at us as they swept by. The sun came full out and shone on the miracle of its huge plaited sail. The dirty Huangpu was transfigured. From a brown flood, turgid with earth and silt, it changed to the fretted bronze shield of a Greek warrior as a little wind lifted its surface waters. For centuries China has stood guarding her heart with this vast expanse of the Yellow Sea, her back to her encircling Great Wall. And behold, it was but a shield of water and over the sea-way have come the children of the silver West. Some have come, purely adventuring, greedy to capture, careless of hurting that heart. Others, a number which grows every generation as is only right, have sought to gather of its riches, yet bringing withal a charity with them in their own hearts. These, when the time has come for them to return to the West, have gone away sorrowful, regretting that they leave behind friends, though of another race. Each side has learned to love the bonds of a common humanity, and to respect the other while they have made mutual efforts and shared mutual interests.

Others have started their infancy under a corner of that shield. The first arms in which they lay have been Chinese ; the first words their lips have uttered have been the short, expressive, easy syllables of Chinese speech. When caught in some childish wrongdoing, they have fled to bury their remorse on the bosom of some largely forgiving Chinese amah. Crumpling their ears against her heart, they have listened to and been comforted by its steady beating.

While I was still dreaming, lo, a little old Chinese woman came and joined the farmer at the capstan : evidently his wife. She smiled up at me and nodded her head a number of times in greeting, and I nodded back. I do believe she would have taken me to her heart then and there, if I had wanted to lay my head there—though she had never seen me before. Pathetic to think that there are children in the world who have not pressed a face against a Chinese amah's tunic ; or watched her peel a delicious clean section of sugar-cane, that they might dig their milk-teeth into it. She would caress those back to the right path who go astray ; not scold them—not when they were very young.

I stayed and thought upon my amah. When Fate takes me to the British Museum, I always visit the corner where Demeter, the Earth Mother, sits, with her ample shoulders draped, and her welcoming knees. And my heart goes back to the shoulders and knees of the amah who loved me so innocently. What do I not owe her? Down there in Wenchow, when I was five, my amah in her blue cotton trousers and her blue cotton tunic once came and sat beside me on the floor of the dining-room, where I had a cave in the hollow of the sideboard. She took me on to her thighs and tucked my feet between her knees.

" Little Precious," she whispered into my ear, brushing my forehead with her lips, which is a Chinese kiss. " It seems that the mistress is truly troubled over thee. Thou dost not try one smallest bit to learn to read. She fears, she said just now to me with sighs, that thou art born stupid, and she says the respected Master will grieve to think he has fathered such stupidity, and she will be much shamed. Indeed the Chinese pastors and friends, they too will hang their heads when they learn that the Teacher for whose learning they have such admiration, is encumbered with a daughter who cannot read. Already have one or two asked me, thy nurse, how many words thou couldst read. I have put them off by saying that it was so much harder to learn to read or write those strange English letters than our comparatively easy Chinese characters: it must take longer to learn them. But what shall I be able to say to them later on, if still thou dost not try to learn? For, since I am now baptized, I can no longer answer them with prevarications when they address me questions. What sayest thou, my Jewel?"

" Amah," quoth I, aghast at the outlook for my future: " all the letters do look alike to me. I cannot remember their names one small morsel. What shall I do?—for indeed, I would not shame thee or my mother or my father."

She took her silver ear-pick from its home in her hair and scratched her cheek with it thoughtfully.

" True it is," she sighed, " that the foreign letters look alike. Only yesterday, when the coolie fetched the mail-bag into the kitchen from the fire-steamer, did he say to me that whether he held the letters upside down or sideways or right way up, there seemed no sense or understanding. Like a spider that has crawled in ink, did he say of them. Yet, truly, there must be sense to them. See, thy mother, a woman, can read easily: and they tell me that there are even Chinese who have mastered their mysteries."

"What can I do?" I whimpered. "I am so stupid—stupid to death. The Elders will lose much face on my account."

"Thou must breathe in wisdom," she said, drawing deep breaths to show me the method, "when the mistress scatters the queer letters round and about thee and Small Brother Didi. Thou must 'eat wisdom,' as we Chinese say."

She fixed anxious eyes on me: I gazed anxiously back at her. She picked up a child's book lying near.

"See," said she, "try to recognize some of the words."

Alas, not a letter, much less a word, brought a gleam of recognition. "Amah," said I, "shall I eat a piece of it and then perhaps I shall have wisdom within me?"

She brightened. We tore off half a sheet, rolled it into small pieces, and Amah administered them to me there on the floor. They went down smoothly: Wisdom seemed easy to acquire. There was a picture of a ship at sea at the top half of the sheet: but she felt this would bring no help. It was calligraphy that was needed internally: not art.

The cure was, of course, almost instantaneous. Within a week I was reading a few words. Amah's homily had focussed my butterfly childish attention on the spider's meanderings. Soon we were packing to go by the small coasting steamer to Shanghai, and thence I was to go to school in the North, far away from the unhealthy heat and moisture of Southern China. My mother came on a torn page of one of my books. The top half of the sheet was a picture of a ship at sea.

"I wonder," she exclaimed, "how this book got torn!"

Amah and I preserved silence.

Do I not owe her something? Had she not given me my first lesson in literature—there on the dining-room floor, leaning against the sideboard? Dear Amah, my blessings be on you. Long, long ago your heart of flesh ceased to beat, and your soul took flight for other heights of wisdom. Up there, in Heaven, are you Chinese put in a separate country, associating only with your fellow-Chinese ? Are we Westerners segregated from you ? Or are there some white babies scattered about for you to give an extra mothering to, because they are so different from your own lovely babes ? Surely the smile of an English child follows you as you sit crooning and swaying, still quiring to the young-eyed cherubims, and singing them to sleep with a song about

> " A bamboo bridge and a big, big freshet
> That washed it quite away."

Bless you for those pills of literature ! Of how much greater worth are they than the gilded pills of immortality for which your Emperors sought during the long centuries ! Did they not give me the key to the immortals ? To Chaucer, who would have placed you upon an ambling grey-eared ass and set you telling one of your Aesop fable tales. Or Shakespeare, who would have made you nurse to Rosalind herself ; let you follow her to Arden, to mend her doublets and ease her heart. Yes, and to your own great Confucius, of whom you knew hardly anything yourself except that he was Great. No mean virtues, those you possessed, of reverence and humility in the presence of true learning. Did not Confucius say, " Sincerity is the way of Heaven " ? Then, surely you have arrived at that goal.

And, lastly, did you not teach me with pulpy pills that no literature is of avail which is not a part and parcel of one's blood : that the Word must become flesh, or it remains for ever mere breath ?

So, floating down the Huangpu from Shanghai, did I stand and look down upon the old man and his wife, smiling unwittingly on them, and never seeing them. Mercifully one can naturally do these things in kindly China. The chair behind me scraped again : and I was back on the steamer, and grown up. I sighed, and turned. I was met with a rush of small feet and children's voices in laughter. Round the deck-house hurtled two Chinese children, and ran pell-mell into my knees. Hot after them pursued their scandalized amah in the stiffest of starched white tunics. But her feet had once been bound, and she would never be any match for her young free-footed charges. Faithfully she began to scold : and at the same time came a voice from behind me. The mother of the two children was the occupier of the creaking chair.

" Oh, Nieh-Nieh, and Yün-Yün ; how can you behave so ? " she said in the language of the South, which I could just comprehend. " You have nearly knocked the foreign lady flat down." The unrepentant imps struggled, captive, in my arms, laughing as ever.

" There is nothing," I said, turning to their mother, " that I like better than to be knocked nearly flat down by how-so-many children ; and when they are Chinese children, my mind has peculiarly golden peace in the matter. You see, I was born in your Honourable Kingdom, so that often my heart seems half Chinese."

" Pu kan tang—we are unworthy," she replied in the Peking speech with which I had answered her. " Please tell me your Honourable name : mine is Sung."

The amah took the children off me. Across the white deck I drew another of the immaculate basket-chairs, shaped like an hour-glass, with white-painted canvas bindings, found on all China's river steamers. I sat down beside Mrs. Sung.

" My unworthy name," I informed her, " is Hsieh "—that soft sighing breath, half hushed between the teeth ; the Chinese name given to my husband when he went so many years ago, a shy young man, to Peking, and chosen for him by the courteous old Chinese scholar attached to the Legation.

Mrs. Sung laughed to hear me utter the ultra-modest Chinese phrase, and picked up her knitting again—a new accomplishment for Chinese ladies. The children were wearing attractive pale-blue woollen jerseys. She had made them, she said, proud like any other mother to let me know her domestic capabilities, her care for her family. In the distance Nieh-Nieh was unbuttoning his jersey, to take it off. He was three years old, said his mother.

" Not till you are cooler," commanded Yün-Yün, aged five and firmly buttoned up his neck again.

Mrs. Sung's eye caught mine, and we smiled.

" Isn't it strange how she behaves like a mother to him already ? " she asked.

I wondered how many mothers since the world began have marvelled in this same tender way concerning their right-minded little daughters.

" Yesterday she gave him a lecture on behaving in company and how to bow. Come here, Nieh-Nieh," she called, " and make a bow to the foreign lady, Hsieh, and ask pardon for falling into her."

The infant came slowly, fixed his bright black eyes on mine, composed his cherubic face, put his chubby folded hands together somewhere down in the pit of his well-nourished baby stomach, and gave a half-squat of a bob. Yün-Yün at once seized his hands and disposed of them in a different manner. " No, Nieh-Nieh," she complained, " what did I tell you yesterday ? You must put your hands higher. You don't try to remember."

" He should ' eat wisdom,' " I murmured *sotto voce* ; but they were off, which was as well, for I do not seriously recommend printed matter as pabulum for children. Mrs. Sung asked what I meant and I told her of what I had been thinking when the children ran into me.

Then she wrote down for me the children's names.

" Yün-Yün means Little Cloud—pretty, isn't it ? and Nieh-Nieh "—she stopped, then half began to laugh, embarrassed : " Well, Nieh-Nieh means Strong. But not strong as a man is strong, or as iron : rather, unshatterable, steady, Strong-as-a-Rock. Do you understand ? "

I understood. She meant Simon—when he had become Peter. That was what she wanted her son to be, was it ?

Ah youth, youth ! From Carthage to Londinium, from Jerusalem to Peking, there 's the test you must all pass through. How many of your Simon-the-waverers will become Peter—Strong-as-a-Rock ? It seems that that is what your mothers, from East to West, desire for you.

MRS. SUNG cast off one sleeve and began another, chatting casually. Now and again I looked at her. I liked her—this lady of China. I liked her face, her expression, her dress, the neat way she manipulated the needles. Her husband came down the deck and she introduced him. We sat, the three of us, talking together. Away on either side, as we turned presently into the Yangtsze, stretched the banks; the further one but a faint dark line on the horizon, so wide is the mighty river towards its mouth. I liked her husband, too. He had quiet frank manners, a pleasant smile. He was dressed in European clothes of unexceptionable cut and wore them as if accustomed to them. Which, indeed, he was, for it turned out that he had been five years a student in London. No, alas, he answered my query, he had made no English friends.

"I was shy," he explained, "and every one in London is occupied with their own affairs, as is natural."

"Englishmen are shy too," I said, in dismay at such a state of things.

"So I know now," he said, "but too late." He turned to his wife, as if to rest his shyness upon her. She understood it and that had helped him to overcome it. It was plain he admired her. Doubtless, like many another wife, she had supplemented what he lacked in social affiliations. She had been partly educated in America, having gone there in the train of her father, a diplomat of renown as I realized when I heard his name. There was no need to harrow them any longer with my stumbling Chinese: and we broke into English, which both spoke excellently.

I told them of the difficulty the foreigner has in making the acquaintance of Chinese in their own land. "So how can we achieve true friendships?" I asked. I spoke of a young

Englishman in Peking, just down from Cambridge, who had dreamed all his life of living in China. He had written to me despairingly after eighteen months that it seemed almost impossible to meet Chinese to converse with, and how could he get to know them? "I have chances of conversation only with my rickshaw coolies," he had written. "They are interesting enough; but how much I should like to talk to some of the scholars' class! Sometimes I meet foreign-returned students at various functions, but, alas, most of them spend their time running down their past Chinese history and tradition."

"It is true, too true," nodded Mrs. Sung energetically.

"Then there is a young English wife, who married when she left college a partner of an old and honoured firm in the South. She wrote to me lately that at last, for the first time, she was to meet and talk to a Chinese gentleman of education. 'The consul has promised that I shall sit next to him at dinner,' she rejoiced. So, you see, the difficulty is on both sides."

We talked the matter over, and then still talked. I liked them separately: I liked them together. The gentle sunshine of their family affection warmed me as pleasantly as the mild March sun. Confucius, austere wanderer from state to state, refers with approval to the Book of Poetry. "Happy union with wife and children," he quotes from it in his Doctrine of the Middle Course, "is like the music of lutes and harps. When there is family concord, the harmony is delightful and enduring." To my mind, it impinges on the ear-drums of all around who are not deaf, and pleases.

Mrs. Sung was nearing thirty—she told me, Chinese fashion. She was, thus, a woman with youthful freshness still upon her. She had lost her first baby, and Yün-Yün was born after they had been married some time. "So she is very precious," I commented, and she threw me a look of gratitude. My eyes lighted on her feet, cased in neat black patent shoes which were cut and ornamented into the rice-ear pattern favoured of China. Her slender ankles in their pale grey silk stockings were half covered by her black pleated skirt of figured silk. I moved my chair to face her more directly while we talked. She wore a tunic of deeply blue silk, as full of colour as the indigo of twilight. It, too, had a figured pattern—plum-blossoms adumbrated over it, as if in shadow. At the neck and wrists it was piped with black satin, against which a hint of white linen embroidery suggested sweetness beneath. Her dress was neat, pretty, suited for the occasion of travelling : it attracted.

From her ears hung drops of pearl and jade, the green giving the touch of contrasting colour needed. Probably they were not her best jewels, for they were simple ornaments. Her hair was brushed smoothly back from her forehead, but had the Chinese rounded dip in front of the ears to mitigate the severity. It was kept smooth by the discreet use of the cosmetic resin which Chinese ladies apply as a pomade. My glance travelled to her face. Against the black hair and dark clothes, it looked out, milky and pale as a pearl.

" I have not been well," she volunteered, " and the doctor ordered me this trip up river to Hankow and back. The fact is we have had too many late nights. My father likes me to entertain for him : we have had a stream of receptions and dinners."

Her voice was gentle and low—proper for a woman. The curve of her lips spoke of good-humour and self-restraint. She looked apt to smile. But it was her eyes which drew me most. Usually cast down on her knitting, they would be raised now and then to mine ; and they were full of animation. Jet-black they were, but alive and sparkling. This woman would poke fun at shams, yet not jest at the principles on which her life was founded.

When I learned who her father was, I looked at her with renewed interest. He was a famous statesman. Educated in Paris in the early days of Western knowledge, he yet cherished China's past. No iconoclast was he. He had lately administered a stinging rebuke to the subverters ; asked them what they had accomplished which might encourage Chinese reliance on their methods.

" You have talked," he had said, in effect : " but what have you done ? Is any Chinese town the cleaner for your presence ? Is justice a fact or a sinecure in the area in which you hold sway ? Rather, is there not a greater oppression of the poor under you than under others ? "

It had been very courageous of the old statesman to speak these unpalatable truths, and in public, so that they were faithfully reported by an approving foreign Press. The Chinese journals let them pass without comment. Even the more thoughtful Chinese wondered if he had not lowered his country to some extent by thus proclaiming to the world that she was marred by any defects. A gentleman does not admit shortcomings on the part of his mother. Moreover, such admissions hurt the susceptibilities of the rest of the family ; they lower, so some of the class think, the respect in which their neighbours hold her and them.

We of the West, who have been born into a generation of exacerbated self-criticism and are pleasantly titillated by outpourings of self-accusation, admired unstintedly the old statesman's spasm of confession.

" That was a very fine speech of your father's," I said to Mrs. Sung. " Foreigners from outside kingdoms respect China the more in that one of her Eldest Sons has spoken out so bravely. I hope he has not suffered unpleasantness for it."

" Nobody has expressed approval, except the foreigners," she replied ruefully. " Our Chinese have kept silence."

" Nobody else would have dared to make such a speech : he has a lion heart," I told her.

For one thing, he is seventy, so age lifts him head and shoulders above the younger politicians. Also, he was one of the earliest reformers ; and, though the modern young men consider him a back number because he believes in constitutional methods, yet they pay him homage for his past fight against " tyranny." Moreover, he is wealthy and his social position assured : so that the most ardent revolutionaries speak respectfully of him, and none of them would wish to ignore his influence. By marriage he is linked up, as is the modern Chinese way which follows an older custom, with many of the leaders of the new factions as well as the great old families. I had talked with him at one of his own receptions—at which Mrs. Sung, for once, had been absent, she said. He and my husband had met on an Opium Suppression Commission years ago, had learned to esteem each other's efficiency, and had ended by working hand in glove for the same beneficent purpose. He was tall, thin, elegant. He had looked tired, I thought: and said.

"My father is weary, very weary these days," acknowledged Mrs. Sung. "The modern movements of thought surging round the world are too full of electric sparks for old people, he says. This speech will be his last effort to keep our country from slipping further downhill. So, at least, he affirms."

The children's dinner-bell rang. Off they went with Amah to the saloon a good hour before the rest of us, including Mr. and Mrs. Sung, went to a tiffin which was prepared like an English lunch. They went to Chinese rice, and good hot fish and minced chicken. Mrs. Sung slipped away in their wake. "I like to see my babies eat," she whispered to me, "and Yün-Yün has not been very well lately. I must keep my eye on her." Mr. Sung stayed a few minutes longer. He was a real estate man in Shanghai, it seemed.

"I buy a piece of land where I think the city will develop, perhaps build some shops or apartment houses on it, and then, of course, sell it for as high a figure as anybody will give me."

Naturally the land near the Settlement is the dearest and also the most productive, as the owners have the benefit of the good roads and water system in it.

His was a new profession in China, he explained—one learned from the West.

After tiffin I lay somnolent in a long chair on the deck. Perhaps our most striking shipmates—though at a table to themselves—were a group of Chinese Catholic sisters, in the charge of an Austrian nun. The captain explained to me that the shipping offices of his company were built on land owned by this particular Catholic community. By leasing their lands in this manner, Catholic missions find funds for their work mainly in the country itself. Berths are reserved for their missionaries, when needed, on ships going up country. The nun sat at the head of their table and was clothed in a thick white woollen robe. A woman of forty-odd, propriety and aloofness were written in every sweep of her voluminous sleeves. Her pointed chin stood out enchantingly, provocatively, against her becoming wimple and coif. Her little flock was composed of girls of twenty or so; very sweet they looked, as did she. It was strange to see them in their cloistered habits sitting there in the public saloon eating the white man's tiffin with knife and fork, and evidently relishing it.

We rose from table about the same time, and the nun and I met at the saloon door. We both tried to give each other the *pas*, and so naturally we fell into a talk. Questions were surging to my lips. Where were they going?

"To the Upper Yangtsze," she said, "to our work beyond Chungking"—the heart of the great river. One or two of the Chinese sisters lingered to chatter with me. She began to marshal them away from me: I felt her doing it. "Yes," they had said, "they enjoyed eating foreign food for a change. It was fun going up the river like this." But the lady called them: and who was I to tempt them to a moment's disloyalty? I made a last attempt. I asked after the fortunes of a dear and lovely Austrian Mother Superior of the orphanage in Taiyuanfu, who used to come and drink tea twice a year with my mother and myself. The soul of frankness and charity, she also wore these white sweeping woollen robes—surely the most attractive, if unhygienic, attire ever invented.

"I do not know her," answered coldly my new acquaintance. "During these years, what may not have happened to her? As you know, we are at the bidding of the Church and may be sent anywhere. We come prepared never to see our native lands again."

I smiled discreetly. I am convinced that the Catholic Church has as large a share of common sense as any other body of saints, and knows the rejuvenating power of an occasional visit to a beloved milieu. At any rate, it is rare for its very faithful and devoted workers—though this does no doubt happen—to be kept immured in one Chinese locality for an inhuman length of years.

This paragraph, you perceive, is the output of a malicious mind, the result of pure pique.

As I lay somnolent on the deck, from the other side of the deck-house I could hear the Austrian sister reading aloud some holy book, and then another voice beginning—the

Photo by Lady Hosie

The Real China. A kindly old farmer on a Yangtsze river-boat

voice of a Chinese sister, who probably owed her life, her welfare and the very goodness of her personality to the loving-kindness of the Faith. They were going to troublous districts : that I knew. I could only hope that the possible martyrdom which they so constantly envisage and refer to did not await them. There have been many martyrs of the Catholic Faith in China : as also of the Protestant. It was a Catholic who knew what persecution and martyrdom meant, who slipped that clause into the Chinese version of a French treaty some seventy years ago by which the Chinese Government agreed to toleration for Christians—Christians in those days meaning Catholics.

" What are you sighing for ? " came a voice, and a cheerful young Englishman, my vis-à-vis at table, planted himself into a chair beside me, bringing a cocker spaniel on a lead which snuggled into my knee as if to make up for my outcast condition.

" O Father Abram, what these Christians are," quoth I, smoothing the dog's ears.

" Are those Christians, those Chinese friends you were talking to this morning ? " he asked. " They look rather nice : and what a jolly pair of children ! "

" I 'll introduce you, if you like," I said.

" Well," he hesitated over it, then rushed out the words : " I wish I could get hold of Chinese like them to talk to regularly : but I never know how to begin a conversation with them. Are they Christians ? "

" I really don't know," I answered. " I am sure they are not ' pagans.' Probably betwixt and between. Funny, isn't it ?—I suppose you are a Christian, baptized and confirmed ? " —he nodded—" and I also profess that Name, and the ship's captain and officers are others, and the nuns round the corner are more to add to our number. I suppose in the long run it must make a difference to people like the Sungs to meet such varying and variable protagonists of our faith."

He looked gravely at me, a trifle startled at the introduction of this subject, but clear-eyed enough and ready to talk of life's problems like any other modern young man.

" Probably people like your friends, the Sungs, don't often meet missionaries," he ventured slowly, " so they depend for their spiritual guidance as to what Christianity stands for on very ordinary Christians like myself. That is what you are saying, isn't it? I always have thought it odd to imagine that the propagation of our religion is a matter only for missionaries."

We exchanged views abundantly and frankly: China our subject, as always happens to two China folk.

Up the river the steamer was pushing. Gradually the banks closed in. Amidst the light green of the low-lying fields, an occasional almond tree was breaking into pink cloud above the spring rice. A low golden-brown group of clustered buildings represented a village. In the distance ahead, a small hill cast its long reflection back into the water toward us. A temple under a gnarled tree guarded the rocky summit from malignant demons. Each bend of the river, each rocky promontory had, in addition to its ancient Chinese, an English name given it barely a century ago by some master mariner of our blood who, first of merchantmen, adventured his cockle-shell and charted those mysterious inland waters for the benefit of other Western master mariners to come.

We drew near to one of the landing-stages which stand at intervals up the river. A large and grimy sampan was waiting. At sight of us, it pushed out furiously in our direction against the swift current. Countryfolk filled it, sitting on mounds of their luggage, clutching more packages and baskets. The steamer slowed down but did not stop. Bound-footed women, small children, old farmers, a young strong coolie seeking work, scrambled or were hauled on to a lower deck—at the very great peril of their lives, or so it seemed to the Englishman and myself as we went to watch. Their bundles were thrown up and deftly caught. Then we were putting on steam again and forging ahead. One young woman, married no doubt "up river" and evidently having been on a visit to her parents—a rare joy—could not contain herself. She burst into a loud wail, and tears ran down her rosy rounded country-girl's cheeks. "Ah pa, ah pa," she wept, and stretched out her arms towards the receding boat in which her father—her "ah pa"—sat; an elderly peasant. "When shall I see thee again? Ah yah! Ah yah!"

The Englishman looked at me, troubled.

"Poor girl," he said, then began to talk of the Chinese poor. "I daresay if I were a Chinese, I should be a Red revolutionary in sheer despair. Of course, being what I am, I know it would only make matters worse," he ended.

We began to walk round the deck: and somehow I thought that the Austrian lady's eye softened a wee towards me, as she found I left her lambs untainted and unattacked. Out of the corner of her eye she was looking after me and my companion. Later on, she half invited me to take their photographs with my camera. Then she again half withdrew when I started to take it. However, by this time I was so provoked with the lady, dimpled chin, wimple and all, that I took it, whether or no. Why need she have considered me a possible emissary of Satan? Mrs. Sung had not acted so.

"About a fortnight ago," I told my companion, "I was visiting a Catholic mission in a city on the Southern coast. The Mother Superior is a charming old lady of seventy-odd who knew Sully Prudhomme and still recites with verve his measured verses. The poet used to frequent her mother's salon when she was a little girl. It is one of the pleasures of foreign visitors, such as myself, in that Southern port, to pay the homage of a call on the old lady. She sends for her sisters to help to receive the visitors and tells them hospitably to bring a little sirop and a precious helping of English biscuits out of a treasured tin for the occasion. Then we go and see her orphans; and the ward for sick prisoners, which the Mission has coaxed out of the city officials; and the dispensary where Sister Marie-Angélique, who is Venetian, mixes simple concoctions from phials or with pestles, as though a trained chemist; and the clinic where a hundred poor come twice a week while Sister Marie-Claire, who is English, goes to work on sores and fevers with lint and boracic, thermometers and quinine. Then we come away feeling humble in mind, and grateful in heart that such women exist." I paused.

"But they have minds of their own, these ladies!" I added, bethinking me of that self-same Mother Superior.

Trouble had been brewing in that city of the South.

Rumours were going about, and the old legends revived that the Catholic sisters received orphans in order to take out their eyeballs for medicine, and that they made more medicine of the hearts and livers of their victims. The old Mother Superior, having been bred in the days of the Second Empire and in France, had no doubts whatever as to what was the right course of action. She cabled, through the Chinese Post Office—which took the message without murmur—for the French Admiral to steam to their defence. He came in his man-of-war: he landed his marines, duly accompanied by their machine-guns, and sent them to the Catholic Mission compound. But the old lady would have none of this. "The people of this city have just as much right to be protected, in case of disturbance, as ourselves," she told him. "If the ruffianly set—which exists in every city—attack us, they will make no bones about plundering and looting those around us. It is the just right and due of this whole quarter that you should protect all within it."

So she made her military dispositions, and had the marines, with their machine-guns, plus barbed wire, placed at the strategic corners of the large streets for a considerable area around her. The peaceful Chinese shopmen crowded to thank her for her kind consideration of their safety in their own city.

At that same time, the English Protestant missionaries, on the other side of the city, realizing that the situation was shaky, asked that one policeman be allotted to stand at the door of their compound—to show that law and order was on their side. Chinese pamphleteers seized on this fact, and printed head-lines and long articles on the wicked imperialism of the English. Every detail was exaggerated. A bicycle pump in the hand of the principal of a college became a revolver with which he pursued his innocent and terrified pupils. This was reported and repeated in the Shanghai Chinese Press with enlargements. And never one word appeared in any Chinese paper either in the city or in Shanghai about the French machine-guns sticking their noses at intervals along the Main Street; or of the French man-of-war lying off the city; or of the machinations and manœuvres of the Mère Supérieure! She, no doubt, was enchanting the admiral's staff with her recitations from the poets in between her suggestions for a little more barbed wire here or there for the comfort and consolation of the tradesmen of her neighbourhood.

Such is the justice of life. So run the tongues of Rumour in the House of Fame, whether this side the globe or that.

My young Englishman listened and laughed and said he was not surprised. He too had been born in China. "How much more interesting it is," said he, "to deal with people who think in such unexpected ways than with dull folk who always do what you expect of them!"

CHAPTER III A YOUNG MAN FROM SHANGHAI

THE young man and myself fraternized. We talked of many things. We talked of Trade, which was his job. He was a junior member of a firm which had been founded by his grandfather and carried on by his father.

"I am one of those persons known as Shanghailanders," he informed me.

"It is a horrid name put upon decent and reasonable people," I comforted him. "My husband was once Commercial Attaché; so you cannot expect me to think lightly of men who have produced the Liverpool or Rotterdam or New York—which you will—of the East, and who at the same time keep a level mind to administer equitably and on the grand scale such a conglomeration of nations as is Shanghai."

He said he thought that trade and more trade would accomplish as much as anything else to relieve China's difficulties—if their leaders could but see this: and with this I concurred heartily. The give and take of trade is not only in that of material fabrics. As our comfort depends on goods from other parts of the earth, so Chinese also can enjoy woven stockings—instead of shapeless socks cut from calico; telephones and leather suit-cases; candles and kerosene instead of the old dip-lamps. There is an exchange of ideas also in foreign trade, which keeps a nation's mentality alive. The hermit nation becomes intolerably stupid and proud. And what do we not owe to the East in Loveliness? Did not Chippendale find his claw-legged chairs first in Chinese design? Who of us is not the more satisfied of soul for having beheld the wonder of a painted Chinese screen or fan?

"But I wish my firm could have left me to pursue my career in Shanghai," he groaned. "There is some riding in my future port, I hear: but I had two jolly ponies in Shanghai and they were entered for the races. My brother-in-law has taken them on: beauties they are. Every morning I used to exercise them at six on the race-course."

Gloom engulfed him at the remembrance of those partings from his beloved. Who could resist the lad? He had brought his dog, and the captain allowed him to exercise it on the deck. He had been at school when the Great War broke out; but he was in the War during its last year, and he had had enough soldier's uniform to last him his life. He was sickened at having to put it on again during these years of discord in China.

"In order to discourage any hotheads from rushing the Settlement and making mincemeat of everybody in it," he growled, "we have had to march about for weeks in full panoply, and waste hours doing sentry. I never can actually imagine myself fighting my friends, the Chinese. Of course, I suppose we should have to if we were driven into a corner and besieged as the foreigners were in the Boxer Year. Strangely enough, you know, most of the Chinese citizens of the Settlement approve of us marching about in military garb. It gives them courage to stand by what they believe to be right, to refuse to be bullied into shouting with the deluded crowd. When we have a dress parade through the streets of Shanghai, we are thronged with crowds of Chinese sightseers who pass admiring remarks about us as if we were a Lord Mayor's Show arranged for their benefit! They certainly feel no alarm or anger at our armour."

Round the deck we walked.

"I 've only had two games of golf all winter," he ended.

"It is a pity the Chinese warring factions don't settle their differences on the golf course," I suggested.

"I 'd settle all wars that way—or the football field, where you get team work," he decided.

Then he told me of the Chinese young men volunteers of his Corps, clever shots, good officers, keen and smart.

"They are the pride of the Corps," he said, "though it seems queer that they should be with us at all, getting ready to defend the Settlement against their own countrymen, if need arises. And they would too. Staunch fellows they are. They vie with us in the most gruelling marches and inspections, and take orders and rebukes like—like——"

"Men," I supplied. He nodded.

That was too sacred a phrase for him to use glibly. I asked him if he had ever heard the story of the raising of the Weihaiwei regiment. My husband used to delight in telling it, and I in hearing it. The colonel charged with the task, whose name is still dear to the Chinese members of his disbanded regiment, had some difficulty in finding recruits. Finally he went forth into the fields to seek them. He came upon a farm labourer at work, hoeing.

"How much pay do you have a month, good man?" he asked.

"Three dollars a month and my keep," answered the Chinese peasant, stopping his work for a moment to look at the stranger. (That sum would not be correct to-day.)

"I'll give you twice that and better food, if you will come and be a soldier," said the colonel.

The man considered the offer.

"Right!" he said. "I'll come. I'll come and be a soldier. But—I won't fight."

My young Englishman laughed. "All the same, the Weihaiwei regiment did fight in 1900, and very well, did they not? Because they could trust their officers to do their best for their welfare. Any general who can assure his men of that in China will get such loyalty as will amaze the world."

I remembered my teacher in Peking. He was a teacher of the old school—going fast asleep if he felt inclined so to do in the midst of my lesson—when my progress became altogether too stultifying and slow. During the Revolution, he came late one morning to instruct me. I hardly expected him at all. He told me the horrors of the times, and ended:

"How dreadful was it last night when the soldiers ran loose and dashed down the streets firing rifles into the air!"

"Into the air," I echoed dubiously. "Why into the air?"

He looked at me, greatly shocked. He was wondering what I could mean, what sort of inhuman monster I could be.

"Surely," he said slowly, "you would not have had them shooting bullets into people?"

I hastily denied this, sinking back abashed at the tone of

reproach. The air is indeed a target preferable to a human being.

The young Englishman alluded to his own experiences. " How trusting they are with us ! " he exclaimed. " I was up in Tientsin a few months for the firm : and the compradore came one day into my office with two of his Chinese friends to ask me, without a blink of his eyes, to receive over a quarter of a million taels into my bank account ! Yes, and without any guarantee I was to put those tens of thousands of pounds into my own name. They took it for granted that I would give them their money back in due course. However, I stipulated that the money was to remain in my account for six months—I was not going to have my passbook upset for a few days' convenience of theirs. Besides, it would not be fair to a banker."

He grinned largely at me, and refreshingly.

" I must say it was a change for me to have sums like that to my credit ! Of course I told them they should have the interest."

A pleasant young man this.

" But the extraordinary thing was why they chose that moment to bring their money to me in the Concession. We were hourly expecting an attack on the Concession by disaffected troops—who had not been paid for months. I said to our compradore, who is a suave elderly gentleman with magnificent manners, that it seemed an inexpedient time for his friends to be putting their money in the Concession, considering that we might be besieged any moment. Can you imagine what he replied ? He answered that it was for this reason they were bringing the money to my bank. ' You, from over the seas,' he said, ' are sure to defend yourselves, and if you do so with energy as undoubtedly you will, you will beat off these red-beards, these wolves, these sons of bandits. They will then, in their disappointment, start to loot our city which is defenceless : and they would assuredly nose out this money. If there is trouble, I and my family have made arrangements to come into the Concession."

" In effect," I interpreted, " they would rather be besieged with you, and would feel safer, than remain in their own homes and streets, unprotected."

"There was trouble later on," he continued. "One night I thought I heard a stirring in my stables. I wondered if my horses were all right. So I went out to see. I found about thirty people encamped in the yard with their possessions. The ma-fu—my groom—begged me to let them remain. They had tramped in from villages around and were friends and relations of the servants. They were refugees from their own soldiers. How could I turn them out? I told him to give them hay for bedding, and said they could stay—so long as no harm happened to the horses, of course! Poor beggars, I believe they slept with the animals for warmth. We were cluttered up for days. I told the ma-fu that if we were besieged they would have to go. How could I have looked after such an adopted family? He said, 'yes, yes'—but it is even betting that he would have got round me when the time came. However, it did not come, thank goodness."

"Did you ever hear the tale of the missionary's boots?" I asked in my turn. "It is a true story, for I had it from the victim himself, who was half perturbed, half in fits of amusement over it."

He was travelling, this missionary, on a very small Chinese coasting steamer—"the smallest steamer you ever saw," he described it. The captain was a Chinese, which is still an unusual appointment in steam-vessels on the Chinese coast. He had learned his job from the foreign captains under whom he had served. He was perhaps thirty years old, and he was determined to do his duty thoroughly in every respect. This had been drilled into him by his former captains. When they reached Hai-men—Gate to the Sea—a crowd was waiting on the pontoon. The people rushed on to the steamer. My friend was on deck, watching. A presentiment told him to go and see if his cabin was locked. Too late: already a pair of brand-new boots had vanished. Now in those days, a pair of leather boots was not to be bought in any and every Chinese city, as to-day. Boots were still mainly confining the feet of the foreigner. He would have to send to Shanghai for another pair. Being an English missionary, his funds were not unlimited: and he felt annoyed. It was also very inconvenient, as he had no other boots with him: the streets were muddy, and he could not land. The tiffin bell rang, and at table he spoke firmly to the captain. He said that it was most unwise to allow such a rabble to pour on board and over the ship like that, pell-mell, and that it would not be allowed on other ships. And, finally, he had lost a pair of boots.

"Leave it to me!" said the young captain, as they rose from table. "You shall have your boots back. It is disgraceful that they should be stolen off my ship."

The missionary sat writing on deck for an hour or two. An unexpected peace brooded over the ship, the quayside, the city. He took a simple pleasure in the lack of the usual uproar. But it lasted so long that he was moved to rise and see if all could be well. Reaching the stern of the vessel, he found the crew. The captain was standing over a quick-firing gun, and the gun was trained on the city. Wide-eyed he looked at it and at the captain. "What on earth——?" he began.

"Hush!" the captain silenced him. "This is my affair. I will not have passengers' boots stolen off my ship. I am dealing with the matter firmly; as foreigners do."

The missionary was aghast. Was a city to be blown up for his boots—and he the messenger of peace and love—and for some crazy notion of foreign firmness? He was just about to protest vehemently, when the captain's face broadened into a smile. "It's all right," he said, "there are your boots coming up the gangway." The missionary looked, and lo, two ragged citizens, each carrying a boot, were hastening towards them. The captain received them, gave them a dressing down, to which they said "yes" and "no" exactly as he required.

"And all was peace and love once more," ended the missionary, "except that I shall never remonstrate with energetic Young China again, however many of my goods are stolen."

"How did the captain recover them?" I queried, interested.

"It is a shocking tale," admitted the missionary. "It seems that he sent word at once after tiffin to the police station up the hill-side, not far from the quay, to the effect that a foreigner's boots had been stolen off his ship, that police existed for the protection of the public and that, if the boots were not forthcoming in two hours, the police station would go up sky-high, for he had his quick-firer trained upon it."

"The blood-thirsty man!" I exclaimed.

"It was not that," the missionary excused him. "But when Chinese catch this modern go-ahead feeling, they take the disease very hard. The police at once sent a message down to the king of the beggars—that head of the roving thieving clan which operates in every Chinese city and has its own guild and officers. They said they wished to see him and his chief lieutenant on an urgent matter: and he, not being anxious to run athwart the police, came. They clapped him into the lock-up. 'Now,' they told him tersely, 'a foreigner has had a pair of boots stolen off the fire-boat lying there in the harbour: the captain has a great cannon trained on this building, the roar alone of which will deafen the province. We are leaving you—alone—in this police station. If he fires, this building will certainly go sky-high, and so will you. He has given us two hours to produce the boots. There is your second-in-command: give him the necessary instructions to retrieve them."

They left the building; and the king of the beggars lost no time whatever in speeding forth his lieutenant to make inquiries in the dens of iniquity in the city. Thus the boots were returned to the missionary's feet.

The young Englishman laughed as had I when I first heard my missionary friend's tale. "What a dilemma for a man of peace!" he commented.

We began to speak of Shanghai. He pitied the thousands of rickshawmen who haul their man-carriages about its streets in such numbers and crowds that the eye becomes at last conscious only of a flicker of slender spokes, of high wheels, wheels and more wheels. "Those unfortunate men," he said, "receive cudgellings from the Chinese and the Sikh policemen on duty for faults of mere ignorance. Raw lads from the country, most have never seen a macadamized street before. The motors, the rickshaws, the rail-less trams careering down the roads, the crowds of people stepping on and off the pavements—they must all be very confusing to them. How can they know by instinct that there exist such things as the rules of the road, especially since they speak some dialect uncomprehended in Shanghai? I take my hat off to them. I rage when I see one of their own Chinese police raining blows on them with his baton. So unnecessary it is to whack anybody—except perhaps a Public School boy—now is it not?"

"Oho, so beatings and such like should be a privilege of the Upper Classes?" I mocked him.

He laughed. "Something of the sort," he agreed. "Did you see what one of the rickshaw coolies wrote after their last Christmas entertainment? You know there is a Mission which provides a jollification for them, to which every one in the Settlement subscribes. After the last festivity," he said, "the company of rickshawmen chose one of their number, who could write, to convey a vote of thanks to the donors. The letter appeared in the newspaper, and this is how one paragraph ran:

"'*We specially wish to thank the two kind foreign gentlemen who came and explained to us the Traffic Regulations of the Shanghai Municipal Council and the Gospel according to St. Mark.*' All one sentence, without pause!"

Both treatises shed light on the purposes of the two mysterious Authorities under whom life in a foreign settlement has, apparently, to be lived.

Thus we talked and jested: and the sun began to sink lower into the river. The air was very still. An odour, not unpleasant, of cooking crept up from the lower decks where the poorer Chinese passengers were preparing their evening rice. The whirr, whirr, of the captain's telephone to the engine-room was the only sound.

At this point Mrs. Sung came along the deck, looking fresh and clear-eyed after a long siesta. She had changed her tunic to one of pale-pink soft silk. My young friend rose at once to flee.

"I 'll see you again later," he murmured.

"Why not stay and talk to Mrs. Sung?" I murmured back.

"I must—er—exercise the dog," he announced, reddening a little, and was off on a pacing of the white boards.

"Your friend has run away from me," she smiled, sitting down. "It is only that he is shy, I think," she added; and I nodded. "What has he been talking about?" she queried.

" He has been giving me his views on China—the views of Young Britain," I reported. " He is a nice lad." I told her what he had said regarding the Chinese members of the Shanghai Volunteer Corps. She blushed with pride. " My youngest brother is a member," she told me : " and we have often teased him for his earnestness in getting up early to drill and being so careful of his rifle instead of merely telling a servant to clean it—as is our Chinese way, when of course only too often it does not get cleaned."

It is indeed a change of mind when young Chinese elegants dirty their hands, and get hot and perspire with marching. Their grandfathers would never have dreamed of behaving so on any pretext whatever.

" Our old Chinese way seems to have landed us nowhere very enviable," she added bitterly. " But I am sure you would like my younger brother. He is so modest. He is so kind, so thoughtful of others."

" In short, not unlike the young man I have been talking to," I mused aloud. " Their daily life is different, their education, interests and pastimes : but their quality seems similar, eh ? "

This time she nodded at me.

" What is this young Englishman interested in—horses ? " she asked.

" Oh yes, and golf and motor-bicycles," said I.

But this was not a fair impression of a gallant and chivalrous young Western mind. I told her how he had spoken to me, compassionately, of the agony of Chinese coolies at their labour. " You know," I related, " how officiously Chinese policemen act towards your own labouring people—their autocratic behaviour. He told me how angry and distressed he felt when a Chinese policeman would stop a procession of sweating load-bearers, staggering beneath a hundredweight sack of flour on their backs, merely to let his motor-bicycle pass. ' I refuse to have them treated so for my benefit,' he said fiercely ; ' I can stop my machine far more easily than they can endure waiting with their awful loads while I pass. I always wave them to go on, and give the policemen a piece of my mind.' "

" Yes," she admitted, " many foreigners truly behave so

towards the coolie. But do not blame the police too much. They are obeying the tradition of our old official days, when the richer and more powerful folk naturally took precedence of labour and cooliedom."

I remembered in Wenchow streets the passage of officials in the sedan-chairs of former days; the shoutings and the whackings on shoulder and arms given in the narrow wayfares by the official's runners to all and sundry who wore the common blue coolie garb, while the Great Man in his enclosed chair sat like a god in a shrine behind his draped silk curtains.

"Tell me more of what he said," demanded Mrs. Sung.

I was not sure if she would see the point of all the stories which we had been exchanging: so replied in vague terms. I am not sure that any of my Chinese friends will comprehend why the stories in these chapters may amuse or interest occidentals. On the other hand, I have no doubt that they will think laughable many of my accounts of their ways of life. Humour is the last morsel of our minds which we can share internationally.

Chinese comments are worth attention. Lately I gave a lantern lecture on things Chinese, and deliberately invited to it a Chinese girl, my friend, because I hoped to learn from conversation afterwards.

"How queer it was of you," said she, "to show a slide of one of our funerals! And you never showed one of our weddings!"

That was fair criticism, indeed. We should think a Chinese lecturer strange who did the same by us.

So, forgive me, dear China, if I seem in your eyes to be drawing your picture lop-sided. Some day there will come another from the West who will have larger skill; by the side of whose artistry my bungling attempts will seem crude and undiscerning. My efforts at picturing you will be comparable with the Saints as portrayed by the Primitives put beside the Sistine Madonna. But I hope they will never seem ridiculous; for love is never ridiculous. If, then, to you these particular stories do not appear in the least humorous, pray go on to the next chapter. Even then, you will doubtless feel the need of much patience!

I told Mrs. Sung one of the young man's stories which I thought she could appreciate.

" He was remarking on the cheerfulness and good humour of your common people, your 'Hundred Names,' " I explained, " and how readily they respond to a joke or chaffing."

A friend of his, it seemed, another young Englishman, was sent during a recent disorder to help to fetch in a party of European women and children from an isolated area some distance from the railway track. It was in the North, and the Northern generals had been commandeering the railway trucks, the engines, the engine-drivers, the coal; everything. Having brought his small group of refugees down to the railway, and found an empty coach, he ensconced them therein, but no engine could he find for a long while. Presently, on a siding, he discovered one, with steam up. The two Chinese manning it looked very sulky.

" No wonder! Probably they had had no pay for many long months! " interpolated the Englishman, with a shrug.

Station-masters had been shot summarily for protesting against the rapacity and the insane muddling of the militarists. Engine-drivers had been forced at the pistol point to take their train out of a station in the direction willed by a self-appointed colonel who was ignorant of time schedules—with the inevitable smash when they met another oncoming train. These two men were glum. Their sole stock-in-trade was one sound engine, and they had seen to it that its bunkers were filled. For the time being, it was in their charge, and they kept steam up so that they could run with it at the approach of any armed compatriots.

" That does not sound like good humour," commented Mrs. Sung.

" Like the Younger Sister who is telling you this story "—I bowed: she bowed: we smiled: I continued: " the young Englishman had had the good fortune to be born in your Honourable Country. It was a hot morning. He had been up all night, and many nights on sentry duty. He was bored to extinction with the senselessness of warfare. It was plain to him that he would never have that engine—except as a free gift. His alternative was to take his refugees down

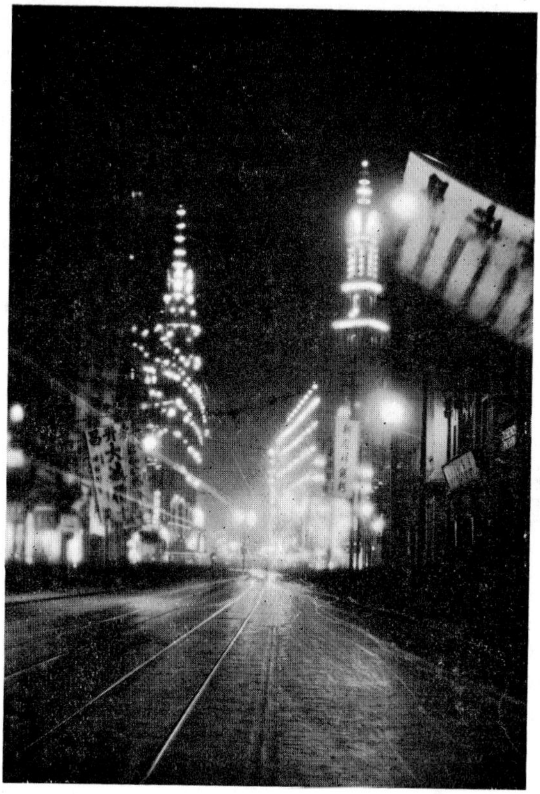

The Nanking Road at night, Shanghai

to Tientsin on foot, or by mule—an alarming and wearisome journey with young children. He pushed back his helmet, mopped his red forehead and groaned loudly, 'What would I not give for a cup of tea?' The engine-drivers pricked up their ears: in an instant the sulks disappeared."

Few are the Chinese who would not answer to that appeal. Tea! China's incomparable gift to parched and fatigued humanity. A fellow-human needed a drink of tea. Immediately the two men called down to him as he stood by the side of the line, "Our kettle is boiling! Will the foreign First-Born care to drink a bowl of our tea?" The First-Born cared very much to do so, was pulled into the cabin by friendly hands, sat himself on a sack on the coal, drank two cups of the weak, refreshing, boiling infusion, felt much better and said so. He proffered a coin—which was indignantly refused. "I must go along, I suppose," said he; "but how fortunate have I been to meet such men who have been as kinsmen to me! Would I might meet more!" They asked whither he was going. He explained that he was accompanying a band of foreign refugees, bound for Tientsin, and that they were sitting in a derelict but usable railway coach; minus, however, an engine.

"But we have an engine here!" they exclaimed. "Why not use ours?"

"That is amiable of you gentlemen, truly," he answered, "but doubtless you need your engine for some other purpose."

Thereupon they pressed their engine upon him. Nay, they waxed fiery, offered to drive him and his friends over the whole line—and run down any ill-begotten general who obstructed their course.

"So he secured his engine—with a cup of tea: and run by a smiling crew," I ended.

"And I daresay they did not refuse the proffered coins the next time they were offered," Mrs. Sung added. The corner of her lip curled in mirth. She looked round the deck. The children were playing with Amah at a little distance. She leaned towards me.

"I coax Amah that way sometimes," she whispered with glee.

" And I," I whispered back, " have employed the same methods in a household in England ! "

" Do certain of the poor people remain always children with you also in the West ? " she asked, still whispering.

" They do," I assured her, and we looked at each other in a common conspiracy of housekeepers.

" But I wish——" she began : " I wish that my young brother could meet more of your young English gentlemen."

" Yes," I said, thoughtfully.

CHAPTER IV THE BONDS OF FAMILY

"YOU learned to speak English in America," I remarked next morning, as Mrs. Sung and I pulled our white-painted chairs into a sunny corner of the deck out of the wind.

"Of course," she said, "why not?"

"There was a Cantonese lady on board ship coming out from England," I told her, "who had spent five years in New York, and could not speak five words of English—and did not intend to try."

"Tell me," she said: so I did, for it had been amazing to me. Yet I suppose there are European and American women to be found equally ignorant of Chinese or Hindustani after living five years in China or India. Still, most women, Oriental or Western, contrive to acquire a trifle of a vocabulary, sufficient to manage their households, buy food and pay wages. This Mrs. Pak on board the ship was a nice enough woman, too, as I had felt when I saw her sitting in a corner of the ship's saloon with her husband. She was unusually intelligent; this her husband, a banker of first-class standing in China, avowed of her.

"When I am in doubt about financial matters," he said to me, "I wait till I get home and then consult my wife. I 've never regretted accepting her advice. She has very sound judgment. She is good at figures, and understands the complications of exchange, even on a large scale, and checks my calculations. She is invaluable to me."

Judge, then, how nonplussed I felt when I discovered she could speak no English at all—after five years of New York. While her husband and I and another Cantonese gentleman friend conversed, she would sit watching our faces with the indulgent amusement of a Mona Lisa, uttering never a word. She had taken careful scrutiny of New York, of her fellow-passengers on board ship, as I realized by his occasional references to her. But she was not to be hurried into any contacts which she had not proved and proved again. He showed me snapshots of their two boys of sixteen and twelve, left behind at a school in New York.

"Yes, they can speak English very well indeed ; the trouble will be when they return to Canton and cannot read Chinese characters easily," he said.

No communication could pass between Mrs. Pak and myself except when one of the Cantonese gentlemen was there to translate. She wore the livelong day a most unbecoming flat pancake of a white satin hat—which was fashionable attire a year or two ago for Chinese ladies who felt it necessary to attempt to follow foreign fashions ; China's first trial at putting that entirely useless object, a hat, on her smooth and comely head. Mrs. Pak wore also a foreign dress, home-made. It was as if all things foreign and her foreign experiences were but the masquerade of a New York night's entertainment, to be doffed and forgotten when she reached her true home again. In this unattractive garb, she sat in corners of the saloon and looked out upon the rest of us with her whimsical smile as if we were children to be humoured. Yet, when I went and sat beside her and showed her snapshots I had taken *en route*, in default of speech she gave me an attention which not only spoke of steadiness and kindness but had charm.

"Some day we may go back to the States to live a few more years," her husband told me.

He spoke of the intense cold of the New York winter. For the first month or so, they had lived in a furnished house where he, unaccustomed as he was, had had to go out early into the cold mornings to shovel away the snow-drifts in front of their house, to keep the stove going in the basement, and perform other trying duties. Then they had found an apartment in some service flats. They paid an unbelievable price.

"But it was worth it," he sighed. "It was steam-heated, so there was no stoking up of stoves to do : the rubbish was shot down a shaft and burnt by the janitor. I ordered the food by telephone, as my wife can't speak English. Occasionally a coloured woman came in to give the rooms a turn-out, but she was so good she needed no directions, or very few. My wife pointed, and she understood. My wife enjoyed cooking our daily meals for us. She had nothing else to do till I came home at night. Sometimes she went with us to a tennis club, or to some American friends who had a court, and watched us play. We like tennis, the boys and myself."

I could imagine her sitting out, saying not a word ; merely smiling gently. He added that they had just persuaded her to follow the fashion of foreign women and play tennis herself, and that she had shaped well—when they were recalled to China.

To hear such a tale, one might think her a fool. Yet by instinct I knew she was anything but that. It had been so pleasant to me, after years of immersement in England, to meet again in my daily walk a Chinese woman, that I took the habit of sitting with her a little every day. She puzzled me. Suddenly I felt annoyed with her and her obstinacy. Learn English she should, whether she wanted to or no. For a fortnight I struggled with phrases which her husband helped me to foist upon her. She repeated them parrot-like, to please us : and next morning never a trace of them was left. "How do you do?" "Good-bye," she would say docilely, and shake her head in perplexity when called upon to produce them at the next conversation.

"You see how it is," said her husband : "she just does not interest herself in such things."

A light broke upon me. Who, indeed, is interested in such phrases—except as a means to an end : and that end friendship and understanding? She wanted neither foreign friendship nor understanding. Her armour in the matter was complete. Ah, but was it? I knew by the way she had taken up the snapshots of her children after her husband had finished showing them to me that she, too, had an Achilles' heel.

"Where are your sons?" I tried next morning, word by word, and taught her the answer.

"New York," she said joyfully—and with the true inimitable American closure of the glottis and curl upward of the uvula, as of swallowing an oyster. " N' Yorrk ! " she englutinated.

We were within three days of Hong-Kong when I grasped this truth : that five minutes' careful study of the psychology of China is worth fifty years of blind patience, or five years of the still blinder impatience which usually follows. For the next three days I would see her white satin hat divergating from its normal course, as its wearer caught sight of me on the deck. From afar she would wave her hand, and smile and proclaim, " I haff-e two son-ners in N' Yorrk."

Mr. Pak preened himself in the sunshine of her linguistic achievements. The last day, as we sat to say good-bye, she caught my arm, turned to her husband and said in emphatic tones, " Hao jen !—she is a good person." She had taken a long time to discover my merits.

" It is true : that was the right bait to catch your fish ! " said Mrs. Sung, her cheeks dimpling into laughter.

" It is a pity somebody did not begin angling five years earlier," I grumbled.

" I wonder how she is getting on in Canton," mused Mrs. Sung.

" An American said to me that it was like going into a power-house to go there these days," I told her. " You have to walk very carefully or you get caught up into some devouring monstrous moving steel octopus that claws you to pulp. All around are hidden fires ready to burst forth, if you lift a lid ; and infernal din and clatter. Inflammable material is lying loose over the whole place."

It was a powerful simile, and he proved a true prophet. Within a year the lid was off and the furnace belching flame.

" The trouble is that half the operatives want the machines to turn out silk, as in the old days, and the other half want only explosives as in these," said Mrs. Sung unexpectedly. " Then they start quarrelling and shouting and push each other into the machines, and the place swims in blood, or half of it blows up the machines. I am Cantonese by origin : so I know my people."

She paused.

" How much better is it to manufacture silk than gunpowder ! " she ended.

" Indeed it is," I agreed : " or to lift a lid and see pretty cheeping baby chickens."

We fell to talking, of Wenchow, of Canton, of homely crafts, of silk spinning, and of the beautiful Cantonese chinaware. The troublous times were very bad for this latter art and trade. Chinaware is delicate fragile stuff to survive the physical shocks of civil war and banditry.

" It breaks so easily, you see," she commented. " When pirates attempt to seize a junk laden with crates of bowls, and there is a fight, there are not usually many bowls left intact, even if the pirates are driven off. Then the ruined china-vendor shrieks to heaven in his despair."

This was a new light on the difficulties of small Chinese traders. No wonder, with the wolves ever pressing on their heels, some throw down the burden of their lives and join the wolf-pack. This may lead to the execution-ground some day : even so, they will die in company with their fellow-bandits, and not alone, in rags, of famine and cold, in the Beggar's Yard, forgotten of men and gods. They may steal enough to give a dowry to their daughters and see them respectably settled instead of having to sell them into slavery and worse, lest they too should die of famine. If they commit their banditries discreetly, in a district not their own, they may perhaps slip back again into their normal life undetected. Of course, in some Kwangtung villages on the coast the whole population turns pirate on occasion : and as all are related to each other, nobody tells tales.

Presently Mrs. Sung bent forward, hesitatingly.

" You are in black," she said, touching my sleeve.

" My husband died a year ago," I answered. Her eyes filled with tears.

" Oh," she said, " it is pitiful, pitiful." She leaned over the chair and patted my arm. She crooned over me, though she is younger than I. Mother China gathered me up into her arms as my amah had gathered me when a child. Wherever I went from North to South those next few months, whenever Chinese women inquired after my family condition—as is their way of politeness—and had to be answered, they wept over me and patted me like that. Humble women, gentle women, Christian and pagan, it was as though I were their sister, to be comforted. Their friendship was mine at once. And for myself—I learned that the surest way of gaining hearts is to give of a piece of one's own.

With one breath, they each and every one agreed, as did Mrs. Sung, that it was now my duty " to return home and serve my parents in their coming Old Age "—that period of life so venerated amongst sober-minded Chinese. I often smiled to myself as these last words so unfailingly came to me. Praise be, if there is one attitude my parents would avoid, would contemplate with horror, it is that of picturesque silver-haired Do-Nothing-ness, of sitting quiescent in the sun, or knitting socks by the fire. Old Age will never come upon them, for their lives are too full of sympathy and interest. They are but typical of their generation. Was there not a grandmother of seventy-six the other day who took her first flight in an aeroplane from Paris to London: and who liked it so much that she immediately booked a return ticket?

China is right with her Categoric Imperative about the proper attitude of children to parents. Albeit, certain Chinese of the poorer classes sometimes fall short of this traditional reverence. Some of them have been known to grudge their old parents a corner in the ingle, their bowl of thin rice, though they will weep as loudly as any when they die. It costs less to burn a stick of incense now and again than to provide daily food. Silver hairs, however, usually gain respect in China. Do they not indicate a maturity, a flavour of ripeness which time alone brings and which properly trained youth should appreciate after the manner of a connoisseur?

Mrs. Sung spoke of her own mother. Terrible to say, she had been a victim of the Boxer troubles. The family were living in a house in a Tientsin Concession. The Boxers had fired into the Concession; a shell had burst through a corner of the room where her mother and the women and children were huddled in terror. A piece of shell smashed her mother's leg, and soon after she died.

" Were you there? " I asked in horror.

" Yes," she said simply: " I was a little girl. My brother was a babe in arms. The amahs were so frightened that I took care of him and saw to him. I cannot speak about it. My dear mother's last look was on me. Mercifully I do not think she suffered long: she was soon unconscious. But that is why my brother and I are such friends. We would do anything to help each other."

"Tell me," I asked, "for I have often wanted to know, but never liked to ask before. He was your brother by your own mother: do you think you love each other more for that? Or do you love your brothers by your father's other wives just as much?"

She pondered a moment. "I am sure," she said, "those who have the same mother love each other better than the others, as a rule. Not always, of course. Sometimes it happens that a sister by another mother is nearer your own age, and you study and play together more than an elder or younger sister by your own mother."

Her father was too public a man for any need of pretended ignorance of his family arrangements. All China knew that, though he had been educated abroad, he had carried on the old Chinese ways of life, and had seen no reason to abrogate the tradition that a great position and great wealth are most suitably adorned by a large household, a plurality of wives, and many children.

To the Chinese, the generation of to-day is but a bridge between the future and the past. In particular, as they reverence their past forbears, so they hope their successors will in due course reverence them. This reverence—which we call, in default of a better word, Ancestor Worship—is largely the reason why rich Chinese officials in the past indulged in a plurality of wives: in concubines. They hoped to have sons who would honour them when dead. A Chinese had not done his duty to his house and line till he had provided men-children to carry it on. Thus only was a happy Immortality safeguarded. While still within the precincts of the cheerful day, a Chinese has lived surrounded by his family. Who can contemplate the chill of possible solitude in the next world without a shiver? The more sons there are, the warmer will be the atmosphere of remembrance in this life, and the more company in the next. True, ghosts and demons, who inflict untold distress according to the ideas of the common people, are the logical outcome for some. No bright angelic visitants wing iridescent wings back from the gloomy portals for Chinese bereaved. Even the fairies are sinister and malignant. But the beliefs in the continuity of life, in the oneness of the living with those who have passed over the bridge, comes with comfort to the thoughtful, whether Chinese or foreign.

"I ONCE stayed as a visitor in a Chinese house," said I to Mrs. Sung: "the house of the family Kung, of whose former head, a Prime Minister for many years, you have doubtless heard."

She was all attention in a minute. "I hope they were kind," she asked.

"Never were people kinder," I said, "and though Kung Po Fu—or Uncle Kung as I came to call him—has returned to the heavens, his son and his daughters are my dear friends to-day. I am eagerly looking forward to seeing them again when we go Northwards."

"I wish I could have stayed as a friend like that when I was abroad," she sighed. "But I should doubtless have made many gaucheries."

"And doubtless I did," I acknowledged: "but they were broad-minded and charitable and put them down to a different standard of manners."

"How did you like the food?" she asked anxiously, and on my expressing appreciation, gave my hand a pat and plied me with a dozen questions, as to my bed, how I spent the time, how I liked my hosts. I described it all, even to the young people's teasings and jokes, the pretty ways of the baby grandchild and the devoted labours of her mother Gentle Calm. The colour came into her cheeks as she questioned and questioned, and found that without exception my replies were satisfactory.

In the midst, her husband came and sat down with us. But he did not enter into the conversation with her vivacity; and gradually a certain stiffness in his pose could not but affect my freedom. Finally, with a bitterness which his studied restraint could not disguise, he came out with the question which I then realized had been disturbing both their souls the whole time.

"And how," asked he, with a sarcastic smile, "did you get on with the Great Man's secondary wives, with his harem?"

Almost brusquely, rudely, he threw the query at me—altogether unlike his usual agreeable manner.

I was taken by surprise and for a moment, foolishly, felt a touch of anger at his thus breaking down our pleasant intercourse. Then I realized that there was pain and wounded susceptibility in the air. I turned my head towards Mrs. Sung, saw the pulse beating in her neck and found her eyes fixed on mine. Quickly she averted them. Mr. Sung was sitting stiffly upright, his mouth set hard. Silence fell between us. What answer would I give? Would I politely ignore those concubines? Or would I do worse—would I condone the hateful system? Out of a blue sky, an electric flash was quivering. Our friendship was on trial. The joy of it that I could answer freely out of a quiet mind, with never a damaging clause—that they could go with me into that beloved household and find only a clean family life, a Puritan disdain of self-indulgence!

"There were no secondary wives in my Uncle Kung's household, and never had been," I said with deliberation.

But that was not enough. Between us must pass the "diamond of sincerity." It was required of me that I must show on which side I stood in this vital question of plural wives—of concubines. So I added, slowly, bowing a little to them Chinese-wise, "Their household was like your own in that matter. The taking of a subsidiary wife was against my Uncle Kung's principles." In a second the strain was over. We were comrades in a common ideal, for a beloved land; nay, more, I was doing them the justice of realizing they desired as lofty a standard of morality for their land as I did for my own. We were allies in a deep distrust of lowering the flag in such matters. Their very anxiety as to my answer had given the clue to their own household faith. However tolerantly they were obliged to regard the arrangements of their forbears and the older generation, evidently there was only the one way of married loyalty for them.

One's heart yearns towards these younger men and women who feel much shame over that ugliness in their people's life. They fear that foreigners will despise their nation as one fit only for lower ways than their own : they are ashamed that curious outsiders should know the state of affairs. They would not have blamed me if I had glozed over that imaginary harem. But they would have known, and to the quick of their hearts, that it was politeness that had bidden me shut my eyes. Who can find any warmth or support in a friendship which pretends to perceive nothing of one's sorrows and sicknesses ? Are we ourselves so free of disquieting shame that we do not need the compassionate understanding of a friend or sister ?

One of the reasons why there is nowadays no real opposition to the Chinese Christian Church among the educated Chinese of the old school is that for these past decades it has stood uncompromisingly for the Christian idea of marriage and the home, as well as against opium. The new younger school of anti-Christian thought easily wins over Chinese whose roots of learning are not deeply established in past traditions and philosophies. But men of the older schools, seeking new learning for their sons, send them to the Christian schools.

" They may not teach the Chinese Classics as thoroughly as our private tutors, but they give us principles," said Li Cheng to me once.

" No, my uncle, Kung Ta Jen was not a Christian : he had had but little to do with Christianity," I replied to Mrs. Sung when she asked me if that was why he had no concubines. " Also he was blessed in his wife. But neither was that the reason. It was because he was of one mind with Confucius in the matter," I explained. " While not condemning polygamy in the ignorant, he considered it unnecessary for a scholar or a statesman."

Uncle Kung would far rather, indeed, read a book of history than play with the tangles of Neaera's hair, as another statesman philosopher put it. " You remember how Confucius shook the dust of one State off his feet when its Duke accepted the present of so many dancing-girls from his rival. No ruler of a State that dallies with dancing-girls is going to accomplish much for that State: such was Confucius' opinion. It was also my Uncle Kung's."

The virtue has gone out of his manhood in luxury. Delilah will shear his locks any moment that she wills. And after that, where is Samson?

> "Look at the great Deliverer now;
> Eyeless, at Gaza, at the mill, with slaves."

From that slavery he will redeem his soul only at the most tremendous price, if at all. It speaks doubly well, therefore, for the older generation of Chinese, who have chosen the way of the many wives themselves that, to-day, they send their sons to schools where they know this ancient polygamous habit is looked upon askance. They might bind their children with cords, hard and fast; for, economically, the Chinese son is dependent on his parents. It is to their credit that, on the whole, when the sons manifest a desire to abide by the one wife, the fathers accept the new rule and respect such a position. Not that that has prevented them from arranging for early marriage and hoping for grandsons. If there are no grandsons, possibly the old parents may press for the taking of a secondary wife. Yet, even so, there is often a way round for the young husband in that dilemma: for, according to Chinese tradition, he can look about and adopt one of the sons of a relative in the male line.

The trouble in a monogamous house arises when husband and wife are unsuited to each other, just as it arises in the West. But in the East a boy is betrothed too often without any reference to his desires and to a complete stranger. One must always be in fear of the result. When he has been educated and she has not, the bonds of such a marriage chafe and fret spirit and nerves. One such young man at a university in a provincial capital seriously wrote and asked his young wife, an unlettered country-girl who could not read, if she would kindly commit suicide and set him free. The letter had to be read to her, and one can imagine her outraged feelings. She did not oblige him.

A scholar of the modern school, who has studied economics, law, philosophy abroad, or a politician leading the free life of modern Peking society, realizes afresh each day that the wife to whom he was bound in his youth by his parents is an illiterate woman. It needs a touch of iron in him if he is to keep to the standards he has set for himself. Well for him if he remembers Zarathustra's cry : " By my love and hope, I conjure thee, throw not away the hero in thy soul ! Keep holy thy highest hope." Nor is it easy for the wife ; for the illiterate have intuitions and passions. She, too, has to exercise forbearance.

Ancestral deference, on the other hand, does not altogether account for the exceeding largeness of some of the older households. How was it that so many of the older generation avoided its logic and abided by the severer standard, as did my Uncle Kung ? He was certainly not alone in his monogamistic preferences. Perchance there is a touch of King Solomon in the habit of concubinage. May it be that there is a certain pride and pleasure in contemplating a garden of one's own, full of variegated plants and flowers with their different charms ? Possibly a man feels a little sumptuous in owning a harem. There is a sense of power over human lives and destiny. Moreover, if one of his worshippers, his wives, fails to appreciate his many virtues, he can turn to another and inhale the incense of her more discerning spirit. Probably, indeed, they vie with each other in offering up that incense. If they become disconcertingly human and quarrel with each other over his favours, the jewels he bestows, or the favouring of the son of one of them over another, he can retire quickly and with dignity to his own quarters and wait till life's exigencies bring them to a less petulant state of mind.

Some marry a second wife because they seek a companionship absent in their first arranged marriage. This is becoming more common now, said Mrs. Sung to me, in troubled tones. Even an educated girl will consent to such a " marriage " these days. To begin with, only the rich can afford a plurality, so she is sure of comfort and a degree of luxury. Secondly, she knows she has been chosen because of personal liking—for these second contracts are made after the parties have seen each other. And lastly, she hopes to be the real mistress of the house. The first wife is the wife *de jure*, the second the wife *de facto*.

That is all very well : but she has forgotten another factor in human nature. Once the standard of a single-wife has been lowered, wife-acquiring is apt to become a habit. Why stop at two ? Moreover, the larger your household, the greater your money requirements. Money you must obviously have : it is your just due from Heaven. So you become, with each wife, a little less scrupulous as to how you obtain that money. Once you have the money, then it is also obvious that another wife lends éclat to your entourage. Yet the more old-fashioned Chinese halted at four or five. This number was permitted by established traditions : after that, plurality without restraint was the hall-mark of the *nouveau riche*. With four or five, you can still implicitly refer to the need of an established lineage, of ancestral obligations. But after that, it is either decadence, or undiscerning vulgarity, and practised by such people as ill-bred militarists swollen with ill-gotten gains. So thought Mrs. Sung.

Though they lack the bed-rock Puritanism of my Uncle Kung's ethical monogamous code, there may be real dignity and kindness amongst some of the polygamous Elders towards their several wives. Mrs. Sung's father was a case in point. He required a certain amount of wit and integrity in his wives as well as more physical charms. Were they not to be the mothers of his children ? He had the sense as well as the means to house them in different mansions, often in different cities. He was affection itself to all his children, daughters as well as sons, and could and did give them impartially the best education within his power. He loved to see his girls polished after the likeness of palaces. This is plurality at its best. It is also rare.

" They say that one of the Shantung generals has sixty wives," said Mrs. Sung to me. " I suppose foreigners, knowing it, and even compelled to meet some of them, will think all Chinese are like that or approve such licentiousness. It makes one sick with disgust. That sort of thing is increasing too as those without traditional learning obtain power and money. Unversed in either Confucian ethics or Western learning, they love display, such as stars on their breasts, glass-windowed motor-cars—and wives covered with jewels."

Young China is not without charm

"Do not fear," I comforted her. "We foreigners very well understand that waves of brutishness seem to sweep over peoples at times: and that it behoves those of the other mind to understand each other and stand by each other, in the common fight."

"Students returned from America or Europe have a higher standard as a rule. They do not always please us—or you. Too often they seem to have forgotten many of our best Chinese ways, but in this they set a good example."

I told her a story I had recently heard of Chang Tso Lin's old-fashioned family circle. Chang Tso Lin, the Old Tiger of Manchuria, five feet high, weighing nine stone, soft of speech, gentle-eyed, mild of manner, yet the absolute ruler of his people, was merciless and ferocious in his punishment of those whom he thought had betrayed him. He shot sixteen Chinese stockbrokers that same year of our talk because they speculated in his paper money, and its value consequently went down in the market . . . a Short Way with your Stockbrokers, as Swift might have said.

Yet he had another side to him. A missionary lady was visiting his home and took some picture cards with her. Chang Tso Lin's youngest little boy leaned against her knee as she showed a card, "Suffer the little children to come unto Me," which he liked. He looked up into that tender woman's face. "We all know," he told her seriously, "that Jesus Christ is the best man that ever lived. But," he added, "my father is the kindest!"

Thus the smallest son, the Tiger Cub, spoke of the Old Tiger of Manchuria, his father.

"Chang Tso Lin is an old-fashioned militarist. He only has five wives," explained Mrs. Sung.

I did not tell her the story of how he took his second wife, as it was well to change the subject. It had made me smile, when I heard it, and from a friend, an Irishwoman. She had known the first Madame Chang, now departed to the world of spirits. Twenty-five years ago, Madame Chang had been a very capable energetic woman, the last to permit her man to espouse another.

Chang Tso Lin was driven into the banditry with which he was often twitted in his later grandeur. There was a vendetta between his clan and another on the Manchurian plains of the Liaotung peninsula. One dreadful day the other clan swept down upon the Chang clan and destroyed it, every man—except young Chang, who happened to be away. He was seventeen, and he came back to find his village full of blood and corpses and blazing homes. White-faced, his heart black with rage, he swore revenge, this young lad of five foot. For his immediate safety he had to take to the hills. His only course was to join the bandits. So able was he that he became in time their leader, and one fierce day of delight he in his turn led his band down upon that other clan. And this time he destroyed them, every single man and boy. None was left to plan revenge. But he had done the unpardonable in civilized countries; he had taken the law into his own hands, and therefore the law from henceforth hunted him and his band. As an insignificant member of a bandit group and inconspicuous, there had been a chance of his slipping back to ordinary life—that pathetic objective in life of all bandits. He had now no alternative but to continue his bandit leadership. Tradition has it that he was harsher with the rich than the poor. Among the Manchurian mountains and in the forests he lived for the years of his early manhood, cut off from the chance of learning to read or write, or the graces of peace. It is a marvel that such an one can ever take his place again amongst cities. During the Japanese-Russian War he caught at his chance of reprieve. With his guerrilla band he helped the Japanese so efficiently that, at the end of that war which brought them triumph, they interceded with the Chinese Viceroy of the three Eastern provinces, which make up what we call Manchuria, and obtained his pardon. His military skill had gained him a share of admiration from the Japanese and they could, and did, recommend the incorporation of Chang, now in the prime of life, and his band, into the ranks of the newly reformed, poorly officered Chinese army. He was given the rank of colonel, and presently settled down to a life of comparative peace as a military official in a Chinese city. His duties now were to hunt the bandits with whom he was once allied: and ever afterwards Chang Tso Lin was a good bandit-hunter. He did not harass the poor wretches till they became too outrageous. Then he was drastic.

At what period he married a wife, history does not say : but married he became and to an extremely efficient woman. Like Mrs. Pak on board our ship coming out, she had a talent for finance. It seems to run in Chinese women. Chang himself, unlearned, could keep no accounts. She it was, Madame Chang, who had the brain for this. She not only kept the accounts but the purse-strings. A very capable and economical housewife, she knew how to save against a rainy day. He trusted her completely, and she was worthy of his trust. But one fine day, in a raid, his band caught a handsome Manchu girl. Chang liked her looks. " A very pleasing secondary wife she would make ! " was his thought. But how could he venture to suggest the idea to the excellent woman who administered his affairs so much to his satisfaction ? He could ride rough-shod over her feelings, of course, this being his due marital right. But she might pay him out afterwards for it in a variety of ways known to woman, especially financially. Ah well, guile often gains far more for its promoters than force.

That night he took to sighing, to looking very thoughtful, a trifle glum ; and he ate a poor dinner. " What is the matter ? " asked his wife.

" Nothing, oh, nothing," he prevaricated, and sighed again. This naturally roused her curiosity. She persisted. He persisted. At last she got his story from him.

" Thou dost share my heart's secrets, so I suppose I must unburden myself. Yet I did not desire to cast this load upon thee : for thou hast borne so many," he began.

" Tell me at once," she fretted.

Then he told her that they had made a raid upon a village and his men had taken a girl, a Manchu girl, intending to hold her to ransom ; and now it turned out that she was the daughter of a rich official whom they could not at all afford to offend.

" In short," ended the wily one, " he demands not only the girl back but a *douceur* of five thousand dollars with her, or he will set the military on our track."

" Five thousand dollars ! " shrieked his wife. " What

robbery ! What monstrous greed ! Surely you can bring down the price of the daughter of such a Turtle ? "

" We have brought it down," he answered, " for it was ten thousand originally."

" Is she a pretty girl ? " asked his wife.

" On the contrary. Quite an ordinary wench."

" Five thousand dollars, and for a plain girl like that ! Why, it will make a big hole in our savings. And here have I been pinching away, cutting down the cook's bills—and all for this ! It is unheard of. Surely there is some other way out. There must be."

" Well, of course," said her husband, scratching his head in a puzzled way, " they did suggest I might take her as a secondary wife, and then they would say no more about the matter. But how could I do that with thee here ? I told them plainly that nothing would induce me to do such a thing —that my Within-Apartment needed no further adornment. Art thou not my Treasure, and sufficient ? Am I not blest in my Jasmine-Flower ? "

Naturally his wife felt complimented to a vast degree. But the matter of the five thousand dollars weighed on her and rankled in her economical soul. All night long she turned and twisted, pondering how to encompass the difficulty. When morning came, she had made up her mind.

" Listen," she said, and woke her husband, " I have come to the conclusion that you must bring this girl into our house. She is plain, you say, so I do not fear her blandishments on you. And she will make a servant for me. It is intolerable to think of paying away five thousand of our hard-earned dollars for her."

" Impossible," said he, " I do not wish any other wife."

But she pressed and pressed. So at last he consented. Thus he obtained his secondary wife—and peace with honours. " No wonder he is ruler of such vast areas," I had commented to my Irish friend. She told me that later, when they had settled down, and the bandit life was over, she went at the request of the first Madame Chang to teach her foreign arithmetic. For, of course, the lady had always used the abacus, which is a mechanical and tortuous method of mathematics. She was forty when she began to learn arithmetic, and it did not come easily to her to write our Arabic figures, 1, 2, 3, 4 : but she worked away till a sudden epidemic swept her away, as epidemics have a habit of doing in the East.

Her husband grieved sincerely for her. "I shall never have another wife like her," he wept, "she was unique amongst women."

Yün-Yün came running up to interrupt Mrs. Sung and myself in our now desultory talk. Her soft Chinese shoes, made by Amah of cloth and then embroidered, padded on the deck. Her chubby knees were slightly grimed with play. Her bobbed hair tumbled about her face like a Little Cloud. Her cheeks were rosy.

"What shall we play next ?" she asked.

Mrs. Sung turned to me and groaned. "This," said she, "is the question I am asked every other hour. And I want to finish this second sleeve."

"Then are you in the position of all other mothers," I mocked her. "You cannot expect the sweets of maternity without its worries. But this time I 'll come to your help."

I bade Yün-Yün fetch Nieh-Nieh and Amah, caught Mr. Sung's hand, and made them stand in a circle to play "Ring-a-roses." They stood looking at me : and I fetched a breath. Suddenly I realized the game had to be played in Chinese. In Chinese—or they would not understand it, except Mr. Sung ! And how could I expect him to translate those foolish words ? To any one who has not been in the unheard-of position I had involved myself in, I can only say : try turning the words "Ring-a-ring-of-roses" at a moment's notice into comprehensible French, German or Choctaw. And with a little group of children gazing at you, waiting. Well, I did it—with variations and permutations, amid bursts of laughter on Amah's part (and Mrs. Sung's as she sat knitting) at my extraordinary phrases. I was obliged to embroider on the original : I said we were flowers blown down by the wind. However, the children enjoyed it. After each bout of "falling down," fat little Strong-as-a-Rock remained pleasurably spread upon the deck like the precious pat-of-butter that he was, rolling about and chuckling. Yün-Yün would tug him to his adorable feet. I had to invent another couplet finally about how

> " Down there came a shower of rain
> Which made them all stand up again ! "

We performed the rite a thousand times, or so it seemed : neither babes nor Amah would willingly stop. Mr. Sung withdrew discreetly after his first blessing of us. It was hot work. The tiffin gong was a welcome sound. Amah bore the mites off to wash their hands. Suddenly Little Cloud broke away from her hand-clasp and ran back to her mother. " Mamma," she whispered with a loud breath, " what shall I call her ? " and she glanced in my direction.

" You can call her Po Mu," answered Mrs. Sung, smiling at me : which means " Auntie."

Old China had cradled me. Very Young China was now permitting me to cradle her in my turn.

WHEN I had come on board the river steamer at Shanghai, it had been night, and the majority of the passengers had been asleep. Entering by way of the lower deck, I had a dim vision of double tiers of human beings in the huge dormitory for the poorer passengers forming the centre of the ship. My mind had been full of a conversation just ended with a friend at whose house I had dined. He had accompanied me to the dock. We had dismissed our rickshawmen, and then walked about together for half an hour in the pitchy night, stumbling over the coils of rope, avoiding as best we could the tram-lines laid for the cranes to run on. He was telling me of New China. He had known and loved Old China: he had begun his life in her service. How about the New?

"Full of impulses and stirrings that lead her into extravagances at times: but she is not the only Youth that reacts that fashion, eh?" We laughed, for we both knew that in his own youth he himself had somewhat disturbed the greybeards. "Old China had some exasperating tricks: so have we ourselves, and had. Youth everywhere, Asia, Africa, Europe, America, yes, Australia too, truly has problems ahead of it, just as we had in our day: with vistas of possibilities. We of the older generation must not but be very considerate. I daresay they do not particularly desire our consideration: but that does not prevent our giving it. It helps more than they know. Impatience is the necessary sap of youth, but patience is the essence of maturity." So he had talked—wisely and well.

My friend had brought me an invitation to dine with Chinese friends of his, Mr. and Mrs. Yang, and was expressing his disappointment that I could not accept, owing to this trip up-river.

"How I wish you could go!" he said. "They represent the new Christian home life better than any I know. You only have to go inside the door to feel 'Here is goodness, here is happiness.' The house is well ordered, the welcome genuine, the wholesome fare is unpretentious but good. These are symptoms of a healthy home life which speak well of a household anywhere. Mrs. Yang is bringing up her children in the way one would wish. She and Mr. Yang are partners in content."

"'The heart of her husband doth safely trust in her,'" I quoted.

They had both been educated in England. The result upon them had been that they had taken the best of our civilization. For the rest, they had grasped that, despite shortcomings, we are aiming at some ultimate good; and they were not of the sort continually to fix their attention on deficiencies. They looked primarily at whatsoever things are right and clean and lovely about us; and found these of no small account. Mr. Yang was not a ranting raving "anti-this and anti-that." He was full of work, and in the evenings he wrote and translated on behalf of his Christian faith. "If any one," ended my friend, "asked me if Christianity had failed in China, I should take them to this house and let them experience its atmosphere."

It was a pleasure to hear the enthusiasm of this seasoned man, who had lately seen mischief working havoc with his dearest aspirations for the nation and church he served.

Yet I could believe what he said of Mrs. Yang, for it happened that a few days before there had been a Girl Guide tea-party at the British Consulate. Most of the ladies in the committee chairs were British or American, but three or four were Chinese. In their dresses of bright unadorned silk and satin, with their sleek hatless heads, they had contrasted charmingly with the hatted and bigger-made foreign women. Half-way through the programme, one of the Chinese ladies on the platform rose to make her speech. I listened enthralled. That golden voice! Those sane direct sentences, in perfectly balanced English, that unconscious dignity of carriage, those quiet hands! The sentiments, and the expression of them, were exactly what they should have been.

The speaker was perhaps not beautiful ; but the turn of her head was full of a joyous graciousness. She was well-built, and her poise spoke better than anything else of a generous mind at peace, of a radiance of heart sufficient to warm others.

" Who is that ? " I whispered to my neighbour. " She speaks like a Portia." My neighbour gave me a wondering look.

" How strange that you should say that ! It is Mrs. Yang," she answered, and added, " She won the gold medal for elocution in England during her last year there, and it was presented by Ellen Terry herself."

That was how the thought of the golden voice had come, was it ? Mrs. Yang rose again to return thanks : and the beautiful modulations flooded the walls of the large room.

" Yes, I should have liked to dine at Mrs. Yang's," I said to my friend with sincerity, as once again we came to the ship's gangway in our peripatetics through the night. Then we had shaken hands, and I had crept softly along the deck, not to disturb those poor folk sleeping uneasily in their tiers of bunks.

After tiffin on the second afternoon, I asked my friend, the First Officer, if he would take me down to walk amongst those lower-deck passengers. I should have felt an intruder, had I gone by myself, as though wishing to pry into their poverty with no semblance of sharing it. Not that the conditions of the ship were themselves bad. The Officer showed me with considerable pride the arrangements made for washing, for sleeping, for cooking—since each family party cooks for itself. They were reasonably good arrangements ; and humanity and hygiene were studied.

" Taps left running again," he said, and turned off a faucet in a wash-room. These were people unused to seeing water run out of a pipe, who did not realize the difficulty of keeping supplies of fresh water on a ship, he explained.

He told me that the foreign shipping company, besides providing the transport, had nothing to do with these passengers. The Chinese compradore it was who sold the tickets, arranged the berthing. He paid the company for these privileges, and the more passengers he took, naturally the greater was his profit. It was to his advantage to see that he brought no great epidemic on board, and no pirates, and that the passengers were not crowded to the point of mutiny. The price he charged for the tickets was left to him, and might vary from trip to trip, according as there was a rush or not. The greater the rush, the higher the charge, as a rule. The Chinese shopkeeper thinks if you want two of an article, he should charge you more : for manifestly you desire it very greatly. Occasionally the captain would call a halt if he thought the boat overloaded. But, as he said, when one of the disturbances from which the Yangtsze has suffered the last few years, was taking place, the boat had to be very laden indeed before he could bring himself to deny a refuge to folk perhaps fleeing for their lives. The ships are well built, and the river journey is not attended with the risks of the open sea. The habit of the various armies, however, of firing at these ships from the shore means that often they are now plated with armour.

Making our way towards the bows, the First Officer and I passed slowly through the ranks. Most of the folk were silent, sleeping amidst the heaps of their luggage, rolled in their padded cotton-wool quilts ; or they lay on the narrow deck, or sat on the floor of the passages, in the sun. We stepped gingerly amongst them. Never, outside a hospital, have I seen so many legs with huge ulcers on the shins. The trousers were turned back to give relief, and perhaps a green leaf was placed medicinally over the wound. Nobody was reading ; few probably could read. Once we passed a little group of sturdy men, better clad than the others, in a coarse navy serge. They had a map of France, Italy and Austria, spread out before them on the wooden deck. They had been labourers in the French Labour Corps, they told us, and they were going over in memory their routes and travels. They derived real pleasure, as do all travellers, in following with their fingers the names on the map, which was printed in both French and Chinese. They spoke gravely with us, with the dignity of men of the world, as if, in effect, they said with Ulysses :

> "Much have I seen and known ;
> Cities of men, and manners, climates, councils,
> governments."

Their enlarged outlook had given them a certain contempt for their comrades of the same deck. You may see the same look in the eyes of an ex-navy man, who comes to read your gas-meter at home and tells you he was up the Yangtsze in such-and-such a year.

"You don't have to mind what people here say about China, ma'am," he says tolerantly and pityingly. "They just don't understand. You should have heard one man jabber at a meeting I attended. I had to come out after a bit. No use arguing with him, you know, ma'am. He never would understand: it isn't his fault. He has not been there."

On board this boat these few men were studying their map of France, talking of "Marseille," and looking with good-humoured charity on the narrow views and incurable ignorance of the stay-at-homes.

Occasionally an old woman nodded to me and gave me a toothless smile, her face a patchwork of wrinkles. So I stopped to ask her, as politely as I knew how, if she had "eaten her rice yet"—China's way of saying "Good-morning." When we had passed on, we could hear her neighbours burst into chattering, asking what I had said. When we came back from the bows, understanding that the First Officer had small time to linger, I bade him return to the Upper Air without me. Several women roused themselves from their semi-comatose state of waiting for the next landing or making ready the next meal, to come and look intently into my face, take my hand, feel the quality of my clothing. Not ungently did they handle me. After all these years of intercourse, travelling as they were on the foreigner's ship, most of them had never yet come to close quarters with a foreigner, at least not a woman. Of course, it may be said with equal truth that few of the inhabitants of Western countries have much contact with such Chinese as are in their midst. Since, moreover, on the whole these Chinese abroad are peaceable folk, their rare appearances in the public eye are only when one of them has run amok and taken to knife or drug. From this comes the very unfair impression that murder and drugs are their chief pastimes. As I write, this City of Learning in which I live is plastered with theatre bills, on which the shadow of a looming sinister Chinese with knife upraised betokens who is the villain of the piece. And it seems the unerring instinct of a white woman when she adorns herself with some Chinese character, in jewelry or embroidery, the beauty of which has caught her eye, to wear it upside down, and never by any chance any other way. As I sat in a bus yesterday morn, the lady opposite wore the Chinese word for " joy " wrong way up on her hat. How should we not expect similar misapprehensions of our mind and manners on the part of untravelled Chinese ?

It will always seem a strange thing to me, however, that after a century of a foreign intercourse which has been so vital, the common Chinese people of the big ports, of the railways and steamers, have had little contact with the foreigners. When they see them, it is usually at a distance. One morning in Shanghai, with half an hour to spare I went down to the creek-side in Hongkew, not far from the ugly iron bridge leading from the Settlement. Foreigners were mingling with Chinese passing over the bridge ; and I was not a hundred yards below it. The biting March winds had parched the city. The river looked attractive, though it was bronze colour. The sun glittered on it, and I went down to one of the landing-stages, looking at the big cargo barges passing easily downstream, well-kept, clean and workman-like. Could I hire a barge for the day, sail down in the splendid sunlight, warmly wrapped up, to the clean air at the mouth of the river, and then come back before sunset ? The wish floated vaguely into my thought. I knew I had neither the time nor the energy to tackle the proposition. At the side of the stage was a big boat being loaded with rusty iron slats, or so they seemed to me ; long awkward, swaying, heavy pieces of narrow metal a dozen feet long, carried thither between two men from an ironsmith's across the road. When the bearers saw me standing, they broke into an incredibly fast walk, they swung their shoulders with a delicious swaggering gait and, derisive of the weight, flung the heavy slats into the well of the boat. In short, they were showing off before me. Sweat poured down their faces. Their trousers, blue cotton lined with white, were rolled to the knee. The sinews and muscles of their shapely calves stood out, and the sweat poured down them also. I wished

I had been taught the use of chisel and marble. They were glorious subjects for sculpture. Pride in their prowess shone in them, from the toss of their heads, to the grip of their slim and perfect toes. God taught Chinese coolies that balance of foot and backbone and shoulder swing, thought I.

They jerked their heads at my smile of appreciation. What artist does not work the better for a meed of applause? Shyly, children that they were in heart, they came across to me. Then more of the Shanghai boatmen came, and still more. In old days they would have scrutinized me to embarrassing point, stared open-mouthed, pinched my clothing in unmannerly way, pressed uncomfortably upon me. Up country, where the white person is not seen even walking upon a distant bridge as in Shanghai, the countryfolk still would do that. But these men clustered about me with a delicate reticence. I knew they were pleased to have a foreign woman standing amongst them, and that it was out of the ordinary for them to be near one—in Shanghai, where there are thousands of foreign women. Only, of course, not many foreign women have the time, even if they have the desire, in the rush of Shanghai life, with all its societies and Society, to stand and be thronged by a group of boatmen.

Their dialect was difficult to me, and we laughed over our bunglings. I had nothing to say to them, except the simple Chinese politenesses with which I had heard my parents and my husband greet the passers-by. "Have you eaten your rice? What is your Honourable Age? How many sons have you? Are your parents still on earth, and do they live in Shanghai? Where are you taking those iron rails? Do you think Shanghai a good place to live in, or do you long for the country again?"

To which latter question they all replied that Shanghai was a very good place to live in: expensive, but then wages were bigger. "Yet the country is the best place to live in, if there is enough food to go round."

"May you put forth riches and save enough to go back home again!" quoth I, and said good-bye.

"Au revoir—and come back to-morrow," they invited.

"I can't waste your time from your running after riches," I riposted gaily. I heard them chattering happily and laughing when I had gone; and to any one who is feeling melancholy and has half an hour to waste in Shanghai, I commend an unstudied colloquy with Shanghai's boatmen as a pleasant interlude in optimism. I went up the road and crossed the bridge. A barge swung through below, between the piers. The man at the big sweep in the stern was nodding at me as if his head would fall off—one of my new friends.

And now, here I was on board this ship up the Yangtsze, once again talking with such folk, simple of heart, but all intent on the same object—"enough to eat" for themselves and their families, and a little store for a rainy day. But what a painful sight many of them presented: and how different was the scene about me compared with the one on the upper deck, not so many feet above! There all was spaciousness, aloofness, cleanliness: the well-washed passengers were sitting comfortably in their spotless clothing, with its fine textures and attractive colours. Probably none of these upper-deck passengers was of the wealthy class. But they had always known the decencies of life, and to them these were not luxuries but necessities. Here were the people who wore cotton clothes: of dark blue, because it does not constantly need to be washed: and coarse fabrics that irritate the unaccustomed skin—as I know, for after half an hour of them once, I put them off as unendurable. To descend from one to the other deck was appalling to the heart. That is true of all such "descents": they appal. From a bird that can soar at will into the untrammelled heavens, one has become an ant crawling on the ground and possibly being crawled over. It is hard to breathe freely; the air seems filled with the sighs of the heavy-laden. With only an occasional visit into such an atmosphere, it would be easy to become sombre, over-sombre. But when one lives a while in close touch with the individuals who form that seething mass, one finds that joy is no plant that grows only on leisured soil: that if stone walls do not a prison make to the brave of heart, neither do days and years of labour stoutly performed. Respect for this courage and cheerfulness, humility regarding one's own poor achievements in that other atmosphere of a luxury in spiritual as well as material things, mingle with gratitude for the unfailing sympathy which these poor give one in trouble. Still, leisure is desirable: it gives labour wings; and stone walls and grinding toil can crush and narrow hearts.

Such thoughts are bound to invade the mind in any crowd of lowly people anywhere in the world. What then of a Chinese crowd? Is it different from any other?

In a crowd of Slavs, or of Hindus, man's, and perhaps especially woman's, sorrows seem the intense note. Not so with a Chinese crowd, for though their sorrows are as lamentable as those of others, they face them with an innate fortitude that has something of French clear-sightedness. Which, however, does not prevent them from indulging in preliminary bursts of hysteria that clear the air for them; a *soulagement* of their immediate feelings.

Yet they are not far removed either from the psychology of an Anglo-Saxon crowd. Lying on the decks, they looked an army battered in the fight, but with no intention of giving up the struggle. Of course occasionally they dally with the thought of abandoning it: who does not? And suicide some do commit. It is not usually from sheer despair, however, but rather from a desire to spite Fate or their adversaries—in a sort of rage with life. They go down fighting, so to speak. Here on this river boat, one saw the army at rest, with time to tend its wounds, in a breathing-space between its combats while it was being transported from one battlefield to another.

a little overdrawn.

CHAPTER VII THE NEEDY WHEN THEY CRY

WHAT then distinguishes a Chinese crowd from any other? One sees plainly the marks of toil, the signs of an exceeding poverty, and yet an inherent doggedness and endurance. "They give so much: they ask so little," as my father put it in my hearing once to a society of students.

Probably the distinctive mark that would strike a first-comer would be the lack of cleanliness and the abundance of unnecessary disease. The countryfolk seem no better off than the townfolk. They are often the poorer of the two; sanitation is less regarded by them, and there is not the stimulus to personal pride in appearance which moves a city population.

The next feature is that there is such a vast number of them. It would be easy to lose the individual in the crowd. Yet as the glance travels from face to face, from figure to figure, it finds many differences in physiognomy and expression. Here is one whose face bespeaks modesty and self-forgetfulness: there is another whose coarsened lines betray self-indulgence. Here is a sweet and shy girl; there a youth, clean-limbed, cheerful—a young god as self-reliant as Michael Angelo's "David": over yonder is a form full of disease, a noseless face, the product of his own sin or another's, or of ignorance.

A legend is current in the West that the Chinese are an inscrutable joyless race, their faces made blank in order to deceive the innocent foreigner. Nothing could be further from the truth. It is, indeed, inculcated in every young Chinese that he should stand with eyes cast down before his elders and betters: and strangers are treated with this aspect of polite respect. But one walk down a Chinese street will dispel the other illusion. Its occupants are laughing, loiter-

Photo by Lady Hosie

A Ningpo Countrywoman and her Two Nephews, who go to school in the town

ing, chattering, calling to each other. There is animation and vivacity. Very different are the passers-by from the silent quick-stepping English folk who hasten down the grey streets of London Town.

But that unwashed appearance, these innumerable diseases! They cannot be denied, and it is not altogether surprising that many people take but one look and then turn and flee. The immensity of the task of showing these crowds the means to help themselves, and the fear of contamination, inevitably cause the great majority of those who can, to pass through the Folk of the Lower Deck, press as quickly as possible to the upper deck, and remain there in a blessed segregation. For these poor and needy of the lower deck are folk who have not known soap, till foreign trade introduced its use. To them it is still a luxury to be used parsimoniously. Often, too, water is another luxury which has to be paid for with a couple of their pitifully few coins. Hot water means fuel, and fuel costs money. Even weak cheap tea is a rare treat to millions of China's Northern folk. We pay for our water in our city rates and perhaps grumble at the price. If our water had to be raised from wells by man power, we should conserve it drop by drop. No doubt our forefathers in mediæval times considered well before they made their scanty ablutions: in the comparatively recent times of Smollett and Fielding, our countryfolk knew much of disease and little of preventives or sanitation. We in the West have had a greater deliverance than we realize. Without water or soap, with a devastating ignorance as to hygiene and infection, quite apart from the superstitions which form the mental outfit of every people, white, yellow or brown, and in the position of being ever but "one jump ahead of starvation," how can the Chinese labouring crowds be other than they are?

Be it also remembered that human labour and human transport are dearer in the long run than machine labour or transport. His well-water, when it has to be paid for by the poor townsman in China, costs him very much more in proportion than ours from a tap costs us. As the American Commercial Attaché reminded me, when we discussed these things together, a Chinese coolie in Shanghai can buy big Californian oranges cheaper than his own small oranges from

Canton, the home of the China orange. Not only have the Canton oranges reached Shanghai from orchards which have not known any modern science to improve the fruitage of the trees, but they have been sent to the coast on men's backs. Men can carry but a small weight in comparison with a railway engine or a motor, however heavy that weight may be in comparison with the man. By sailing junk, by rowing sampan, not by quick steam, those oranges reached their markets, the men on the boat having to be fed during the many days of the journey while the craft was at the will of wind and tide. Tonnage for tonnage, it takes fewer men by far to bring a steamer than a junk from one port to another, and the cargo can therefore be sold cheaper. But on the other hand, fewer men have been receiving wages directly. The middle course between this Scylla and that Charybdis is as difficult for China to find as it is for ourselves.

We of the West have envisaged for a century such elementary facts, but they are amongst the most upheaving factors in the many different sorts of revolution through which China is passing: and particularly for the very poor do they shatter the old systems. The simple luxuries of a soft towel, soap, and an enamel basin seem very desirable to a Chinese peasant, as also to his wife. Both he and she would like to possess them. Yet are they originally articles of foreign trade. Possessing them, they find there is economic revolution bound up in them. For they are brought up the rivers in steamers, and thus they bring home the hard truth that presently the ancient junks will have to vanish. Meanwhile, however, what of the living and the wages of himself, or of the junksmen, descendants of generations of junksmen? Ah yah! It is not easy to solve—this riddle. Well, the peasant will scratch his head no more over it, he thinks. He will set out upon his daily toil with his heavily laden groaning wheelbarrow, with its iron spike to give a good grip on the road when he rests a minute now and then from sweating and straining. But here are all his wheelbarrow friends grouped together and talking excitedly: and one of them, who can read, is slowly spelling out a proclamation fixed on the city walls, which seems addressed to them—the men of the burdened wheelbarrows.

"All wheelbarrows," reads the treatise, "must now be provided, upon pain of confiscation, with rubber tyres"—of such and such a width and thickness. "This is decreed because the wheelbarrows of the ancient type are destroying the new roads."

"Oh! Ah!" groan the men, their faces worn to a constant look of endurance because of the weights they have shoved and pushed since they were little fellows.

"And, pray, what is that idea going to cost us?" one of them demands of the universe, mopping his head and neck. "Mei fa tze—there is no help for it! These young foreign-trained rulers of ours have no pity for us of traditional ways!" "These new children of ours, they never cease to astonish us. This is what they call Progress, I suppose," bitterly comments another. "It is not the least use kicking: the tyres will have to go on to our wheels. Well, I suppose they will make the barrows easier to push!" says a third. "It must be admitted that the macadamized roads are less labour for us than our old ruts," says another. "But I am in debt for my father's funeral up to my ears: how shall I raise the money for tyres? Shall we go on strike and refuse to pay?" anxiously a troubled one consults his comrades.

"You remember when four motor-buses first came to our city three years ago," advises the foreman. "The rickshawmen let them ply for a day or two. Then they found that their usual passengers were taking the motor-bus instead of their rickshaws: and how they did beget angry breath! There was much brawling in the streets as they cursed their former passengers, running beside the bus to shout. The third day they met the buses at dawn coming out from those great sheds. They threw the drivers off the seats and they drew the buses into a side-street and wrecked them entirely, so that only tangled iron remained. They fired the wood-work. And then they were satisfied. But, look now, it must be that over the seas a vast family and army of buses are daily begotten.. Ant-hills of motor-buses! For they came back; and lo, our streets are full of them to-day. Nor are they altogether bad. I myself have sat within one and been driven fast as the wind, faster than the Emperor's horses! Even so is it useless for us to resist this decree of the new city fathers, though we shall all be in deeper debt than ever."

Yet progress it is ; for a wheelbarrow with a tyred rim progresses faster than with an iron rim. It will be able to do several journeys more in the day.

China, like the rest of us, is enduring growing pains. Meanwhile in the present conditions it is not easy for the Chinese peasant to keep himself and his house clean and sweet. In the filth of Flanders, behind the sun-smitten sand-bags of Mesopotamia, men of our own race were made wretched by undesired companions of enforced dirt. They can compassionate the soapless peasant. They know that torturing biting parasites breed with horrible velocity in the habitations and clothing of the unwashed. True, the Oriental seems to have been lulled into partial indifference by generations of endurance. The beggars at the sunny gates of the cities sit unabashed to rid their ragged garments of vermin. But, as the years pass, in the short space of half a lifetime, each visit to the East brings the realization that a cleaner standard of living is within sight, and with it a comforting knowledge that the fatalistic Oriental acceptance of the flea is coming to an end. There is less dirt : there are fewer bugs than there were in the past.

But to-day the Chinese labouring crowds are still the result in clothing, food and physique of those older conditions of economic life. Yet shall they not be always as they are now. More and more, during every succeeding decade, East and West become bound together. There is a traffic of the material and the spiritual between us which is welding us in a union which can never be dissolved, except at huge cost to both. The wooden houses of America are painted with oils which come from Central China, in casks which are carried down this very Yangtsze River. The English housewife lays down in her kitchen linoleum which has been made waterproof by the oil of the soya-bean of Manchuria : her husband's collars are stiffened with the albumen of Chinese eggs in the starch. The Chinese housewife, on the other side of the picture, wears the fine cottons of Manchester for her better clothing and they are stitched together by a sewing-machine from the United States. Her husband's long winter gown is made of good Yorkshire woollen cloth. To look at her sleeping babe, she lights a candle moulded by an English firm.

It may be that it is the foreigner who, with all his revolutionizing ways, will help these Chinese peasants as much as any of their own countrymen, in return for what he has received from the East. Infinite gentleness, an inexhaustible supply of sanity, patience and common sense are needed before there can be brought healing to this army of workers wounded in the fight for mere existence, their wounds unclean and suppurating through ignorance. Yes, and the tender jestings of a friend are needed also to elicit willing Chinese smiles. Mirth heals the heart as sunshine does the body. Such are the oil and wine with which the foreigner can sustain those so much less fortunate than himself. Palliatives they may be: but they help, as does the touch of a mother's hand against a sick child's face. Gradually it is dawning upon the foreigner that he must set this man of the East, who has lain so long sick on the road, upon his own grey ass: that they must keep company in things economic and hygienic; of this life as well as the next.

Is it a dream? Better a dream than a nightmare which the first sight of a crowd on a Yangtsze steamer is apt to be. A mother with uncombed hair—toilet is difficult to perform in her circumstances—patted her baby over her shoulder and took my hand and felt its texture. "How white, how white and soft!" she said, and exhibited it to all and sundry. Yet, being an Englishwoman's hand, it is not at all so white and soft, for it passed not so many years before, during a war, the test of sweeping and plate-washing, of the spade and hoe. But always there had been soap and hot water to cleanse it and a towel to dry it. To that Chinese mother a towel, a small one, was a treasure. Thanks to Japan, these small soft towels are gradually becoming possible, owing to their cheapness, even to China's poor.

The gentle wind on the river blew away the smell of humanity which clings to every crowd, and of the diseases too. While I stood there, I knew that at that moment in every mission hospital there would be people who had not run away to the upper deck, people who would be giving brain and heart and hand to cure, to prevent these preventable diseases. *Sursum corda.*

I was back in a mission hospital in Wenchow, to which I had recently paid a ten-minutes' visit. The staff consisted of one English doctor, a handful of Chinese students in training, and one English nurse newly arrived. Their only helpers were four or five willing but inefficient coolies and a couple of kindly but equally untrained old Chinese women. The hospital was the solitary centre of modern medical science in a district the size of Wales. There passed through its wards, dispensary and operating-theatre many thousands of sick folk each year—sick, who were terribly, unbelievably sick; often with strange diseases; brought to the hospital usually at the last extremity and perhaps carried on a friendly back twenty miles over mountain tracks. I knew that hospital; for when I was eighteen, there being then no nurse, something of its fabulous task impinged on my spirit. For shame I could not but offer my inadequate girl's hands. For two paltry years I had swabbed and bandaged in the women's ward every morning under the direction of one of the young Chinese students in training. At a pinch I had helped with the anaesthetic during an operation. It had been for me to do then what many other young girls were later to do and for long hours when the call came to them in 1914, and which they still might do, if they would, especially if they live in the East. I had gone back for a flying visit just before this Yangtsze trip. The nurse, an Englishwoman, had begged me—after the fashion of clever enthusiastic nurses—to give myself the treat of admiring their new operating-table. It was her idea of a compliment—of a pleasure. On the way up, we passed the out-patients' hall.

"Say good-morning to the doctor," she said, and opened the door quietly. Never shall I forget the sight. The doctor, his thick black hair scattered with silver, was standing in his white overall, which showed the marks of a morning's out-patient work. He was holding a Chinese child in his arms, bending over it. His strong and rather serious face was lighted with pity. His finger was raised in raillery. He was trying to provoke baby to a smile before he probed into the nature of a festering wound in its neck. The mother, a poor woman of some back street of the city, stood anxiously by, trying to read his face. Another older child, sucking a stick of sugar-cane, was leaning against his knee. It seemed a children's day, for more mothers with babes sat around, on the narrow backless benches. At the other end a child was wailing as an assistant put drops into its eyes. There was an overpowering smell, for the sick and untended had filled the hall all morning, and the weather was growing hot. In the midst was the tall form, the grave kind face, and the ailing babe beginning to dimple into a wan smile. We shut the door.

"A good shepherd," said I. The nurse caught my eye, and gave a tiny nod and smile.

"Yes," she said simply.

With a few of the lambs that had been caught in the thicket.

While I was writing the last words, came a letter, not from the central Yangtsze zone, but from the North, from Manchuria. During the late wars and oppressions wretchedness exceeding the ordinary difficulties of everyday human toil and sorrow claimed its victims in the far South and the West—in Kueichow and Kwangtung, Szechwan and Kansu. Many of the poor within these provinces were almost beyond the relief of groaning. But in Shantung, in the North-east, things were said to be worse. Here in this letter we can read the tribulations of all as instanced in one area alone, except that the trek from Shantung into Manchuria has been the result of sheer desperation, and is probably the greatest trek the world has yet known. Thirty-three thousand emigrants passed through Moukden every week going North. "You would be touched to see the multitudes of Shantung refugees trudging through Moukden, parents and little children," so runs the letter; "I am glad to say the T'ung Shan T'ang—the Hall of Universal Goodness—gives them a night's lodging and two meals as they go North seeking a new home. My dear friend, if the opportunity comes, speak of them. You can picture the little families with babies, bundles and tins, in their winter padded garments, with honest faces; footsore, sitting down by the side of the road—an unending procession of them. No food, no produce, nothing left which they could give to the unpaid marauding soldiers, or the bandit bands, in their own province. Stripped of all, they have fled North. When one sees them struggling beneath such a cross, how can one not try to lift it by however so little? You will think this letter exclamatory, but when one sees these things, one must cry out."

CHAPTER VIII COUNTRYFOLK

AS I reached the upper deck, I nearly fell into Amah with Yün-Yün and Nieh-Nieh in her train. Amah's washing must have meant a considerable item in soap and starch to Mrs. Sung. Much boiling water must she have used in her life in the interests of personal cleanliness. Her hair was neat beyond praise: her teeth gleamed with her daily ministrations to them: her hands were smooth and spotless—not to be mentioned in the same breath with those grimed wrinkled claw-like hands that had taken mine and felt and patted them five minutes before at a depth of, say, fourteen feet below where we were now standing.

"What a number of country people are on this ship travelling in the third class, Amah," I said. "I wonder where they can be going to and for what purpose?"

"Oh, the populace!" she said. "Such crowds and heaps of them! They tumble together like fish in the sea for number. Goodness knows why they go on having such a lot of children, when there are far too many of them already!"

"They are quite good people," I ventured, "lao shih—you know." Was it not Lincoln who said the Lord must have liked ordinary people since He created so many of them?

"Full of sores and vermin!" she exclaimed. "What on earth do they want crowding on to ships like this? Where on earth can people like that be wanting to travel?"

"Perhaps they have business on the River, even as we are here only to take pleasure," I suggested.

She went towards the companion: she hung her nose elegantly as might have done Coriolanus over the well below her, and took a whiff of the odours from below.

"Ch'ou!" she exclaimed—"Stink! Why can't they

wash themselves and be decent members of society? Come away, Yün-Yün and Nieh-Nieh to the other end of the ship. You might catch any sort of illness from that smell."

She was, of course, perfectly right, and I went down to my cabin and washed before seeking the upper regions again. Mrs. Sung greeted me as I came on the deck.

"Amah says you have been to visit the third class," she said inquiringly.

"I did," I acknowledged, and we looked at each other, and were silent awhile. No need for me to tell her what was to be seen there.

"When I think of our people, of my people, the dear common people," she said presently, and her eyes were full of tears, "and their conditions, I fall into despair. What can I, or even the two of us, my husband and I, do? We give what we can, when any special need comes to our notice, and in our homes we try to teach those we are in contact with to be clean. But how little is all that?"

This would never do. Giant Despair plucks the bones of his victim bare. Vigorously I combated her, taking Amah as an instance. "Twenty years ago, could you have found an amah like her, demanding cleanliness above all?"

"N-no," she admitted.

"Seven years ago," I went on, "there was not, I vow, a single shoe shop for women in the whole of China. Lately in Shanghai I went to buy a pair of shoes for curiosity's sake, at a Chinese woman's shop, and I had to wait in a queue! Pretty shoes too, the purchasers wanted. Twenty-five years ago, going for a walk one Sunday, I counted in the main street of Wenchow the number of people who had something the matter with their eyes: from mild ophthalmia to dreadful diseased eyeballs rolling on the cheeks, ghastly sights. Exactly half of those I met had some eye disease: mostly the result of ignorance, of infection, of dirt. To-day I should not see a tithe of such terrible things."

"True," she said, "and my rickshaw coolie often makes me smile. We keep a coolie to draw my husband to office. If you please, he takes a bottle of water and a tin of tooth-powder, and he spends the time of waiting in brushing his teeth. Ten years ago he had hardly heard of a tooth-brush.

Now, all the rickshawmen keep one under that flap hanging from the cushioned seat of the rickshaw."

" Yes, and the older people are having artificial teeth, too," I added. Few things used to be more distressing than the broken teeth and festering gums of rich and poor alike.

" If only our countrywomen would unbind their feet," she sighed. " It seems as if they needed a bomb to make them alter their old ways. And they form the majority of our women."

We wandered on to the folly of forcible conversions in politics—the bomb method versus the growth of ideas, the short cut versus the slow making of a great highway for halting feet.

Later, an Englishwoman, who had gone up the River in the boat ahead of us, told me a story to the point. She had gone much higher up, to see the great gorges, which it is the desire of every foreigner in China to visit. Sitting on deck one morning at a river port, her feet on the rail, the ship fastened to the embankment, she perceived that the array of Chinese men who come to sit and smoke and spit were focussing their gaze on her feet. She is a dainty lady, her feet are the mice of Herrick's poem, and her spirit is elvish. She let them have a long look at her feet, then she slipped down and changed her shoes to stout brogues, came up and placed her feet ostentatiously on the rail once more. Exclamations, discussions, much attention, while she, in apparent unconsciousness, read a chapter of her book. She slipped down again, changed to her smallest, softest, prettiest evening slippers, and once more planted her fairy feet on the rail. A delighted burst of laughter answered her puckish humour, and many ejaculations of appreciation. One by one she worked through her *chaussure*, and the onlookers were ravished. Their excitement to see what next she would wear and their admiration of her footgear were beyond doubt.

" I reckon I struck a stroke for hobbled Chinese women," she said to me with justifiable satisfaction, " performing like a mannequin before their husbands. For I have some very attractive shoes, let me tell you."

" Also feet," I thought. " And face : and heart."

Mrs. Sung would have enjoyed that prank. She and I told other stories to each other to hearten ourselves, however.

She remarked on the posters which were then displayed on every tram-post, every municipal building in the Shanghai Settlement. " Look on this picture, and then on that " was the motto. For there were two Chinese babies displayed on the poster : one was thin, crying, covered with spots. He had smallpox—" heaven's flowers," as the ignorant call it. The other was pointing with a chubby finger to a chubby arm, was jolly, smiling, announcing to the world, " I have been vaccinated ! "

" You are right," said Mrs. Sung, " our people are beginning to understand about infection."

" And how considerate are they for each other ! " I said, " which is what we can say in the West of the poor and hungry also."

I was thinking of those wrinkled claws of Chinese working-women's hands which had just been handling mine. But none had touched me so much as those belonging to a girl of twelve whose cottage, with its mud-beaten floor, I had once visited far in the mountains of North China, where the summer heat is intense, where the winter cold is even more to be remembered. For, in the North of China, the ground is frozen so that no pick can pierce it, and the dead must await sepulture till spring. The sea is frozen three miles out in the northern Chihli Gulf. The rivers are frozen, the cascades of the streams are caught by King Frost and remain still and silent, carved in ice. Where should a child-woman find cold water to wash in, much less hot ? Why, the villagers sold the little fuel they had, the charcoal, down into the plains, for money to live ! To cook their home-grown millet and maize they used dried grass and bracken from the hill-sides.

When I first saw her she was tugging and half-carrying a heavy baby, her brother of two. She had come to the door at the first glimpse of me in the village street. Her mother had died when her brother was born. Her father worked in a primitive mine for a fractional sum when the sowing and reaping months were over ; half farmer, half miner. She looked tired : I doubt if she had enough to eat, this young housekeeper and proxy mother. All the clothes-making of the house, her own included, all the washing—such as it was—

had to be done by her, as well as the cooking. Her success was partial, but her spirit was willing.

"The neighbours are kind to me: the woman next door cut out this tunic for me," she said proudly pointing to it. She deposited the baby on the k'ang, the family bed of warmed brick, as I peeped inquiringly in at the door. My stock of tiny gifts was running low. Once, in a similar predicament, I had been reduced to safety-pins, and was touched to see the particular girl with whom I had forgathered wearing the two I had given her pinned in parallel lines down the front of her tunic for ornament. I had, on this occasion, a few sugar biscuits left. I offered one to her. Out came that eager skinny claw, wrinkled and grimed like a hen's foot far up the wrist.

"Eat," I invited. She thanked me very politely, and at once took it to the k'ang and gave it to her small brother. I gave her another, and she was proceeding to do the same with that, because he had enjoyed the first so much. But I was firm and saw that she also tasted its sweetness.

When I left her, I wandered down the village street. Across the gully dividing the village in half, an old woman stood at her door and waved to me to come in. Just as I was opening the crazy wicket of her so-called gate, a large dog, a mixture apparently of a sheep-dog and a chow, sprang down the path barking fiercely. Long and bitter experience renders the foreigner something of a coward in connection with large barking Chinese village dogs. Moreover, they are usually so full of mange as to warrant their avoidance. The old woman waved me to come up her path. "But—what of your dog?" I suggested.

"Oh, he won't hurt you. He would not hurt a baby!" she answered. "Look now."

She called to him, and the creature bounded back to her. She took him up into her arms, and into her breast, staggering with her small bound feet under his weight. Over his nuzzling head she beamed at me. I opened the wicket and walked in, and we sat down on her k'ang. The dog had a beautiful coat, and she brushed him with a broom made from "Burning Bush" while we talked.

"What do you feed him on?" I asked.

" Just the same as ourselves," she replied, " millet and whatever relish we have to eat with it."

I could not comfortably sit cross-legged like her, with my leather shoes on, though she begged me. But we sat and swapped doggy stories, she boasting of this one's intelligence, I of my Caesar far away in England, till it was time to make her son's dinner. She invited me, with all the grace in the world, to stay and eat with them, but meanwhile began filling the one-roomed little home with smother from the bracken-roots which were her fuelling. The acrid smoke poured into the room, the tears flowed down my cheeks, and I pleaded an engagement, though I should have liked to accept.

" Were they Christians, this little girl and the old woman ? " asked Mrs. Sung, as I told her of them.

" No," said I. " The inn at that village was so intolerably dirty that the Boy, our temporary servant, came to me and said the Master could not possibly be put into any of its quarters. He did not mind so much about me ! "

She laughed.

The Boy had been ashamed of the condition of things he found in those far-away villages. He was from more sophisticated neighbourhoods and had lived long in foreign homes in a city. He wearied me with unhappy protests as to the impossibility of that inn.

" Well, Boy, go and find a better, if you can," I dismissed him. " You know very well that the muleteers, who come this way every ten days, say that all the inns round here are bad and this is the least bad."

" Yes, but perhaps they are relatives of the innkeeper and it pays them to bring us here. Truly they cannot all be as bad as this," he wailed.

" Well, well, go and seek," said I, for I had come half a mile ahead of my husband, and I wanted to rest.

Soon he returned, crestfallen. " The others are worse," he said gloomily.

I had a happy thought. " Boy," I said, " ask if there are any Christians in the hamlet. Perhaps they would allow us to use a room in their cottage."

" Would that be better ? " he asked.

" Think now," I said, " is not every Christian's house

cleaner than its neighbours whenever you have known one ?"
He was not a Christian, that Boy, for, though he had lived most of his life with foreigners, they had not considered any information as to their faith a part of their dealings with servants. It takes a St. Paul to discuss religion with Onesimus.

He considered the matter. "I don't know many Christians," he reflected, "except foreigners: but, yes, I realize now those I know are clean people."

He went forth, seeking for a Christian. The village elders and their wives were coming to visit me and he met them *en route* with his demand for a Christian. I heard the palaver going on in mid-street. They trooped into the court, where I sat on a narrow bench amongst the mules nosing for their beans in the open mangers. With many apologies they came to me; with regrets they informed me that there were no Christians to be found in the neighbourhood.

"The nearest Christian," they said, "is five days' journey away, beyond Lai Yuan. You will have to put up with us as we are."

"Five days' journey away to the nearest Christian," exclaimed Mrs. Sung. "Oh! though I am not a Christian myself, I wish there were more Christians in China."

I smiled at her naïvety and thought of that Christian whose light had shone five days' journey away. Not a bad distance for one small candle to be shining. Five days away—and in a distant village they knew where he was to be found, though they may have known nothing about him or his faith.

"Tell me," she asked, "are there any Christians amongst the people in the third-class passengers of this ship, do you know?"

So I told her I knew of one—no, three. A simple woman, with pretty, rosy, oval cheeks, bespeaking the healthy life of sunny field-work, her head bound in a clean white kerchief, had come up to me as I stood talking. She wore the blue cotton tunic and trousers of the Ningpo countrywoman, and she had two boys by the hand. one, her nephew, the other her son. "I am a Jesus-Way-person," she announced to me unasked, and said it many times, both to me and to all around. " And these boys are going to be Jesus-Way-people too," she added. " They are teaching me to read: they both go to the primary school: and I can read three hymns!" The crowd stared at her, with no sign of understanding of what she was saying. The boys beamed intelligently enough at me; but she seemed so simple, so innocent. I liked the three of them. As for the crowd, they gazed upon her dumbly, as if she was some fortunate one who had been granted some boon, or she would not have made such a point of it. They did not grudge her it: but such favours from heaven had nothing to do with them.

" Amah," whispered Mrs. Sung to me presently with a flight of pretty laughter, " was a countrywoman originally. But we don't mention it. She is most townish and modish these days."

" So I gathered," I answered. " But she is a good amah."

" She is," agreed her mistress; then sighed. " But I do sometimes think I know why her husband left her. She is so very firm on occasion."

" All Chinese people do not refuse to acknowledge their connection with the land," I assured her. " You know the British Consulate in Shanghai. There is a Boy who opens the door to you. He wears a long blue silk gown, and is girdled with a gallant red sash. Quite the man of the world he looks, very superior in that uniform."

" Tell me about him," she said: so I told her.

He greeted me with smiles of welcome when I called, for he was lent to us for a few weeks once when his master and mistress were on furlough. He is a servant without peer; cheerful, efficient, loyal, gentle-mannered. But he and I once held an illuminating conversation on that very trip which my husband and I took into the mountains south-west of Peking.

The land we had to pass through was very poor, the mountains were barren, the soil thin. The mountain streams swelled into freshets in the spring after the frost broke, and swept away from the valleys what little soil there was. The farmers, if wealthy enough, built dams of stones. The only shrines and gods in good repair in the whole neighbourhood were at the bends of the stream, where propitiation might reasonably be expected to effect something. No god likes to sit with his feet in a flood! Lonely, lonely were the little farmsteads. It was a very quiet land; there was nobody to make a noise, except the donkey caravans passing through on the atrocious goat-tracks which are called roads, and the shouts of the muleteers.

"These people here have my admiration," I remarked to a Chinese merchant in our train, "for truly is their courage great."

"How is their courage great?" asked Wang, the Boy, joining in the conversation, striding along. He had a walking-stick in his hand. He had confided to me that he intended to take this opportunity to walk five miles every day. "Like the Master and Chu Ta Jen—Sir John Jordan"—he said. "It is a very good foreign custom for the health. And only will I carry a little stick in my hand to defend myself from attack, as they do. How much more manly is it than the way of our great officials who never go abroad except with a bodyguard!"

"How is the courage of these country people great in these parts?" he now asked me. "The muleteers tell me there are no thieves at all. Nay, even the officials hereabouts are good people and do not over-tax, or lack in justice."

"They are brave to remain in these cold mountains and work with such endurance in their poor fields," I suggested.

He snorted in scorn. "What else can they do?" he asked, "they have nowhere else to go. Besides, it is always better in the country than the town. I am from the country myself, so I know."

"They might," said I pointedly, "do as others have done: go and hire themselves out as boys or coolies in towns, perhaps even under foreigners. Would they not be earning more money that way?"

"Yes, perhaps they would," he conceded: "but they can make enough on their farms here to give them food and clothing. And if you have sufficient to eat and wear, how much better is it to remain a farmer in the country! I am from the country originally myself, from Southern Chihli, so I know. Only, alas, in my home there was not enough to eat for all: so one of us had to go into town—and it was my lot."

He is in receipt of a wage which would seem fabulous to his brothers: and the money is mostly going home to the tiny farm of his fathers, where his wife and children are deposited. When he has served the foreigner long enough, or when that particular foreigner of his loyalty goes back to his own country for good and all, Wang will also take himself back to his own country home. He will doff his blue silk gown and red silk sash and wear grey cotton lined with white. And may he have better luck than my husband's old Boy! This Boy served with a faith surpassing praise, accompanied him through the perils and discomforts of long journeys inland; but put the accumulated savings of those sixteen years of service into a mulberry orchard for the rearing of silkworms the very year that a blight was to fall on the mulberry trees about his native country of Ningpo!

All of which I faithfully related to Mrs. Sung. Whereupon she gave me that reward than which none can be sweeter to a teller of tales.

"Tell me some more," she asked: "some more stories like these—tales of my own people."

Tales of her own people!

"As they appear in the eyes of a foster-sister, eh?" I queried.

CHAPTER IX AN ENGLISH GENTLEMAN SEES CHINA

IT was time to leave the ship. On our arrival at the Nanking pontoon I went to the lower deck. So eager was the crowd to land that many had leapt from the deck to the pontoon the instant that the boat drew alongside. One held one's breath in anxiety. " Don't they ever get drowned, or crushed between the ship and the dock ? " I asked the Captain. " Yes, they do sometimes," he answered, " but how can I prevent it when they behave like this ? If they fall overboard, nobody stays to pick them up, except one of our crew, because of the tradition which is the bugbear of China's rivers."

" You mean about the devils dragging them under ? " I queried.

" Yes," he nodded.

Sometimes one hears of Chinese boatmen apparently in cold blood leaving each other to drown. But such boatmen believe that there are devils inhabiting the water, who put out their arms and pull down their victim when they need a human life. If they save a drowning man they anger the demon by depriving him of his appointed victim. The result is that the demon, refusing to be mulcted, follows the rescuer on his watery way and, sooner or later, grasps him instead of that other who has been saved. Such stories as that of Jonah do not seem strange or fantastic to these men. Indeed it makes an appeal to them which we can hardly comprehend. They are capable of appreciating its agony of the castaway, its drama of the worn sea-traveller arriving at the bustling city of Nineveh, the contrast of the burning sunshine withering the gourd after the episode of the stormy rain-swept ocean, in a way that astonishes us who have lived in another atmosphere.

With my heart in my mouth, watching the men leaping

seven, eight feet, across the intervening space, I heaved a sigh of thankfulness when the boat was tied up alongside. Then came the rush off the boat by other third-class passengers, who met in the midst of the narrow gangways the rush of the passengers coming on. Some of the latter leapt the bulwarks and were pushed *a tergo* by friends, their bundles being handed afterwards to them. The noise and shouting were incessant. The young Englishman pointed out a line of wire being laid aboard, and said it was the telephone. It was evident that it must be some time before I could join my father on shore, wherever he was, and I slipped down to the steward's galley to telephone. It seemed doubly strange to find that modern appliance in the midst of such un-modern lack of organization. And the telephone was already going back into the past in some things, for pieces of its apparatus were missing or broken. One wondered at its functioning at all. With cheerful good-will, however, various Chinese friends and relatives of the steward kindly held portions of it together, or fastened other portions with string, so that I could get my message through. I felt as if I were back in the booking-office of one little town at home in England, where the clerk never fails to come to the help of any of us. What do mechanical arrangements matter, so long as the kindness in service remains the same ? Is not the man more than the machine ?

It goes to the heart of every Occidental to see the mismanagement of delicate machinery by the Oriental. Perhaps disintegration comes so quickly to pass because the Oriental only knows the price of the machine : he has no notion of what it has cost the Western world in thought, in inventive powers, in patience, or skill. He has received these machines ready-made, and has no conception of long years spent in study of nature's mysteries, of the lives given to such discoveries. When he begins to probe into them himself, when he too is given lessons in scientific accuracy and research, his machines will no longer be maimed and lamed in a sorry shortness of time. He will perceive that these machines are not merely material objects, but the manifestation of ordered thought. On the other hand, we are apt to shock him and seem equally and sinfully wasteful in many of our daily ways.

He wastes machinery, we say : we are wasteful in clothing and food, he thinks. We neither of us realize sufficiently what these items have cost others.

I came up again from my telephoning, wondering how I should reach the shore. " I will wait till the crowd is off," I said easily.

" The ship leaves at once then," said Mr. Sung : " and that will be too late. You had much better tip the steward to smuggle you off the moment he thinks fit. He has had long experience."

" After seeing this scramble, I shall not go off the ship at all at Hankow," said Mrs. Sung. " I could not possibly drag Yün-Yün and Nieh-Nieh through the crowd to the shore. We shall wait and come back on the same ship."

And this actually was what happened, except that Mr. Sung went off the boat to visit friends. The young Englishman had uneasily bidden me earlier a farewell. " I promised to go with the engineer," he said, " or I would have seen you safely over the gangway."

The only way off the ship was to go down into the crowd, and through it. On this occasion the Chinese steward led the way, and the people gave way a little more to him than was usual. It took under half an hour to pass through the crowd of outgoers and incomers. Once upon a time, on leaving the small steamer at a small port on the coast, a ship's officer, a son of the Levant, had offered to see me through the shouting, pressing crowd. He yelled in vain for a passage through. Men, women, old and young, he had shoved with his arms till he was weary. They took no notice though he shouted in their ears. Then, to my unspeakable dismay, he took his stick and whacked and cudgelled a way for me. Still the crowd closed in behind him, and I was left.

" Come faster, closer behind me," he shouted, turning back his head. I shook my head.

" Don't beat them ! " I screamed it at him. But he did not hear. At last he looked back, missed me, and saw that something was distressing me and waited. He had meant kindly by me. Mercifully the people were in their padded winter garments, but it would have been the same if they had been in thin summer wear.

"It will take you an hour to get through, if I don't make them give way," he stammered, troubled.

"Never mind," said I.

"But you can't be left for an hour in this crowd," he said, looking at the scab, the ringworm, the sore reddened eyes of the folk that pressed about us.

"Yes, I can," I replied. "I can have a bath afterwards, you know; and these people can't. Leave me, and never mind me, I beg you."

He was too chivalrous for that: and we wormed through eventually. Yet one must remember that the crowd was not shocked by his methods. For centuries they have been the methods adopted by their great ones and their richer classes.

Only two days later at Nanking, Fate was to lead me down to the pontoons again, and there I saw, waiting for a steamer that delayed its coming, the tall figure of a foreign man. It was the Head of the Commission on which my father was working. The rest of the party had gone by train: he had elected to go by boat. The only white person in sight with the exception of his valet, who was at a respectful distance, he was standing in the midst of a surge of unwashed but happy Chinese children. He looked like a poplar in a field of moving rye. They were craning back their round dark uncombed heads to smile into his thin fair-complexioned face. He was bending his six feet odd to smile back at them, and was saying in English, when I approached, "Well, thanks awfully for your company. I 'll look again to see if the steamer is in sight." He waved his lean hand, stalked to the side of the pontoon, and the crowd, which of course understood not one word except the look and tone of kindness, oozed away, amazingly docile. Most travellers have a difficulty in ridding themselves of too close attention from such onlookers.

On board ship Mrs. Sung had spoken of Lord Willingdon, whom she had met at one of her father's dinner-parties.

"You will like him," she had said to me sagely.

Knowing that he had been but a month in the country, and could speak no Chinese, like my Levantine helper I felt aghast at the tribulations through which he would have to pass in order to board the Yangtsze boat. He had been twice

Governor of provinces in India ; he was to be Governor-General of Canada. It was a trial to the soul to think of such an one struggling through the suffocating, seething, deafening maelstrom of those most unfortunate of unfortunate people. Besides, I, born in China, was hurt that he, used no doubt to the bejewelled company of Indian princes, should see my China thus, in its least attractive state. One wanted him to understand something of the Chinese poor and needy, but this was going altogether too far in realism. One did not want him to be nauseated by certain of their habits and aspects. Who would wish a Chinese or Indian to receive his first introduction to our own toiling men, for instance, shouting their way home on a Saturday night in Glasgow? Another Englishwoman with me was equally troubled at the prospect before him. She, we arranged, should bring up the rear, and I would be the pilot—but he should not know of our manœuvres.

In the meantime he talked to us freely and candidly, while we watched the speck in the watery distance grow bigger till it gradually became a steamer. He told us what his Commission had been doing and seeing. For myself, I was deeply interested to know what such a man would think of the China which had been a second Motherland to me. He had been visiting many Chinese government and provincial colleges. Some of the establishments were said to be centres of revolutionary projects : and certain people had criticized the visits. The pernicious beings who worked in those colleges should be consigned, they averred, to moral isolation, and material too, if possible. It may be that at times this is the only course to pursue : but a preliminary raid of courtesy upon such an enemy has also been known to have had good effects. " I wanted to find out," said the Chief of the Delegation, " first, if they were ' Reds.' And secondly, if so, why? Nobody becomes a Red from sheer *joie de vivre* that I ever heard of."

" And what did you find ? " we naturally asked.

" We found," he said, " groups of young men, and some not so young, who had been working as teachers in those colleges, testing seeds and researching into plant diseases in the agricultural departments, without a cent of their rightful pay having reached them for seven months. Plucky is not a good enough word. They are living as best they can. The richer among them help the poorer—and for no reward, but to promote knowledge and to bring science to the help of the Chinese farmer. What is more, they say they will struggle through and keep on somehow, living on the produce of their hands—till a Government comes in which will pay teachers their salaries again. Red! They are not Red at all, half of them: but burning with proper indignation at the mis-treatment of their country by their self-appointed rulers. Only a very few are Red. When they have seen for so long their country eaten up by undisciplined armies, and the money for education and agriculture going to buy munitions instead of books and seeds, it is not surprising some of them see Red on occasion, and are willing, in sheer despair, to listen to the honeyed offers of the Communists."

Apparently a man does not arrive at the post of a high official of the British Commonwealth without being able to grasp the points of a situation, or discriminate between the workers and the drones.

One could wish every high officer of every world-state to come at least once in his life to China; to broaden his out-look. And I would have Chinese officials meet him and then visit him in his own land, so that they might learn something from him of his ideals of service. Few of our most valued public men come East of Singapore. Kitchener came during his retirement, and, when war broke out, readily understood that the contribution China could make was by her unrivalled capacity for labour. Lord Ronaldshay made that difficult, dangerous journey through China to Burmah by way of the deathly valleys of the Mekong and the Salween. A student of the world of Eastern men, he realized that he would learn more that way than by looking on from an office in Peking or Calcutta. Curzon saw Asia, and to him the earth was ever a spacious place. And now here had come the Head of this Commission of service, to see for himself how best we could help China in her present difficulties, in return for the many gifts we have had from her. The next visitors one could wish to see in her lands are the recognized and solid leaders of our great Trade Unions. Those who know what labour is in the West have many lessons they could learn ; comradeship, for instance, with their fellows in the East who bear such intolerable burdens. We should hear no more disparaging words about " yellow labour."

The steamer arrived, and we started on our way through the throng, warning the Chief that it would take some little time and patience. " Go ahead ! " he said, smiling. It takes considerably longer to corkscrew a passage, calling interminably, " Chieh kuang ! May I borrow your light ? " than by mowing a way with a stick, but it was the method of our choice. With the full flavour of the miseries of the Chinese poor breathed literally upon him, a man who has captained the Eton Eleven may be forgiven a certain fastidiousness urging him to extricate himself as quickly as possible from close physical contact. It is a strange, psychological fact, however, that the gentlemen who hit cricket balls on to the pavilion at Lord's are usually the last to wish to cudgel their way through a crowd of the burdened and the poor. One sportsman, I fancy, hates to see another sportsman in the great Game of Life needlessly and unduly handicapped. Viscount Willingdon's face, as he came slowly through, showed nothing but a deep concern. Compassion was piercing his heart with its red-hot needles. He drew a breath as we gained the Upper Air.

" Poor souls, we 've got to alter life for them a bit, if we possibly can." That was his comment.

The next time I saw him was when I again joined the Delegation. We were to visit a silk factory. It was at Hangchow. In that factory hundreds of women sit daily, dipping deft water-wrinkled hands into small vats where thousands of silkworms are simmering in their cocoons. Rickshaws had taken us there a couple of miles, in a hot sun, over terrible by-paths. It was by a miracle of endurance that the rickshaw coolies reached the goal. The English visitors would infinitely have preferred another mode of transport : but if there had been one, which there was not, these men would have gone riceless that day. Lord Willingdon unfurled his long legs and stood for a full minute looking at his coolie, the pick of Hangchow rickshaw coolies as he was. The man's naked chest was heaving, his breath was a sob, his back was streaming with sweat, but his eyes and lips were smiling with pride in his achievement. " Stout fellow ! " at last said Lord Willingdon, the product of such a different stock, yet recognizing a fellow in the same school, that of willing submission to discipline. He put a finger on the wet shoulder and turned the coolie about, the better to look him in the face.

" You deserve," he said slowly, " the best that earth can give you." The man beamed. He comprehended nothing of the words : but he understood the look on the face and the ring of the voice.

Once again I was to see how such a man, a visitant from England, viewed the impingement of East and West. It was on a steamer going up the coast to Weihaiwei. A few of the passengers were sitting after dinner in the saloon. The wireless operator, a Chinese, sent down a radio message to one of them, an Englishman, by the hand of his assistant, also a Chinese. The recipient, whose name I never knew, a traveller for a firm, had told me over the dinner-table that he had only been out in China a couple of years. He was probably a respectable member of ordinary society in his home town. But he snatched the radiogram so roughly from the uniformed young Chinese assistant wireless operator that I bit my lip and hoped the Chief of the Delegation had not observed it, for I knew such rudeness would set him a-quiver. But he has quick eyes. When the Chinese was at last allowed to go, after being kept standing unnecessarily long, the Chief called him across to give him a special word of good-night. Then he came and sat down beside me. The affair had fretted his nerves and spirit. " Now what," he asked in low, vehement tones, " in the name of common sense is the use of behaving like that ? Is that sort of thing going to get anybody loved or liked ? It would have cost that fellow even less trouble to have taken the telegram gently. But no, he must try to feel important, being rude to a servant who can't be rude back to him ! It is insufferable. That is the sort of thing that makes people go Red."

" In the West as well as in China," I appended.

It takes a fund of sincere goodwill to sit through a dozen big formal lunches and dinners, one after another, trying to converse intelligently with a Chinese official through the medium of an interpreter : then rise and make a fresh speech every time and convey, also afresh, a conviction of unwearied good faith, of unshakeable friendliness. While England can breed men to behave with this courtesy of soul, her service to the world is not yet ended. The Chinese generals conducting a war between Peking and Tientsin had, shortly before our visit to the Yangtsze, held up their battles for this particular representative of England when he wished to pass through their lines and return to the South of China. They had mined the mouth of the Tientsin River, but they let the ship he was on pass through unharmed. The guns at Taku held their fire, though the infantry could be seen crouching behind their sand-bags, ready with rifles for the next ship. It was not because he was a high personage or because he represented Britain. They fired on a Japanese gunboat two hours later and killed some officers. It was because the leaders had met him in Peking : because they liked him—and for no other reason. They had an instantaneous perception that good manners are but the outward and visible signs of an inward and spiritual grace. The East knows by now without a doubt that we of the West set great store by Truth. But Truth may run lop-sidedly, shorn of the wings which ought to be part of her heritage, and which render her acceptable to perverse humanity. When the East finds sincerity and the grace of good manners happily combined in one person, of whatever race he may be, French, English, American or German, it gives its heart freely and at once to that visitant to its shores.

CHAPTER X HOW AN AMERICAN SERVED CHINA

ONCE on the embankment, or Bund, I salvaged my baggage from the onslaughts of innumerable work-hungry coolies. The driver of one of the disreputable victorias standing by, which I found later were much patronized by such in Nanking as had to have regard for the shallowness of their purse, held up an envelope to attract my attention. I deposited my suit-cases on his seat amidst the torn horse-hair stuffing, and found directions for my movements.

Accordingly I ran my father and his Commission to earth in the science laboratories of a university, a magnificent gift of American philanthropy. As sincerely as he, I delighted in the rows of bottled chemicals, the well-arranged charts of study, the airy rooms with their big windows. Above all we took pleasure in the sight of the many Chinese students at work in their clean, simple, grey cotton gowns, who smiled at us, wishful to please visitors. The comradeship of science, of a common search into natural laws, does more at this difficult stage of his growth to rehabilitate the Chinese student into the vivifying sense of the dignity of his calling than can be easily realized by outsiders. His old empirical learning has fallen in ruins about his ears : he has been shorn of his ancient and very worthy pride in his Classics. It is well for him to realize that it has never been the quality of his brain which was criticized—only the enforced narrowness of his objectives. As my father puts it, the Orient has never had the chances of cross-fertilization in its civilization as has been given to the Occident. China has perforce been self-contained, owing to geographical and historical accident.

We shook hands with librarians : we rejoiced in their well-filled shelves—nay, envied them. But when the next move was to be across the lawns to inspect more laboratories, and trays of seeds being tested in the agricultural department, I reminded myself that, after all, I was not a member of the Commission; and therefore I need not undergo all its labours, but would simply cull such of its flowers as came my way.

An elderly American gentleman was also lagging behind, and to him I whispered my conclusions. "Continuous and intelligent appreciation of educational facilities," I said, "is an exhausting process." He had a twinkle in his eye.

"Come with me," he whispered: "I too have admired excellent institutions in vast quantities."

We crept up some stairs, and more stairs, and so came out upon the floor of the tower which overlooked the great quadrangles. The flooring was not finished, and he was gallantly careful of me as we dodged scaffoldings.

"Come and look out," he said: and through the dormer window we gazed straight up a long avenue between the university buildings. He showed me this building and that, the science schools, the lecture-rooms. He gazed and gazed, and said he had just been in America raising more money for it. He dreamed over it.

"You see that south-eastern corner: that would make a fine medical school. I wish some one would give us some old Chinese stone-lions: they would look well at the entrance. We can't afford such ornamentation yet. But it is good for present-day China to learn to love its past treasures, its sculptures and architecture."

He told me how this department grew, and how that one was still growing. His fatherly face grew more fatherly as he looked and talked and pointed out various of his cherished projects. "I wish we had a chapel as well as an assembly hall," he sighed. For half an hour I listened and felt infinitely humble. For he was so modest, so mild, this man who had spent his life in building up this great and wonderful institution, so great that it had made me tired to think of it.

We spoke of New China and understood each other. I told him of my friends, Mr. and Mrs. Sung.

"I am Nationalist in my sympathies," he said, "for I want China to be great."

" I think during the War we learned in Europe that it is only as a country serves the rest of the world that it is great," I said diffidently. He was so humble it seemed odd to hear him claiming greatness for any people : but I knew he meant no greatness in land or riches or even learning.

For all time, he stole a piece of my heart for that Nanking University, as he uttered so simply his dreams for it. It was the look of a lover that he gave it—this Vice-President, as I found he was. Little jokes, too, we made. From one window we looked across some of the handsome roofs to the hill under which nestles the city, providing it with the good-fortune which such a position gives a city in Chinese geomancy. On its crest stood a famous pagoda. Alas, it was in a shocking need of repair.

" Oh, what a pity it is that it is in such a state ! " I exclaimed, " it will be falling down completely soon. Can't anything be done ? "

" I agree with you," he said, roused almost to wrath, and reverting to pure Americanisms, " I get real mad about it ! Why, I was so ashamed that this city should have such wreckage overlooking it that, only last Fall, I sent word to the leading gentry here, and the Governor, that it was a downright disgrace that a city like ours could not keep its public buildings in better order. I said, I, an American citizen, a missionary, would willingly put down ten dollars towards its repair, but that I should expect the Governor and the gentry to head the list with a heap more dollars than that. Well, they say they will start work this spring."

" And do you mean to say that you, a Christian missionary, are not only urging the Heathen to rebuild their pagodas, but putting down dollars yourself towards that nefarious end ? " I mocked him. Pagodas are definitely of Buddhistic origin and purpose : they are supposed to contain sacred relics. It is an act of merit for a Buddhist to build a pagoda. The tired grey face lit into a smile.

" I did," he teased. " And I 'm going on stirring up the gentry till they do repair our Nanking pagoda. What would Nanking be without its pagoda, pray ? It is one of our chief beauties."

" You had better begin on the Buddhist temples, then," I

girded at him : " they are in a most ruinous condition over half the country."

He smiled his paternal smile at me, and we sat down on the attic stairs, after he had flicked away the dust from my step with his handkerchief.

" I almost wish I could : I almost wish I could," he admitted. " I feel real sorry for some of the priests : they look so forlorn and underfed, some of them. I suppose I feel sorry for them because in a way they are of the same Trade Union as myself ! And some of them do try to minister in holy things with a pure heart."

" Not too many, I fear," said I, thinking of the cathedral of Buddhism in Canton where the abbot frankly says that ninety per cent. of the monks are there because they want to rid themselves of family squabbles, or are wanted by the police, or are in such debt that they must seek sanctuary in a monastery to evade their creditors. " But it is true that the Buddhists are neglecting their ministers of religion shamefully. I went to see a Chinese tea factory lately, run on modern lines in Wenchow, and behold, a nun sitting with the other women picking over the tea. The temple funds were so low that when the tea season comes round and extra hands are called for, the nuns take the opportunity of earning a little money to live on. There she was in her grey nun's robe and round cap sifting tea—and rather pleased to be at the work."

" All ministers of the Word should sift tea or plough fields now and again," he affirmed. " Did you hear of the priests going on strike lately, was it in Hankow ? They made a procession and carried banners, saying ' No more prayers except at enhanced rates. The rising scale of living forbids.' "

I laughed, and told him more of our recent visit to Wenchow : and how pleased we had been to find that the grey old city wall, the parapets and the ramparts, had been recently repaired with fresh, good stone.

" It is safe now for some hundreds of years more," I told him. " We used to love to walk on the wall : it is wide enough to drive a carriage and pair on it."

Gradually it has been crumbling away, and nobody has cared for it. It is archaic, and modern Chinese are not proud of the fact that so lately it has been considered necessary to a city's defence. The huge gates are still shut at night and only opened at dawn, but there is talk of doing away with this custom as mediæval. So we congratulated the present foreign residents in Wenchow that the city wall had been repaired. It is the only cool place in summer where they can walk and catch a breath of air, blowing fresh up river from the sea twenty miles distant, beyond the humping hills scattered on the rice plain. Spring violets and little ferns grow in its crevices, and of them I had picked many a bouquet joyfully in earlier days. "The city wall is repaired. How splendid!" we had exclaimed.

"Yes," replied our English host who has some humour, the missionary principal of a Chinese college. "To our lasting gratitude. It seems, however, that there are two societies in the city. One is a Society for the Preservation of the Wall as an Ancient Monument. The other is for the Tearing Down of the Wall and making a Road or Tramway in its place, after the fashion of the old city wall of Shanghai."

"A good thing the first society won," we commented.

"Y-yes," he said hesitatingly, "but, you see, the same man is the chairman of both societies!"

The attic stairs shook beneath the Nanking Vice-President's enjoyment of this.

"I suppose he was the leading gentleman of the place," said he, "and so did not like to refuse an invitation to be chairman of any society formed for the good of the city."

"He was," I admitted. Then I went on to relate how the Buddhist temples in that city were also repaired.

"They have services every Saturday morning at ten, and sing Buddhist hymns," I informed him; "they are not going to let the Christian Church have it all its own way and all the good methods, as General Booth might have said. Just above where we stayed, up a hill-side, was a temple, newly painted, the gods newly painted too, the courtyards made spick and span. It was a pleasure to look up at it. Every Saturday morning came the throbbing of the big drum calling the faithful to worship: and up the steep, winding, stone pathway they would toil."

"Were there many? And who were they?" he asked.

"A handful of women," said I. "Mostly elderly."

" Dear, faithful, elderly women, what should we do without you to keep the flames of faith and love alight ? " he mused.

" It seems," I continued, " there were two societies concerned over the Buddhist temples also. One was for the Maintaining and Restoring of the Temples of Our Old Faith, and the other society was for The Turning of Effete Buddhist Temples into Hospitals and Schools of Modern Learning."

" And the same man was chairman of both these societies also ? " he queried.

" Yes," said I : " he was again the same leading gentleman." There had been schism in our host's college, I went on. Some of the students had been there the full number of years, but they had not passed their examinations successfully and had been required to try again. " We have spent all this time here," they argued in excessive annoyance, " and we demand our certificates, whether we pass or no ! " Finally, they had gone off to form another college of their own where discipline was less rigid, where they could elect their own teachers and dismiss them if they did not like their teaching. " So, as they had to have a Board of Patrons, of course they asked this gentleman to be their chairman also," I ended.

" A pity the Christian college did not do the same. Doubtless he would not have refused," suggested the Vice-President with vice-presidential guile.

" I will write and suggest it," I said, as we came down the stairs and joined the returning band of inspection just as if we had been with them all the time, and feeling much fresher than they looked.

" Au revoir, my partner in duplicity ! " he said.

I have never seen him again, and never shall. When the riff-raff portion of the oncoming army was let loose on Nanking only a year later, and permitted to work evil on the foreigners, they came to that University. The Vice-President, who hoped much that the Nationalists were going to deliver their country from its wretchedness, who had never hurt a Chinese in his life and did not believe a Chinese would hurt him, went to meet the bands of the conquerors. He spoke courteously to them. He could never have spoken otherwise to any one. He was beginning to joke with them —as he had joked with me. But one boor, from a far-distant province and city, snatched and dragged at his watch-chain. Possibly he made some involuntary start: who would not? He caught the man's hand, but he did not make any violent motion: so all agree. He was about sixty; his heart was not strong, as he had told me in the attic. And the boor shot him without more ado.

What can be the mind, the future outlook of a being who can do such a thing as that? Did the soldiers who diced for a seamless robe, in the intervals of watching a long-drawn death, look back aghast upon their callousness? Shall the torturers never blanch in memory over their work? And what is to become of them, either in this world or the next? Will they ever grow a soul that shall know remorse?

At the gate, then, of the University, which was his life's devotion, his joy, his crown as another apostle put it, the Vice-President fared forth into the sweet and blessed country. His wife, they said, could not believe he had gone, and would not be induced to leave the dear image of what had been most dear to her, when the others implored her to flee with the rest of the hunted little community. She felt no hatred, for she said he would have been the first to forgive them for knowing not what they did. She stayed: and thought. And presently, so one told me who met her many weeks after, she came to a conclusion in her thinking.

"With my husband's death," she said, "the violence of the hatred of foreigners abated. The wantonness of the murder struck all with shame. He would have been glad to think that by his manner of death he had helped China to turn her face from hate."

When my other Chinese friend of old days, Li Cheng, was in England—for his first visit—three springs ago, he accompanied the head of his Mission, a Mission of inquiry into foreign economics, to the Tomb of the Unknown Warrior in Westminster Abbey. There, in the name of China, they laid a choice bronze plaque with a Chinese phrase upon it. A few days later, Li Cheng took me to see it. A group of Britain's women, many quite poor, stood, as they always do, about the place where the body of the son of our race is laid.

"Will you tell me, sir," said one of them to him, "what those Chinese words say?"

Willingly Li Cheng translated them, and the crowd stood listening.

"This hero led his people to victory while he lived: in death he will ever be a guiding spirit to them."

"I call it beautiful, sir," said the poor woman.

And to me it is almost impossible to imagine that the loving thoughts of the American missionary will not make, now and again, a traffic of Jacob's Ladder between the Eternal City and that Chinese city of Nanking to which one might give the name of Eternal Hope, so often has it been destroyed and then rebuilt. That sunny day, as he looked down from the tower upon the work largely of his heart and hands and brain, he had found it very good. It was so great a work that it had tired me to think of it. But was it deeply founded, or only ephemeral? You shall judge.

How did his students, his children, behave when the awful catastrophe rushed upon them: at least, the majority of them? Brought up in a tradition which abhors physical violence of any sort and is only beginning to admit it in games, they clustered round their foreign teachers. They shielded them with their own unarmed bodies from armed attackers of their own race. Some of them paid down every cent they owned in the world and promised to bring more than they owned, borrowing from the future, to buy the lives of the men they had learned to honour. The girl students met the insistent marauders and led them into the rooms of the women's college, except into the room where their foreign staff was gathered silently.

Ah! that was the real work accomplished by such men as the Vice-President, not the mere buildings, nor even the science laboratories. The storm blew, the sea rose, but that building formed of quivering young hearts shook not. The foundations of faith and hope and love had been dug too deep; and these rest upon a Rock.

The other citizens of Nanking, who knew little of the foreigners personally but had become used to seeing them walking peaceably in the streets and knew by hearsay of their good works, behaved with equal integrity. They took them into their homes when the marauders were pursuing them, gave them their own clothing, hid, fed them ; till they could be conducted to safety. A Buddhist priest—Dr. Williams, do you now know this, I wonder ? Perhaps he was one of the very temple priests you had pitied—invited some foreigners in danger of attack into his temple, behind the shrine of Buddha, and hid them till night : people he had never seen before. A carpenter took a wounded American woman lying in the street into his carpenter's shop and covered her with shavings and tended her. Surely Another Carpenter would have approved. Common humanity it was which stirred in them. Dr. Williams, do I hear you say that they are a people worth dying for ?

In another city of the South, after the foreigners had returned to their ruined filth-covered homes, the ordinary innocent citizens stood at their doors to see them come back. And they wept.

" Ah ! you have lost your goods, your furniture ! " they said. " But we—we have lost our good names, which is far, far worse."

Of course, not all held firm in the day of trial : one could not expect that anywhere. A story I heard sears my mind. One young Chinese, of twenty or so, preparing to be a pastor, who had during his short life lived with kindly foreign folk and known only affection, was caught by the oncoming Army at its most anti-foreign moment. It was at Changsha, I think. He was howled at for having consorted with the foreigner : he was stripped naked, bound, insulted, and marched the livelong day at the head of the mob, about the streets where he had walked in honour before. At the end of the day they beat him : and contemptuously let him go. And the poor lad went to the river and drowned himself.

That day from the tower of the University Dr. Williams pointed out to me, with pride, the new tomb which was being built for Dr. Sun Yat Sen. He has a right to be buried there at Nanking, the heart of China. His tomb is a very great one, is very beautiful ; in short, it cost a million dollars. I was glad when they chose for it the design of a Chinese architect who, though a modern student, has based his plans upon the ancient rightful splendid lines of great

Chinese tombs. I was glad that the dwelling-place of the dead still means so much to modern China.

"My friends! Despise not the narrow laws of the elders," says Schiller. Strange, however, that the revolutionary who gave the death-blow to a dynasty should lie in a tomb of regal traditions and dimensions!

It may be that history will forgive him his short-sightedness, his destructive methods; for the sake of that love for his country and his desires for her progress which were the truest and most abiding portion of his soul. When he knew he was dying in Peking, whither he had at last attained, he sent for a Chinese Christian minister and said that he would wish to have a Christian burial. He asked that there should be sung over him his favourite hymn, "Jesus, Lover of my soul." And so it was done, with a surpliced Chinese choir to sing it amidst the grief of thousands, there upon an ancient altar in the Forbidden City, both Christians and others listening. The minister, as he told me of it, wept. Dr. Sun died in the midst of an adoration which would make any man sure he was a hero and a deliverer.

It is not only in China that patriots do some odd deeds or that there are incomprehensible Christians. Should we like to sit in judgment?

Yet there was another who loved China, whose heart was stilled by a bullet in Nanking—at the gate of his University: a modest elderly man of an alien race. His family has put up a memorial to him in his home town in America, I hear: and the words on it run: "The servant is not greater than his Lord."

CHAPTER XI MODERN NOTIONS

ONE of the Chinese women on the staff of the women's college where I was staying in Nanking was a Miss Wu. A very different sort of person she was from Mrs. Sung. She had discarded the resin which keeps a Chinese woman's head sleek. It has been an object of foreign criticism—this resin. Truly it is more cleanly to keep one's hair washed than gummed. But without this species of brilliantine a Chinese woman's hair, taken close over her head to a knot in the nape of her neck, is apt to stray and become untidy.

Miss Wu was neatly dressed and suitably, but her clothing, which was very clean, was more serviceable than dashing. She was a brown worker bee, not a butterfly with pansy wings. She was saving her money for a trip to America, where she could take some extra courses in education, so she told me.

Oh, but she is a fine woman—Miss Wu : a dauntless worker bee, flying straight for her objective, and laying up honey—for others. When the soldiers came with evil intent upon the college, which has her love and service, she was amongst those who led them to every room except where her foreign colleagues sat silent, trusting in their Chinese women friends.

That evening, after my adventure in the tower of the main University buildings with the Vice-President, my hostess of the women's college asked if I would like to accompany them to a play. It was being given by various members of a neighbouring branch of the University for some charity : tickets, one dollar each. " Miss Wu has bought a ticket and is going too," she added, smiling, for I had hesitated. Like a good hostess, she had seen that Miss Wu and myself had taken each to the other. Indeed, just before she spoke, Miss

Wu had begged me to give her the chance of a long talk, saying that she so much hoped that my father's Commission apprehended how greatly Chinese women needed educational encouragement. My hostess, seeing our interest in each other, had invited Miss Wu to dine with us at the foreign staff's table, and had put us together. The Chinese faculty naturally ate Chinese food, so they usually dined in their own dining-room conveniently for their cook. The American faculty could hardly have supported life if deprived too long of waffles, just as the British feel the hardest part of a foreign diet to be the incomprehensible divorce from the rightful union of bacon and eggs at breakfast. Miss Wu had accepted my hostess' invitation to dine with us. Nor was this unusual, for the faculties were often guests at each other's tables, so happy were the relationships between the Chinese and the American staffs.

Off we set, then, after dinner, down a lane and up a lane: half a mile's walk to the assembly hall, which was nicely full of various portions of the American staff. There was a goodly sprinkling of Chinese, interested either in the charity or in the actors whom they knew in daily life. I sat amongst charming American women, and next to the fair English girl who was my immediate hostess—the only English girl in that hall, and on the staff of the women's college. The play was a simple three-act affair, innocent and amusing, about a Southern family in Carolina and their coloured servants, and it was acted with verve. After the first act, one after another of my neighbours moved away to speak to friends in the hall, and there was a space about me. I rested. The curtain went up again and darkness came down on us, except for the lighted stage. Presently I became aware that the chair next to mine had been filled: and then, gently, a hand slid into mine. I took it. That was a Chinese hand. I knew that at once. The rounded wrist fell soft on mine. The fingers were so small. It reminded me of a hand that had slid often into mine, as mine into hers, years before: of Flower's hand, my Chinese blood-sister's, in Tientsin. There was, again, no lack of decision in that quiet, steady Chinese clasp. Yet there was appeal. The edge of a short Chinese coat-sleeve brushed my wrist. Without turning my head, I knew it must be

Miss Wu who was asking my friendship, though she knew we might have but a few brief days together. I drew her arm through mine, and together we watched while an American woman, with a soft contralto voice, dressed like a darkie Mammy, fat and comfortable, made quaint and humorous remarks on life. At least, so I gathered by the laughter around me. My ears had not become sufficiently attuned to the unexpected accent, for they were obsessed with Chinese as the other language that called for my attention, and it was difficult to switch to yet another range of speech. To Miss Wu also, excellent speaker though she is of our tongue, much passed not fully grasped. Drama is the final test of the understanding of another language.

In contented silence Miss Wu and I sat and looked, rather than listened. It seemed so very odd to be sitting in the middle of China amongst a large number of Americans, mainly New Englanders, watching a play about Southern gentlemen and their delivery from uncomfortable straits by those dearly loved children, their darkies—Chinese all about us, in an unhappy China, a Chinese woman's hand in mine. It hardly seemed real. Yet it was good, this interlude from another atmosphere, helping to keep those present proportioned and balanced.

When the play ended, three American girls on the women's staff offered to see me home, as my English hostess was detained. They were bound for the same dormitory as myself. They caught up Miss Wu and myself, and began to walk fast, singing, down the lanes. It was very dark, but I heard soon a pant beside me, and I felt like panting also. Miss Wu and I were the same age, as we had discovered in the country where one's age is an item of polite inquiry at the outset.

"Youth must be served," I said, "America leads the way. China and Britain will creep slowly after."

They protested, but Miss Wu stumbled into a sandy hole. I stumbled in after her. We sat down and laughed and refused to let them wait. They linked arms, and sped light-footed down and away. From far ahead we could hear faint strains, soprano and alto, of

"All through the night."

America brings up its young girls to be very charming.

" But we 'll reach home finally just as surely as they, Miss Wu," said I. " Now what we ought to start singing is

> ' Through the night of doubt and sorrow.'

We English went through a shattering war, you know : and it took the youth and spring and freshness out of our generation just as these years of your country's distresses have taken it out of your thoughtful people."

" How does that song go on ? " she asked.

> " Sister clasps the hand of sister,
> Stepping fearless through the night,"

I paraphrased. Arm and hand entwined, we walked leisurely. The clear singing of Young America came to us down the warm breeze.

" I am not at all a fearless person," said Miss Wu. " I am often very much afraid."

" So am I," said I ; and we paused. " But what is the special fear in your heart just now ? "

" I fear for our women : China's women. We are in the midst of such difficulties."

I knew what she meant. The coming of Liberty—what does it not entail, anywhere, everywhere ?

In the course of our library inspections, I had come upon a student, a Chinese girl of nineteen or twenty, looking mightily perplexed in the beautiful latticed and painted room. She had won a scholarship from a mission school in a distant port. She sat surrounded by a pile of books and studied intently one in her hand, sighing after the manner of Bunyan's burdened Pilgrim. Like the Evangelist, I had asked her wherefore she sighed, and she had yielded up her book for my elucidation. It was on very modern American psychology, as were all those about her. Long involved latinized sentences and repetitions met my eye and fuddled my wits. She had looked so overwhelmed that, taking the law into my own hands, I had urged upon her notice the heavenly translucence and simple utterance of William James. But when she heard he was " dead," again she sighed and intimated in her beginner's English that in such a case she feared he must also be " finished " in psychological circles of to-day.

Now another book lay open on her table : a book of many close-printed pages. I took it up—the English of it was indeed different from the others. It was the *Forsyte Saga.* " Do you enjoy reading this book ? " I asked her. She looked at me with the frightened eye of a thrush caught sitting on its nest in a trimmed box-tree. Then she whispered half-ashamedly, " No, not much. But it is our literature book in modern English. Our teacher says it is so well written, we must learn by it."

Feeling more and more like Alice in her rabbit-hole, I asked myself if it was the Red Queen or the Mock Turtle or Father William who said " Take care of the sounds and let the sense take care of itself."

" Why don't you like it ? " I asked, tormenting her like any inquisitor. She hesitated, then broke out :

" I did not know how unhappy English wives are. And they seem to have as many husbands as our rich Chinese have wives ! Why do English women behave so ? "

" They don't, my child," said I : and burst out laughing, because otherwise I might have groaned. In a minute the girl flung back her head and laughed too.

" Well," she said, " I did not quite believe it. Of course I have only seen one or two English women, but they cannot be so very different from us as that, or from American women. We meet many American women here in Nanking, and not one of them has been divorced, yet the newspapers would make us think all American women get divorces. Of course divorces are good sometimes," she reflected.

" Dear me," said I : but had no time to continue the conversation. I felt as if suddenly young again, in an English college, discussing with friends the seriousness of Life. On the way back through the lofty room I saw her again, and she looked round her pile to smile at me.

" Have you," I asked in haste, " read *Tales from Shakespeare* by Charles Lamb ? You would enjoy them."

" Is he dead ? " she asked, doubtfully.

" He will never be dead," I assured her, and was going on my way, but turned back to add, " and neither will William

James. Read what he says to teachers about 'the nightingale of life's eternal meaning singing in one's heart.'" She had told me teaching was to be her career.

Of course, after I came away I remembered all the things I might have said to her. How often have I yearned for my mother's quick wits! How she would have pierced the clouds for that girl with a shaft of sunlight in a twinkling of an eye! I ought, I can see, to have talked to her about this being the Age of Revolt in literature; revolt against hypocrisy and man's tyranny and nineteenth-century self-satisfaction. I ought to have said that this did not mean that possibly the nineteenth century had not something to feel pleasantly smug and self-complacent about; but that the next era in literature would no doubt contrive to achieve that most difficult ideal, absolute sincerity lit by the fires of growth and conception. I might have added, however, that since God alone is Perfection and Pure Enlightenment I feared that mankind, East and West, would yet have to endure a few more centuries of ebb and flow, of growth, restriction and revolt, before perfection in literature was realized.

"But now," I might have ended, if I had had the sense, "it may be that the winter of our discontent is passing. Meanwhile, do not take the frost and ice too seriously to heart. Winter is good. Look within, says Jeremiah, and see how full is your heart of evil and meanness and selfishness. Even at your best, you are a poor thing, a sham; so Juvenal scathes you. It is wholesome that certain eras in literature should thus chastise human frailty. But beneath such icy breath tender shoots are shrivelled and vanish from sight. Yet are their roots deep in man, and with the roll of the earth into warmth and light, out they will put their buds and flourish—till at last their harvest also is gathered, and the nip and frost come again, and the purifying cold of the snow."

It was perhaps as well I did not say all this to the girl—she might have been more dumbfounded than by her reading. As I went away, I remembered a French girl who came to a friend's house in England to study. The solitary English book she possessed, amongst her collection of her own great literature, was *Jude the Obscure*. "It is the modern English book set for our baccalaureate degree," she explained to her captious hostess.

People had told me in Shanghai that books translated from the English on birth control were selling by the hundred thousands there, and in Peking and every modern centre in China: that they were the best-sellers on an immense scale. One must read them, or be considered incapable of sound judgment on any modern problem.

In Shanghai I had been out to a dinner given in honour of a deservedly renowned preacher from the West, something of a saint, by a renowned modern Chinese preacher, a leader of the Christian Church of China. Friendly conversation had flowed as we sat about the round polished table, under the lamps, with modern appurtenances around us. Our bowls of Chinese food and the chopsticks and the Chinese gowns and faces were the only intimation that we were not dining in Europe or America. A lull came, and the noted Chinese Christian, a man of forty, turned to the noted English preacher and asked in a bright conversational way, with the courtesy of a younger to an older man, " I suppose, sir, you have read this book we are all talking about, *My Sex Experiences*: or is it not translated into English yet ? "

A missionary's wife opposite me, also a guest, remained stock-still, her chopsticks in the air, her eyes round and aghast. The saint, however, was a trifle deaf. To my ears the question had been put loudly enough to penetrate a battleship. Or was it that he could not believe his ears ? Or did he remember another Saint who wrote on the ground when He was asked questions He preferred left in silence ? " What did you say ? " he said, turning his hearing ear. At that moment the telephone bell rang and the leader was called away. Indeed he was a very conscientious and clever man. He had stuck manfully by his religion in the face of much difficulty, and it was because of a real appreciation of his character and work that he was now on demand for every important wedding or funeral, and that the telephone hummed, day and night, with communications and requests from his innumerable friends.

So I never heard how saints of to-day deal with sex problems at dinner-tables. The leader's wife was near me, and, amidst the confused table chatter concerning the nuisances of telephones, she tried courageously to follow her husband's lead and asked me if I had read the book. I confessed I had not: and she cast me a pitying look. What sort of an adviser could such an uninformed person be to modern China? "The people who contributed to that book have had their names and addresses printed in it to guarantee their *bona-fides*. Is it not brave of them?" she asked me.

"It is," I agreed: "almost rash." She looked at me, shocked at my flippancy.

I was not even a representative of modern England in her eyes; for with a pang I realized that the leader had thought our normal dinner conversation in the West ran on the lines he had indicated.

For my own part, I am at one with C. E. Montague in such matters. Wittily he says, "There is a time to embrace; and there is a time—*and a much longer one*—to refrain from embracing." Similarly, to my mind, there is a time to discuss embraces, and very many more times to refrain from such discussion. Is the Majestic Phenomenon of Love a thing to be cut up with a knife and poked into one's mouth on a fork or a chopstick at a dinner-table as if it were a slice of pork? Are its mighty pinions to be minced into small talk as if they were the wings of a groundling chicken?

So I did not undeceive my Shanghai Chinese hostess at her interesting dinner-table, much though I liked both her and her husband. But out on a dark road with Miss Wu was a very different matter.

"I fear for our women: China's women. We know so little, and we need much help," she said.

I knew what she meant.

Did you ever go up into the working chamber of a ship's wireless operator? High up there, above the floor of the sea, he knows that a call is coming: and then he shows you how it comes. He opens a cabinet door, and, within, is flame—flame and lightning, unspeakable; brilliant, blinding: orange and pink and violet, zigzagging, crackling, in sheets from floor to ceiling. Who would ever think that behind those quiet mahogany doors such power was ambushed, waiting till a young man brought it out from its secret tabernacle. He, the young man, flashes a quizzical smile at you with his gay eyes, and makes the electricity leap and splutter and flame more, in his content at your wonder. He deals with death and destruction and those immense forces as though they were a bagatelle. He is aware that they are always around us, living, vitalizing, ready to leap out: rejoices in them, and swims and dives and immerses himself in the thought of them, ever striving to draw out more of their inner possibilities, by his logic and his thought, his concentration and his intuition. The ether is to him as a bride, whose flame answers back to the eternal flame of the youth within himself. With his sleek head, his thin cheek and the neat tailored clothes of modern youth, who would know that that flame burnt within him any more than we who gaze out into the atmosphere are thinking of the angels of hidden fire speeding through its electrons? He puts the ear-phones over his narrow head, his eyes grow quiet, he handles his love so carelessly, yet so surely. Our middle-aged generation can die in tranquillity, when the hour strikes. The Flame, which lit us in the way required of us in our time, has already caught and lit the souls of those who shall follow us. We trod the road of mud and wounds, and of Great War. They—who can say how and where the Flame will lead them before the trumpets of the Bridegroom sound for them also?

Yet can the power of that same flame be destructive, terrifying, blasting and withering, when ignorantly handled. The desire to rid the earth of oppression, how beneficent it is—a warm fire we would fain keep alive and leaping in every heart! But it can make such a bonfire of a man's soul that he becomes a raging sheet of destruction to a civilization. He can bring his country down to despair. The flame has not been pure enough: it has not included in its love all God's creatures: it has set aside, as dross to be burnt, things which it did not know were a precious heritage.

Was it Voltaire who said no woman could ever understand the cry: Liberty, equality, fraternity? Perhaps not—for what woman does not know that the freeman is for ever bound, and with a yoke he has fitted on himself? Yet the electric thrill of the new Liberty has flashed into Chinese women's minds. They are staggered and confused by its dazzle and glare.

CHAPTER XII MISS WU OF NANKING

AS we walked along, Miss Wu and I, the opening sentence of the *Inferno* came to my mind. Centuries ago similar problems disquieted Dante's mind. He might have been writing of China to-day.

> " In the middle of the journey of our life I came to myself in a dark wood where the straight way was lost. Ah ! how hard a thing it is to tell what a wild, and rough, and stubborn wood this was."

" There are so many new ideas to perplex Chinese ! " sighed Miss Wu. " It is so hard for us to tell which are good, which are bad. You in the West have had a much longer time to prepare yourselves to understand them. We are unprepared ! "

> " But after I had reached the foot of a Hill there, where that valley ended, which had pierced my heart with fear, I looked and saw its shoulders already clothed with the rays of the Planet that leads men straight on every road."

Dante believed that a Planet would surely shine upon the seeking heart. There are many seeking hearts in China. There is more than the one " Miss Wu " in China. Myself, I was to meet other Chinese women as modestly desirous of good for their land, and as convinced as she that a Planet shone somewhere, however dimly they might apprehend its light, which could lead them straight on every road.

" Oh, if only I had the chance to speak to the women of the West ! " she cried again.

" What would you say ? " I asked, moved deeply.

" You must say it for me," she said. " Tell them to stand by us, to help us, to put their hands in ours and show us what path to take."

Then she—that Chinese woman—began to talk of Florence

Nightingale, of Josephine Butler, of the pioneers of women's education in the West. " You have received so much," she said vehemently. " It is not so long since Florence Nightingale lived ; but, look what a tradition you have already in your nursing profession ! You know your nurses will behave in such and such a fashion. We have no professional traditions yet, for we hardly have begun having professions." She almost wept.

" Do you know what I heard lately ? " she went on : " that many wounded Chinese soldiers arrived in a city after a serious battle. They sent for all the nurses and doctors of the locality, and a few newly trained Chinese nurses went too, glad at last to show what they could accomplish. And what happened ? When they saw the dreadful conditions, and the numbers of the wounded, and the lack of facilities, it broke down their hearts. And very soon they had to be sent back, because they first lost their heads and then they could do nothing but weep and wring their hands."

" Poor girls," I whispered.

" Yes, but no foreign nurse would behave so. Yet it is not of herself that she has the virtue, but because she has been brought up with traditions and knows that Florence Nightingale would never forgive her if she acted otherwise."

I smiled a little. But I had to acknowledge the justice of her contention. Strange that it should be Modern China who was insisting thus on our debt to tradition, while throwing her own glove in the face of her own forbears.

" I see," I said ; " you have been bound-footed for many generations, and it takes time for you to become used to the loosenings of the bandages and to walk as free women do, unconsciously, without thought."

" That 's it," she said eagerly.

" But, you know," I began warily, " not all Chinese girls or women would speak as you do, or want foreign women's advice and friendship."

" Oh ! " she cried in exasperation, " you will have to have patience, and much patience : especially with some of the very young ones, and some not so young either, who call themselves Advanced Thinkers ! "

" I know," I told her, " people who plunge over the nearest

A Young Wife of To-day, who is also a mother and a student

precipice in their eagerness to advance. We have people also like that."

"Yes, but they have the chance of a solid education first," she replied. "They do not do it quite so blindfoldedly as ours do. We need more of your company, and not less of it. And educated foreign women do not possess that Superiority Complex which foreign men are supposed to have. I know, for I have met them." At which I smiled again, in the dark.

What treason! Yet I suppose it is true that our sex not so long ago honestly felt itself an Inferior Sex. It may be that though our present generation of women has never had the slightest feeling of being crushed, possibly a dim racial remembrance of those other days makes a certain proportion of women tread a little more gently to-day, for fear of hurting other people's susceptibilities.

"Education, and more of it, and more deeply: that is what we need," went on Miss Wu. "Do tell your father this, over and over again, so that we women shall share in any funds for education which are going. Where can we find help as to what we shall study, and how, except from you foreign women?"

She, who was speaking, was the lecturer in Chinese Classics at her college. She probably knew her classics better than any other woman within a radius of many hundred miles. Yet she could plead like this for Western knowledge.

Thoughts crowded on me. I believe I groaned. She pressed my hand, and we walked in silence. In her own college, American women were standing by Chinese women, with brain and heart and soul. She herself was well done by in the way of foreign comradeship. It was those others, millions of her sisters, she was thinking of and pleading for: she knew their lack because of her own riches.

"We must be able to stand on our own feet economically too," she said. "You know our marriage customs. You spoke to a girl in college to-day, when you asked her to lend you her hockey-stick for a moment. She is working so hard, so hard; she does not want to be married. Her mother, a Christian, had only the one child, herself. Her father took a concubine. Their house is a misery, for she is a coarse woman. She has seen what her mother has endured, and she hates marriage."

Story after story she told me. Another girl, such a pretty gay spirit, had been betrothed to the son of a famous modern Chinese diplomat ; but, alas, he was not the least like his father. He was not vicious, but he was stupid—" stupid to death." She had tried being betrothed to him, for her parents were advanced enough not to wed her against her will. She had met him, and the more she met him the worse became the thought of marriage to him. Her parents had allowed her to break off the betrothal : so far they went. But they did not approve of her ideas, and it was her longing to earn her own living that had brought her to college, after an incredible conquest of difficulties. Another girl had been unhappily married, and had managed to obtain her divorce —a new step for Chinese women—and was now in college.

" You cannot imagine what it is to be married to a complete stranger," cried Miss Wu. " Why, there was one woman I heard of who never even spoke a word to her husband till after the birth of her second son. She knew it was her duty to have children, if she could : but an agony of shyness took her when she tried to talk with her husband."

" I can tell you a story, also," I returned.

" A friend of mine from Peking was married at eighteen to a young man of very good family : and for two or three years they lived amicably together. But gradually there came a shattering. The young husband showed some signs of mental trouble, and he quickly became worse. His worst symptom was a hatred of his wife : till, at last, he tried to kill her. More than once he tried. You can imagine her anguish, for she had been happy with him, and she had borne him a son : and she was but young. This state of things went on till her nerves were frayed, and her father, one of the early Moderns of China, took the tremendous step of saying that she must be divorced. For divorce in Modern China is granted on other grounds than infidelity. Indeed it is rare for a Chinese woman to seek divorce because she has fallen in love with a man other than her husband. To begin with, she would not probably have much chance of meeting him socially !

At any rate, this Chinese father considered homicidal

insanity a sound reason for seeking for the divorce of his daughter. But she, poor girl, was torn in twain, and would not consent for some time. Alack, she would have to leave her little son behind : for he did not belong to her, but to his father's family. Not that she feared he would be treated with anything but kindness, for his grandparents would see lovingly to his welfare. It needed another attempt on her life by her distracted mate to show her that he would kill her and that her child would then be parted from her that way. So with unspeakable sorrow she sought her divorce and went back to her father's house. Later he persuaded her to a second marriage, which proved a truly happy one, her husband being a man who had studied abroad, rested content with one wife, and cherished and loved her. Indeed she had five children when I last saw her. The terrible thing was that the first father-in-law procured a second bride for the demented young man, during a time when he seemed to have recovered. All went well for a few short weeks, and then he came to hate her also, and injured this second girl for life. That was tragedy, truly."

"There, you see," said Miss Wu, "we must be able to earn our own living, or we shall remain in our fetters for ever."

"Miss Wu," said I, and hesitated. "Our forerunners in women's 'freedom' used to talk in that way. But things are not so easy as that. You in China seem to think every English and American woman is happy and contented. Because she has had a better chance of education than Chinese women and can therefore usually earn her own living if put to it, you think all is well with her. Think now of many of our unmarried women in the West, teaching when perhaps wearied to death of their profession, being typists and secretaries in cramped offices year after year, washing dishes in restaurants ; and often leading very lonely lives, going home to a small bedroom or a cheap woman's club. These are the facts, you know. Do you really want us to help you to that destiny ? Are we justified in stirring your ambitions to such an end ? Would we not be better to leave you in your old ways, and trust that Providence may supplement our cowardice towards you, and find you some other way out of your impasse ? Perhaps you do not realize how lonely the life of a single woman earning her living can be."

"I think I do," she replied quietly. "I am one myself, am I not ? Yet of course I am not lonely, for my foreign and Chinese colleagues are so very kind to me. Besides, there is always Christ, and the Father, and the Kingdom of Heaven within us, is there not ? Foreign women know that."

Still, even in a mission college, where the members of the staff are amongst those who know that through every cloud one may glimpse, if one will, on the rocky way, the footprints of divine feet which also have bled, that a pierced hand is stretched through every darkness to uphold the lonely heart, some foreign girl comes now and then to lose her hold on joy.

"Often people need not be lonely," went on Miss Wu. "If they will only give out of their own hearts, others will give them of their hearts."

"Think well now before you answer," I urged, however. "Do not speak for a minute. Would it not truly be better even to be a concubine, a part of household life as in the China of the past, than a single woman earning her own living as with us, with however brave and generous a heart to those around her ?"

On the dark road we stopped. Uneasily she moved her hands. I could feel, though not see, that she had turned her gaze to the abyss above.

"At least she would have the chance of bearing children," I went on remorselessly. "And, as you know, it is not altogether shameful for a Chinese girl to be a concubine as it is with us."

The clear singing of Young America had long since been swallowed up in the night.

Dark were the heavens overhead. Was there no Planet shining for us, as for Dante ? Must we grope in the twilight ? I looked up too. Yes, there were a few stars. Dark must be the night that shows not a single star. But when Miss Wu did speak it was not the starry heavens above that framed her answer, but the moral law within.

"Better, far far better," she burst out, "to wash dishes in a restaurant all the days of one's life, however lonely, than be a concubine."

The voice of China's modern woman is the same as that of her Western sister.

She gave a deep breath, I took her arm, our fingers clasped, and once again we went, swaying down the uneven unseen road. But now the curved roofs of the college were in sight, silhouetted against the sky.

"You Western women cannot, cannot understand what it means to be a concubine. How could one have self-respect left? Bad enough to be married to a man one has never seen before: but how smirched one must feel as his secondary wife! There is no drawing back either: it is for life. You never heard of a secondary wife trying to earn her own living. She has lost both the will and the capacity."

Then once again she began to plead. "Speak for us. I am not a clever woman," she added.

And in a flash, I knew she spoke aright. She is a plodder rather than a winged soul mounting into the empyrean. Later I was to hear she had addressed a delegation, half English, half Chinese, on the subject of women's education. She had been so deeply in earnest and had tried so hard to give the whole of her vast subject, that she had confused her audience with much speaking. Mercifully she was addressing herself to those already converted to her cause. If she had spoken to them, simply, as she spoke that night to me on the road, they would have learnt how noble a noble woman can be.

"Western women," she said, "have had so much given to them. They ought, they should, help us, and give us to understand the secret of their courage. They must befriend us. It is our right."

When we had left Wenchow, that port in the South, just before starting this trip to Nanking, a former schoolgirl of ours, a young mother and a Christian whose faith shone in works of love in her own family and in the church, saw us off at the steamer. The tears rolled down her cheeks as we stepped on the gangway. "Oh, whatever should we have done if you had not come to us from over the sea-way?" she had said. "What should we do if the foreigners had to leave, as is threatened? We should be orphans—orphans!" Hearing Miss Wu, my mind went to this girl who had uttered the same sentiments.

It seems that friendship is, after all, what people want—a friendship that will go a-seeking for the friend.

We crept to the door of the college building and came to our everyday senses, for, search as we would, we could not find the key where Miss Wu knew it ought to be hidden. Laughter took us. We had to throw gravel at a lighted window above: and she was a much better shot than I. Young America poked its head out of the window. "Where have you been?" it asked. "Your conduct is reprehensible." At last we were allowed in, and the Three Graces stood aside to let us pass. Miss Wu went down one dim passage, while the Graces turned to lock up. I crept down to Miss Wu. "Good-night," I whispered.

"I have talked much," she answered. "Forgive me. It is for China—for those who might have been my daughters."

I laid my cheek down to hers, and we kissed. Chinese do not approve of kissing as a rule. It is altogether too familiar a thing, an infringement on personal individuality. But Miss Wu turned the other cheek for a second kiss, before Young America had pushed the last bolt.

A light was burning in my dormitory bedroom, and Young America had made hot cocoa. "Well," said I to the youngest, "you always knew that the British Empire lagged far behind America in every sort of way; but now you realize that it is even slower in gait than you imagined."

That is the worst of colloguing with Americans. For some curious reason—is it affinity?—it is almost impossible to forget one's British origins and be unconscious of race. One is less aware of nationality with French or Chinese than with our kin over the water.

"I do wish," said the youngest slowly, looking at me with distress in her sweet eyes, "you would not talk like that. You hurt our feelings."

"Forgive me!" I said, with contrition, and ruffled the forelock of her shingled head. She put up her cheek with an obvious invitation.

"Two minutes ago I was embracing Miss Wu. Who next?" quoth I. "Do you or do you not agree with Miss Wu, I wonder? She says it is better to type figures in an office than to be a secondary wife."

The second of the Three Graces answered. "The question does not arise for our Lucy," she announced, "for the deluded child imagines there is a man in the world good enough for her." She tugged at a reluctant hand and showed me an engagement ring on Lucy's hand. "He is much too good for me," stoutly asserted Lucy.

Lucy, it seems, had taken her college course, become affianced, but had felt she would like to help to set some other women's feet on the path to happier times before she entered on her own happiness: so she had come to this college in China for a year. This is a method of staffing mission colleges unknown to English organizations, and it obviously has its drawbacks. Yet one's heart warmed to the girl who wished to do this thing.

"I am," I announced, "a firm believer in matrimony, in thorough-going, abysmal and mutual enslavement." I warmed to the theme. The Western romantic idealistic notion of what marriage may mean appeared to me that night, after that walk, a very beautiful and precious heritage of the West, while its sons and daughters marry, and are not given in marriage. Oh, yes, there is plenty of poverty and selfishness in our thoughts concerning it, and cracks and fissures in our practice: but it is a sunlit dream, more sacred and sweet than any other of which I have yet heard. I blessed, in the name of Europe and America, the age of mediæval chivalry. I became extravagant. I extolled the troubadours: I said no young man knew love who wrote not a sonnet to his mistress' eyebrow. I lingered on Sir Thomas Mallory and clean-hearted Arthur. I gave homage to Spenser, with Una the Innocent and her knightly lion. I said that Thackeray's insipid but constant Amelia would no doubt be a pleasanter member of a household than any Dark Flower of depraved vampiredom. I bowed my knee to Meredith's memory. "And if your lover is not called Richard, oh my Lucy, he ought to be! May you be bound tighter than by hempen ropes! May there be all give and no take between you! Away with liberty—she is a useless jade, a stone of no worth till set and held in bands of gold!"

At the end of this rhodomontade, the two unengaged American girls fell upon me and embraced me. "Our sentiments precisely!" they cried. "Lucy, bring this Englishwoman more cocoa!" Then we laughed. The brotherhood of man—perhaps it is not the worn-out phrase some suppose. But the sisterhood of women—it certainly exists. And it can be sweet.

When they had gone, I went to the bookshelf of the unknown American girl whose room I was inhabiting, and found Bunyan. What a tender heart he had for us women! Things were always easier for Christiana than Christian. I read of Christiana and Mercy starting off together, and how Christiana went first through the wicket-gate.

> "Now all this while poor Mercy did stand without, trembling and crying, for fear she was rejected. But when Christiana had got admittance for herself and her boys, then she began to make intercession for Mercy.
>
> "And she said, My Lord, I have a companion of mine that stands yet without, that is come hither upon the same account as myself—one that is much dejected in her mind. . . .
>
> * * * * *
>
> "Now Mercy began to be very impatient, and each minute was as long to her as an hour; wherefore she prevented Christiana from a fuller interceding for her, by knocking at the gate herself. And she knocked then so loud that she made Christiana start. Then said the Keeper of the Gate, Who is there?
>
> "And Christiana said, It is my friend. . . .
>
> * * * * *
>
> "So he opened the gate, and looked out; but Mercy was fallen down without in a swoon, for she fainted, and was afraid that no gate should be opened to her.
>
> "Then he took her by the hand, and said, Damsel, I bid thee arise. . . .
>
> * * * * *
>
> "Then said he to those that stood by, Fetch something, and give it to Mercy to smell on, thereby to stay her faintings. So they fetched her a bundle of myrrh, and a while after she was revived."

A bundle of myrrh!

I am not sure that that is what Miss Wu wants: she cries out for something more solid. Education was what she mentioned to me.

That is not the end of Miss Wu—nor will be for a long while yet, please goodness. She is still very much alive.

After the College and University had been impounded and filled with the anti-foreign, anti-Christian wing of the oncoming Army in 1927, she had to flee: and she went to America. Word reached me of her now and again. She thought of coming to study politics and economics in England, she wrote. But a friend told me more of her doings than she did herself. One evening, for instance, at a large meeting in a large city, when China was being discussed, an American judge stood and inveighed long and bitterly against missions in China.

"I challenge any one in this audience to tell me one solitary good thing they have ever accomplished," he ended, dramatically and rashly. Up rose Miss Wu in righteous wrath. The brown worker bee would fight to the death on behalf of her beloved hive. Usually shy and unready of public speech, she was now in a blaze of indignation and cared not what she said. Before them all she called out in a clear voice, "I am a living example of what good they have done. They have given me, at the very least, liberty: they have given us Chinese women a chance to rise into a free air we did not know before." Then she started out and gave the critic a very feminine scolding without more ado: till he hung his head and could not reply. For fifteen minutes she flayed him.

She ended with such laughter at the unbeliever as must have been more convincing than her diatribe, for her audience rocked with laughter with her. How many of the enemy's heavy guns has not our own Mr. Thomas Atkins spiked with the same weapon?

Doubtless the American judge wished that Miss Wu had been left in her pristine unemancipated condition.

Another middle-aged Chinese spinster body in France told me how she, too, had felt impelled to speak the truth to a compatriot of hers. I knew him: he was a person of importance. But she thought he had been remiss in some duty.

"So I assembled together our Chinese in the city——"

"That would be in lieu of a family or clan gathering," I interpolated.

"Yes," she said. "Then I stood up and I called him by his name and asked him why he had not done such and such a thing. He could not answer. So I scolded him. He had to listen."

"What a ferocious woman you are! And does this sort of Chinese torture go on in Europe to-day?" I asked.

She was five foot, if that, plain of countenance, wore spectacles, and looked over the top of them at you when excited.

"Oh, he had to listen to me," she jerked her head.

"Did he repent?" I asked.

"He did," she snapped: "and how much better for him that he should thus repent and walk on a right road afterwards than be allowed to go wrong, to the detriment of himself and us all!"

I knew he would not have taken such a talking from any but a woman of mature years. He must have been conscious that if she reproached him, there was reason for it. To my mind, it shows a certain amount of grace in him that he was willing to appear "before the clan" in an alien land and hearken to the voice of a righteous spinster. There is no doubt about it, the worker bee, even if she does not sting, can make life very unpleasant by flying and buzzing in one's face far too closely for comfort.

Yet, in a dark passage, one such had leant her cheek on mine and put soft arms round my neck.

"And Christiana said: It is my friend. . . ."

OH, the lovely new Chinese girlhood !

"Flowers, aren't they ?" said one of the foreign lecturers to me, glancing at my face, as we stood looking at a group during some games. One of the first things I had seen when I had landed at Hong-Kong, on the Kowloon ferry, was a young Chinese girl with shingled and waved hair powdering her nose and rougeing her lips by the aid of a mirror in her handbag. "Modern Chinese womanhood," I had smiled to myself. For she was plainly a shopgirl—a fresh institution in China.

Here in this Nanking women's college was the new educated woman, whose personality was in the process of being polished unto the likeness of a palace. Not one of them looked the bluestocking of tradition. There was almost envy in the voice of my companion. To her life had come to mean responsibility, courage, generous fulfilment of duty. She had brought much more for the help of China's girls than she had set out to bring. She had expected to add fine things of the mind : and behold, health and radiance danced in the eyes of her pupils, in their laughter, in their lovely limbs, as well as in their souls. "Blossoms of girls"—and perhaps the thought came that now she was only the gardener, who had digged about their roots, and become rather tired after years of toil. Is not the rose more entrancing than the gardener who has tended it ? Yet who knows how the two will compare in the tribunal of eternity ?

Some of those girls had tasted disillusionment : but physically healthy youth can at least play games, although disillusioned. The joyous freedom of Western pastimes, the charming surroundings of the college with its buildings and its green lawns, the friendliness of girl companions, the personal ease which the college life gave, combined to give those Chinese girls the attraction of vitality. Gone was the pallor and silent demureness which were their chief enticements of old. Life had become something to be gathered like dewy flowers, in careless armfuls. As they scuttered and romped in a bunch from one corner of the large hall to another in some game, laughing, glowing, fresh-eyed, rosy, their happiness was infectious. Their heel-less shoes pattered on the parquetted floor like rain on leaves. They were clad in the white blouses and balloon-like knickerbockers which American girls use for drill. Their combined laughter was the prettiest sound I have heard in my life. I wanted to radio it through the world—that cascade of music from twenty soft throats: a breath of innocence like a phrase from Schubert. Its harmony penetrated my heart. "No country can go far wrong," I said to my companion, "with such loveliness possible to it. And it has been your love that has waked it to life."

A year later, and these girls were in the midst of whirlpools of hate. They must have seen the bodies of other Chinese women and children floating, murdered and mutilated, down the great river that washed their walls. Bandits worked not far away from their gates, with whom was nobody able to deal, for civil war was occupying the attention of Chinese armies and officials. The foreign women who had been their leaders had to leave, under the protection of shot and shell.

Well, beauty remains and remained. Nothing can ever take away their beauty from those girls—the development of which they owe to the thought of others. Is not beauty better ammunition than gunpowder, for its effects remain when the explosions are finished and forgotten? China's crafts, her arts, her delicate porcelain, her poetry, her embroidery—do they not speak louder for her, when she asks for a place amongst the nations of the world, than any political slogan or painfully achieved militarism?

Political turmoil was swirling round these college girls, as round their brothers, while I was still there in Nanking. Some of China's newly freed women were swept off their feet. They walked in processions of hate and cried "Down with the foreigner!" as excitedly as others. But not all. Some had already received so much training that they had begun to realize they knew very little—that chief end of education. When they were asked to sign grandiose resolutions on national and, particularly, international questions, very naïvely these women held an hour's service of meditation ; and their leaders read what the Master said concerning the Kingdom of Heaven. After this, they began to discuss the vexed questions presented them about the foreigners within China's boundaries. They always ended by making large modifications in the resolutions sent them by the men students.

Not always did their ideas win : but they persisted, and not once or twice they altered considerably the temper of their menfolk and the tone of the resolutions. A Chinese woman understands the psychology of her own men—it would be a pity if she did not. There are few more delicate compliments that Mr. John Bull pays to Mrs. John Bull than when he turns to her on public committees, whether on education or social hygiene, and asks her opinion. She appreciates the compliment. It is a happy day for China that young Mr. John China is learning, equally in public matters, to turn to young Miss China, and requiring that she shall sanction his resolutions before he despatches them by cablegram to the ministries of an amused or annoyed world. Brave girls they are, for it does not make them popular with eager, dashing young men, when they assert and re-assert that the cause of right is not helped by shutting the eyes to the other person's point of view, that ingratitude is ugly, and that wild words lead to wild deeds for which remorse must follow. These facts appear incontrovertible when one is sober. After years of war and banditry have produced an intense consciousness that the outside world has become scornful or impatient, that the leaders of one's country are impotent and are sadly misapplying their energies, then the nerves become frayed, the least exasperation sets them on edge ; and ardent youth throws aside the soberer virtues. Tolerance and temperance seem as useless as do the older men of staid tradition.

Sick to the soul have the lovers of China been the last few years, not only at the sight of her distresses, the needless and unspeakable sufferings of her magnificent working-classes, but even more at the evil things done by some of her sons. One hoped after the Boxer Revolt that there could never again be possible within her borders the spirit of unbridled and studied cruelty of which one has had to read. To the great mass of the kindly Chinese peasants and the educated thoughtful classes, cruelty is as repugnant as to us, and it has seared their souls as deeply as ours.

Hurt to the quick were we when China turned away from us who loved her and chose the company of those who only pushed her into more misery, who administered the hashish of hatred and rejoiced in her madness. The thing weighed on us. The old joyous friendship seemed blotted out behind a black cloud which that friend on the other side did not even wish to pierce. Then through the hampering fog would come an echo : the laughter of those girls at their sports, the memory of their free limbs and careless lithesomeness. And sanity and hope returned. Oh happy games, oh lovely laughter ! Chinese girls had played with free hearts before woe fell on their country in diabolical blackness : they would do it again. The morning is as sure to come as the night : and dew will be as fresh on the flowers to-morrow as if the storm had never beaten. Laughter would fill the mouths of Chinese girls again, and the dance of their free tripping feet would echo from parquetted college floors.

And Chinese girls will once more conscientiously kill themselves, or try to, with overwork, as Miss Lucy had reported of them to me that time in Nanking. She, fresh from an American college, spoke almost in awe of the desperate eagerness of those other girls to fill themselves with the New Learning.

For on the morning after our symposium on marriage, Miss Lucy and I set off together to visit the historic and ancient examination cells for which Nanking was a famous centre. We started out in one of the dilapidated barouches. We might have taken a motor-car in Nanking, modern city that it is ; but how much more expensive ! Working women cannot afford to hire motors negligently. However, I had traversed Nanking streets in a motor-car ; paid for by others ; officially provided. Motor-cars had not been long seen in Nanking, and were hardly then a common vehicle. The city had vast open spaces, owing to its many destructions : but that did not mean roads. We wanted to see the city and its

Photo by G. V. Kitson, Esq., H.B.M. Consular Service, China

Big Sister and Little Sister at the gate of their modern home in Hangchow

scholar's finger-nails, wrote and corrected and wrote again, hoping to pass into their country's Civil Service.

With a clatter of its hoofs on the wide old stone pavements, our Chinese driver stopped his ungroomed shaggy horse. Behind the painted wide-spaced wooden railings, we saw that the big courtyard of the examination halls was full of folk. A few young men in the straight gowns of students stood at a blackboard at the other end on a raised parapet, with some Chinese sentences chalked on it. Other students were unfolding posters with more sentences. At sight of us, they hesitated. One of them carelessly flung a poster, with its back turned, so that we could not see its wording, over the statements chalked on the blackboard. Then he flung a flag over a poster, as though casually. Where had I seen that flustered, conscious look on a young face before? In an instant, I was back in a Young Men's Club in a coffee tavern in a Walworth Settlement—my own weekly club and my own young men. I had come in sooner than expected, and there was a pernicious drawing on one of the marble-topped tables. For a second my eye caught it: but the perpetrator had looked so horrified that I gave him a chance, turned away, and it had been washed out in coffee when presently I turned back. Very well; this was evidently another occasion on which it would be well to be blind. On the other hand, if this was an anti-foreign meeting, what about pretty Miss Lucy? It might be wiser to turn tail and go back to the carriage. But when should I have another chance of seeing those wonderful halls? The driver was evidently non-plussed and stood looking doubtfully at me. Miss Lucy's sweetheart seemed to lift an eyebrow at me from over the Pacific. "I love her. I have trusted her to you and China: be careful," young Richard called to me.

The courtyards looked full of Chinese men through the wooden grille. I wavered. Then I caught sight of a group of countrywomen, come a-gallivanting in their bright-dyed clothes. Then three or four others, decent poorish women of the town. No decent poor woman, town or country, will let a man hunt down or annoy her sister—not even from over the seaway—without telling him what she thinks of him for it. Her tongue is more powerful as a protection than scorpions' stings. In my soul I smiled. In Canton once a crowd of urchins and grown men had much annoyed me, though I had not uttered a word to a living person and had kept humbly to the side of the road. They jeered and crowded, till I was almost frightened, and my heart beat painfully. I espied a fishwife, a buxom barefooted Cantonese quean. I went and stood beside her, and with a bow saluted her. Then without a word I flung a hand out in the direction of the crowd—"one woman to another." She gave me a serious look. Then she lifted her voice and began to address the men. I did not understand a word she said, for Cantonese is as closed a book to one who speaks the language of Northern China as Italian is to us. I have no notion what she said. She spoke: she continued to speak: and soon there was no audience. When it was over, I tried to thank her. But she looked at me with scorn and went away. Once again in her eyes I was a foreigner, not a woman. "Cast your gaze down, Miss Lucy, my child," said I: "do not look about you at all, except with the veriest tail of your eye. Do not smile: and we shall yet see these famous halls." Then "Chieh kuang—allow me to pass," I said in cool tones, and we insinuated our way towards the three or four women nearest.

Is there anything less inviting either for attack or delectation than a woman with downcast eyes and an impassive face? Chinese women found that out long ago. No Chinese woman of breeding would dream in the old days of behaving in any other way in public places. Heads had been turned at first in our direction and voices raised, and for a moment their owners had evidently wondered if they might jape with us. Miss Lucy was puzzled at first by my un-American tactics, but she soon entered joyously into the by-play. As soon as the men saw that we were, like decent women, making for the neighbourhood of others of our own sex, they gave way before us respectfully, and silence fell. Every ear was cocked to hear what was said.

"Ch'ing wen! Please, ladies, can you tell us how one can see the examination cells?"

The women were a trifle flustered, but took us under their wing, and at once bade the men move out of our combined way across the courtyard. Another Chinese girl in a clean tunic, newly washed and ironed, and a pleated skirt, detached herself from the crowd and joined us. We marched, a solid phalanx of respectable women on our lawful occasions, wishing no truck with that disturbing graceless creature, Man. We scorned him, we looked down our noses at him, as he pressed about our flanks. He was reduced to vain aspirations for but one human glance from our stony eyes. He offered advice, information, gratuitous kindnesses. We accepted them all, but gave the coldest word of politeness in return. What is the use of having a sex if you cannot make some use of it occasionally ? We feigned hardness of hearing and addressed ourselves to our women friends. We encased ourselves in femininity as in a fortress. " Talk of race psychology ! This is where we older civilizations have the advantage," I gibed under my breath to Miss Lucy. " You are so busy with self-expression that you forget how to express yourself in terms another race can understand. You have become so used to friendship between the sexes that you do not realize how useful a little antagonism can be."

However, she had her revenge on the way home, later, for she taught me quite a fair amount of school psychology of the modern type, and then it was my turn to listen meekly.

The girl who had joined us was about eighteen, and presently Miss Lucy and she were poring over a notebook between them. They showed it me : it was a drawing-block. The girl was, it seemed, in a normal college and was to be a kindergarten mistress. Especially, however, did she love drawing. This foreigner's method, which has been introduced to China, of setting down with a thick black pencil anything that catches the eye in the street was delightful to her. It was more interesting than only copying at home the old scrolls, lovely though they are.

" Y-e-es," we agreed, hesitating.

When China at last bestirs herself, she does it whole-heartedly. On fine days, the bridges, the pleasure-grounds of every Chinese city are to-day the scenes of artistic efforts on the part of every school of any repute or ambition in the neighbourhood, and working in every medium—oils, pastels or chalks. It does not always make the foreigner happy to find himself the " onlie begetter," after this manner, of crude oil-colour paintings of outdoor scenes. How much lovelier are the old scrolls, is his first thought. It makes one sigh to be presented at the station at the hour of departure with small baskets of gilt-ware holding pink paper roses, the special achievement of a class of young ladies studying " Western Art." One wonders if we make as many *faux pas* when the West discuss the Art of the East.

This young lady had not contented herself with scenic efforts. She had drawn the faces of men in the crowd, and with bold vigorous strokes which pleased both Miss Lucy and myself. Moreover, she had chosen her subjects aright : an old man in his winter hood, a child looking down. Unwittingly, one gives offence to educated Chinese by showing pictures or photographs solely of their poor. Chinese society no more consists of unwashed babies and wheelbarrow-men, beggars or tousled priests than does any other society. It is these, however, who attract the attention of the foreigner—to the indignation of the Chinese student, who would prefer that we made pictures of the well-dressed, the clean, the handsome. " There is not a single photograph of a decently dressed and washed Chinese in this book of pictures you own," had been the heated comment of a frowning young Chinese to me once, his face flushed. And I had had difficulty in pointing out to him how the kindliness and cheerful courage of the poor and old of his countrymen shone so from their faces, that to us they looked far more interesting than many of the well-dressed.

This girl had seen the strength and endurance in the peasant faces, and had chosen them as her subjects. At my request she stood against one of the old doors of an examination cell, and laughed as I took a snapshot of her, with her pad in her hand. Then she said, " You will have a picture of me, and I none of you. May I try to draw you ? "

So she posed me against the old wall, and began. The other women examined Miss Lucy's hat meanwhile, and hands and petticoats ; good girl that she was to permit it. Very courteous she was with them.

It was an extraordinary sensation to me to keep meeting the absorbed eye of that Chinese girl-artist. She lost herself completely in her work. When her eye met mine, it was dead to me, yet amazingly intent on her work, hypnotically entranced. She took infinite trouble, and both Miss Lucy and I grew weary : but we dared not break the spell. She worked fast : she blocked out, she smudged in shadows. Finally she was satisfied, nodded, and handed the result to us to inspect.

Miss Lucy gasped, and then bit her lip. To me came the realization of the tremendous steps which Art must take to bridge the limitations of nationality. The girl had made me Chinese—against her desire, and unwittingly. My eyes were the conventional almond, my cheeks the true Chinese oval : but she had tried to stress the English features and had enlarged my jowl, my nose, my mouth and ears. Yet undoubtedly there was myself in it. It made one ponder. Do Chinese look on our artists' occasional portrayals of their flesh and blood with the same dismay as we looked on that picture? We see our racial features with eyes accustomed to our racial traits, and unconsciously. Are we as blind to the essential lines of Chinese physiology as this girl was to mine ? Is that really how we appear to them ? No wonder they have called us "devils."

"Ask her for that picture of you, and tear it up !" whispered Miss Lucy. "It is excruciating."

But I left it with her as a souvenir, and I thanked and praised her with sincerity, for she had given of her utmost effort. She had done her best to make me, a foreigner, good-looking—and how could she do it better than by making me as Chinese as possible ?

I took her block and begged a souvenir from that. She willingly tore out two or three pages of her black-and-white rough drawings of the crowd. She signed her name and address on the back. When I look at them here in England, I once more see myself with her Chinese eyes—in not too flattering a light.

A Chinese artist, not a Christian, of his own accord once drew a picture of Christ at Gethsemane for a friend of mine, a missionary who had been kind to him. It was Christ with a Chinese face that he drew : but he had put his heart into making it the most perfect Chinese face he could conceive.

Ah, that was different. He was expressing his ideal: not a fact.

We said good-bye to our artist and the other women, and made for the gate. They accompanied us through a lane formed by the interested men: and we passed out through the grille. The girl came, too, hesitating. But our little play was over, and the carriage waited. Well, the spectators should have a good curtain. I turned to her, raised my hands clasped to my bosom, Chinese fashion, gave her the stiff, jerky, unsmiling, ceremonious bow with which I myself had been dismissed often enough at yamen arches, when a visit was definitely ended: then turned on my heel sharply, still with downcast eyes, drew my skirts about me, and sat down with impassive face in the carriage. Miss Lucy acted her part gallantly. Imagine my intense gratification when I heard an elderly gentleman, with the long straggling white moustache and beard of the old school, who had been standing at the road edge, say to his companion:

"What excellent manners these foreigners have!"

"Did you hear that?" I asked Miss Lucy, with awe. For he had used the word *li*—one of the most expressive words in the Chinese language. If he had said *kwei chü* we might have well felt flattered: for *kwei chü* means Correct and Proper behaviour. But *li!*—which is pronounced *lee*—it is the word of the Classics which means that your manners are right because your soul is right, or at least taking the right direction. It means Right Behaviour, Right Relationships between yourself and others, and Right Manners, which are the natural consequence. There is the root for worship in its written character: indicating that you reverence others in something of the same way that you reverence the Perfect One. *Li*—it is the foundation of all right human relationships according to Chinese ideas; the keynote of Chinese civilization. It is the perfume of the spirit breathing through the flesh. "Those foreigners have *li*," said the old gentleman. Miss Lucy and I kept our eyes downcast, but our hands slid into each other's in a joyful pride, seasoned with a sense of unworthiness.

CHAPTER XIV DINING OUT IN SHANGHAI

ON my return to Shanghai after various wanderings, I rang up Mrs. Sung to inquire after her health. I wondered to myself if she still desired our further acquaintance.

" Oh, it is you ! " she answered immediately and warmly ; " when will you come and dine with us ? To-day ? To-morrow ? I want to ask Dr. Yao to meet you. He is a returned student from England, and we love and respect him very much."

" To-morrow will do admirably," I replied with pleasure.

" Have you some adventures to tell me ? " she asked.

" Ten thousand—*i wan*," I boasted.

" Tell me them all, won't you ? " she asked, over the wire.

" Not I ! Is a woman to put on the whole of her jewelry at once ? "

" Then, come early so that you can see Yün-Yün and Nieh-Nieh before they go to bed. They want to play ring-a-roses again, they say."

" Ah," said I, " your two jewels are worth all mine put together."

She laughed happily. " They 've both such rosy cheeks with the trip. In fact, Nieh-Nieh is becoming obstreperous. Yün-Yün is busy keeping him within bounds. He goes shouting and skipping and singing over the house."

" Bless him," said I, his radiant infantile image in my mind's eye.

I arrived early for dinner. This is Chinese correct behaviour. You converse first and meet your friends. Then you eat, and after that go away. The reverse system of ours, it may be, but the essentials of a friendly conversation and a shared meal remain. Even then I had not arrived early enough for Yün-Yün and Nieh-Nieh. They were brought in by their starched amah for but a few moments and were disappointed with me on the score. However, we rode a cock-horse successfully, and the children put their soft, warm foreheads to mine in the Chinese baby's kiss. Nieh-Nieh gave his famous squatting bob, and Yün-Yün sat on my knees and gripped me by the shoulders to see herself—" little, little, quite little "—in the pupil first of one of my eyes, then of the other.

Dr. Yao was a thin, alert man of forty-odd, with a few grey hairs at his temples. It turned out he was a lawyer of wide repute in Shanghai amongst his own people. He was deeply interested in his subject, and in Chinese history as related to foreign affairs. He had been in constant correspondence with a learned professor of Chinese in England, Professor Parker of Manchester. They wrote to each other about once a fortnight on matters of Chinese lore. He had brought with him in his breast pocket the professor's last letter to him, punctuated with Chinese hieroglyphics, as was his bewildering way. The professor had recently died. I had written a short appreciation of his character and learning in a Shanghai newspaper that very morning. Dr. Yao told me he would have done it if I had not. Truly, he had more right to do it, for he had been his pupil and loved him personally. The professor had been kind enough to write me letters on various occasions. He sent me sometimes his treatises and brochures on Chinese history ; and he and I thought it a good joke when he used to write on these erudite pamphlets "Hommages à ma chère collègue ! " I to be called a " colleague," indeed, by a former member of the British Consular Service who was a sort of walking encyclopaedia in Chinese culture !

" But Dr. Yao is very bad," said Mrs. Sung, looking at him affectionately. " He never goes to any of my father's dinner-parties to meet foreigners ; nor, in fact, to any parties of any sort, Chinese or foreign. Foreigners do not know how famous he is amongst us. He stays up till all hours of the night, not for company's or pleasure's sake like the rest of us, but to work. You see, he is a bachelor."

" He is better occupied," her husband said in defence. He is our most trusted lawyer. He is really terribly honest—which no lawyer is supposed to be." He shook his head at him with smiling eyes. " And he makes money, too, though he is honest. He took a very good degree in England to start with : and he is the busiest of our lawyers, because he works so hard for his clients."

" Tush ! Tush ! Fine words—*hao shuo*," said Dr. Yao : not altogether displeased at the warmth of the regard he was held in by his friends. Who is ?

" Now I will tell you a tale about him," said Mrs. Sung, pointing a finger at him. " He was very puzzled over the evidence of one witness in a case he was pleading. He wished to believe him, for he seemed an honest sort of man, a farmer, but all the other evidence was against him. The whole case depended on the time it would take to walk from one village to another in Chekiang between Chuchow and Wenchow."

" Chekiang ! That is my country," said I, pricking up my ears.

" Yes, the district in question is noted among us for the shrines and temples built amongst jagged crags and in clefts of rock. Our artists love to paint it on our scrolls, you know," interposed Dr. Yao.

" Oh, bamboo groves and streams swirling round boulders and soaring curious rocks with their heads in the sky," I ejaculated, while Mr. and Mrs. Sung beamed at us both. It is pleasant when you take the trouble to introduce people and they complete the circle of friendship and take to each other. Dr. Yao and I gazed at each other, and warmth flowed between us.

" It was raining a fine rain while we were there," I told him, " and we saw it in a mist. That was aggravating, for we had to hurry on after only a day. Yet I never regret the rain ; for it was spring-time and the mist floated about the hills and valleys like the scarves of Kuan-yin, Goddess of Mercy."

" Ah, we had sun : but not too hot, for it was autumn, and the leaves were turning."

" What of your evidence and the farming man ? " I asked.

" Well, now, it was strange, but my instinct was truer than my logic—as is so often the case. I was glad I went : and this is how I went. It happened that I had been overworking—— "

"Happened!" jeered Mr. Sung, on whose rounded pale townsman's face pride in his friend's adventuresome spirit shone.

"Well," amended Dr. Yao, "it suddenly occurred to me that I was becoming very tired, and that a holiday like the white man's appeared desirable. The case was not coming on for some weeks. So I persuaded an Englishman here in Shanghai, the son of another learned British former consul in China, to take a holiday too. He had a right start in life and knows something about Chinese history, and, in short, is one of my few real friends like Mr. and Mrs. Sung. Off we went, down the Ch'ien T'ang River, in a house-boat of very simple style—none of your floating hotels!—and then we struck across the hills, tramping. I wanted to tramp the distances my villager spoke of so assuredly, and which the other man pooh-poohed: and my witness was right."

Few Chinese have the opportunity to visit that beautiful spot of Chinese soil of which we spoke. How many English saw Wordsworth's Windermere before the railway or the automobile gave them their opportunity? The way in China is arduous, the journey very uncomfortable. There are no hotels, and the inns are mere shelters from the weather, and unkempt at that. The roads are but a foot-track. Yet the temples, when you finally arrive, are so exquisitely placed, on exactly the right ledges and in such picturesque clefts between the rocks, and the country is such a giant's tumble of crags and dales, that it is worth the trouble and discomfort, provided you can give the time to reach it.

"Did you see the stone on the tableland like a praying priest?" he asked. I nodded.

"Did they point out to you the clusters of little hanging green orchids, their tuber roots in air?" I riposted.

"And the temples up, up, between the crevices, one after another?" he added.

I did not tell him how we had come into a cliff temple at evensong; or how my father had afterwards taken the worn handwritten holy Buddhist book in his hand, and had explained to the large and fat abbot the portion of the Sutra which was the allotted scripture for the day. The abbot had read and chanted, and understood nothing of what he had read. The sacred mumbo-jumbo was enough for him. When we left, he was still turning the book pages hither and thither and pondering the fact that there was indeed some meaning behind the chant.

Mrs. Sung began to tell me more tales of Dr. Yao's passion for accuracy, and the pains he took to prove the innocence of an accused, when he was convinced of it. To amuse them, I told them the story of the British judge in India who discovered that an entire village was perjuring itself. You remember it? The plaintiff declared in court that while his men were one morning working peacefully on his fields, the defendant drove his cattle among them, into his crops, and beat his men when they remonstrated. The defendant counter-replied that while his servants were driving his cattle quietly along the road, the plaintiff's men rushed out and attacked and beat them. The whole village was called in witness. Precisely half the villagers gave evidence on behalf of the plaintiff and the other half for the defendant. So utterly at a loss was the judge, an Englishman, that when he found himself by chance in the vicinity of the village one week-end, he determined to look into matters for himself. He discovered that the plaintiff possessed no fields or men, and the defendant no cattle. In British disgust at such a plethora of lying, he summoned the village to his court next morning and asked them what they meant by their perjuries. They were abashed for a few minutes. Then the oldest men quavered how their headman had died, how these two men were continually keeping the village in an uproar as to which should be his successor. So they had devised this law-suit. "We decided to elect headman the one you gave judgment for," they ended deprecatingly. "We do not mind which it is."

I am glad to say both Dr. Yao and Mr. Sung enjoyed this tale thoroughly, and we then fell to comparing China with India, which was interesting. Dr. Yao and I had both visited India, and the Sungs plied us with questions. By this time it was the dinner-hour, and we left the salon, which was singularly like any English room, with its comfortable Axminster carpet and its walnut glass-cupboard for curios and pieces of porcelain. Well-made English carpets and furniture appear as desirably exotic in Chinese eyes as Chinese blackwood and camel-hair carpets do in ours. In a Chinese city, an English house would have shown green or red lacquered tea-poys from Foochow, brass-bound cabinets from Korea, a cloisonné bowl from Peking, or an embroidered silk curtain from far Szechwan province: trophies of journeyings hither and thither in a land that was first known to Europe by its beautiful handicraft. My Chinese host and hostess had travelled abroad too, and they had brought mementoes of their journeyings in ideas of solid Western comfort and large easy-chairs for their home.

We went in to dinner. It was *pien fan*, as they had promised me—" convenient rice "; that is, their usual family dinner, and not a specially prepared feast, which would be the right way to entertain distinguished strangers and which can cost the host a fortune. Rice, boiling hot and sticking together in glutinous lumps, very easy to pick out of a bowl with the chopsticks, was the main dish, and renewed at intervals, with the " five " dishes, as they are called, of meat and fish and relishes. When we had finished eating as much as we wished of a big bowl of fish stewed in gravy with a pleasantly sweetened flavour, it was taken away by a manservant in a clean blue cotton gown, and replaced by another of stewed pork with delicious little puddings, mushrooms, chestnuts, and pigeons' eggs floating clear and pearly in the brown luscious gravy. The bowl was set in the middle of the table, and we took good-sized pieces of the meat with our chopsticks and put them into our smaller bowls on top of the rice. It pleased Mrs. Sung, a good hostess, to find that Dr. Yao was hungry, and she heaped more on to his bowl, and edged in wise words about men who overwork and do not take proper care of themselves—for he lived alone in a flat. Undoubtedly he enjoyed being thus cosseted. The table was guiltless of cloth or mat: and the servant wiped away with a napkin the splashes of gravy which I, the clumsy foreigner, made between the middle bowl and my own.

" This is very simple," apologized Mr. Sung, enjoying bean curd.

"You would have a bowl of flowers in the middle," said Mrs. Sung

"How much more comfortable a bowl of hot food," quoth I—"and such a bowl!"—for it was of beautiful Cantonese porcelain. She nodded contentedly, for it was plain by my abandonment to the contents of the bowl that I was happy. Mr. Sung and Dr. Yao occasionally made desultory conversation, but the time for serious talk was past and the time for digestion arrived. There was peace at that moment in China, and a man could shake off political and national cares in homely joys. The general in command of the province was Sun Chuan Fang, and his name cropped up with praise for the condition of his troops. I told them I had passed a couple of his soldiers at the door of a barracks in Nanking, when driving out to the examination cells with Miss Lucy. One soldier was on sentry duty, and armed *cap-à-pie*. His friend, off duty, squatted the other side of the gateway, and was helping to pass the time for the sentinel by playing him a tune on a newly-bought flute. Spring was in the air—the time a man feels inclined to buy a flute from a pedlar and play an air or two. He was *déshabillé*, his grey cotton jacket open at the neck, his trousers slack at the ankles instead of bound neatly in cotton puttees like the man on duty. They were happy children in the sun; though they were grown men as were General Sun's troops, and not boys of sixteen or seventeen as in many of the other Chinese armies. The sweet thin whistle of the pipe had followed us and called above the dull thud of the horse's semi-shod hoofs in the dust. So I had stopped the driver, and we had gone back on foot to the barracks door. The piper stopped in confusion at such an audience, and refused to pipe his song again. I begged the courtesy of a snapshot of him playing. He declared this an impossibility.

"Take a photo of my comrade," he said; "he is properly dressed as a soldier. The general would be furious if he saw a photo of his soldiers in undress like mine." I cajoled. He went, finally, and fetched his coat, and tidied up. But he had fetched his rifle also and put down his flute.

"I can take photos of any number of Chinese soldiers with rifles," I protested. "I want one of a Chinese soldier with a flute. How much better—to soothe your countrymen with music, instead of terrifying them with rifles ! "

" True, but too idyllic for our China to-day," commented Dr. Yao.

" Confucius tried to persuade the China of his day to yield their anger up to music, and even he failed," added Mr. Sung.

" Oh, I hope there will be no wars in China when Nieh-Nieh grows to be a man," sighed Mrs. Sung. And I looked at her.

" That is what every mother in Europe says to-day," I appended gently, " and every father also."

Dr. Yao and Mr. Sung began to talk to each other, and Mrs. Sung asked me why I could not dine with them the night before. " Because I was dining at a Chinese restaurant with the uncle-in-law of another Chinese friend of mine, and his two daughters, and a sister-in-law," I told her. " Hardly a friend, perhaps, because I have only just met him, but the women of his family are relatives of my uncle Kung. It was very kind of him not only to invite me out to a Chinese supper, but to go himself in feminine company. We went in their Rolls-Royce car, attended by two chauffeurs in uniform, to that new Chinese restaurant in the Settlement. He had the first Rolls-Royce ever brought to Shanghai, he told me. He had engaged a private room : the Snow Room, it is called, because the pictures on its walls are on Hangchow glass and of snow scenes, a kind of corrugated painted mirror that gives the effect of falling snow when one moves one's head. We had a simple dinner, for I had begged for that ; a dollar a head, you know," I ended.

" I know that restuarant," said Mrs. Sung : " you have a good dinner for the money."

It had been an interesting experience. The Chinese garçon was a friendly person, who recommended this and that dish to the patron, with interest in it and a sense of savouring the good dishes himself. He came expeditiously up the stairs and across the linoleum-covered floor of the " private room " and set the dishes down, took off the covers as if to say, " Now you will certainly enjoy this ! " He received a dollar at the end and thanked our host courteously, and yet as if sure it was his due.

Mrs. Sung knew of the family slightly. All China is a whispering gallery ; so one discovers after an immersion into its female society. When their cousins' cousins and the nieces-in-law of these, together with their daughters-in-law, are considered kinsfolk, one of the ladies you dine with casually in official circles can nearly always tell you the family histories of half China—if she cares. You mention to a Chinese lady in Tientsin in the course of conversation that you met some Chinese lady in Hangchow : and after listening to you with interest as you tell of your doings together, you perhaps mutually reach the subject of divorce by quite a different thread of thought. And perhaps an hour later, as you are leaving, she casually mentions, with the smallest twitch of a malicious smile at your surprise, that your Hangchow friend divorced her husband. " Oh, did you not know ? " she asks with elaborate carelessness. " And a very good thing too. She is a clever, sweet woman, so I hear, though I have never met her. He neglected her disgracefully. I don't know what more he wanted : she had had a Western education. And she is noted for her wit. He is clever enough, too : but it was notorious the way he hung round everybody else and was scarcely ever at home. Oh, she has done quite right to finish such a marriage."

This from a model wife and mother : but then her husband admires her capabilities and is not above asking her advice on important matters of life. She thinks all the more of him for his common-sense in so doing and his power to appreciate her usefulness in the old-fashioned way.

" Let me see, your friends with whom you dined—they have no son, I think," said Mrs. Sung. I paused, uncertain whether to let that pass. But one could trust Mrs. Sung's discretion. The servant was out of the room.

" They have a son," I admitted, hesitating ; then continued, " but he was born deformed, and has never grown up, mind or body. He is nine years old now. His mother loves him dearly."

" Oh," she said, and again, " Oh ! " Her face quivered. She set down her bowl and chopsticks. " Is it not strange ?" she queried. " Everybody knows how rich they are, and sees their fine house and many servants and their luxuries.

And behind all is this mother's breaking heart. I shall always teach Yün-Yün that: never to look only on outside things. You cannot know what the happiness or unhappiness of a man's heart is by looking at his clothes or his motor-car or his house. On board the boat you mentioned meeting Mrs. Wei. Her mother-in-law is an old-fashioned Chinese wife, a lady who has had a large family and is so kind—beyond words considerate to everybody she meets. Kindness flows from her. Her husband, now that she is no longer young and though he is not young either, has taken a pretty house on the lake at Hangchow, and has bought two concubines and sends them there to stay in the spring and goes to visit them. Yet he will never take his own wife away; he grudges her any outing and will share none of his pleasures with her as he does with them. She is a stately, fine lady, and so respected. Many relatives have spoken to him and told him how wrong he is, but he only loses his temper and will not listen. He is throwing away gold for rubbish! Meanwhile her inmost heart is sad, though she smiles at us all and is as kind as ever."

The conversation became general again. Mrs. Sung stood up to take more pork from the central bowl to put into mine and Dr. Yao's. He looked up at her with a friendly smile. They chaffed each other a trifle but with great politeness. She was an admirable hostess.

Mr. Sung turned to ask after my Nanking experiences, so I told them how my father and I had gone to visit the Ming Tombs there, or what remains of their once glorious ruins. A soldier, a Northerner, attached himself, uninvited, to us and kept up a running commentary on what we saw, addressing himself to my father. Now my father was more than distrait in his replies: he plainly did not listen, and finally, afraid lest the soldier's feelings should be hurt, I said, to excuse him:

"Ah well, you must know that my father speaks the Southern speech very well: he has not listened to the Northern talk for some time, which you are speaking."

The soldier turned a haughty eye on me, and easily disposed of females.

"Hu!" he said contemptuously, "whatever he speaks, it is a great deal better Chinese than any you talk."

Photo by Lady Hosie

Two Chinese Soldiers in Nanking. But one is playing a flute—he prefers it to a gun

Mrs. Sung doubled up with laughter.

" Oh, what did you do ? " she asked.

" I went behind a large stone dog and laid my head upon its shoulder in delighted silence : and the two men marched on. If the soldier only knew how honoured I felt : mentioning me in the same breath as my father ! "

Directly dinner was over, Dr. Yao slipped off to his work. " But first," he said, " give me the prescription." A mutual friend was ill, and a foreign doctor had been called in that afternoon and had written a prescription. And Dr. Yao, whose doctorate was of laws and not at all of any science, was going to compound it !

" Certainly," he said to my look of surprise. " I like to do these things for my friends. When I was at my English school I learned some chemistry : and surely you did too."

" Y-yes," I hesitated : " but are you not afraid of making a mistake now and then ? "

" Why should I ? " he asked. " Is it not more likely that I, who love my friends, will make up the prescription right and with accuracy rather than some slovenly youth in a shop who cares nothing whether it does them good or not ? Besides, look at the exorbitant prices chemists charge ! Now, I find I have most of these chemicals ready in my cupboard ; for most doctors give much the same prescriptions ! I shall send out for the quantities I want of the others. Then there is only the mixing to do. Good-night."

To a European, trammelled by custom, who had thought of the Institute of Pharmacopœians as sacrosanct, this blackleg attack on their trade union seemed audacious in the extreme.

CHAPTER XV THE LEPER DOCTOR OF HANGCHOW

I STAYED on after Dr. Yao had gone—foreign fashion, as Mrs. Sung said, of dining out. " Now tell me your stories," she commanded. I told her of Miss Wu, of Miss Lucy, of the girl-portraitist and her conception of a foreign face. I brought out some snapshots, and we chatted away about the beauties of Hangchow, its lakes and hills and temples, for thither the Commission with myself in its train had gone after Nanking. We came to a photograph at which she stopped. " That is a Buddhist," she said.

" Yes, a Buddhist nun : a woman of thirty-five," I told her, and she exclaimed in surprise. I was out early one morning, watching the pilgrims going by, doing their round of the Buddhist temples in the Hangchow country-side. Most were elderly ladies, in sedan-chairs, earnestly using their rosaries ; some of them ill and praying for health, with thin, tired faces, or accompanying their daughters-in-law who suffered from some disability.

" One's heart goes out to them, doesn't it ? " I asked.

She nodded. " They wore yellow silk sashes from shoulder to waist, with prayers printed on them, didn't they ? " she asked.

" Those yellow bags at their sides are painted with more prayers, are they not ? " I said.

" They hold small change to give the beggars en route, because Buddha loves the charitable," Mrs. Sung replied.

" Oh, the beggars ! " I said, " with their sores, and stumps of limbs, and even leprosy ! "

" Terrible ! " she said. " I never go to temples, and I will not go, for I hate to see them ; and what can I do for them ? Nothing but give a few cash ! "

" When I first saw this nun," I went back to the snapshot, " she was sweeping out the front of a closed building near our hotel on the lake side, and we greeted each other, she and I, in the early morning sun and dew. The lake at our feet was limpid and lovely. Here was this slight and, I thought, young person sweeping. How better could one be employed in the early morn ? I took her for a boy of about sixteen, just beginning to grow, so immature did she look. 'Is this a temple ?' I asked. 'A nunnery,' she replied : 'come in and look.' So in I went and found she was a woman, and thirty-five years old. The temple was being enlarged : there was to be a sleeping hall added for ten more nuns up the hill-side behind, so Buddhism seemed to be progressing in that neighbourhood. It was all very clean, with a smell of fresh wood. Moreover, she was a proper and well-behaved person, very decorous," I added.

Mrs. Sung understood. "You mean she was not deserving of the bad reputation which some of the Buddhist and Taoist nuns have. How did she get there : did she tell you ?" she asked, examining the face of my nun friend.

"She led me into her own room behind the image of the Kwanyin, the Goddess of Mercy, who was her particular deity," I told Mrs. Sung. "Very clean and neat it was, with the bedding rolled up at the back of the well-brushed fine straw matting on which she slept. She had a gay painted clock on a shelf and some framed photos. She took one of them down and said, 'This is myself, when I was in the world.' I was so surprised at the vivacious plump face of a girl of seventeen or so looking at me that I thought I had heard wrongly. I could not believe it was the same person as the serious, rather sad, thin woman now before me. She was proud of the photo, and it showed her in her student's best flowered dress, standing in a *dégagé* attitude, one arm over a picturesque rock, made of cardboard I suppose, and a pictured waterfall : all done in a photographic studio. She showed me another with a young man. 'My brother,' she said. She told me how it was that she was now a Buddhist nun. 'I was ill, very very ill, so ill that I was unconscious and it was evident I would die. So my parents promised me to Buddha if I recovered, and Buddha revived me.' Her engagement had to be broken off, of course,—but as she had never seen her betrothed, this did not affect her deeply. Besides, she was weak so long that she ceased to wish ever to be married."

" Was she alone in the nunnery ? " asked Mrs. Sung.

" No, and I can tell you a charming sequel. While we talked, in came a Chinese woman and a little girl of eight, skipping and chattering. ' This is our nunnery ahma,' said the nun. ' She does the cooking and helps me with cleaning the temple and the shrine. Look, we have had enough money bequeathed by pious women to put our gilded Kwanyin behind glass and keep her immaculate and clean,' she said, ' and we hope soon to have enough money to buy glass cases for these other smaller Kwanyins,' pointing them out at either side the great central benign woman's figure. ' And the little girl ? ' I asked. She called the child to her knee, put her hair straight, smoothed her cheek, made her give me a bow of ceremony, and put an arm about her. ' She is Buddha's too,' she said. ' She was so ill when she was five that her mother vowed her to Buddha if she lived. She was brought here very ill : and I nursed her for a long, long while, and did not think she would recover. But Buddha willed that she should live. She will be a nun when she grows up : and now she is strong. I often think how good is Buddha. I had no home, no child : I have here a quiet, happy home, I can pray for others and be useful, and Buddha has sent me a child for my old age.' "

" Was the child well ? " asked Mrs. Sung, touched.

" She was jumping and singing, as jolly as a cicada. The old woman went to wash the vegetables she had been down to the market to buy. The nun had some piece of piety to perform—the morning incense and tea to renew. There was a piece of thin cord in a corner of the clean court, with its latticed partitions. So I showed the little girl how English children skip. But I fear the nun thought this rather too boisterous and indelicate for decorous Chinese girls, when she came and saw us."

Mrs. Sung laughed. " Of course she would : she was a nun ; not a modern mother. Where is the child's own mother ? Does she ever see her ? "

" Down in the city she lives : and every now and then she brings her daughter a fresh coat. She was wearing a pretty flowered cotton tunic that day."

I thought of Hannah and Samuel.

"I took a young English consular friend with me next day to take a snapshot, as he has much pleasure in taking photographs of Chinese people, especially the labourers: and I suppose a nun who says her prayers is that, eh? Of course I asked her permission first, and she brought him a cup of tea with both hands and set it before him with the grace of a princess receiving guests."

Mrs. Sung was silent a moment. Then she gave me again the tribute dearer than all else to a spinner of tales.

"Tell me some more," she said. She wanted to know why there were no stories in Chinese books like these. She complained that there were no novels suitable for the refined female mind in Chinese literature: that one became tired of novels of the ancient or mediæval days of Chinese history: and anyhow they were not very easy to read. "If only we had a good outpouring of novels, in heaps and floods like you!"

"Oh!" said I, taken aback.

"At least some of them are readable, and they are all in plain language, not dressed-up literary exercises for the brain as ours arc," she continued.

This was a fresh point of view on the output of modern literature. Better too many books than too few, evidently.

"But what about this new Pai Hua, the White or Clear Language, the language of the people put into writing?" I objected.

"Oh yes," she said impatiently, "but it is still so new that there is no real literature in it. Essays—but what housewife reads essays? There are a few stories set as exercises in it, but what we want is something we women can read and warm our hearts by and spend leisure hours over, and rub our brains against. We have nothing to do but sew and talk, and then talk and sew. No wonder we almost cease to be able to read after a while!"

I spoke of an earnest man I had made friends with at Hangchow, the headmaster of "the only government secondary school for girls in the province," as he kept telling me, so eager was he to impress on me the need for more such government schools. He had suffered political proscription for his ideals in education. He had been a tutor in a university, the dean of which had been suddenly turned out of his post by political jobbery : and at once all his staff resigned to show their loyalty. This is a wholesale Chinese fidelity to a chief which is very praiseworthy, but it must be disconcerting to wives and upsetting to the family budget. His school, which was financed by the province, was always the last of the schools to receive the small pay which was due to it, and the pay did not invariably arrive even when money was in the provincial treasury.

" But never will we give up our work," he asserted.

He was in such dead earnest that I asked him what had made him so interested in women's education.

He was a schoolmaster : he had learned Method in Teaching. He said, " I can tell you in three sentences." He fetched a piece of chalk and wrote thus on his blackboard, for my instruction :

" (1) My parents died young : I was brought up by my grandmother. Though she could not be expected to know what we know now, yet she did her best, and I owe her very much."

He then erased this sentence with a duster, took his chalk, and wrote :

" (2) I have been very fortunate : for I have been given by Providence an excellent wife : she is charming, she is pretty, she is sensible. I cannot be grateful enough for this. How easily it might have been otherwise ! "

And lastly, he wrote :

" (3) I have three children, all girls, no boy. Their future, their education must necessarily be my care. I shall have no money to leave them : I must earnestly wish, therefore, to give them a good education. If they marry, they will then wish to marry sensible men, not fools or knaves : if they do not marry, they will know how to support themselves."

" Your reasons are perfectly sufficient," I agreed with him. " May your efforts on behalf of Chinese women be successful and you be honoured."

" I envy you," Mrs. Sung continued, harking back to literature. " On the boat, there, you talked with us, then you picked up a book. You went for a little walk, after which you read your book again, and you were so interested in it that your face was absorbed and you did not hear me speak. I tell you, we Chinese women have nothing like that, and it is such a simple pleasure."

"You must ask the Pai Hua scholars to translate our books for you."

"We have some of your books. But they are about life outside of China, about foreign men and women. We would like stories of our own people, of to-day, and stories that could be true: not heroics like the old tales of fairies and dragons and snake-women and monks defying them. Have we no heroes of our own to-day? Did all the generals and scholars live in past centuries?"

"I 'll tell you a story of to-day," I said slowly, "heroic enough for anybody. And true. Of somebody I met at Hangchow." I paused. "It is so heroic," I went on, "I hardly know how to tell it. I am not worthy enough."

"Try," she said seriously. She realized from my tone that it was my heart's blood she was asking. "But perhaps I am not worthy to hear it."

"Nonsense," I said, and began. I do not know how I told my tale to her. It was disjointed, for I kept breaking off from Chinese into English and then into Chinese again, and very halting Chinese at that. So I will not tell it as I told it Mrs. Sung.

She had met Lady Willingdon, of whom I spoke, and who in India had become greatly interested in a Leper Asylum, which is called by her name. Lady Willingdon had received the yearly report of this Indian asylum the day we left for Hangchow. Now at that city English missionaries have founded an asylum for lepers. So when we arrived she said to me that, while the others went looking round the hospitals and schools there, she would like to go over the Leper Asylum with Dr. Main, its founder and mainstay. It is one of the few asylums for lepers which exist in China. She wanted to compare it with others she had visited in India, and one on an island off the South African coast. "Our King's son—our Prince of Wales"—as I told Mrs. Sung, said that he might forget the grown-up lepers' misery, but that he could never forget the look on the leper children's faces. And so he is the President of the Leper Help Society of the British Empire.

When Lady Willingdon took it for granted that I would accompany her to the Leper Asylum on the hillside apart, I am ashamed to say I hesitated. I had never seen a leper : my heart failed. She had seen many. To her, lepers were like any other fellow human beings, to be cheered by a little attention from the outside world ; liking small kindnesses as do other sick folk, and especially entitled to them considering the awfulness of their affliction. She sent to a Chinese confectioner's for packets of sweet cakes and dainties, such as she used to give her Indian leper friends. The packets were wrapped in the gay red paper proper in China for such occasions, one packet for each of the seventy lepers.

There are two homes, one for men, the other for women, next each other, on the hillside overlooking the Hangchow lake, with its boats and white sails and curving parapeted bridges. Dr. Main thought lepers should have lovely surroundings, needing them more than other folk. One of the accusations brought against him later by the ultra-Nationalists was that he, a foreigner, had bought up the best sites round the lake. To be sure, they were waste land before, and are being used for hospitals and convalescent homes and leper asylums. But Hangchow nowadays is developing into a summer resort for rich Chinese from Shanghai—and lo, the lepers have the finest views. Needless to say, only the few and the prejudiced talk like this. The real China speaks far otherwise : rich and poor.

The lepers, knowing of our coming, had put on their clean clothes, and those who could awaited us on the veranda. Lepers, it seems, like to look as pleasing as they can. Also, even among lepers, social distinctions weigh. Two of the women had put on fresh tunics of silk for our coming. They came from genteel homes, and they spoke differently from the other women—who respected and looked up to them. One of the men had been a professional acrobat, and on our arrival he gave a display of his prowess, standing on his head and doing somersaults for our entertainment. The doctors encourage all possible muscular activity, as it helps the lepers morally and physically. Lady Willingdon, surrounded by her red packages, dropped with a kind word her presents into each leper's hand. She did not touch them, for, though leprosy is no longer supposed to be highly contagious, it is wiser to avoid contact. One of the most trying aspects of caring for lepers is the dressing of their terrible sores.

In the meanwhile I made the acquaintance of Dr. Wang, Dr. Main's assistant. He was a man of thirty or so, clad in the long grey Chinese scholar's gown : of no great physique, but with an amazing sweetness and serenity in his quiet eyes and on his face. A sort of heavenly candour shone in him, a spiritual illumination which nobody could mistake. He told me something of the treatment of leprosy. If a leper comes to the hospital before his leprosy has been developed seven years, thanks to modern research, the doctors can check the disease. The injections will not, of course, restore a finger or nose, or bring elasticity back to a solidified joint : but the disease can be arrested—at least for some years, perhaps longer. There is hope that the day may come, with research, when the patient can return to life in the community.

In China, as yet, there has been no law making any disease notifiable. Public Health is only beginning to be a matter for public attention. We in the West cannot boast of being very many decades ahead in this matter. We have, however, had more scientific doctoring than the Orient and more understanding of the dangers of infection. When Chinese become lepers, they usually seek the neighbourhood of temples ; they lie on the temple paths exposing their sores and misery to move the hearts of the compassionate and draw a coin. How else can the leprous father of a household keep his family going ? When a patient came to the hospital on whom the dreadful disease was discovered, Dr. Main had not the heart to send him away. He determined to grapple with the problem. Hence the asylum. Yet it is of their own free will that his patients remain under its roofs. Many of their fellows cannot bring themselves to give up lying about the temple precincts : the free life of a beggar, though it means rags and pain and lack of attention, is a more paying proposition.

Unspeakably bitter must it be to leave wife and child and human intercourse and enter for ever, confessedly a leper, into a segregated colony. It speaks much for Dr. Main's influence that there were no unscaleable high walls or locked gates to that asylum. The lepers rarely disobeyed the advice not to go beyond a certain point lest they bring harm on those outside. It is an appalling sidelight on Chinese poverty and Chinese ignorance about disease that poor folk from the peasantry around have climbed over the asylum wall and stolen the lepers' clothing.

It was evident that the lepers loved Dr. Main and Dr. Wang. Not that they are always amenable. One of the difficult symptoms of leprosy is that the moral sense, owing to physical causes, is apt to become perverted. Lepers, for instance, in Africa, are subject to ungovernable fits of black rage, which lead to murder sometimes in a leper colony. Yet here were these Hangchow lepers living peaceably together on the whole. Ah, but a large proportion of them had become Christians! Two were baptized that very Sunday morning of our visit.

On the wide veranda of the women's house, a group came around Lady Willingdon and Dr. Main, and asked me to photograph them with my camera. I did so, at a little distance. As I finished, there was a commotion, and down the stair was helped an elderly woman whose face was a heart-rending spectacle. Her sightless eyes were without their lids; she wore a woollen mutch to conceal her head; her lips were shrunken over swollen gums; her nose was affected. I could hardly restrain my tears. "Ah yah! Chang ma has missed having her photograph taken!" was the sympathetic comment of the other women: "Oh, T'ai T'ai, take another with her in it, and closer up to us, so that it shall be a good photograph."

What could I say to such an entreaty? I half thought I would make a pretence about taking the film: but the poor creatures sat down in a row, the elderly woman in their midst, trusting me. As I was focussing them, that woman in the middle, blind, the worst leper of all so far as her body was concerned, began of her own accord—it seemed almost incredible—to sing that hymn of our childhood, the song of the Desired Country, "There is a happy land." I took the snapshot and suddenly I saw, not the maimed and seared bodies, minus toes and hands, fingers or noses, but as Dr. Main and Dr. Wang saw them,

> "Where saints in glory stand,
> Bright, bright as day."

The others joined in, and I left them singing with their harsh, toneless voices : not lepers, but loved ones . . . nay, lovely ones. So thought St. Francis, at any rate.

The others had gone ahead ; Dr. Wang and I followed hastily. We came to a ward where one elderly man, with a fellow-leper sitting beside to help him, lay semi-comatose. The footsteps of Dr. Main and Lady Willingdon had roused him, and he was raising his head with its sightless eyes an inch from his pillow. One glance at his face, and I knew that his spirit was loosening its bands. Dr. Wang stopped and told him, for he was wondering evidently at the footsteps, that some foreign guests had come to pay a visit and bring gifts. Then Dr. Wang looked seriously at me and whispered, "Speak to him. He is dying. Soon nobody will be able to do anything more for him." My heart nearly failed. What could I possibly say ? This was beyond speech. But the Chinese doctor kept his eyes earnestly on me. That Eastern Christian, so short a time a Christian, took it for granted that any woman from the West, with its long tradition in the Faith, would answer to his call. Very rightly we revere the names of Father Damien and other Europeans who have left all to work amongst lepers. Yet they were like us, products of centuries of Christian faith and charity. How can we sufficiently give tribute to one such as this chance friend of mine, Dr. Wang, a Chinese whose Christianity is only one generation back ?

So I steadied my voice, and lifting my head called to the dying leper, with the politeness which China teaches :

"Elder Brother, art thou at peace ?"

And from that frame almost unrecognizable as human, with an affected tongue and from a lipless mouth, came a voice back to me, cracked yet steadfast :

"Yea, at peace, at peace. And I shall soon see my Lord."

"The Heavenly Father support thee !" I called again.

Unconquerable, wonderful spirit of man—truly a candle lit by the Lord ! Exult, oh dust and ashes !

I went out with Dr. Wang, clattering down some wooden steps. The sun was shining. We came to a gate and a boundary wall. The bricks looked so clean, so wholesome. I put my head against the bricks and wept.

The others had gone up the hill, to the Tuberculosis Sanatorium at the top. Dr. Wang waited beside me, looking at me weeping. I tried to murmur apologies for breaking down. He quietly stood by and looked at me. Then presently he put his hand on my arm. He broke the silence, and this is what he said : " T'ai T'ai : only Christ can help those poor people. But He *does* help them."

I took his hand, English fashion, and from the bottom of my heart answered :

" And you are truly His disciple."

He gave a little smile at me, and we went on to see his tubercular wards, for he was in charge of them too. They were not easy to visit, either, for many of the sufferers had come to hospital far too late.

It was this story of the faith of those scarred women singing their hymn, of the dying leper, and of that Chinese Christian doctor serving in that angelic manner, which I told Mrs. Sung that night in Shanghai.

I have heard of him again. Three months after our visit, his wife died of typhoid, and he was left with two children.

" My poor friend is in sore grief," Dr. Main wrote.

Dr. Main himself retired to England soon after this, for he had reached the age of seventy.

" The lepers came to see us off at the station," he told me later, " those that could walk the distance, men and women." Once more they put on their best clothes, and, keeping in a little band to themselves, walked through the streets and on to the station platform. The medical school, pastors, school boys and girls, all were there in flocks to see off this man they loved and his wife whom they loved also, for she had been an equal worker.

" The last people we saw when the train left were our lepers,'" he said. " There they were, waving their stumps of arms, the tears running down their disfigured faces. Tears ran down my cheeks too. And Dr. Wang was standing by them, looking sorrowfully after us."

When the Nationalists first came to Hangchow, they took down the Ten Commandments from the Lord's Table and put up the portrait of Sun Yat Sen instead. They earmarked the mission hospitals for special rigour. They made some attempt to keep the Leper Asylum going: but a number of the lepers, fearing them, fled to their homes, taking their disease with them. Those who remained wrote sad letters of the treatment which they were given.

One of the complaints which the lepers in the asylum made against the oncoming armies was that they were forbidden not only to hold services but to sing hymns. They would quaver away now and then, to keep their courage up. "Jesus Christ," said one poster in the streets of Hangchow during that period, "was born in Palestine, which is under British mandate: and therefore He must be a British Imperialist." Another informed the citizens that Christ and Plato, on whom Western civilization was built, died two thousand years ago: so what had Western civilization to give to Modern China? Nay, one poster ran, "Down with Heaven! It is a dream" —in which case lepers certainly should not be permitted to sing about it.

And the lepers' second complaint was: "They have ringed us around with barbed wire!" So they wrote, and wrote again and again as if in tears.

Barbed wire! Ah, what it has meant to this generation!

Dr. Wang, because he had worked under a missionary society, was a Christian, and remained steadfast to his foreign friends, nearly lost his life, and had finally to flee to Shanghai. Yet Dr. Wang is a Nationalist. It seems there are three classes of Nationalists in the world—and not only in China. The first thinks greatness means possessions and power, which must be maintained by show of military capabilities. The second is characterized by suspicion of every other nationality, and is susceptible to every imaginary pin-prick: this sort is pervaded by race-consciousness, as the modern parlance has it. The third has discovered that the only measure of greatness is the measure of service rendered to the world:

that there is no other greatness at all in any nation except that which says, " I am among you as one that serveth."

Dr. Wang belonged to this last class. It is not so small or select as one might imagine.

Well, that barbed wire has been taken down now : and he is back with his lepers again, Dr. Wang—the leper doctor of Hangchow. I suppose he has his faults and deficiencies, but I did not see them.

" Is he not a hero, that doctor ? " I asked Mrs. Sung, " and he is of your own race."

She nodded. She did not speak.

MR. and Mrs. Sung sent me back to my hotel in their four-seater coupé, driven by their liveried Chinese chauffeur. Their house was in a pleasant section of the French Concession, embowered in trees ; with a public park near at hand. The wide roads were smooth and easy. I leaned back and tried to put myself in Mrs. Sung's place, visualizing the kind of life which she, a modern Chinese woman, lived. Her setting perhaps differs from her grandmother's even more than it does from ours. Yet from the days of Pompeii down, and before that, and from Shanghai to New York, I suppose if the women of a certain comfortable social class met, they would understand each other's lives. Like a Western woman in similar circumstances, she was fond of a reasonable amount of society, and sometimes it became rather burdensome. Her children's education lay on her mind ; so she had told me. Which would be best : a school, or a tutor at home ? If a school, which one ? Some of her friends sent one child to a school in France and the other to Germany. Dr. Wei had sent one son and daughter to America, the other son and daughter to England to college. She was not sure that this was an unqualified success, for they grew up, these children, out of sympathy with each other's mental development. Still, with such a choice, surely one child would receive the best education the world had to offer. She and her husband had both had the advantages of travel abroad : her children should have the same advantages, if it could be managed at all. It would cost plenty of money. Better not be too extravagant now, even if Mr. Sung had had a windfall or two lately, selling land. However, as a fairly young mother, it would be a pity not to go out into society a little and enjoy herself with her friends, as Western women did. It would never do to shut herself up as her grandmother had been obliged to do, clever old lady that she was, and a power in the family notwithstanding. It kept one's brain alive making new acquaintances, and life in Shanghai could provide such a variety of brains. It meant rather more dresses, of course, but her " son's father " liked her to look pretty, thank goodness : and he was so shy, it was good for him to go out sometimes with her. She had many mercies to be grateful for to Heaven. The servants were occasionally tiresome and the head amah a tyrant with the others, but she was clean and careful of the children. She was not sure if Nieh-Nieh had bad tonsils which ought to be taken out, in the foreign fashion—but there was time enough.

For a moment the motor stopped : a red light shone at a cross-road. But a Chinese policeman soon flashed up the green, and we sped on. I imagined myself Mrs. Sung again.

If only her country would remain at peace as at this moment. Better not think of other possibilities. How terrifying it was when Li Ching-lin was fighting round Shanghai! There were far too many diabolical kidnappers in Shanghai, where otherwise one might feel safe. How could any human being be so inhuman as to steal children? She heard that they shut them up in foul dens, cut off an ear or a finger, and sent it to the parents as a foretaste of what would happen if these parents did not pay ransom promptly? It turned her sick to think of her darlings within the least danger of such happenings : she would go mad if such a thing happened to her. The Li family opposite sent their children to school under the guard of one of those unfortunate Russian men who had flooded Shanghai since their Revolution : and he went with two pistols ready loaded in his belt. If she were a judge she would have no mercy on kidnappers—none. But it could surely never happen to her.

If she could only do more to bring peace and beauty back to her country! She seemed to do nothing; merely run her household as best she could, and be happy with her husband and her children and her friends. Well, the Lord of Destiny had put her there. But how would she feel about life if she were poor and ill and lonely? Yet such folk were often astonishingly brave, as though they had some inner strength to uphold them. She did not see what other sort of

Photo by Lady Hosie

Miss Way considers the Outlook

life she could lead, at any rate. What could she do? She was not very wealthy or very clever, and she had children to tend. She could only be kind and compassionate as opportunity presented itself.

Moreover, there were these stray foreigners who wandered into her life now and again, who wanted to understand Chinese life. If it helped the world on, she would let them see what was to be seen in her household. Funny ideas, the foreigners had of Chinese: especially that they were mysterious. That was because Chinese had nice warm black eyes, not eyes of every sort of colour, and they thought these black eyes unfathomable. What pretty eyes Yün-Yün had! She looked very well in her knitted jumper suits, but it would soon be "the festival of the excited insects" and warmer weather. Perhaps she might find an inexpensive piece of flowered silk in that sale on the Nanking Road. As for Strong-as-a-Rock, she would buy him a foreign engine when she went out shopping next morning. How her brothers had loved the mechanical toys her father had brought back for them from abroad when they were small! What a wonderful man he had been! She hoped Nieh-Nieh would grow up as wise and liberal-minded.

Thus I sat in Mrs. Sung's seat in her car, thinking of her life and pondering on the friendly homely evening I had enjoyed.

"No," I said aloud. The Chinese chauffeur turned questioningly to me, so I shut my lips and answered Mrs. Sung in the quiet of my mind: "Certainly you are not a useless creature." She had spoken thus of herself to me.

What would this earth be without the grateful shade and the healthful beauty of its gentle laughing birch-trees, its spotted deer, its pomegranates, its comforting and comfortable homes? How poor would be the world without a happy woman's warmth and levity of spirit, her womanish frights and her sudden daring! Is not a "lady" one who kneads the bread of household sustenance, and makes enough and over to give away to those less fortunate than herself?

So I argued in spirit. Is not a home as important a part of the world's frame as a constitution or an empire? Is it not the epitome of the ideal republic? Did not Heaven, praise be, create the water-spring as well as the wild typhoon;

the delicate-stepping racehorse as well as the draught bullock; the pied and soft-winged moth as well as the ant; the jessamine as well as the cabbage? Not one of them can we spare from earth, and not one of them can live or have its being without dependence on other varieties of creation differing from itself. "Live your innocent life; enjoy your home and make it as fair as you can; be compassionate with your servants and the poor at your door; use your wit and laughter upon everything that passes before your quick eyes. 'Love one another with a pure heart fervently,' says the apostle; and while you do that, you can never be useless. Far beyond the confines of your own walls your perfume blows. You help man as does the lark which fills the sky and earth with its pure song:

'True to the kindred points of heaven and home.'"

The car bumped over the tram rails of the Nanking Road, and a myriad electric lights glared and flashed in my eyes. The place was as bright with electric signs as Piccadilly. The big Chinese departmental stores were outlined dazzlingly from towering cupola and mansard to pavement and basement. A Chinese cinema palace was a glittering Aladdin's cave. The silk and the gold shops had their shutters up in a decent darkness; but in the big stores one could see the wax figures, the dresses, the piles of suit-cases and rugs, the model dining-rooms, yes and the motor-cars, which we find in departmental stores over the world. No city outdoes Shanghai for shop buildings decorated with electric lights. A childish taste, no doubt: but therefore to be enjoyed frankly and childishly, an entertainment as entrancing as the transformation scenes in the pantomimes of our youth. The illumination is partly due to pleasure in the magic flowering of electricity; partly the pleasure of a new toy, a new power; also vanity, in that the shopkeepers can afford such costly toys; and finally, good hard Chinese commonsense in the excellent advertisement which the light throws upon them and their stock.

For you see, the Orient—and Africa too—has leaped full-grown into the tremendous stream of our material progress. It has not crept by way of gas to electricity. The railway has not broken it gradually into aviation. The East has slipped a century or two of our physicists. We came slowly to petrol and electrons. It has, so to speak, been suddenly brought face to face with Einstein without any introduction by way of Newton : to Lenin before it knew Rousseau : Karl Marx before it had met Descartes.

This is very upsetting. It speaks much for the essential courage of the human intellect that, after the first shock and a few years of trouble and worry lest the dragons and protective spirits should be put out by the innovations, China has taken the innovations with ever-growing calmness. To our dim sight, China hardly seemed ready for such vast changes of thought and life. Providence evidently thought otherwise. And Shanghai is an epitome of these changes.

Shanghai in early spring is full of whirling dust. Also I often waked in my hotel bedroom opposite the Soviet Consulate-General to find its thick morning smoke driving full into my windows, which made me unreasonably annoyed with Communism.

Moreover the hotel " Boy " required much patience. My mother had been taken very ill on arrival in Shanghai. She had needed ice, and needed it often. The management had thoughtfully ordered the kitchen to send up invalid delicacies. But after the once, the kitchen had forgotten us. It was the duty and privilege of the Boy attached to our room, according to every tradition of service in the East, to fight such battles for us ; to see that every necessity, nay luxury, within reach of his hands, came to us. Instead of this, in our need this Boy failed us. He sat, well nourished himself, dumped on his haunches in the servants' corridor, discussing politics with such of his fellows as were of his own mind. He looked at me with dulled eyes of dislike when I bade him fetch ice : and he delayed two hours over the little errand. I asked him once what was the deep matter which kept him so long talking and talking, squatting with his fellows. He laughed sardonically.

" What is the use of talking ! " he sneered at himself. " That is what we say ! Yet we talk ! We are trodden down, we Chinese. But how can we fight ? There is nothing but death and burial for China. Anybody can do what he likes with our country. We have no strength. China has no strength—mei yu li, mei yu li."

He pulled the corners of his mouth down: he was a hysterical child. The room coolie came from behind my door at the moment. It was the Boy who ought to have made the room tidy, and dusted, the coolie only sweeping. Out of the commonsense and goodness of his heart, the coolie had done the Boy's work and abstracted a cloth for me to help finish off the dusting. There was unspoken alliance between us. My anxiety over my mother had touched him: he had given me of such strength and thought as was his; the English nurse and I had leaned on him in many ways during that heavy illness. Once he had jerked his head in the direction of the Boy, and whispered with curled lip: "That Boy! A worthless creature!" Then he had added: "But they are all alike, these Boys here, and the cooks in the kitchen are as bad these days. I wish I could find respectable service, I do, with respectable folk in the kitchen, not these--these—patriots, as they call themselves! Ai-kuo! Patriotism! Tchah! I would not be a patriot—an ai-kuo man--for anything!" That was because his son, aged fifteen, had been impressed into one of the armies fighting for the unification of China.

He used to slip down to coax fresh ice out of the cook, which the Boy should have taken by right. The time came when he, the coolie, had to say to me, "Mississy, you go catchee ice from kitchen. Velly bad Chinese boys these: they talkee me plenty swear words and chase me with knives and rolling-pins. I say, foreign missis velly ill: they say, No care: foreign mississy all die, velly good. They make me wait long long time."

So I went myself: and they were courtesy the first moment, obstruction the next—till I said it was my "elderly mother," and then old training broke through and filial relationships conquered.

"Mei yu li—no strength," whined the Boy, and the smoke blew thicker than ever from Soviet Russia upon my window the morning after my dinner at Mrs. Sung's. The coolie went out, keeping his eyes down respectfully while passing his superior, but when he reached the door, he turned them up cornerwise, very comically, at me and gave me a glance conveying total scorn.

"Come here, Boy," I said, and made him look out of the windows, round the smoke. "Do you see that huge city—two million people are about us? Do you see those junks and Chinese ships? Are there not many huge cities and many junks in China? Who built them—a people without strength? Good work is much stronger than swords. China has very great strength."

"Yes, but only Bitter Strength—K'u li," he sulked; that biting pun on the word as we know it: "coolie."

"Oh, then there is no strength or wisdom in the stomachs of men who build cities and junks?"

He became a trifle more accommodating: but he was far from the friendliness of most Chinese servants.

"No strength!" I said to myself, as I called a rickshaw and went shopping. I thought of the limbs and chest and shoulder-muscles of the brave man pulling me and running fast. Food and transport and shelter one owed to such men's strength: but more than that, there was his courage, his cheerfulness, his willing service. There passed and repassed me hundreds of his comrades: and I was ashamed to be bad-tempered any longer. They might so easily have given way to despair. I leaned on their spiritual vigour. Sanity, temperance and tolerance emanated from them to me; and I took these virtues from them gratefully, humbly. I rested my weak heart upon them, and found hope, just as happens when one sets forth in Western lands to take material comforts to the poor. So often they give in exchange the qualities of the soul.

The cold wind blew particles of dust up the Bund into my face: but my rickshaw coolie trotted along, battling gamely. The black grit settled into the trickles of perspiration running down the back of his neck. He beamed with pleasure when I spoke pidgin English to him.

"My no savee ploper English," he had confided; "no savee Amellican. My likee talk pidgin English; belong all same old fashion. Velly nice talk."

I agreed that there is a kindness and quaintness in pidgin English which pleases us humble folk when we forgather.

" Mississy go see almond blossoms Lunghua—the Dragon Flower Pagoda ? " he insinuated, head on one side. " Catchee plentee Spring joy ! "

" Spring joy, indeed, in this blasting black Shanghai dust!" thought I.

" No, no : go silk shop ; then Wing On's," I said. He took up the shafts and ran so beautifully.

I wondered where he lived. He would be buying his rickshaw on the hire-purchase system : or had he finished his payments ? Then there would be its licence. If he lived in his own Chinese-administered area out of the Settlement, that would be no trifle, and no fixed sum. I bethought me of a shopman I knew in Tientsin whose son would settle to no business, a trying young man. One day the shopman spoke to me cheerily about him. " It is all right now," he said ; " his uncle has found him an official post."

" Official post ! " I said, surprised.

" Oh well, quite a small post ; but, still, now he is an official under government. He has been granted charge of the bureau of rickshaw licences, and perhaps he will get the sing-song girls as well, with their licences. So he will be in clover and able to help his old father now and again, eh ? "

The uncle had paid cash for the privilege of that post, and of course he would have to be repaid in time out of the difference between what the licences brought in to the collector and what he sent up to his administrative superiors. I wondered who were the sing-song girls who would also be paying for licences, and then my heart failed me as I realized what was, at bottom, their dreadful trade.

We came to the narrow outlet of the Nanking Road, where the big bearded Sikh policeman flashed full black Indian eyes and shouted incomprehensible guttural Indian anger at the congestion of China's rickshawmen who held up the sacred trams. My temper flamed again at their ruthless bludgeoning of the toiling rickshawmen, stupid and heedless though these latter no doubt were. More trams arrived, driven by Chinese drivers with the insouciance of a London bus-driver ; packed so full with Chinese passengers that portions of these passengers protruded from every square open window. More passengers clustered on the steps, hanging on precariously, arguing with the conductor as to the particular brand of cent-fare that happened to be legal tender at the time.

Shivering, we waited till the fracas should die down : discovered that it was a permanent feature of that bottle-neck corner, so plunged into the fray.

" Chieh kuang ! " shouted and shoved my man.

A truck came heavily alongside us laden and piled with vast packing-cases, on the way from some steamer tied a little further up the Bund, Shanghai's quayside. The truck was pulled by human horses. Five or six Chinese were harnessed to it with ropes over their shoulders, and were straining every muscle to move it along, bending almost double in their struggle. Sweat poured from them. Yet they laughed and chaffed with my man as he swept me in my little carriage out of their stride. He retaliated good-naturedly—though possibly it was better for me with my English ears not to understand the actual terms of their badinage. A motor-lorry, or even a horse, would have dealt with that cargo with a fraction of the effort.

We swung by the head of narrower side-streets, and I twisted to look down them. Lacquered shop-signs, hanging, bore the handsome Chinese gilt characters : and much bunting was witness to a forthcoming spring sale. This is a form of shopping lately introduced to China, and with great success, although naturally only possible in the newer establishments where fixed prices are the rule and the old-fashioned exciting bargaining is done away with. The foreigner has indeed conquered in this—he who was rarely matched in bargaining powers with any Chinese vendor, being either too soft or too harsh and humourless. Of late years he has taken to offering so little, in his fear of being overmatched, that often no sale is achieved at all.

Chinese establishments have their own method of advertising their wares. In Hangchow, while I was looking at the exquisite fans in its famous fan-shop down a narrow street, a band started playing on a balcony opposite. Cymbals, pipes and drums made the street lively. " Foreign music," said a fan assistant to me with some pride. The band was playing " Ye banks and braes." Scottish tunes, with their lack of semi-tones, are practically similar to the Chinese pentatonic scale, and come most easily of all foreign airs to the hard-working and aspiring Chinese bands ; those last products of Chinese modernity. When the band had finished playing " Ye banks and braes," it stayed for breath for a few minutes : then started it again. Six times running it played the self-same air, and I left as it began a seventh time. What impressed itself on my mind, however, was the fact that the Chinese shopman did not recognize it, even at the seventh time—it was so utterly bizarre and foreign to his ears !

" The band is hired to mark the opening of a new shop selling electric-light appliances," he told me. I went across to peep at the glass shades, portable electric lamps, electric fans, and what not, offered for sale. If extra advertisement were still needed, the band would parade the street, blowing instruments. I glanced up, and the bandsmen smiled down on me from the balcony. They were clad in the gayest uniforms, made from cheap and flimsy materials, and modelled on some memory of the French Foreign Legion in full dress, with a British general's cocked hat, the feathers done in paper, thrown in. Now, again, as I looked down a side-street in Shanghai, a band arrayed in such attire issued prancing from a shop and began to blow its instruments. There came to my ears the achromatic full-tones of " Auld Lang Syne."

One day I had taken a fancy to explore these side-streets. Dismissing my rickshaw, I had wandered away and away from the narrow fringe of the Bund and from the quarter of the foreign shops. Three-quarters of a million Chinese have overflowed into the foreigner's Settlement, the piece of waste-land which he leased seventy years ago, and where he is now but a drop in the sea—albeit a vital and colourful drop ; perhaps one should say, rather, a morsel of yeast in a measure of meal.

I walked for an hour before I again knew where I was. Perfectly safe was I, but after that first fringe of foreign banks and shops I was in true China. For a vast distance the foreigner's Settlement is inhabited by Chinese alone, and those mostly natives of Ningpo, Soochow or the outlands of

Shanghai, talking a dialect of their own, and not understanding any other Chinese. If a Northern man comes, or a Southerner from Canton, he has to communicate by the written word. Again and again I inquired my way, for I grew tired and knew I was late for tiffin ; but away from that fringe none spoke English, even pidgin English, or any other form of Chinese save their own. Kindly busy folk, they would have liked to help me, but shook their heads : and, alas, I had not enough command of Chinese character to write the name of the hotel. No other foreigners came my way : and it was long before at last I reached a street I recognized. So might a Chinese who had only learned broadest Scots wander bemused about London. We used to say that the Shanghai Settlement was not the real China. To-day most of its streets are pure up-to-date modern China.

CHAPTER XVII NEW LAMPS FOR OLD

SO, gradually, my rickshaw-puller drew me down the Nanking Road.

A lady with white hair, luminous hazel eyes under arching eyebrows, and an expression of taking vivid interest in everything she saw, stood waiting outside Wing On's door. I jumped out towards her, and turned to pay the man. She had arrived at our rendezvous first.

" Old lady belong your ma-ma ? " he queried. I nodded, and smiled to myself at the respectful term " old " : nobody is more youthful. " I wait," he said grandly, with that deep satisfaction which fills the Chinese heart on perceiving filial relationships. I sighed, for I knew it meant paying him for that long waiting ; but how could I dash his simple pleasures ? We left him sitting between the shafts of his man-carriage, contemplating the world with calm and approval. Foreigners had parents : the world was populated by kindly human beings, even outside the Middle Kingdom.

My mother and I went through the store, passing the food department, with its piles of coloured biscuit-tins, its jars of sugar and coffee, its cheeses and lard. The clean-washed tiling echoed under our leather-soled feet. A store servant in short workaday cotton coat over baggy trousers was sweeping up the sawdust in one corner. He saw foreigners and turned a sulky face : we evidently were not popular people at the moment. A chill air surrounded us. Any friction between nations always irritates most the semi-educated. Shop assistants, male and female, stood behind their counters clean, spruce, neat-fingered : but we sensed that they would rather not serve us, as we inquired our way or prices. It was early, and we seemed the only customers in the shop.

Then came our deliverers. There wandered into the shop two old Chinese countryfolk : and such countryfolk. First sauntered an old man with grizzled locks. He wore a pigtail—in Modern Shanghai; oh, how shameful! And such a pigtail. It was the last faded scrap of hair possible to plait, and was eked out with what had once been black cord but which now was brown with age. His monthly visit to the barber was greatly overdue. He wore the thick bulky winter blouse and baggy trousers of the peasant, of coarse dark blue cotton, quilted and padded with layers of cotton-wool. His teeth were broken and missing. He had a long pipe stuck into his belt, and his leather pouch containing flint and steel hung at his side. True, from his wrinkled visage looked out humour, endurance and bonhomie, with a large percentage of commonsense and shrewdness: but for the moment these were mixed with a sort of fearful pleasure.

There also walked his short-statured wife, of his own age, in the right place—behind her lord. Wonder filled her, and a secret mirth at finding herself in such a building. She too wore her winter clothing, and her dark blue cotton tunic bulged out in front of her person above her trousers. Unashamed of labour, she had tied a clean dark blue cotton apron about her middle. Her hands were wrinkled and seamed with work. She had done her best to smooth her hair, but the cosmetic resinous fluid of the Chinese lady was beyond her purchasing power. And oh, horrors, she had bound feet! Bound feet—that symbol of the past which, quite rightly, New Shanghai would fain forget. On her trousered sticks of legs she stumped with hoof-like feet.

Every assistant behind every counter stopped dead in his or her tracks, for a second held the breath, and went hot and cold. Imagine the feelings of a member of the decent, respectable staff of a London store whose parents persisted in coming to visit him in his place of business, the father with corduroy trousers tied with string at the knees, and the mother with apron and basket. The pit from which he was digged would appear to be full of clinging black clay.

The shop-walker in his well-creased grey flannel trousers, into which his pin-striped American shirt was tucked, pulled nervously the ends of his butterfly bow tie. He wore the tortoise-shell spectacles which China invented, America remodelled and sent back to China—type of this vast traffic in ideas which is flying faster and faster each year, weaving East and West together. His hair was cut in foreign masculine fashion. We saw the blood flush darkly his jaw as he led us two foreign women swiftly to the lift. Possibly we would not see the full blackness of the pit if he enticed us away in time.

" Hi ! " called the old farmer. " We are going up too. Is not this the self-raising room ; the lift of which my son told me ? " Into the lift he walked, and the little old woman scurried after him. The Chinese lift-boy in his grand uniform and peaked cap pulled the gates together, and we started. He was a pleasant lad, and turned politely to ask which floor the old folk wanted. He enjoyed a visit to the country himself, he added, and jerked his head at us knowingly. The lift was very fine : one of the largest I had been in anywhere, carpeted, with mirrors, and easy in motion.

" Our son told us we could come and see these wonderful things free ! He said nobody would charge us a cent. So here we are ! " the old woman informed me, beaming. I took her hand, and we compared hands as is customary for us women to do in China. She held on to mine as to an anchor in an unknown sea. We were nearer to her spiritually than these bright young people—and she knew it.

" It is very good-to-see, this New China," I said comfortingly. My mother, not too strong, sat on the upholstered bench and smiled at us.

" Where shall we go ? " they asked. " Now what do you advise ? "

" Up to the top with us," I answered, " and walk down through every department ! You may as well see all you can—— "

" Seeing there is nothing to pay," he chuckled.

" It is like fairyland, a dream, so clean, so fine-to-look-at, such wonderful things," said the little woman. " Fancy there being such a place in the world—and here in our China ! Our son told us it would amaze and delight us. He would not rest till we saw Shanghai : told us it was marvellous. He is one of the crew of a boat bringing grain here, and his master is a kind fellow, let us come on the boat—— "

" Without paying ? " I asked, and patted her hand : and felt her son was a good fellow, also his master.

"Yes, yes! My married daughter is home with her boy for a visit, and is looking after the pig and the chickens, and persuaded her father to come, and our son would not be content till I came too. His father will be busy enough presently with the spring rice. We brought our food with us and bedding in the boat: but really we could have bought food here in this city after all. Well, well, what wonders, what wonders! Ch'i kuai: Ch'i kuai te hen!"

The lift reached the top: and we turned to do our business while the two old folk wandered about between the long glass cases and counters. The grandmother was enraptured by a row of the new-fashioned babies' hats which Modern China has adopted: round straw hats with very small crowns and adorned with woolly pompons of bright colours. How she would have liked to take one for her married daughter's baby! What a sensation it would cause in the village! But it must be far beyond her price: she could feed the pig for six months on the money. Still she could stand and look at the bonnets and imagine how lovely her grandchild would look in one such.

The old man wandered on. The assistants stiffened around him, and those serving us bent with assumed attention towards us. The climax came. For some reason which remains incomprehensible to the European, the men of Old China experience constantly an uncontrollable desire for expectoration; a vast and deep expectoration which is excessively disagreeable to foreign ears and eyes. This habit was taken for granted in every class: but those who have mixed with foreigners are ceasing it, and realize that its inhibition is desirable. Whether it is the dust, or that Chinese suffer from catarrh or bad throats more than others, or sheer unchecked, unnoticed habit, one cannot say. As the old man walked on the soft carpet in the semi-religious hush of the store, he grew nervous in his unaccustomed surroundings, and the expectoration came naturally to his lips. He looked wildly about. Heavens, this was not the clay-beaten floor of home! A shop assistant was, however, prepared just for such a contingency, and rushed forward with a spittoon. The management of the store knew the habitual frailty of its older customers.

"It is not allowed to spit on the carpet!" hissed the assistant, and scowled. That would teach the old man what his proper place was and show him he had better not leave it till he could do so without bringing blushes to the cheeks of the new young people who have so vastly improved on the old. Especially in the presence of their "enemies," the foreigners. He succeeded in making the farmer feel ashamed. Trouble was replacing the naïvety of his enjoyment. He was beginning to realize that his young compatriots preferred his room to his company. He looked about him dazedly, the light gone from his eyes.

"Come and see what we are buying," we called to him: and made the assistants set chairs beside us for the two countryfolk. And gradually, as the younger folk saw that so far from despising we even admired the noble clay from which they were formed, they too came in a more friendly way about the four of us. Presently the old people grew tired of our ideas of shopping. Imagine bothering one's head over amber beads while such modern luxuries were heaped around! Off they went exploring on their own, happy, at ease once again, and perhaps none the worse for the chastening. We smiled at the young folk, and indicated, Chinese fashion by tilting our noses in their direction, the bulging country backs.

"Country folk," we announced, explanatorily: "and very good people." Young China smiled back, and forgot that it did not desire to sell goods to foreigners. It is very hard on young people over the whole globe when they have to endure their elders committing social solecisms: making noises over their soup, blowing on their tea and dropping their aitches. The solecisms loom as large as mountains. Youth has a sad time of it: it is apt deliberately to try to push away every remembrance of such forbears. Which is a pity, and a loss.

The Shanghai lifts have far-reaching fame in Asia. The Tashi Lama, for instance, a great man from Tibet, came visiting Eastern China. His secretary and man of affairs met all the men of position, Buddhist and non-Buddhist, from Peking to Shanghai. Their talk was of boundaries, tariffs, railways, foreign treaties, concessions: and he listened. His master sent him back on his affairs up the two thousand miles of Yangtsze—" Son of Ocean." He travelled through great cities, he visited officials *en route*. But when he reached Tachienlu and the bourne of his own country, and met gatherings of interested compatriots wanting to know of his travels, he had but one subject : the lift at Sincere's store in Shanghai. Up it went, from one storey to another, each storey as fair as one of the ascending planes of the Nine Heavens of Buddhism. He preached sermons from it. To him it was the most amazing experience of his travels. Trains, trams, fire-ships were banal compared with a lift. It had engrossed and swallowed up every other phenomenon.

Li Hung Chang, truly a great man, came last century to Europe. In England he conversed on lofty matters with the Marquis of Salisbury, in Russia with Count Witte. But when he returned to China, the solitary outcome of his introduction to European civilization was a determination to found a Zoo in Peking; which Zoo is to be found there to-day, though shrunk in size. Was it not he also who, seeing a British man-of-war, for the first time, in the Shanghai Roads, sent to ask for how much he could buy it as it was, all standing? Oh, Shanghai provides many marvels!

Down again in the lift we sped, my mother and I; in her hand a rope of burning amber, boxed up to hide its living fire. And there at the bottom stood Mrs. Sung and Little Cloud! A fortunate meeting, for I could introduce my mother and let her see why I so much liked my new Chinese friend.

" Auntie! Po mu!" Yün-Yün plucked my arm, with flushed, excited face. " Ma-ma has been buying me some silk with chrysanthemums on it for a new dress. And look what I have bought Nieh-Nieh with my own money"—it was a mechanical frog that jumped.

We hastily arranged that Mrs. Sung was to come to tea next afternoon, and towards the lift she went with Little Cloud, just as the two old countryfolk came down the bend of the stairs. As we went towards the door we waved: and two little groups of Chinese people waved back to us—unconscious of each other, and so different from each other. It was very pleasant.

My rickshaw coolie had slipped inside the shop to look at the biscuits and tinned crabs and other luscious foods while he waited, his weather eye cocked on his rickshaw out beyond the pavement. He had studied us intently while we conversed with Mrs. Sung.

" Old mississy, young mississy, both can talk with Chinese lady ? You savee Chinese lady ? " he now queried at me. And when I said we did and that she was a friend, our stock rose high in his estimation. All foreigners were not, therefore, creatures strayed from some curious land, whom Heaven had endowed with more money and less sense than others. Some foreigners were fit folk to be known and acknowledged by ladies of his own country. Astonishing. Then he would behave to them as he would to his own ladies. He went out at once and put his little carriage at my mother's feet—my mother's, not mine—and regarded me with an air of fulfilled duty. He would show me that he knew how to reverence the elders amongst us. Only after he had ensconced her, did he summon another rickshaw for me, the younger woman—as a favour. He pleased me so much that when we reached home I bade him come in the afternoon.

" I will go and see your Lunghua and the almond trees," I told him.

It was a fearfully long ride thither. After we left the Settlement bounds we came to deep ruts. He staggered, but he would not allow me to descend. That would be a slur on his powers of endurance. In Peking, rickshawmen sometimes pull their fares over the miles of shocking road to the Summer Palace, and back. No human being outside China would dream of attempting such a thing.

At last the Lunghua Pagoda loomed ahead. It is not beautiful compared with other pagodas in the heart of China: despite its pretty name—Dragon Flower. The unattractive flats of Shanghai lay about it, very dreary at that time of year, except for the almond blossom on a number of trees which lay in pink clouds about its gauntness. It was the day of a fair, and the roads leading to the temple precincts, in which the pagoda stands, were lined with beggars demanding alms. Lusty folk they were, particularly the women who ran alongside our rickshaws and held out buxom arms demanding charity as a right, and who were not too weak or emaciated to do some good sprinting. They wore plenty of wadded clothing, if patched : and generally bore an air of prosperity and success in their trade which was not amiss after the soul-racking sights one sees too often at such temple fairs up country.

"Mississy go in, look-see Buddha," advised my rickshaw guide, and tucked his chariot into the queue of its waiting fellows. He took out a cigarette to while away the time, for he had deserved the luxury after that long pull. There was a snorting from the gate, and through the crowd of peasant pleasure-seekers with their common blue garb, their lined and unwashed faces, rode in two examples of Young China on a motor-bicycle. In Canton now, they tell me, you may see a Chinese young lady riding pillion behind a man. But at Lunghua that day the pillion rider was a young Chinese man. Both of them were in khaki and wore shorts. They were a sturdy pair. Trial by oil and speed and grittiness had made very different men of them from the other young students who had come to see the sights of Lunghua. They talked a little loudly perhaps, in their exuberance and nervousness at their new method of progression. They stalled their amazing machine : and gave me a glance to see how I was taking in their new Chinese young manhood of the carburettor and the spanner. The countryfolk looked on, stolidly, as if they had ceased being surprised by anything.

Into the temple courts I went, skirting the crowds as far as possible ; for there was smallpox about, and the unwashed are liable to pass it on. But though the crowd was dense, the worshippers were few. The priests looked harassed. One of them confided to me that many people came to the temple to see anything that might be seen, but few nowadays bought incense or gave money to them for prayers : and how were they to live ?

"Look," he said, "the roofs need mending, and we have not the money ; and all these people here who give nothing !"

An elderly woman, however, was going from one shrine to another, burning incense and strings of silvered paper shoes. "Amitofo, Amitofo, Amitofo," she kept calling. I never saw a sadder face. Accompanying her was a girl of eighteen or so with a terribly disfigured visage, which must have been burned in some accident. She, too, appeared to be very heavy in spirit. The two women went round so religiously, they besought Buddha's help in whatever it was they desired so earnestly, that my spirit yearned with them. What could it be? The girl had slight chance, surely, of being betrothed. Was there some one else ill in the house? Had the head of the house gambled away his all? The older woman's eyes met mine once as she walked fanatically and despairingly from one image to another and cast strings of sacrificial paper into the huge incense brazier, so that the air was filled with smoke. She muttered her " Amitofo " incessantly. I drew behind a pillar, for her eyes, catching mine, seemed to flare at me: " So you have come to witness my desperate need—you, foreigner? " She had to push her way through the throng that was not worshipping, only looking on. But they were her own people: and that was different. They could and did understand her need better than a foreigner who ate beef and mutton as though they cost nothing, and washed all over every day, and rode in rickshaws like the lords of the earth.

Then came forward out of the crowd a young man of twenty-three or twenty-four, with a candid, receptive face. He was dressed in a navy-blue suit of woollen cloth, the uniform for one of the Shanghai public services. Postmen wear green, so he was not of the Posts: but he had the undefinable air of being under discipline and minding his own business. His uniform had been made by a Chinese tailor, so that its cut had not been much studied in the making. The priests were saying prayers; the sticks of incense were smoking amid the white ash of previous oblations. The shifting crowd chattered outside; but not so much inside here. Buddha sat, calm with his eternal smile of acquiescence in Heaven's will. The young man felt the call to adoration. Simply, naturally, he stepped out from the throng: raised his joined hands as if to say, " Well, had we not better perform some of the worship for which this temple was erected? " He strode to the mat of thick plaited rush in front of Buddha's altar: and knelt. Three times he prostrated himself, forehead to the ground: rose, with calm on his brow, raised his joined hands again to Buddha, gave a coin to the priest, and went back into the crowd quite naturally. An old man and a middle-aged one then came forward and followed his example.

As for me, my feelings were mingled indeed. For, as the young man knelt, one could not but note his foreignized clothes. The soles of his leather shoes were of rubber crêpe, that latest modern production. His action reminded me of a young soldier saying his prayers in barracks, as his mother had taught him. But above everything, I realized that opposite to me, also somewhat retiring behind a pillar, was the young man of the motor-bicycle, his bare knees, unaccustomed to shorts, showing white where the khaki ended. His whole attention was riveted on that other who prayed. The colour flamed into his cheek, and he drew a sharp breath. He was sick with shame of his countrymen for bowing down thus, and publicly, to stocks and stones. He had no use for image or incense himself. But he envied that other young man for being able to kneel and adore—yes, though he knelt to clay smeared with pig's blood, and possessed no such thing as a motor-bicycle!

Sheepishly he looked across at me, his motor-goggles dangling from his hand, his leather helmet pushed off his brow. He waited to see if I was laughing. If so, he would have been the first to laugh with me. But I withdrew further behind my pillar, avoiding his eye. Laughter was far from me.

To-day the youngest Chinese iconoclasts are going round lassoing the gods, pulling them off their perches, sawing off their heads. "See, no harm has come to us!" they say triumphantly to the troubled peasants. "There are no gods; there is no God. There is only man."

Only man. What a thought for despair!

As the rickshawman began on his long, patient, homeward trot, my mind turned with sympathy to this young New China. From shopgirl and postman, through every grade of the social ladder, these changes and innovations are a sharp test of their mettle. A day or two before I had called in at a newspaper office and sat amongst files and paste-pots on a high office stool, while a young English journalist had discoursed to me on how difficult it was for young Chinese who have been educated abroad to adapt themselves to their old home life.

" It is always hard for the young to adapt themselves to the old ways at home after college," I said, to provoke him to more speech.

" But much harder for them than for us : do believe me," he pleaded, and ruffled his hair at me. " When I think of Chang, I am appalled. Let me tell you about him, and you will see how hard it is for Young China."

Chang was a friend of his in London, but not a close friend. He had been born in Hong-Kong but was educated in Scotland. He returned to Hong-Kong a few months after the journalist had been sent there himself, and they had been pleased to meet again. Every time they met, however, Chang seemed more silent and depressed than the last time. In Scotland he had lived in the home of some decent ordinary middle-class folk, a father and mother and two children. They attended a Presbyterian Church on Sunday morning, lived useful quiet full lives, and were kind to him. He had been with them from the age of fourteen to twenty-two and taken a degree at a Scottish university. Then he had gone back to his home in South China. His father, in the years between, had grown very wealthy, had built a fine house, with any number of wings, containing rooms and bathrooms. Electric chandeliers glittered in vast salons ; priceless blackwood screens stood majestical with inlay work, and cabinets displaying *objets de vertu* lined the walls. What more could a young man of taste and education want ? Alas, together with bijouterie, which displayed his wealth, his father had taken unto himself much other goods. Chang's mother had died during his absence : so much he knew in the rare letters which his father wrote him. His father had married again, which was only to be expected. But he had not been content with one substitute ; he had brought three concubines into his household : and the house was now full of wives and small babies and the necessary serving-women. Into this species of household, which he had forgotten existed, came the boy back from Scotland. His spirit rebelled within him. The bathrooms, the electric chandeliers, the *articles de vertu* revolted him. Far better the bare Chinese mediæval home than this. He quarrelled with his father from the first. Bitter things were said on both sides : which, coming from the younger, amounted to an atrocity in the ears of Old China.

"You are become a foreigner !" shouted the old man. "How dare you criticize and look down on the ways of your fathers ?"

"How can I endure this household with its innumerable women and babies ?" shuddered the young one, and almost hated his parent.

"I have spent gold upon you without stint : and provided a home here which is the envy and cynosure of our whole clan," bellowed his father. And so it went on : till at last the old man told his son that he never wanted to see him again, drove him—nothing loath—from his gates : and swore to disinherit him.

"Never does another son of mine go to the West to be educated, and learn to sneer at his father," were his last words.

The young man had but a small store of money. He went to Hong-Kong, and there he shut himself up in a top bedroom in a foreign hotel. At first he came down for meals, and in his despair told his young English friend his tale ; for here was one man who knew how different had been that life in the quiet Scottish home which he had come to think of as second nature. The Englishman would know how much of a shock it was to another young man of twenty-odd to live in a polygamous home after a monogamous.

Gradually he took to making a meal in his bedroom. His funds grew lower. He hated to face the world : his nerves were aquiver with shame. Presently he would hardly open his door to his journalist friend, and the latter became afraid that he would seek relief in suicide. Then the father was stricken with an apoplectic fit—the result, doubtless, of his storm with his son. There was added the sting of remorse.

A month went by : and the old man died. He passed away before he had time legally to disinherit his son. But of course the family knew of the quarrel and of his intentions. They held a family meeting ; they sent the son a reasonable lump sum of money down, and bade him go away and never come near them again.

"Where did he go?" I asked.

The young journalist's hazel eyes looked troubled. "He went back to Europe, but not to Scotland, because he could not bear to tell his old friends all the shame. He bought a small farm, and he is trying to find balance and peace and solace in the cultivation of wheat and turnips and potatoes. So he wrote me. Now you will believe that life is very difficult sometimes for Young China, will you not?"

ONE afternoon Mrs. Sung telephoned she was coming in to town: was I likely to be at home about tea-time? I was, and we sat an hour talking. She spoke of wishing to pay a visit to Soochow, the home of her childhood. She had lately received a letter telling of the death there of an aunt-in-law of her husband's sister. "She was a Buddhist, a very pure soul. She loved Buddha dearly. She gave—how she gave!—to the poor. She was the most beloved woman in Soochow. She fed the hungry daily at her door. When she knew she was dying, her last request was that her body should be wrapped in cotton, not silk: and the difference in cost was to be spent for the poor."

That was noble. Silk was the funeral cerement due to her in respect of her rank and wealth. Moreover, it would have been ghostlily transmuted for her use in the social ranks of the next world. Now her spirit would face the turn of the Wheel of Life in cotton, as though she were a beggar woman. "Nor was it only to gain merit and a step further in sainthood, but from pure benevolence and compassion," Mrs. Sung proffered. She had a snapshot of the saintly lady in her bag. I could believe any goodness possible to that sensitive sweet face, which yet looked forth with a certain intentness of purpose.

"A good Buddhist is as good as a good Christian," next announced Mrs. Sung, and cast an eye at me to see whether I would accept her challenge. I merely laughed: too wily a fish to rise direct to such hoary bait. Craft for craft! A touch of malice gives piquancy to any dish. "Strange," I ruminated aloud, "this sudden enthusiasm of yours for Lao Fo—Ancient Buddha. Yet have I not seen an image of him in your house, or even a scroll. You do not, like my Aunt Kung, lead me imperatively by the hand to your private altar and kneeling-mat, and tell me how you reiterate 'Amitofo' forty times on your rosary each morning. Never a whiff of incense lingers in your hair. I do not believe you brew a single cup of daily sacrificial tea to Buddha, or the goddess Niang Niang or anybody else. She—Heaven keep her honoured and treasured head!—sits me down on her bed and impresses on me the fact that Buddha, also, saves souls—with a stress on the 'also.'"

"Does she?" asked Mrs. Sung, her interest in sheer Buddhism abated at once. "And what does her son think?"

"He thinks Buddhism retards progress, to put it plainly. I am not sure myself that she and her daughter Gentle Calm have not taken it up with ardour these last few years partly to keep him from joining the Christians."

Mrs. Sung knew, she said, the wiles of women. Did she not employ them herself?

"In his opinion, Buddhism has been a hindrance to China. It teaches that it is ideal to renounce the world. Very few, like your old aunt-in-law, go on to the next process of sacrificing themselves for it, and thus acquiring special merit. Li Cheng says that China's best and most honest officials, when trouble comes—such as a Revolution—use the cloak of Buddhism to retire from the struggle. They leave their country to find her way out of her difficulties as best she can herself. Naturally the bad officials remain, to prey like tigers upon her blood. The Buddhist says he is sincerely regretful this should be so, but that it is no longer a concern of his as he has finished with earthly entanglements." "Li Cheng speaks quite truly," ejaculated Mrs. Sung. "What! Is not a good Buddhist as good as——" I began. "Ah, do not tease," she petitioned.

Now it had happened that, just before we left England for China, my father had finished translating, with a Japanese Buddhist student, the Lotus Sutra. Its versicles are exceedingly difficult to turn into another tongue. A scholar who attempts them must be versed in Buddhist theological terminology as well as in the Chinese language.

"I want you to read our translation," he said to me one day: "Tell me if I have made the English of it plain to your intelligence. Moreover, you ought to read it. For it has been rightly called 'the gospel of half Asia': it is the Sutra read by Chinese and Japanese Buddhists in their daily temple worship. It is the nucleus of their thought."

Fascinating it was. Sometimes it became wearisome. There is much repetition in it: there are long lists and enumerations of devas, saints, boddhisattvas, demon-kings. At intervals, too, it surprises. Buddha, or some great manifestation of a Buddha with special attainments, springs into mid-air, sits cross-legged on a throne there, preaching. Flowers and jewels and wonders rain round and about him, and on all the myriads and ten thousand myriads of buddhas and saints on earth listening to him. A cadenza often ends such scenes of apocryphal marvel by declaring that to fashion one single image of Buddha or say such and such a prayer is of vast merit.

Yet Buddha's words, when allowed to stand by themselves, the sermons he preaches when sitting thus in mid-air, contain great beauty and consolation. One of the central doctrines of Buddhism is the gentle persuasiveness of Buddha: his grace going seeking men. This parable will illustrate.

A Father had a house full of children. The house, though large, was very old and decrepit, filthy and rotten. A list follows for many versicles, of the various bats, foxes, demons, rats and other ill-things which infest its boards and rafters. There is but one small door to the house. One day the Father sees the house is on fire. He argues within himself in this fashion: "If I call and tell my children the house is on fire, they will not believe me. They are running about, playing, each attentive on his own affairs." Thinking thus, he goes to the door, claps his hands and cries, "Children, outside this house I have very beautiful presents waiting for you"—and he tells them of three wonderfully caparisoned chariots, drawn by different animals, for each child. The children will surely be willing to run out of the narrow door, and be saved, he thinks.

Thus Buddha persuades rather than drives man towards salvation.

The Sutra continues with a theological disquisition, quite after the manner of Aquinas. It seems that there was but one vehicle for each child, not three; but is Buddha to be accused of deceiving ? The one vehicle is of the most superb excellence, much finer than the three with which he had lured his children to safety. Many versicles are devoted to the description of this wonderful vehicle : its jewels, tassels, flowers, silken cords and curtains. By this side-path one comes to the great division of the doctors, and learns to differentiate between the Mahayana Buddhism, which holds to the Greater Vehicle, and the Hinayana School, which prefers the Lesser. Just so you may choose in the Christian theologies which you prefer to follow: the Greek Orthodox, the Roman Catholic or the Puritan School. And controversy is not without its interesting features.

In any case the tremendous conception stands : that the Father cares for his children and seeks their welfare. Yet another plain inference of the story is that this world, by which we enter through so small a door and go out, is a hideous, shaky and rotting hovel.

" To the Christian," I commented to Mrs. Sung, " since Life is the Father's house, there must be something of essential beauty and hope in it, or He would not have put his children into it. It holds the seed of heaven. The wheat will yield a greater harvest in the end than tares. Despite sin and pain, there are great spaces of sunlight. Above the nettles tower the oaks, and the singing-birds outvie the serpents."

Mrs. Sung had listened with wide eyes. She, a modern Chinese woman, knows little of the older religions of her land : its legends and parables have slipped from her memory and her mind. This story of the House, one of the central allegories of Buddhism, she had never heard.

But Buddhism is hardly a subject to be dismissed with a story on a spring afternoon. Buddha's influence on Chinese thought, art and philosophy has been vastly ennobling and civilizing. It was a blessed dream which caused a Chinese Emperor many centuries ago to send to India for enlightenment about the golden image of his vision in the night. Through whom else but Buddha have stricken Chinese men and women caught a glimpse of heavenly kindness, or nursed the hope of a happy issue from their earthly sorrows ? He gave forth the message of a Father's compassion, and it was benediction and illumination.

Superstition and the general hardness of men's hearts have blurred Buddha's teaching. Can we cast a stone ? Ignorance and debauchery have brought down his doctrines till they are despised by the keen of thought—who are not lacking in China any more than elsewhere. The Buddhist Pharisee has bound intolerable burdens on the backs of the poor and the widow. Their priests have demanded much money for masses for the dead. Their boy acolytes look half stupefied with inanity while they cast the chasuble over the backs of the priests at the altar, and swing the censers and tinkle the holy bell at the right moments of the service. A pious Buddhist will buy snakes, at the due season, and acquire merit by setting them free, thus showing mercy to animals—snakes caught by a sagacious peasant for the purpose. Do we of the West never cheat our own souls ?

Nevertheless the image of Buddha—dumb though it be, and lifted into a nirvana above ordinary human life—has breathed assurance of a final answer to the riddles of existence, and has spoken with calm smile of ultimate benignity. He who implanted in Sakyamuni, an Indian prince, a mind to preach self-forgetfulness, and gave him the will to perform it to a divine end, knew the world's exceeding need of such a lesson and such a hope—even though those other precepts of his, of resignation and quietude, have degenerated into the fatalism and unwashed apathy so easily besetting to the Mongol nature.

If Mrs. Sung were here in England with me to-day, I could tell her still more of Buddhism. But a few months ago it fell to me on an afternoon to play guide to one of the most devoted and intelligent exponents of that religion : T'ai Hsü, the abbot of the Nan Tu Pu monastery at Wuchang. He had journeyed to Europe to explain the excellences of Buddhahood to our religious leaders over here. Unfortunately he had left but a single week for England ; and our leaders are apt to be deep in engagements. This is wrong, according to the East. They ought to sit still and let earnest seekers come and listen to them. But I found that a religious meeting was to be held at the Mansion House in London. The Lord Mayor was to take the Chair, and the speakers were to be the Prime Minister Mr. Baldwin, the Archbishop of Canterbury and the President of the Methodist Church. T'ai Hsü could, at least, look at them. He arrived late for the meeting, having first arrived too early and then gone away and been begged by me on the telephone to return. He entered noiselessly, accompanied by his Chinese secretary, who spoke English and was garbed faultlessly in morning suit and striped trousers. T'ai Hsü was a pleasure to behold. He wore a long abbot's robe of orange satin : immaculate, enchanting. Amongst the dark-clothed Englishmen, he stood out like a piece of carved amber. With eyes meekly down, a black beret on his shaven head, a string of wooden beads as a rosary round his neck, he slipped quietly in, gliding into a chair. To show his tolerant spirit, he, a monk, a Chinese, took the hand of myself, a woman, a foreigner. Around us the people stood ; they sang a hymn.

" What are they singing ? " he whispered.

" Thou of life the Fountain art," came from about us.

" They sing that Je-su Chi-tuh is as water : clean, quenching thirst," I whispered back. " It is a *pi-fang* : an allegory." He nodded. Water is an allegory in every religion. He fingered his rosary. Surely John Wesley, with his seraph heart, would have liked to see T'ai Hsü, the Buddhist, at this meeting—for it was being held in memory of the man who called the world his parish.

When the audience applauded, T'ai Hsü looked round at me to indicate that he could sympathize with the stirred emotions of a large crowd, though language might fail. He was so anxious, however, not to be late for a second appointment that fully ten times did he imperceptibly slide his wrist out to look at his watch. He left the hall as noiselessly as he came, and stepped into a taxi-cab. I wondered if T'ai Hsü, abbot of Nan Tu Pu, would succumb a victim to time-machines and other mechanical devices like the rest of us, if he remained long enough within reach of their tentacles.

At this other appointment, it was he himself who gave the address. He spoke in the tongue used in Central China, so that few present could follow his periods. Orange against the flat blackboard he stood, exquisite. Every five minutes he sank gently down, and his interpreter, under a reading-lamp, read a translation, while T'ai Hsü kept his eyes down, like the well-bred Chinese gentleman he is. But when he spoke of Buddha, of the Perfectly Enlightened Conscience, of the All-Pure, he raised his pale moon-face earnestly, boldly : his gaze travelled far beyond the confines of the stark, drab amphitheatre of a London lecture-room. He moved his hands delicately, freely, opening and shutting them like flowers, to illustrate his points.

As for me, watching him, great texts came pounding through my head, and with new significance. The pure in heart shall see God. The mighty law holds. The pure-hearted Buddhist sees God, by whatever name he calls Him.

In a China paper I had lately read of three old Chinese women : Buddhists. They had walked, though the youngest was nearly seventy, on their torturing bound feet, from the province of Hunan to the border town, Tachienlu, of Tibet —as if from Copenhagen to the Carpathians. They were making a pious pilgrimage to save their souls, three innocent enough old women. Having reached the border of Tibet, they were now about to join the annual religious circumambulation of a sacred mountain, which it takes three days to walk round. But these desirous souls were to do it by prostration. They would lay themselves on the ground, and thus measure the circumference with their bodies. My husband had met such pilgrims when he travelled the Tibetan marches : their foreheads bleeding, their looks vacant with the horrid, senseless strain on nerve and muscle, their clothes dirty and worn to shreds. What did the Voice speak in Luther's ear in similar circumstances ? The just shall live by faith. T'ai Hsü evidently was living by a different interpretation of faith from that of the circumambulatorians.

The worst of such asceticisms is that the pilgrims feel no better for it in the end, which is tragic. Their souls remain as hungry as ever. Some go on to further feats of mortification : others give up the struggle and hope for the best, very uncertainly. Obviously T'ai Hsü was not in this class : or he would not have come to tell Europe about Buddha. Perhaps that was it. Whosoever will save his life shall lose it. Sakyamuni had been willing to give up riches, home and royal prerogative for the world's salvation. Those three elderly women were intent on their own safety and merit. T'ai Hsü wished to save others, to show others the glory of his vision of the Perfectly Enlightened Conscience. The fruit of the spirit is love, joy . . . peace. Peace he certainly possessed.

I doubt whether T'ai Hsü is a very profound thinker. His reasoning left me cold. The history of Buddhism which he gave was hackneyed—the tradition common amongst unscientific commentators, full of loopholes for attack by modern historians. But one could wish there were more Buddhists like T'ai Hsü in China. During our visit to Hangchow, I met one who might have been his pupil. We had looked in at the city temple, set on the hillside on which the city wall is built. Up, beyond, was another building, swept and garnished and smelling of its fresh, newly-built wooden balconies. A gentle-faced neophyte, a young man of twenty-two or three, was coming out of the doors.

" Foreigners ! " he exclaimed. " A fortunate day, this ! Pray enter. I will fetch the head of our small society here. He likes greatly to speak with foreigners."

He sped within and presently came escorting his superior : a mild, elderly man with a goatee beard, inclined to a trifle of embonpoint. He was engaged in buttoning his ceremonious long gown of pale blue calico about his comfortable stocky person, and looked as if his enthusiastic junior had roused him from an afternoon siesta. He was amiable : but the spiritual fire of that place very evidently flamed in the soul of the young rather than the old.

The neophyte led us eagerly to a courtyard within. He fetched for our inspection two long yellow banners written over with characters.

" Look ! " he said, and spread them out. " They are our two prayer flags for the souls of all the men who died in the Great European War. There were thirty-seven countries involved. What an awful passing of souls ! It is the least we can do to pray for them."

" Do you pray for them all ? " I asked, considerably touched.

" All," he replied : " enemy and ally. Every year we

hold two special days for them. Don't we ?" He turned to his superior.

"That is so, that is so!" nodded the Director. The building, we discovered, was a Retreat. It had fallen into disrepair, but some well-to-do and religiously minded merchants had lately set it on its feet again. They had clubbed together to make it a place whither they could resort now and again, when life became burdensome and meditation desirable. "Let me see: the day is soon approaching, is it not?" asked the Director tentatively.

"In two more days' time," replied the young man rather reproachfully. "Then you will know that we are remembering your brave English dead also"; turning and bowing to us.

"That is a very beautiful and holy purpose of yours," I said, returning his bow.

"It will surely help to stop wars, will it not?" he asked wistfully. We agreed without hesitation that it would.

He led us up steps and down steps, determined to show us everything, including the rambling prëmises at the back. When we reached the reception room, we sat and drank tea, while he fetched the Book of the Society for Praying for the Souls of All Killed in the Great European War. He ran his fingers down the lists of the countries, many of whose names were unrecognizable to us in their Chinese transliterations.

Next he said to me, "We have a wonderful thing up this next stair." Curious, I followed. In an upper storey sat a small blackish god, with not too pleasing a face. Curtains were looped closely about him. Instead of the usual handsome, narrow, long altar-table, with its pewter or bronze candle-holders and incense-burners, in front of his shrine stretched a table at right angles. On the table stood a tray of sand, with a pointer of ebony poised over it, one end fashioned like a bird's claw. It was a planchette. I had never seen Chinese using this method of inquiry, so agreed that it should be worked. Two men were fetched in from another court. When told that they would be needed for working the planchette, they hastily went to don clean tunics.

"You have to be very courteous and reverential before this god," explained my neophyte. "He is extremely particular."

He lit a stick of incense. The god began to work at once. The man who held the inert end of the pointer looked now and then inquiringly at the other, by whom the spirit was supposed to be writing. There was a deep silence, except for the young priest who had undertaken to act as note-taker and set down on paper each character as it appeared on the sand. But the young man who held the power end of the planchette pointer looked sulky to me. He had been interrupted in his afternoon leisure, and I could not help entertaining the idea that, so far from the god directing operations, this young man's own will and hand were the sole originators of the prognostications. However, he was liberal enough; and poured out such a quantity of foretellings that I grew weary and wished him a less luxuriant inspiration. Even the young priest became a fraction bored, though he looked at me with smiles of pleasure when the planchette said that most of my male relatives would shortly become Members of Parliament.

" There! Listen to that!" exclaimed the Director to me, who had joined the séance. I bowed at these honours about to descend on my family. Secretly I wondered whether they were not probably the only titles of foreign honour known to the sulky youth.

Having duly paid for my somewhat disappointing flutter in divination, I rejoined my party. We came down again to the temple which overlooks and guards the city: the shrines where the everyday folk of Hangchow resort in their difficulties and bring petitions. It is not a place sought by the pilgrims, who come from far and near. Such visit only the famous altars to Buddha of the neighbourhood.

The city temple was full of people. Especially were there small groups of women, doubtless desiring children, health or riches. The images grew more hideous as we went along: till we came to a narrow opening with grimy looped curtains, and saw, within, a cave in the natural rock, with lights flaring and women bowing and kowtowing to the ground. Inside was a monstrosity of human misconception: a detestable idol, a perversion of devilish imagination. Its black grinning face, the blood painted on its bird-talon feet, its bulging stomacher, proclaimed an expeller of demons, masters of un-

T'ai Hsü, the Abbot of Nan Tu Pu Monastery, Wuchang

bridled cruelty. It was being propitiated by women lest, unpropitiated, it bring malignant disease upon some loved one.

Nauseated by the stuffy air, the horrid figure, the sickly faces of the women who looked at one with the dazed eyes of a bird caught in the claws of a cat, we turned to go. There, at the opening, half hidden behind the looped curtains, two more loathly figures lurked hidden. They held hammers and prongs up high, threatening to transfix each passer-out. Instinctively one stooped to avoid them. They were the guardians of hell's gates.

It will not be altogether regrettable if ultra-modern Young China drags these images off their pedestals. To such distortions has the mysticism of Lao Tzŭ fallen.

As we came into the freshness and sunlight of the large central court, an elderly Chinese man called to us to come across for a talk. He sat in front of a table covered with slips of bamboo, with writing on them.

" Do you see what I am at ? " he inquired. " I 'm telling fortunes. Doing the devil's work. And I shall pay for it some day ! " " Don't you believe in your fortune-telling, then ? " we asked. " Believe in it ! " he cried derisively. " I 'm a Christian. How can a Christian believe in such trash ? " He flung a scornful hand at his bamboo slips, then gathered them up for the next victim. " I go on Sunday mornings to the Happy News Hall and listen to true doctrines. Then I come up the hill and deal out lies to ignorant fools full of trouble wanting to know the future. How do you think these slips of bamboo know everybody's future ? I serve God one hour a week and the devil the rest of the time. I shall certainly go to hell when I die. But what can I do ? I have five children, and we are not young, my wife and I. As I ask her, who will fill their rice bowls for them, and what other trade can I ply ? Nevertheless my children shall not learn this trade and ruin their souls with lies too. Better be honest coolies, however hardly they earn a living."

He was savage and sore at heart. It was astonishing to hear him. He had no doubts about hell whatever. He had looked at it reproduced in clay and painted wood the other side of the courtyard all his life. To us it seemed his hell had begun already. Nor did it sound as if this hatred of his trade had been put into him by others : he had developed it on his own account. There was nothing one could say to him. His conscience it was, not ours, which was troubling him. Would ours have been so sensitive, in his circumstances ?

That is another thing New China is doing—putting down the fortune-tellers and soothsayers. To be sure, the blind and old members of the professions are sending in pathetic petitions, pointing out that their starved corpses will be found littering the streets if they are not allowed to pursue the only trade they know. But even they wish humbly to mention that they try to give harmless advice.

" If a young man consults us as to whether he should go to law, we nearly always contrive to find that the month is unpropitious ! " they plead.

That afternoon in the hotel at Shanghai, Mrs. Sung and I talked of these things. I could not tell her of T'ai Hsü, because I had not met him. But I told her of the young priest who prayed for the souls of all killed in Our War, of the grim city gods of Hangchow, of the fortune-teller. She dreamed : she paused.

" About religion," she said at last : " it is very hard for us to-day to know what to decide about it. I think mine is to do the best I can, always : to be kind, and just : to bring up my children to be kind and just also. Then, when it comes to the end of life, if there is a judge and tribunal, He will not be too hard on me."

The idea of a Judge is deep-rooted in China. She paused again. " I cannot be a Buddhist. I cannot be a Taoist. Not these days." We fell silent. Like a flash the unspoken thought went between us, that there is another possibility for her—these days. But I felt she was afraid. Christianity might entail strange hard sacrifices, difficult decisions. How could she risk it with her children to consider ? The Hound of Heaven was at her heels. She felt His breath. I wanted to tell her not to fear ; to say that gentle persuasiveness and the outstretched arms of grace are not only the birthright of Buddha ; that there was One who said He would gather His children under His wings, as a hen calleth her chickens.

CHAPTER XIX TWO LADIES AND A PROCESSION

WE left Shanghai, and without a proper farewell between Mrs. Sung and myself. I caught German measles and had to go into quarantine. The day after the infection was over, we took ship for Tientsin. Mrs. Sung had telephoned that she was coming to the steamer to see us off—" sung " us, as the Chinese phrase and custom is. My mother's cabin was a bower of lilies and carnations and smilax, with baskets and garlands sent by her Chinese admirers.

" Mostly young men," we teased her. My father and she had taken charge of a hostel in London for Chinese interpreters, young liaison officers attached to the Chinese Labour Corps during the War. These men, no longer so very young, had not forgotten this hospitality, and had flocked about them now they were in China once more: and very pleasant they were.

But just before the boat left, a young man came to me with a bouquet from Mrs. Sung; pleasant, modest, rosy-cheeked, as if he played outdoor sports—her young brother, in fact. Alas, he also brought a note from her, which she had insisted on writing before taking to her bed. She was prostrated with one of her headaches. She sent the flowers to convey her joy in our friendship and her sorrow at our farewell.

I did not expect to meet her again—for years, if ever. Gather, then, my pleasure when three weeks later and we had reached Peking, a hand came from behind me and gripped mine at a *recherché* and gilded evening reception at the Chinese Foreign Office.

We had eaten a sumptuous dinner, cooked by the Chinese pupil of a French chef, who fashioned the menu into a judicious and happy blending of East and West. During dinner an excellently staged Chinese band from behind a group of palms had discoursed soft national music, thin, plaintive and sweet, on quaint and unique ancient instruments lent for the occasion from a national museum. We had met, after dinner, the Swedish, American, English, German, Belgian and Russian wives of various Chinese members of the Government. A trifle overwhelming, this. One Chinese gentleman, indeed, had taken to himself a second European wife while the other was still living in Europe. The first wife, being a European, had wept and was, we understood, inconsolable, for she loved him and had never thought to be displaced. As a Chinese, however, he was within his rights to have more than one wife, and there was no more to be said about it. She could, he implied, feel her nation flattered in that he had chosen, as his second venture, another of her own race and not of his. Meanwhile his Chinese relatives were furious over his marital affairs altogether. They were convinced that a Chinese gentleman is best mated with a Chinese partner.

After dinner there was dancing. I was standing with a few friends watching, when this womanish hand slid into mine. At the same time, its owner hid her face silently between my shoulder-blades. I turned quickly, startled, but my adherent turned with me, with a titter at my stupidity : and the hand waggled. I looked down at it. A large and fine pearl set in a platinum band encrusted with diamonds glimmered on it. Where had I seen it before ? I puzzled. A well-bred Chinese lady, using her quick perceptions, is able to recognize any of her acquaintances by her jewelry. So Mrs. Sung told me later—for, by all the stars, Mrs. Sung it was ! She came from behind ; she put both hands into mine, swung to and fro a minute like a pleased schoolgirl ; and we withdrew into an alcove to talk.

"Are you glad to see me ?" she asked, knowing the answer. I had never seen her look more attractive. Her face was lit with animation, her cheek was rosy. She was sparkling, and happy, because she and I had met again. How delicious ! Suddenly I bethought me exactly what it was in her which had drawn me from the outset. Indefinably, she reminded me of Helen—my kind, my English friend. There it was, that same happy curve of the upper lip, the tender candour of the eyes, the modesty and elusiveness in the bend

By permission of Li Cheng

The Five Sons of Li Cheng. "Particularly naughty and noisy," their father writes of them, "but happily not without brains"

of the neck. Helen is beautiful in features. Mrs. Sung's charm was mainly in her expression. Her countrymen may not think her as fair to see as I do. Her chin, her nose, her brow are not classically chiselled according to Chinese views. Yet, as she stood, leaning back, both hands in mine, an arch smile on her mouth, her eyes soft and shining with affection, I heard my voice saying :

> " Helen, thy beauty is to me
> Like those Nicéan barks of yore . . ."

Was it on a perfumed or a desperate sea you roamed hither ? " I demanded. She looked puzzled. " That is a famous poem," I appended.

She was flattered, as anybody might be. " It was a most disagreeable sea. Do not speak of it. Off Weihaiwei it was abominable," she answered.

" Ah ! you are a slow person and very unobservant ! " she next tackled me. " You have been looking at me all this time and never mentioned my hair ! "

" Thy hyacinth hair ! " I dreamed. " What is the matter with it ? It looks very nice." She shook me, enraged.

Then I saw. The dear girl had been shingled !

" How do you like it ? " she pirouetted to show me back and front. Earnestly I regarded it, and gave my approval : the fashion suited her well. Altogether, as I told her, she looked ravishing. She wore a high-collared tunic of apple-green figured satin, falling over a pleated skirt of crêpe-de-chine of the same tone. A Chinese lady's evening attire is in a state of evolution. Mrs. Sung's sleeves were of diaphanous stuff through which her arms gleamed—an impossible revealing of them in the old days. But the material had been made less transparent by delicate lines of beads scattered beneath the green, which sparkled like dew-drops.

As I stood taking pleasure in the sight, a tall man came into the alcove. It was the Chief of the Commission. " Mrs. Sung ! " he cried. " How did you come here ? Come and dance ! "

Away she went, honoured and charmed at having been recognized by him like this. Pleasantly they danced together, the thin English face so high above her sleek black Chinese head.

Back she came to me. She told me she was staying with relatives attached to the Chinese Foreign Office, that she had arrived that very afternoon, too tired to be ready for dinner.

" But I flew here after I was rested, knowing I should catch you all, and determined not to lose any of your gaieties ! "

" Where is Mr. Sung ? "

" In Shanghai."

" Where are Yün-Yün and Nieh-Nieh ? "

" Also in Shanghai." She made a *moue* at me.

" And you—wife and mother—leave them to the care of servants in order to come a-dancing in Peking ! These modern women ! They care nothing for the most sacred ties, their duties, their husbands, their children. Is this what China's home life is coming to ? "

She laughed. " Very well, then. I am up North to see if I can lease a house for the summer at Peitaiho, and if I can, I shall then go back for the children—and face the sea at Weihaiwei twice over on their behalf ! If that is not being a model mother, what is ? And why may I not dance ? You know how our older folk thought dancing such an immodest affair. I used to myself, but now I know that dancing is good : it is only bad for bad people. I like it ! "

" Oh là, là ! " I waved my hand at her. " Continue this green grasshopper whirling by all means. Dansez ! Chantez ! "

Her friends found her, and we parted with joyous promises of reunion.

It was interesting to find that she was taking a house at the seaside : and she, the woman of the family at that, making the arrangements. Well, it was Aunt Kung who decided what apartments to rent in Tientsin when their family moved at the Revolution. But the seaside ! That announcement of hers brought me up sharp against the enormous influence which Western ways of life are having on the Orient. Imagine the time when every Chinese family expects a holiday by the sea : when the Chinese artisan takes a day off, travelling to and fro—whether by railway or his own family car—for a few hours by the coast ! Who knows ? It may be by aeroplane soon. A few years ago, and he would have found no scrap of pleasure whatsoever in a day by the ocean. And this new spirit in a land which never had a popular holiday, no Saturday, Sunday or Thursday afternoon : which worked the year round, except for five jubilant days at the New Year. The migration of Mrs. Sung and her family to the seaside is as the first trickling drops of a very flood-time of changing habits. Who can avow that we of the West bear no responsibility ; or that all the changes in China are due to indiscreet missionary propaganda ?

The next day I went to pay a call on the wife of one of my father's colleagues, whose home was in Peking. He was a railway expert, and had been the director of one of China's most successful lines. We found a wide spacious court in which four strapping children were playing catch, two girls running quite as fast as two boys. These children, we found, went to their school on bicycles : through the dusty narrow Peking lanes down which motors come shrieking and bumping : the only Chinese children so to do. The director's passion in life is railways : and it is shared by his children, who manipulate model engines. His wife, a woman of forty odd, had been brought up in an American mission college, as had he. " He was the top scholar," she informed us. " There never was any one who passed examinations better than he did, wherever he went." She was proud to give us a fragmentary biography. " And you : were you not the top scholar among the girls ? " we asked.

" Well, I was," she admitted : " but we had much easier lessons than he."

They had seen each other at various Church meetings, at which both girls' and boys' schools attended : but at a discreet and proper Chinese distance.

" So we knew about each other. When it was time for him to be betrothed, our parents thought it a good idea——"

" And neither of you disagreed ! " we filled in the hiatus.

She laughed gaily. She is a happy woman. Her days are full : she has a large household to care for. Her one worry is her husband's health, which is not good. But he does not lack for means. Also, she has taken to heart the lessons of social philanthropy which she has seen exemplified in the American ladies who gave her education. She is a member of several committees—the Y.W.C.A., homes for blind children, a women's hospital board. She has a cherished look, the free, spontaneous joyousness of a woman who is trusted by her husband and cherishes him in return : a woman who is not afraid to give of herself.

She takes life easily. The last time I saw her was at the station at Peitaiho—a suitable place for the wife of the director of a railway line. It was the end of the summer, and I was making inquiries as to departure. There she stood in her clean unadorned travelling dress, by a mound of luggage, warding off a porter who made efforts to put it into the waiting train. For once she looked almost agitated.

" Oh ! " she called to me, " if you see my four young scamps anywhere, do hurry them here, will you ? They coaxed me into letting them take a last ride on the donkeys, the bad children. I honestly believe they are trying to make us miss the train. They don't want to leave the beach. They are capable of anything." Even then she laughed. She was prepared to be philosophical.

I met them at the top of the street—four young people, the girls looking pretty in clean pink cotton dresses. They were sitting their donkeys and riding leisurely as if they had all the time in the world.

" Hurry ! Hurry ! " I called to them. " The train is starting. Your mother is getting cross."

They looked surprised at me, and roused themselves to hustle their steeds. But plainly they did not believe about their mother's failing temper.

She and Mrs. Sung were to meet under my auspices—also on a railway platform. The occasion was the departure for England of various members of the Commission. Farewells at the station or at a ship's side are nowadays a feature of social life in the Orient. It is a far cry from Peking to London, New York or Rome. Who knows when one may meet again one's cosmopolitan friends ? It is quite far enough from Peking to Shanghai, Hankow to Canton ; a good deal further than setting out for France from London : also expensive.

Here, then, on the Peking platform that day, every one of note in its social world was gathered : every nationality ; diplomats, consuls, commissioners of customs, heads of the post office, of business-houses, of banks, together with the Chinese élite. The train was waiting. Ahead of it was another : an armoured train, grey and harsh, manned by Russians of the shattered White armies, who were then serving Chang Tso Lin. On the other side of the platform an empty Chinese troop train stood silent, its doors locked, save where one group of soldiers were performing their laundry, hanging out their clothes in a flat open truck. On the very wide platform walked tall clean men from the Occident. Westerners in the Orient are men who carry themselves, on the whole, finely, and look at life with straight discerning eyes. They are men who have not been afraid to venture into the wide world. They are used to keeping steady in unusual circumstances, and to managing large concerns in a large manner. They are men who have faced loneliness while their wives and families have had to go back home to the West, and they have conquered it. Yes, a distinguished-looking set of men, if at times a little impatient of other folks' theorizings, for they have learned by much experience. Generous, good-humoured, loyal, with brains that easily attack big problems and administration, they perhaps expect a little too much of a nation that has only begun to realize with bewilderment that it is not the only nation in the world that matters. Better, undoubtedly, to expect too much than too little ; and they are men who love very deeply the country of the East in which they have served their life's apprenticeship.

They take pains to dress scrupulously, in white drill in summer, or suits of butter-coloured washing pongee silk. Their sun-helmets and their shoes are pipeclayed white every day.

The Chinese talking with them that day wore silk gowns, dark and neat, costing a good handful of dollars. They were all moving about the platform chatting affably together.

Mrs. Sung arrived : and presently I spied the wife of the railway director. He was not well, so she was representing him at the farewell. She came forward to greet me cheerfully : then stood by herself awhile. I went to her, and she told me she did not know many other people there, and none of them well. She was the real Pekingese : she lived in

Peking. These were all people who stayed a few months or years, and then were gone : even the Chinese élite. I led her to Mrs. Sung, and introduced them to each other : then walked away. They should have a clear field, and I saw by the first glance they gave that all would be well between them.

" Those are two nice women," said an English voice near me : the voice of the head of an English bank. I smiled.

" Yes, they are," I thought, and while walking with another friend cast a pleased and proprietary eye now and then at them.

They stood together, both of them bare-headed as is Chinese fashion, their hair smooth and neat. Mrs. Sung had a parasol in her hand. The other held a large white-covered umbrella. Eagerly they were talking, smiling occasionally. They spoke of their children and schooling, Mrs. Sung told me afterwards. They both pleased the eye : yet in differing ways. Mrs. Sung, born into smart political circles, was a thought more radiant in her attire than the other, who sat on Committees for teaching blind boys a trade and helped in Y.W.C.A. classes. Besides, Mrs. Sung was the younger and had just come from gay Shanghai, the Paris of the East. Mrs. Sung, however, was paler than my other friend, whose clear, honest eyes and warm complexion gave an impression of health and staying power.

Then—into the midst of the gathering, or rather off the side, there came such a procession as would be possible nowhere else than in China. The well-dressed cheerful people, foreign and Chinese, walking easily, chatting in discreet tones, or grouped on the wide platform, came face to face with such misery as sears the soul. The death's-head is not to be forgotten, it seems.

From a level-crossing, round the head of the silent troop-train, there came, mostly in single file, a procession of perhaps twenty refugees from some village which either was expecting a visit from Chinese soldiery or had recently received one. Swift as the moving shadow of a cloud they filed. Unkempt women, with straggling hair, clutched poor kitchen tools, a kettle or a pan ; a bundle of precious clothing was fastened to their backs, the knots cutting into their breast, and on the bundle a baby sat, tied pickaback. Husbands, also unkempt, carried a spade, a digging fork, more bedding, another child. The women walked amazingly fast, considering their semi-bound feet. Countrywomen have never bound their feet as tightly as gentlepeople, for they have to follow their men into the fields at sowing and hoeing and harvesting times. Still, all their toes are broken and bound beneath the foot. One girl of nine or ten was half running, then dropping back, as if she could go but little further. Boys of twelve marched, carrying bundles. An old woman with wan face, but with determination in it to go on or die, hobbled at the tail of the file. Swiftly they came : like a grim band of the Furies—haunting spectres. They kept closely to the side of the troop train, as if to avoid notice. They never paused, they said not a word : they never looked our way, or asked for help. It seemed but a moment ; and they were gone.

Gone ! A sigh, a groan, burst from the lips of every one. Tears swelled in the throat.

" Did you see them ? " my companion, a young Englishman, said to me in constrained tones. " What ghastly useless wickedness has driven them to this ? Which army is the culprit : the so-called oppressors or the self-named deliverers ? "

The two Chinese ladies were standing stiff, their speech stopped. Mrs. Sung was white as a sheet, helpless with anguish and sympathy. Her eyes were straining after that procession of sorrow. The refugees had sped by so fast that not one of us had had time to think of finding a coin for their immediate needs.

It was the older woman who gave us any glimmer of hope. They would probably spend the night lying in a corner of a temple or street. Mercifully it was warm weather. When they crowded in during the cold weather, sometimes they would be found dead in the streets. Sooner or later, they would discover that a few charitable people had put up a mat shelter for such as they, and given firing so that they might cook their food. It was always hard on the old people, and rather than flee they usually preferred to risk being shot at the door of the little farms where they had lived their lives, each sod of which was dearer to them than the whole continent of Asia. Sometimes these people had almost no money to buy food : the soldiers had robbed them to the bone. So they spent their last cash on opium and died, as a united family.

How long would it be before they could return to their holdings ? It might be months. Not much comfort this, you may think. But here was some one who had at any rate thought about the matter and was trying to ameliorate things.

" Oh ! " said Mrs. Sung, " our poor people." She could only, like myself, give compassion at the moment. Is that of no use ? It is, at any rate, a foundation for deeds.

The train began to show signs of departure. Good-byes had to be said cheerfully and good luck wished. There was stir and bustle, as though the procession had never passed. Yet no one forgot it.

Both ladies thanked me, separately and in private, for their introduction to each other. Each summed up the traits of the other in apt terms, which was interesting.

Said the wife of the railway director :

" I am truly grateful to you for introducing me to Mrs. Sung. Her father is famous and a scholar. I do not often meet women like her. She is pretty and chic, and clever : but she is sweet and true also. I wish all the ladies in our political circles were like her."

Said Mrs. Sung, fourteen years or so junior :

" What a kind, sensible woman ! I like her. I wish I lived nearer to her. She would give good advice, and yet be cheerful with it. I would willingly join any of her committees."

" China cannot but resurrect herself out of her troubles eventually, while she has such women managing her households," was my comment to each of them concerning the other.

By permission of T. Butler, Esq., F.R.G.S.

A Statesman of the Past. Carved in stone, he stands sentinel at an Emperor's tomb

MY mother and I had entertained the railway director to lunch once in Shanghai by ourselves, and had learned much from and about him that way. He was the tallest of my father's Chinese colleagues, being a Northerner.

" From almost the border of Manchuria," he enlarged : " right on the northern edge of the Gulf of Chihli." I took out my husband's map, and we found the spot.

After being educated at an American mission school, he had made his way to America, like so many others of China's promising young men. That was twenty years ago, when scholarships were fewer than now : and he had earned money at first by helping in the China section of an exhibition, and then had still to work his way through college. His name, he told us, meant " Spring Landscape."

" But railways have always been my delight, so it seems almost a misnomer on my parents' part, eh ? Which reminds me "—he turned to my mother—" I am hoping you will talk well to your husband, and impress on him that, when he has the chance, he should use every atom of influence he has for the extension of China's railways."

Truly I believe this man thinks the extension of railways is synonymous with the extension of the Kingdom of Heaven. He may be right : who knows ?

" This is sheer corruption," quoth my mother, looking pleasantly at him with her large hazel eyes. " But people ask what is the use of putting more money into Chinese railways when nobody can foretell what destruction may not befall them, as has already happened."

" It is true that they are in a dreadful condition now," he assented. " Who should know better than myself ? But though many of the engine-boilers are burnt out, the coaches fit for nothing but the scrap-heap, yet the permanent way and the station buildings remain—the most expensive part of the outlay. The only way to outwit destruction is to go on constructing. It may be that one-third of our work may be ruined in civil war: two-thirds will remain. If two-thirds of our constructive work remains, shall we not finally beat the forces which ravage the country? Of course we shall. Persistent construction must win eventually."

This is a cheering philosophy of life, at any rate.

"Now," he said, "let me tell you my own story: and you will see how vital it is for us to have more railways—more vital than anything else. In China we have less than eight thousand miles of railway in our whole country, and three of those few thousand miles are outside the Wall, in Manchuria. Little Roumania, in Europe, has the same mileage as all ours put together. India has five times our amount: and nobody thinks she has builded enough."

He told us that his father, now dead, was an old-fashioned Chinese doctor.

"We lived in the country, and the farmers about us were poor: very poor. We have scorching hot summers and bitterly cold winters. When the sea and the rivers and the very ground were frozen, we used to seem cut off from the world. Our main crop was millet. But we could not grow cotton. That came from far away and was dear, for everything had to reach us on men's or mules' backs. We grew a coarse sort of hemp, which our women wove into cloth on hand-looms. It took a long time to weave, of course, and when it was finished it was harsh to the skin. In winter we wore sheepskins, if we could afford them, the wool side turned in. We used to say the weather was 'three-coats cold,' wearing one coat on top of another. The farmers in summer wore straw sandals on their feet to keep out the thorns, and in winter very hard boat-shaped shoes made of uncured leather, fastened with leathern thongs. Their farm implements were primitive. Salt we had in plenty, for we were near the sea: but little sugar, for that came from hundreds of miles away; from the semi-tropical south, in slow-going junks that had to wait for breezes. We kept bees, but the honey was precious: my father used it for his prescriptions. No rice we had, but we did not miss that much, though it is a treat to us now and again : for we are a millet-eating people. We grew indigo to dye our clothing. We had only a poor sort of soap to wash our clothes.

" Coal came from a fine mine some fifty miles away : but as there were no scientific methods known of mining it, and it also had to be carried to us on pack-mules, it was too dear for constant ordinary use. We burnt brushwood and dry grass from the hillsides to cook our food and heat our beds. We village boys had the task of collecting it—and we rather liked it. For coal, the miners dug a shaft where the seam was and shovelled till the shaft fell in. Then they dug another. Sometimes people were killed by the earth falling, for the propping was crude. There was no ventilation : and the air in the deeper shafts was fearfully hot and foul. Little boys carried the coal to the surface. The shafts were necessarily as perpendicular as could be. I cannot bear to think of the numbers of boys staggering up those endless broken steps with their heavy loads of coal on their backs, as they did, bent under their weights and dripping with sweat. In the mines away from the railway areas, they still do this to-day : for machinery is prohibitive in price, because of transport as much as anything else.

" But ah, how different is that mine now ! It is one of the finest and most up-to-date in the world. I have told you about it, because China owes her first successful railway to that mine. Some Cornish men came, foremen, to show the owners how to make a modern mine. One of them—Heaven bless him !—constructed an engine, out of scrap-iron almost, and set it running secretly upon lines he laid down. In those days our people were full of fear of disturbing the dragon which guards the soil. When the Chinese saw that drilling a hole into the ground brought no disaster on them, a few of them abetted the English foreman when he laid lines to run over the dragon's back. He had to do it as best he could without drawing attention to his doings. He wanted the engine and lines to carry away the coal from the pit-head. Some day we will put up a statue to him—that foreman worker. He called his engine ' The Rocket.' "

We had heard of him, this foreman who could not bury his talent.

" It is hard to be the son of a doctor in localities like that!" went on our friend. " It is difficult to make a poor farmer pay his medicine bill. He always has his rent or the interest on his mortage, or his father's funeral expenses : or it is a bad year. The doctor comes off badly."

" We have heard this complaint from doctors in parts of the globe where railways function daily," we interpolated.

" We were truly a poor community, nevertheless," he asserted. " Every one had to work hard to make a living : and my father knew it. The soil was sandy and light. The farmers would try to grow other crops on it, beans, Indian corn, a little wheat. But they were fighting nature. One crop, beside millet, grew splendidly : and that was ground-nuts."

" In England they call them monkey-nuts," I told him.

" Yes, and pea-nuts in America," he added. " We made oil of them : we used this as our cooking fat, the illuminant for our tiny wick-lamps. We ate the nuts roasted, we made paste of their flour. Ground-nuts all the time it was. We grew far more than we needed : or Nature grew them for us. The land seemed intent on producing ground-nuts."

" It is an agreeable picture, notwithstanding, which the villagers make, when they harvest the crop," I broke in. " I love to see the women squatting in groups with their children —and often the old men too—sifting the sand from the nuts."

In their red trousers and gay old-fashioned tunics, with big sleeves, they are very picturesque. They sit round the threshing-floor, which is in the midst of their small dwellings of mud-dried bricks, and which has been swept very clean with the millet-head brooms. They shake the great wide sieves, very light and flat, sifting the ground-nuts. The sand drops through like rain.

" We had one other crop," he smiled across at me, " a women's crop ! That was pongee silk. They call it tussore abroad."

Tussore is from two Chinese words, *t'u ssŭ*, or wild silk. My husband had told me that.

" Scrub-oak grows on the hills in our vicinity, and our farmers' wives would put the silkworms to eat oak-leaves. This silkworm is quite a different species from the other of

By permission of T. Butler, Esq., F.R.G.S.

The Cart Traffic of Peking

the South, which spins the fine strong beautiful silk made there. In the mornings the women put the silkworms to feed, then gather them at noon, and again at sundown. When the grubs have wound themselves into their cocoons, the women spin their silk and weave a length of it on the looms, and finally dye it with home-grown indigo. But, in those days, they could never afford to wear a piece of the silk themselves. They had to sell it—to help pay the mortgage or to put by for their daughter's wedding dowry.

" And then—ah, then "—he waxed lyrical—" came the railway. That railway, I want you to know, was built with British money and under British supervision, and it is built as solid as eternity. Well built it is, and the British engines are good engines. I am telling you this, to make you sympathize with me more : but it is true !

" When the railway came, we found there were other people in the world who could use our surplus ground-nuts : make them into margarine and artificial olive-oil : people who liked to eat them roasted too, as we do. So we stopped fighting nature, and let the soil grow the ground-nuts it wants to : and now we export our nuts by the train-load, and they help to nourish other peoples. Our folk, who were so poor, are now a well-to-do farming community. Life there is different from the old days. They can afford to run village schools and pay a teacher. Our teachers had a worse time than our doctors before.

" And our women can wear a piece of their own silk at their daughters' weddings. That is what I want for all our Chinese women ! Now you know why I am so enthusiastic over railways."

" May you get them," said my mother.

" Amen," I echoed.

Later, I was to learn more about these ground-nut matters. When strikes and warfare were rending China, no ground-nuts came through to Great Britain, and one large buyer told me with heaviness that no other ground-nuts suited his purpose so well. In Shantung province, again, I learned that an American missionary, deploring the small size of the ground-nuts there, sent for American seed and greatly improved the quality of the crop.

Our friend, Spring Landscape, the railway enthusiast, was not, however, wholly occupied with iron and steel and coal. His poetic name was not given him for nothing. He had visited Hangchow the same time as myself, and it was there we first began to be friends, he and I.

" Hangchow ! " he mused aloud to me, in the lounge of the hotel where we were staying, on the edge of the lake. He crossed his legs and showed woollen knitted socks, foreign fashion, and leather boots, beneath his long Chinese gown. Nay, more, he wore, as did all the Chinese gentlemen of the day, foreign striped morning trousers under his national robe. If he had but kept to Chinese customs and sat with feet squared and knees out, these discrepancies would not have leaped to the eye. But no, to-day he crosses his knees —with the foreigner's abandoned etiquette.

The matter of dress interested me. Not that this particular friend of mine of the railways had hard and fast principles about wearing national garb. But he naturally wished to avoid being conspicuous. The thing was nothing to him, a man of sterling sense. At that time, however, it was deemed the very essence of patriotism to wear the long Chinese gown. To appear in foreign coat, collar and waistcoat was despicable. This ban did not apply to the head : for hats might be, indeed invariably were, soft trilby hats. Nor did it apply to mackintoshes, gloves and umbrellas. Try how they would, it seemed as though no patriot, however determined, could wholly escape foreign influence. There are even numbers of Chinese factories to-day which weave vests for Chinese use after the foreigner's pattern. But after all, there is not one of us, of any nation, who does not on occasion join the " noble Order of Ostriches." As well try, meanwhile, to prevent the Atlantic and the Pacific Oceans from meeting and mingling at Cape Horn as stem the natural flow and interchange between nations—with all that this entails in evolution of ideas and manners and dress.

My railway friend would be the first to support these notions about trade. He lit his Manila cheroot with a Japanese match while he poetized to me aloud about Hangchow.

" The hills around are crowned with temples : in every

picturesque spot they grow as if naturally. The steps are terraced into the hillsides ; the roads wander through shady woodlands, amongst bamboo groves. We will visit the temples ! They are well kept, and the priests are self-respecting folk, good administrators of their lands. There are shrines in caverns and grottos, cut in the rock—very romantic. And ah, the women—you know the women of Hangchow are noted for their beauty ! I shall hire a boat and be rowed under the arched bridges and look admiringly at these human flowers of our countryside."

Later in the day, I met him and asked him if he had taken such a boat.

"Certainly," he answered, "and as I lay in it, I made a quatrain to the ladies of Hangchow."

"How many did you see ?" I persisted, for I had not caught many glimpses of enravishing charms myself. It seemed to me, alack, that here was another legend done away, another illusion shattered. I told him I had seen a larger number of charming Chinese women in the Nanking Road in Shanghai in five minutes than in a whole day at Hangchow.

He was pained. He had, however, to confess that but few Hangchow ladies were that day visible wandering lonely—and lovely, of course—as a cloud on the marges of the West Lake. He hoped for the morrow. He had seen one dainty maid walking on the raised causeway which has been cleverly built to cross the water.

"Pray read me your quatrain," I begged. After a little literary hesitation, he did, half singing it, Chinese way. It was very engaging, reminding one of Herrick or Watteau. The lovely woman of his fancyings was all daintiness and withdrawal. He was paying homage to Beauty in the abstract : and his homage was a tiny vase of fine porcelain, so to speak. The maid had lingered a moment on the water's edge : a willow had mirrored itself darkly beside her. A young moon had risen, crescent in the sky, and a fleecy cloud had scudded across its face—and hidden the face of the maid. How could mortal man with immortal soul fail to delight in this picture ? So ran his quatrain : one picture to each line.

No wonder his wife has a happy, infectious laugh and a young spirit. She would have to keep them, to please him.

Yet was his passion railways: railways, so that China's countryside might prosper.

I could wish that this book of mine might last a century or two—to be modest and precise, say five centuries! Then some young Chinese would be bidden to read it by his tutors for its "portraits of twentieth-century life in China." With due annotations and footnotes, of course, as loved by the commentators; such as, "It must be borne in mind that the author is speaking of very ancient happenings." "Bad harvests, inhumanity, homelessness," my young man will be puzzling—so I hope—"what are such things? I must look them up in my dictionary of antiquity. The conditions of life then are incredible. What a different world we live in! We have, indeed, changed all that."

And this book will seem unreal to him in those matters. I pray it may.

They say that no woman has written a dream of Utopia. A man, when he imagines new worlds, creates some very exotic and surprising localities. The people's food makes them enormous giants, gives them abnormal strength. The marriage customs are totally different from those which hold on this earth—and the author's imaginings never commend themselves, let me say at once, to the women who live on this earth at present. In those dream-books of man, life seems very much cut to pattern: and one might as well live in the awful exactness of a bee-hive. Rarely does fear seem finished with, and war still shakes his skeleton hatefulness.

A woman, when she dreams of the Country-that-shall-be, is far less exigent in her requirements. She thinks how good it will be when every child in the world—of every colour—has as much food to put into his mouth as will make him grow a pleasantly normal size, with strong legs and a shouting voice: when each family has a book of poems in its cupboard, a flower growing at its door, a pot of honey in its larder. When every man has a piece of work to put his heart into with pleasure: and every working-woman has a breathing-space from the job that is hers from sunrise to sunset.

We women who set down our thoughts on paper to-day have been left a sentimental sort of tradition by our predecessors. Mary, village maiden, when she sang Magnificat,

Photo by Lady Hosie

The Wife of Spring Landscape

did she put in dashing verses about spears and bows and galloping horses ? Did she call on the planets and Pleiades ; on Leviathan or chariots of fire ? No, no : she must, forsooth, when all the glory of Heaven came upon her, look down on her little brown hand and bethink herself of the needy and those of low estate. Her spirit went a-singing because the hungry were to be filled !

Take our English women writers : Jane Austen of the piercing wit, Charlotte Brontë of the sensitive soul, George Eliot who was so utterly woman. Poor-spirited females writing of life exactly as it is ! If by any chance they induce us to throw our imaginations forward, it is over some absurd trifle : such as the time when orphans and governesses are to be treated like human beings, when girls have the sense to think before they elope with bold bad men, and young men take heed lest their fair charmers turn out cold-blooded gorgons. Even our young hot-bloods of to-day are mostly breaking a feminine lance against hypocrisies or injustices, as they see them. Never a Gulliver amongst us to shake a limb or take flight to the country of the Yahoos, to Mars, to the land where they manufacture robots, or even to the tree-tops of Peter Pan. In short, we are precisely the sort of prosaic, unimaginative persons who can appreciate the mild Utopia of a Chinese railway expert : his dream of a time " when every Chinese woman shall wear a piece of silk at her daughter's wedding."

A humble ambition, is it ? Oh, young Chinese man—who will not, I fear, be reading this book one hundred, not to say five hundred years from now—is that ambition fulfilled yet ? Is it half-way to realization : this womanish sort of Utopia ?

" Spring Landscape " does not seem such a misnomer for a railway expert, after all.

THE next time we all met was at a garden-party, when another of my father's colleagues was present. He is a very famous man in China ; a philosopher, a logician, a professor. When he stands up in a lecture-room to discourse on topics of national interest, young Chinese students flock by the hundred ; and thousands hang on his lips. Every word he utters at his lectures is flashed from one newspaper to another throughout the country. He is noted as a revolutionary and rationalist in philosophy. If a proposition has been generally accepted for some centuries, it at once is suspect in his eyes. Truth at any cost is his motto ; and if a hypothesis is highly disagreeable to most people, he thinks it the more likely to be true. When such a man, therefore, makes an occasional remark on behalf of any of the structures of society, the students at least listen to him respectfully. Some may sadly think that he has not thrown off all the trammels of a hampering Past : but others stay their course for a minute or two to wonder whether Wisdom did actually begin in this generation. Is it possible, the thought comes, that once or twice some thinker, who is now dead, had a flicker or two of intelligence which may be of use to those living to-day ?

The Professor is a slim, pale man, in the thirties ; afraid, perhaps, of growing middle-aged now in his views, and therefore conscientiously asseverating his most revolutionary notions whenever possible.

" Fame has come too early in life for some of us," he said once, wistfully.

If fame can be consolidated by sheer industry, he has more than earned the right to a lasting niche in its temple. His philosophic and historical output is enormous. One of the few American-trained Chinese students who has a deep knowledge of his own language, he is a leader in a school of modern critical methods which has dynamited and blown sky-high the old commentators on the classics and the old historians. At least, so one understands. As our exponents of the Higher Criticism would pish and tush at mediæval theology, and others go further back and tell us that St. Jerome in the Vulgate translated various Hebrew words wrongly, so these modern Chinese protagonists of textual criticism pick large holes in their historians and classicists, and darn them together again with very different thread from that traditionally used. Then they bring forward a less-known literary light of the seventh, or the seventeenth, century to prove that, as he did not accept these traditional commentaries, the Chinese mind has always contained the element of rebellion; that it has never stopped growing, as some have said of it. No doubt they are right: and it is all very interesting, also instructive. Very welcome, too: like any new growth of learning. The fall of Constantinople and the scattering of the Greek Scholars of 1453 led to no greater Renascence than did the crash of the Manchu dynasty of China in 1911.

These young, or youngish, protagonists of Truth are not content with hurling Chinese names into one's consciousness; they quote Jean-Jacques Rousseau, Herbert Spencer and Hegel. It is obvious that such folk are indeed blessed with brains: and it is great impudence on my part to attempt to argue with them on any subject on earth. I ought to listen.

"Women," one of them said, looking at me with cold eyes, "are notoriously incapable of logic."

"Women," announced another, "never understand international politics." That was when I objected that some premise on his part with regard to foreign dealings—in which these thinkers like to dabble—hardly seemed to me clean-cut honesty. For it is strange that this doctrine of Truth-at-all-costs is to be kept to the regions of pure science and philosophic speculation: not necessarily is it to enter practical politics or the life of the world. Compromise is the motto, then; it is more reasonable.

"Do introduce me to the Professor," asked Mrs. Sung at the garden party. "I should very much like to meet him."

We walked down the lawns and found him: and he was pleased to meet her; for—such are the queer tricks of our brains—the modern Chinese philosopher affirms that women ought to be given a chance to know what clever men are talking about. Besides, Mrs. Sung is both charming and looks it: and that has an effect. Moreover, he had met her father.

Have I given the impression that the Professor is a narrow, pedantic and haughty soul? That would be totally wrong. He is a very pleasant man to meet. He is at heart a little shy; he has a sensitive soul. In short, there is nobody who can help feeling affection for him, though differing from him radically in opinion. He is gentle in manners. And one glance at his face stirs every woman's heart, for it is plain he habitually overworks.

The first time we met was in a train going through a fair countryside. The fruit orchards were in flower: the trees carefully, yet unscientifically, tended. Not a weed to be seen in the land: every row straight as a die. A cuckoo called.

"Listen!" he said. "Do you know what it is saying? 'Sow the seed, sow the seed!' The legend is that once there was a lazy farmer whose land fell into a shocking state. When he died, he was condemned to come back every spring as a cuckoo and call to the other farmers not to copy his example!"

"That is a charming story," I said.

"Yes," he replied, "and, like all our legends, very practical and materialistic. Your poets call the cuckoo 'a wandering voice': for us, the voice gives solid advice. That is the difference between us. We Chinese are intensely materialistic. The West talks nonsense when it turns to the East for mysticism and spirituality. As for the Indians, they are less spiritually-minded than even we are."

"Oh, come!" I demurred, thinking he might be, Chinese fashion, covering his real feelings by polite modesty in speech. "There is Ancestor Reverence. A people that believes so completely that death is not the end of human life has surely gone a long way from materialism."

But he would have none of this.

"You know very well," he answered, "that our ghosts are the most materialistic of people. They need food and drink and money; motor-cars and servants too, if they are ghosts of rich people on the earth, sent over to them as burnt paper forms. The ancestors are as gross: if they are not laid in the right direction or buried at the right date or with the due ceremonies, back they come to haunt the houses of their descendants and upset their material affairs. No: in this matter of the dead, our Chinese people have nothing spiritual about them."

I told him I was writing some descriptions of Chinese life for an English newspaper. Might I quote him?

"Certainly," he said: "I have said these things twenty times in my books—which you have evidently not read. But you had better write a proper interview with me."

That would be a new experience, I assured him: and was entertained by the idea.

"Very well," he ordained: "ask me some questions. I have been interviewed any number of times for Chinese and American papers." Later, he was to be interviewed also in Europe.

"About China's materialism?" I asked diffidently: "you have forgotten the Christians, I think. Ten thousand of them died in 1900 rather than give up their faith, you know. That is hardly materialistic, do you think?"

"Religion," he laid down, "is the opiate of the people. That has been said before, and I repeat it, with conviction. A man drugged will perform any brave rash thing. All religions are founded on myths. Look at Genesis!"

"I look at it, and I read it!" I flung back at him. And thereupon I took up the tale and warmed to my theme. "I also listen to Beethoven's Fifth Symphony, look at Raphael's Madonna of the Chair, and delight in other interpretations of the divine. Thank heaven, in my youth, like other Occidentals, I was flung into both Genesis and Revelation, and can never brush the colour and glory of them out of my eyes. There are, so they say, people who seriously inform us, laying heavy fingers of lead on living beauty, that the book of Revelation is an allegory. Soon they will have discovered—those earnest souls—that saints and angels did not literally embrace each other under the thatched shed at Bethlehem, as Botticelli drew them."

Few things, I averred, gave me more satisfaction than to contemplate the devil being flung by St. John the Divine into a bottomless abyss and bound with chains : that this indeed was imaginative genius of the highest, which might well lend itself to a fresco befitting the chambers of the League of Nations. That a still more encouraging frieze might begin with a glimmer of the Light which dawned on the world's dim and humorous origins : shining more strongly through perverse Israel—no whit more perverse, however, than he or I—till it was manifest in the Light that lighteth every man that cometh into the world : and which shall at last fling everlasting jewelled towers high on the bastions of the New Jerusalem. I asked, meanwhile, since it was for us to see that the house of the Lord be builded exceeding magnifical, what more he could desire, pray, of any philosopher or poet, musician or artist, than that he should add his pillars to that building in his own fair way ? I reminded him that there were twelve gates into the deathless city, and said he had entered well in by the gate of St. Thomas the questioner : and a very good gate, too—which frequently entailed martyrdom for its disciples ! That half my Chinese friends at the moment thought the only possible gate was that of Simon the Nationalist—one of the least of the apostles, but whose gate of sacrifice was also of the nature of a pearl.

He looked at me : he listened : he urged me on. That is the worst of this very engaging philosopher. At the moment when you expect him to out with all his daggers of metaphysics to slay you, and to wipe his blade upon your corpse, he sends a sweet and gentle beam from his eye, and says something far more disarming than any ratiocination.

" The mystic," he now said to me in a detached way, with a mildness and humility which, one may believe, lies hidden deep under all his tremendous and provoking implacability, " the mystic is the one person who makes me consider sometimes that there may be some sort of a God."

In these days it is exceedingly trying to be labelled theologically or any other way. But this was making handsome amends. The Way of Beauty was not closed to him after all, it seemed.

He went on to say, however, that the chance of God's existence was so slight that to his mind it was not worth taking into account for practical purposes.

"I am an atheist: not an agnostic," he affirmed. "I will not pander to make-beliefs. I do not say I do not know if there is a God. I say I am convinced that God is non-existent. There is only the material life: there is no spiritual."

My father happened to be passing at that moment, and heard these words. He put his hand on the professor's shoulder and looked down on him sitting there: so sincere, so pale—almost to luminosity—with continued effort and study of books and philosophy, his body so unimportant except as an instrument to carry out the will of the spirit enclosed within. Looking at him, one wondered where spirit ended and matter began.

"My dear fellow," he said with affection, "no human being who sees you will believe you are material at all. You are the contradiction in person of your own theories."

The Professor laughed. Nor was he displeased: which was illogical. But life is not logical: it is biological. Always there is the unforeseen: there is the element of growth. Nobody can say what is round the next corner of life for anybody or any nation. Who could draw an exact picture of the most scientifically grown rose before it has bloomed? So I argued with him.

"Women's reasoning!" he scorned me. "But about religion: thank goodness, I have done with churches and such fetish for ever. It is ten years since I entered a church, and I hope never to enter another."

Somebody had told us that this bitterness of his, which has made him encase himself around with a hard shell as regards to religion, was because a Western Christian, who had been his friend, had proved himself a hypocrite. This would shake any young man's faith in either a friend or a friend's Creator. Yet the Professor can be fair-minded enough. When he was in England, a newspaper debate was in full swing as to the value of missions. One party declared that missions were responsible for all China's troubles. And our Professor took up his pen in their defence! As an atheist, he had no use for their doctrines: as a lover of his country he declared that they had done more for its progress than any other body of men.

"Thank heaven, however," he cried fervently to me, "that I can say that I have never been missionized, that I owe not a cent, not an hour's schooling to any church or religion!"

His father was a country official, but with some means, he told me.

"My mother," he went on, for as a realist he must lay bare the whole truth, particularly if not too palatable to himself, "my mother was a simple country-girl of eighteen. My father was an old man when he married her: he died soon after I was born." From which he meant me to infer that his not overstrong body is due to such wedlock. But it appears to have had brilliant results in brains, and the Professor is not excessively delicate or he could never accomplish all his work. He had been betrothed in early youth to a country girl he had not seen. When he came back with his honours upon him from his American studies, he kept the bond which had been made by the Elders in his name. The honour of his country's institutions and his family's pledges should not be violated by him. A clean, austere mind he has. Learning is his real spouse. As for the wiles of Delilah, he is adamantean proof. Five minutes of her company would bore him to extinction, though she came

> "Like a stately ship
> Of Tarsus, bound for th' isles
> Of Javan or Gadire,
> With all her bravery on, and tackle trim."

His favourite reading in foreign literature is, so he said, "the works" of the Pessimists. He mentioned Thomas Hardy and George Bernard Shaw in particular. "They have looked at life at its worst," he put it; "if they can find any cause for optimism, there must be grounds for it. I am of the same school. Yet I am known as The Incurable Optimist in the newspapers."

Photo by Lady Hosie

A Professor of Logic

The writer and thinker which our Professor loved best was Huxley. He actually quoted to me what Huxley wrote to Gladstone in their Victorian controversy over Science and Religion.

" But, Professor," I cried, " you cannot think that a biologist and a politician somewhere about 1870 or 1880 settled for all time in a few letters a question which more accurately belongs to the realm of metaphysics or theology ? I implore you to read authors a little more modern than that."

Again he proved his innate worth by acknowledging his deficiencies.

" I daresay I am behind the times in the matter of religious theories," he said : " they do not interest me enough. My mind is made up. I have little time to read modern English authors. But nothing can shake my faith in Huxley. He and Darwin have the type of mind which China needs."

Then he stopped and laughed.

" If this is an interview for the Press," he interjected, " it is a very poor one ! I do not think much of your ideas of an interview. Who on earth wants to know my views on Genesis, or materialism, pray ? "

" Personally I have found them very illuminating," I replied.

" You ought to ask how many books I have written, and what they are about," he informed me.

An amazing list it is. Books on logic, metaphysics ; critical essays on the methods of the classical commentators and historians ; theses in political science. His works are in Chinese, and also in English, and such English as needs not a word of correction, although on the most abstruse subjects. When I eventually wrote an account of these books and the author, after the style of interview approved by the Professor, the editor of the English newspaper brushed the whole thing aside. " It is impossible," he said, " for any one man to have accomplished all that." Which made me wonder if my idea of an interview might not be more efficacious than the Professor's. He has published a million Chinese words—ideographs. That is simply stupendous industry. Some of his most famous works have been put into the League of Nations

Library at Geneva, as representative of modern Chinese thought and style.

He has even written poetry. I took a breath of relief on hearing this.

" Then you love Nature ? " I queried, happily.

" Not particularly," he shrugged, dashing cold water in my face.

His poems are about human beings, I discovered later : about a woman's smile, about a rickshawman at his toil.

I met his wife in Peking, a kind and domesticated little woman. She probably finds her brilliant husband a handful. Chinese society's demands, for instance, on its heroes are very exigent. The Professor would be invited to six dinner or supper parties in one evening : and it would be very discourteous, an insult in fact, to refuse any !

" In the same way, a noted friend of mine has been asked to be chancellor of twelve different universities. He has had to accept the title, but he has lately issued a circular, regardless whether he gives offence or no, that from henceforth he will accept no more. There are forty so-called universities in Shanghai alone, and he vows he will not be a party to such incompetence as that must mean. It is the old tradition, that you may write once to a great scholar and for ever after call yourself his disciple." So the Professor explained.

" But you cannot eat six dinners in an evening ! Your poor digestion ! " I suggested.

" No, of course I cannot," he replied. " I take a pick with my chopsticks from a bowl at one dinner and then go on to the next. It is the conversation which is the heart of the invitation. I stop and talk a while. Even so, it is not too good for one's digestion. My wife says I must have the stomach of a buffalo, and I really think I must have."

" It is a dreadful life he lives," she assured me : which was credible. " He comes home tired with his succession of entertainments, for at each they expect him to talk and talk sensibly, and then he stays up till three in the morning writing his essays and articles. He says it is the only time when the telephone is not ringing."

" When I come to England," he said sagely, " I shall go to

the British Museum and stay there: where nobody can interrupt."

He told me that at their marriage he had informed his bride that there were to be no religious teachings or ceremonies in his house whatever, not even the New Year honours to the dead. They had three sons. Children, he held, had the right to independent thought and should not be prejudiced in favour of any religious dogmas. It was positively wrong to give them a religious bias in their youth. If they liked to indulge tastes that way later, it should be their own doing.

"My wife, I must say it of her, has stood by me honourably in this," he added. "I will also say I was surprised when she uncomplainingly agreed to my laying down the law over it."

"Perhaps she knows that the root of the matter is not only in observances and ceremonies," I parried.

He hoped his children would be "advanced thinkers," and be able to teach him presently. (This is often said by parents while their offspring are young.) He feared that otherwise he might, in time, become bourgeois in his ideas, which was the worst that could befall a man.

"Suppose the Red revolutionaries sweep China?" I suggested. "You might be amongst their victims."

"So be it, then," he accepted. "If it be for the advancement of my country, I shall be willing." He thought the Russian Red Terror had been grossly exaggerated. That was before the Terrors took place in the southern provinces of his own land. And such sentiments, so a hard-headed Occidental feels, cannot be authenticated till they have been put to the test.

Yet he is a gallant soul. When the Extremists came into power in China, and he found what the logical deduction of many of their ideas was, he withstood them to their faces—our slender overworked materialist. He told them that, though they killed him for it, he would not join their political caucus. Because of this, he lost for the moment some of his popularity amongst the younger members.

He deserves his popularity: for he has given his time and strength, and the ægis of his name, to a movement for simplifying education for the masses. The illiteracy of his people has weighed on him. He well knows the years of intensive study it means for a man to become only a moderate scholar in Chinese. My friend, Li Cheng, shuts his small sons up, year in and year out, in a room with an old teacher of the Classics. To be sure, they run out and play with balls, in a way which would shock their grandfathers. But they must study their Chinese writing, reading and literature the best part of the year, and after that they have little time for other subjects. They begin at five years old.

" I regret it," says their father, " but I know it is the only way they can ever learn to be good Chinese scholars. There is no other method than being soaked in it from babyhood."

How can a farmer, tradesman, hawker, pursue such methods ? He cannot. Must he, therefore, remain unaided, illiterate ?

The Professor, in one of his outbursts of generous admission to those he half considers his foes, asserted that the dissemination of the Bible, which is written in the " vulgar tongue," has accomplished more than anything else to help China out of illiteracy as it did England. But as the men who first translated the Bible into the common speech were despised by the scholars, so the Professor has had to face the same narrow prejudices. There is nothing mean or petty about him. He fought the battle for this simplification of the written language of which he himself is a past-master. He took part in founding a system, the White or Clear Learning —Pai Hua—which is likely to be the basis of education for his less fortunate countrymen and the beginnings of a new and readable modern literature. The classicists pour derision on what they term his betrayal of pure learning. In a way they are justified, for he frankly denounces much of the old learning as useless. He would have the Four Canons —the foundations of China's ancient education—relegated to the universities, to be studied as now we study Greek or Latin. Like Plato and Aristotle, so Confucius and Mencius are to be the hobby and discussion of the learned, not the food of the everyday citizen. In short, science is to oust the classics in China as it has largely done in the West : science, which includes economics and political science as well as the natural sciences. It is to be taught in the vulgar mother tongue, and not the classical language, which is as difficult to write well as classical Greek is to us, and as hard to understand as the language of *Piers Plowman*.

If a foreigner regrets that Confucius or Lao Tzŭ, Mencius or Moh Ti, should be thus pushed into the background of China's future culture, the new leaders reply : " You scoffed at us before, because we were under the dead hand of the Past—your own words. Now that we have shaken that gripping, chilling claw off our shoulders, you foreigners have nothing but praise for our worn-out old ethics. You sentimentalize over the legendary figures whom we now propose to study as interesting literary antiques. Is this logical or reasonable on your part ? How would you care to be tied down to the philosophy of the fifth century B.C., wonderful though it was as an era ? "

" It may not be logical, but it is very human," you whisper in the secrecy of your heart, feeling as though you had met a ship on the high seas with neither captain nor rudder, and with a crew that has steamed out on the strength of written examinations.

Strangely and significantly, the Professor's name translated into English means " Whither goest thou ? "—*Quo vadis?*

After she had been introduced to the Professor, Mrs. Sung walked down the lawns with me and asked me what I honestly thought of him and other members of the intelligentsia whom I had met. She plied me with questions mercilessly. I told her of my interview with him in the train. She laughed immoderately and clapped her hands when I spoke with any acerbity. She confessed to understanding my feelings of affection for him, since all China possesses them. When I ended by saying such men would never be quite grown up, she took me by the arm and cried :

" Right ! He is very clever, very earnest—and oh, so young ! "

Being women, we both suddenly felt excessively old and maternally-minded toward the whole school of realists, logicians, metaphysicians, modern educationalists and economists. Not for worlds would we have allowed any of them to know it : that would have been the last insult in their eyes.

" Did your brother, when he was young and you sent him

along a dark passage at night, go down it whistling ? Yet, as you knew well, he was feeling frightened ? "

" Yes, of course," she nodded. " They are rather like that, our modern thinkers : children walking bravely in the dark, whistling to keep up their courage—bless their innocence ! And there is the warm light shining within a few yards of them the whole time ! "

I might have left my tale of the Professor at that, had it not been that the last two years have seen his country torn and spent. With what eager hopes he greeted the early stirrings of upheaval ! How he clung to every sign that all was going well ; and how bitter must have been his heart when, brave thinker and questioner as he is, he had to part company with some who had been his close friends, his admirers and colleagues !

Lately he has broken forth into a very desperation of humility on behalf of the country he loves so dearly. It is noteworthy that when a Chinese departs from that pride or self-respect, or " face," the armour in which he lives protected against outside criticism, he throws it away with a fury of humiliation. When he realizes, for instance, that the foreign ideal of truthfulness in daily speech is desirable, in his intense self-disgust at having failed, he will cry, " I have sown lies ! " when he has been guilty of some small exaggeration.

The Professor has recently cast aside all pride and has written things, in English, and in a published book, which must have drained every drop in his veins to indite, and which must horrify a great number of his compatriots. Not because they think them untrue : but that in their eyes they are too ruinous to admit. This is how he writes :

> " What is needed to-day, it seems to me, is a deep conviction which should almost amount to religious repentance that we Chinese are backward in everything and that every other modern nation in the world is much better off than we are. We must confess that we are terribly poor and that our people are suffering miseries which justly horrify the civilized peoples."

But when he goes on to say that

> " most of our homes are nests of crimes, of injustice, oppression, lynching, and suicide,"

a foreigner feels that his picture is painted in too gloomy colours. And yet—and yet. There comes to my mind a story which I could not bring myself to tell Mrs. Sung: about a wife of nineteen. She came to some classes held by a foreign woman, and then she ceased to come. The foreign woman knew the girl was soon to be a mother, and had seen that she was ill and lack-lustre; and she had been troubled over her. Presently she asked the other woman where and how she was.

"Oh, she is all right now: she will be coming back presently," they cajoled her.

Dissatisfied, she said no more. Soon she heard them talking amongst themselves, and, shocked and sick, pieced out the story. It was evident, they had said, that the girl could not come through maternity alive. She had fits, everything had gone wrong with her. The family talked it over. They were alarmed at the prospect of having to provide a coffin for her. They were very poor. A coffin is costly. There is no Poor Law Act yet in China. If she died, moreover, there would be the cost of installing another wife. So they called in an old woman: and she pierced the girl with a long needle—using no anaesthetic, of course: and she had been lucky. The baby was born dead, and the family had been saved the truly unendurable expense of a coffin.

That was misery and poverty and suffering: it was not meant criminally, however. It is also true that many a daughter-in-law has taken opium and died rather than live longer in the home of her husband's mother. On the other hand, I have known some girls who loved devotedly their mothers-in-law.

The Professor continues his accusation of his people:

> "For all this, we have only ourselves to blame. We have bound the feet of our women for a thousand years, and smoked opium for centuries, thereby greatly weakening the race and polluting its moral fibre. . . . We are only reaping the fruit of the sins of our fathers and ourselves.
>
> "Let us," he ends, "no longer deceive ourselves with self-complacent talk about imperialistic powers hampering our national progress. . . . Let us read the recent history of Japan and bury our conceit and self-deception once for all in shame and repentance.
>
> "And then, when we have fully and whole-heartedly repented, let us resolve, solemnly and religiously, that we must learn."

The Chinese professor who wrote that is a brave man. The thinker who with puritan fire worships at the feet of Truth as at the feet of God, will not go very far astray ; nor will he be without a message which shall help his generation and to which they will do well to listen. If ever a god demanded sacrifice and service, it is the God of Truth : and in the long run, the same God gives a just reward.

Never again will Mrs. Sung and myself smile, as if maternally, upon a young creature walking wide-eyed and whistling to keep up his courage in the dark. Rather, here is the Baptist calling, although not clad in skins or living in the wilderness. His cry is Repentance—in the name of Huxley : his gospel, the laws of Evolution—according to Darwin.

He has weighed and pondered, during the late days of stress and bluster : and he has decided that these are greater names and more lasting forces than Marx or Lenin—which is a tremendous decision of the soul.

CHAPTER XXII THE WAY OF TWO WOMEN

NATURALLY our first thought, on arriving in Peking, had been to seek out old friends : in particular, Miss Lo and Miss Way. Sir Thomas Wade, one of the earliest British Ministers to Peking, and afterwards first Professor of Chinese at Cambridge University, would have spelt Miss Way, " Wei." As he was learned in Chinese beyond computation, I for one will not dispute his spellings after the manner of the Younger Generation. But as every one makes the obvious pun on the names of my friends, and asks, " Lo, is this the Way ? " I acquiesce for convenience' sake.

Miss Lo is known more familiarly to me as " Scented Blossom," being the daughter of a Manchu official, a former friend of my father's. My mother and I had been able to be of some small service during what were dark days to Manchus during the Revolution. Scented Blossom was the student of the family : she knows the Chinese classics, she speaks and writes a little English. Her talents are to-day being put to usury in a girls' school hidden up a narrow tortuous, dusty lane in the north-east corner of Peking. Her two sisters were married before Lo Ta Jen and Lo T'ai T'ai, the parents, died : alas, both married unhappily. One of them, Fragrant Lily, used to be such a sparkling, pretty, witty slip of a girl that I felt stunned when Blossom told me of her death on my arrival. Blossom has steadily evaded betrothal, and her solitary brother being younger than herself, he cannot make the arrangements above her head. So she has never claimed her marriage portion, and she lives in a small wing of the family mansion with her own old amah to attend her : the head of the household being her sister-in-law.

" Your sister dead ! " I exclaimed. " She was only thirty-five, surely. And so bright a spirit. What did she die of ? "

" Of her husband," said Blossom grimly.

Then she enlarged. This is, literally, what she said : " He was a cruel man, though I, also Chinese, say it. The finale came over a dog, which he said was disobedient. He took nails and hammered them into its head, though my dear Flowering Lily knelt and wept and implored him not to do so wicked a thing. She could never forget its shrieks. She was poorly before ; but after that, she became so full of sorrow that her stomach swelled and swelled, and then she died. She was glad to die, and to leave no children."

That was a pleasant tale to hear of a friend's passing after seven years' absence from Peking. I leave to the initiated what was the actual physiological cause of her death. In the midst of the telling, arrived the second sister, Flowering Plum, having been telephoned for to meet me. She had been a plump, jolly, sensible girl, direct and frank, healthy and bouncing, with flashes of mischief. She shrugged her shoulders when, after a while, I now ventured to hope that she was happy besides being well in health. She had been married soon before her father's death. The last time I had seen her she had not been married very long : she had just lost her first baby, and it was doubtful if she could have any more. Knowing how great anguish this is to Chinese women, I had tried to comfort her as best I could : and I had been surprised and a little uneasy when she said earnestly and finally, with a few slow tears : " Listen ! I do not mind so very much if I do not have another child. Life is not so delightful that one wants to hand it on."

There is something the matter when a Chinese woman speaks in that way. Flowering Plum was thin and sad-eyed then : but I put it down to the loss of her baby. But here she was again, years later ; and heavy-eyed, silent. I thought her mother would have wept to see her. It was plain that life had come to mean doggedness and endurance for her rather than radiance. She had been married to a widower, I knew, so was his second wife.

" Second wife ! " she derided. " Fourth, or fifth, or sixth, you mean ! "

Blossom explained to me that though her sister, owing to her rank, was the legal wife, her husband had used the excuse of her first child dying to take two concubines into the house and so secure children if possible. But already he had two concubines, having taken them in his first wife's days before his second marriage. Mercifully prognostications had not been fulfilled: her sister had borne a son. She could now require respect not only from her husband but from the other women in the household, over which she was head. Some of the women were harmless and kindly; uneducated, of course: but some were ambitious to have the "Master" in their pockets. As far as she was concerned, they were welcome to the whole of his company: but she dared not let them go too far, lest she should jeopardize her son's future. More than anything on earth did she desire for her son some inculcation of modern ideas, so that he should be "different from his father . . . if he lives. But he is very delicate. How can he be otherwise?" she ended sadly.

"My sister is kind and good to the other women in the household: too kind, I tell her," added Blossom.

"It is not their fault if they are stupid and small-minded," said her sister. "What chance have they ever had to be anything else? Now we had such a mother—and father, too! My mother could not have been harsh to any one."

She had kept her head erect and proud, while each bitter sentence with its awful realism fell from her lips. Nay, she had smiled disdain of her painful situation. Now she turned and put her arm round Blossom's shoulders.

"So you see why, at the family conclaves over Blossom and her refusal to be betrothed, we sisters of hers have stood by her when our brother and our sister-in-law felt she ought to be married," she said. "Our own lives were spoilt: and we are very willing that she should teach instead of marry. The only remedy is for girls to make their parents require at their betrothals that their future husbands shall take no concubines. That is what Blossom is doing in our name."

Which brings me to Miss Way and Miss Lo—Blossom being Miss Lo in academic circles. A Manchu woman, Miss Chi, the friend of a friend of mine, Miss Bowden-Smith, was the founder and first principal of their school. During the Revolution of 1911, she had been so sure that China was rushing to destruction because of its neglect of Confucius, that she had wished to commit suicide in a public manner in order to draw her country's attention to the Sage. Miss Bowden-Smith had been largely instrumental in preventing this catastrophe : and Miss Chi had, instead, lived to give her school-girls a good foundation in the Classics. The school had increased. To-day there are two hundred on the roll, though attendance is not always regular. It is carried on, week-days and Sundays alike, Chinese fashion, from morning to dusk. But Miss Lo and Miss Way are beginning to find a Saturday afternoon, after the manner of the government schools of the new foreign order, a pleasant interlude for all concerned.

The object of the school is education—not profit. The school fees are microscopic : a dollar per girl per month. The result is that Miss Way, the principal, has occasionally to supplement from her own small personal property, left her by her father in lieu of the dowry which she has never claimed. Her father was head official at the Palace, in charge of the tribute rice which used to be sent in barges from South and Central China up China's wonderful canal system. Miss Way is pure Chinese : Miss Lo is Manchu—which is as if one said, the one is English, the other Scotch ; or the one American, the other Canadian.

Miss Lo—Blossom—is Miss Way's right hand on the staff. For ten years now, like Miss Way, she has given her services free : but the rest of the staff are paid at current rates. Not only do the pupils pay so little : the school supports another, attached to it, for poor children who pay nothing. The elder girls eke out the teaching in this school, the staff of the parent establishment give their services free, the richer pupils bring clothes, and others contribute in kind.

" Our children are having their playtime," they say with an indulgent air, when the ragamuffins in the adjacent court are vociferating and rushing about in a manner which Miss Way's own " young ladies " would scorn.

I had told Mrs. Sung of my two friends. " Ask them if I may come with you one day and see their work," she had demanded. " I should like to see the Chinese women you think of so highly."

She was charmed with the school and full of admiration for

my friends. The two features of the institution which inflamed her ardour most were the girls' manners—of the old style—and their Chinese exercises. Trained herself mainly in America, or in an American-run school in Shanghai with its enviable endowment of apparatus, she told me that her great regret, educationally, was her lack of any genuine knowledge of her own literature. Not that she was ignorant, as, alas, many are : her father had provided his daughters with a Chinese tutor as well as his sons. But Miss Way's school, divorced from foreign influence—which Miss Way regrets—maintains the high standard in Chinese exercises of fifty years ago, set by Miss Chi and her fathers before her. In fact, when Mrs. Sung went away, she bore a large bundle of the girls' Chinese exercises under her arm, to show her husband and father.

" If Yün-Yün and Nieh-Nieh do half as well as these girls in their classics, I shall be content," she said : " and it is almost time for them to begin—my babies."

A great statesman, Chao Erh Fang, once Viceroy of the province of Szechwan, a friend of Miss Lo's father, was their school patron, and distinguished guest. An amiable and polished old gentleman, he yet used a certain strictness in examining the girls at their annual recitations. The last few years, being paralysed, he had been of no practical use to the school. But his name awed the vulgar ; his photograph, prominent in the guest-hall, gave a blessing to the establishment ; and the tradition of his high learning set a criterion. Alas, since then, he has died. He had been Viceroy of Manchuria also, and had stood sponsor for Chang Tso Lin when he was seeking pardon for his outlawry. The great Dictator of Manchuria, now himself dead—bombed as he was leaving Peking, a beaten man—did not forget his old patron. In the midst of his turmoils, he went personally to bow before his coffin, and he gave the old statesman a statesman's funeral, which is to his honour.

If the standard of Chinese is high in the school, what of the rest of the curriculum ? In the days of the school's beginnings, this did not exist. The classics came first, last, and altogether : as sufficient in themselves for education as in the scholastic days of mediæval Europe. But the two ladies have other ideals. Their girls are mostly of their own class, daughters of the Chinese and Manchus living near, with some moderate means. Such families have enough to do these days to keep things going: the future is very insecure in the chaotic new republic. They cannot spend much on that luxury, desirable, no doubt, of their daughters' education. But Miss Way and Miss Lo want their pupils to have at least a share in the wider horizons of Modern China. Ambitious they are for their girls. They hope enlargement will bring wiser judgment, a steadier poise, more finely-developed minds and heart—the something which changes iron into steel. Then, in the day of pain and trial, there is that within the soul which remains indestructible and bright; in the day of loneliness, there is fortitude and self-dependence. They said something of this to me. It was beyond my power of Chinese speech to quote them the chapter of Proverbs which leapt to my mind.

> "She is not afraid of the snow for her household;
> For all her household are clothed with scarlet."

That was how these two steadfast women wanted to send out the daughters of China who were in their charge—clothed with beauty and usefulness against all the snows of winter which would surely come upon them sooner or later. And having no other Tyrian dye at hand, they clothed them with the wisdom of Confucius.

Somehow they had contrived to extend the curriculum. Blossom, the shyest speaker of English in the world to an English person, taught English grammar with accuracy. One never-to-be-forgotten year, she told me, an English girl came to work in the Y.W.C.A. in Peking. "She came to our school, and she taught English twice a week—and for nothing! For love, not pay—just like ourselves," she said, pink at the remembrance. For Blossom blushes with any excitement. "But she got married and went away. The Y.W.C.A. girls keep on getting married; so that there are always fresh helpers, and now we do not know any of them."

Beautiful drawings we were shown, too: and again Mrs. Sung accepted a handful, to Miss Way's amusement. "Does nobody draw in Shanghai?" she asked. "There is nowhere any school quite like this," replied Mrs. Sung. "I am so happy that you are old-fashioned!"

"But we are not old-fashioned altogether," Miss Way demurred, bridling. She brought forward more drawings of flowers this time, dissected. Sepals, petals, stamens were correctly named: there was a butterfly, a bee, carrying off pollen. Next came a series of chemical drawings: of retorts, gas-jets and boiling flasks, with gases issuing therefrom: and legends beneath of the experiment. Startled, delighted, I asked Miss Way who was the teacher in botany and chemistry and where were their laboratories.

"We have no teacher," she sighed. "Where could we find one—even if we could pay her? No; the girls copy the experiments and drawings out of the Commercial Press Primers."

The Commercial Press is a mighty institution, the biggest printing-press in Asia: and at Shanghai it keeps a staff of Chinese editors translating school texts, sending out education in Chinese form to Chinese schools as best they can. It reminds one of Victorian times when the earnest learned chemistry and optics by post. Pathetic? Yet it was by such Spartan methods that Fabre learned algebra and trigonometry. Take up Turgeniev's *Fathers and Children*, and you will find the intellectuals of his novel offering each other a book on Chemical Experiments for private reading. It was certainly to the good that Miss Way's girls should know that there are such aspects of Nature in the world as we tabulate into botany and chemistry; that the earth is larger than what can be seen while walking from one courtyard to another in Peking—if only by book-lore.

Very exacting were those two schoolmistresses regarding manners: and their pupils seemed to acquiesce willingly. In accordance with modern notions, they ran into the large courtyard for recreation. But their demeanour when a teacher or visitor appeared was truly deferential. Mrs. Sung's praises grew louder with every step. Myself, I do not disapprove of a modest bearing in the young towards their elders. Deference to whom deference is due. But we both jumped while we were sitting listening to Blossom at an English class. She suddenly rapped with a ruler on her desk in a most ferocious way, scowling like Dr. Busby at a wrong parsing. The idea of the mandarin banging his baton on the table, with the culprit kneeling in the hall of justice before him, still permeated that class-room. Blossom Lo, off her dais, is, in ordinary life, slight, pale, hesitant, young-looking for her years, with an appealing face: a fragile flower, in short. With an English exercise before her, she is Boadicea.

Miss Way is a woman of eight and thirty. She is a tall, shapely, generously-made woman, with a comfortable yet tricksy smile and a rosy glow of good health in her cheek. She lives in the same well-ordered patriarchal home as her brother with his wife and children, her mother being alive and the head of the family.

"My mother is resigned by now, also my brother, to my refusing to be married," she explained.

Miss Lo is in a different plight. Her brother's wife has become a little *difficile*. Custom keeps her confined to her courtyards most of her time: and this is trying to any temper. She disapproves of and nags Blossom—"jang" is the short expressive Chinese word—for her school-teaching fads.

"You ought to have been married like every other reasonable woman," she scolds, all with the best intentions.

Blossom is entitled to her share of her father's estate with her brother, in lieu of dowry. She might with it have even fulfilled her dream of coming to a woman's college abroad. But her brother, who is the trustee of the money, followed the advice of some cousins and joined with them in putting the family funds into a new pawnbroker's establishment near Tientsin. The Mont-de-Piété has always been a most strictly respectable and the safest investment for Chinese gentlepeople in the past, like government stock in foreign lands. But, on account of the recent troubles, pawnbroking in China has ceased to be what it was during the dynasties. The first place which the unruly loot are the pawnshops of a city. These are strongly built and surrounded by high and impregnable walls, like small forts. Alack, the West has sent rifles across to the East; and a looting soldier or bandit now blows the locks of the gates open with shot and shell. Blossom's brother had invested all the family money thus, without asking her—which was not etiquette, for he is the younger. For the sake of peace, however, she preserves silence in financial matters and tries to avoid any discussion of them. One seems to remember similar embarrassments in non-Chinese families. Moreover, a perturbed sister-in-law, when one is obliged to share her roof, is more agitating than any lack of money, thinks Blossom.

Miss Way understands. She and Blossom love each other dearly, engrossingly. As my mother was not very well and could not go to see them, they came to see us now and again, to take tea. One day they commented on a new dress of mine. So I expressed my admiration of a charming thin tunic which Blossom was wearing of lavender silk.

" Miss Way gave it me," she said at once. She raised her eyes to Miss Way, as might a younger sister to an older.

" She does look so pretty in pretty clothes, does she not ? " asked Miss Way, who smiled maternally down from her height upon her.

True friendship, that : the one loved to give, the other to take. Damon and Pythias ! So struck was I by their pleasure in each other's company that I led them across the paved court of the Chinese house, in which we were staying with Western friends. Up I pulled the heavy-weighted hanging rush-screen which fell over the doorway, after the manner of the East, to let in the air but keep out the heat. We went into my darkened bedroom—a Chinese room with pleasing rough pillars holding up the roof, the walls papered with white in Chinese style. In the bedroom there hung Calderon's picture of Ruth and Naomi standing at the parting of the Judean roads, with a servant watching. Ruth, the younger, is saying, " Entreat me not to leave thee."

The two women listened while I told the story and tried to turn the lovely words into Chinese. Then Miss Way put her arms round Blossom, and said, " We also will never part from each other."

" Show our English sister your arm," said Blossom.

Miss Way thereupon smiled upon her again and pulled up the sleeve of her best party tunic. There, at the top of her moulded arm, where a woman of the West may show vaccination marks, was a big patch of tiny scars.

I was taken aback. Surely, surely . . . Miss Way ? Oh, no, she could never be a morphia addict : always a possibility amongst Chinese ladies. Another old acquaintance of mine had appalled me by the thinness of her arms, her sagging skin ; yet her eyes, so dead and sombre one day, would be replaced by brilliance the next. I had spoken in alarm about her looks to Mrs. Sung, who also knew her, wondering if some grave disease threatened, which had made of her a strange and unaccountable woman. Mrs. Sung had looked a little queerly at me, but had expressed no sympathy, which seemed to me unkind at the time. I cannot tell how it was : but suddenly, on seeing those ghastly spikes of arms one day, the truth flashed on me. Opium ! Nothing else could produce that lifeless skin, those alternating bursts of depression and amazing energy. But Mrs. Sung, with Chinese loyalty, would not speak of it till I spoke first.

" I thought you never would guess ! " was her comment when I suddenly thrust my suspicion at her.

Here, now, was Miss Lo's arm patched with pricks. What fresh story of human psychology was Peking going to produce ? Never could it be opium or morphia ; for that woman looked at me, straight of gaze and noble of bearing. It is usually ill-health, pain, or sorrow which first drive a man or woman to the drug in a country where medical aid is as yet unscientific, where toothache, dysentery and malaria rage, and opium eases pain for the time being. There is, too, boredom : a very insinuating disease, and the opium pipe cures that—also for the time being. Shut in their courts, Chinese women with vitality and intelligence have too little outlet for their powers. The tempter in the occasional pipe becomes the fiend which drags them daily and hourly down to a world of shadow and final despair.

Blossom Lo began to speak. She looked upon that patch of pinpricks in her friend's arm with a look of adoration.

" They were all for me," she said, love shining and trembling from her as from a star.

She made Miss Way, ever the more energetic spokeswoman of the two, tell the tale. It seems that Blossom, two or three years ago, became " very low in her mind." She was having a particularly difficult time with Sister-in-law. " Myself, I would never meekly endure being scolded for my vocation," affirmed Miss Way: "but Blossom, here, cannot stand up for herself at all. She wilts, like a flower, and becomes ill."

Once again, physiologically I cannot tell what ailed Blossom. It is very difficult to diagnose a disease from Chinese descriptions of past symptoms. Her stomach did not swell and swell. But she grew weaker and weaker, paler and paler, and more listless. One day, when she failed to come to school, Miss Way went to seek her, made her way quietly to Blossom's inner courtyard, opened the latticed papered door, and found her unconscious on her bed: and alone. Thereupon she poured forth the vials of her wrath—to excellent effect. Blossom's brother has real affection for his sister, and is innocent of anything but good-natured ignorance. He at once fetched the Chinese doctor demanded by Miss Way.

"Chinese doctors are very good for some diseases," Blossom here interposed timidly in my direction, knowing that I should have preferred a gentleman trained in a foreign hospital. This doctor reached the same conclusion as the rest of the assembled group about the bed: that Blossom was near death.

"Is there nothing that can save her?" asked Miss Way, in deep grief. Sister-in-law too was alarmed and shocked. Indeed, she has been much gentler since this illness of Blossom's.

"There is one chance," admitted the doctor, and said that if some one gave her fresh pure human blood to drink every few hours, she might rally.

Hence those pinpricks on Miss Lo's shapely arm. Three and thirty times had blood been drawn to the extent of a Chinese wine-glass each time—the size of our liqueur glasses—and administered to her friend. At first, it had been hard to make the unconscious girl swallow. But in the end she had revived—thanks to Miss Way's blood, of course. She had not known what her medicine was till she was better. Then you can imagine her feelings towards the woman who had loved her so generously.

"I actually have her blood in my veins," Blossom almost sang it.

" She is part of me," said Miss Way in antiphony.

They intertwined arms, and then Blossom put her arms up to Miss Way's shoulder.

" Like that picture," she explained. " What were their names ? "

" Ruth and Naomi," I said.

By permission of Mrs. Calhoun, formerly of the U.S. Legation, Peking

A group of Manchu Princes and Princesses in the modern setting of Peking at a lunch-party given by an American lady

CHAPTER XXIII A PRINCESS MAY HOLD VIEWS

I SAW little of Mrs. Sung in Peking, and was glad to think we should meet again at Peitaiho : for she told me she had secured a house there, when we met at a mah-jong party given by a particularly charming American woman of taste and discrimination. This lady has leased a deserted temple, put central heating along its latticed passage-ways, and furnished the broad niches, where once the gods stood, with hanging tapestries and divans covered with brocades. A delightful home she has made of her temple : the only approach to the glories of the silken East—alas, so often a matter of the literary imagination—I ever experienced. Under a huge elm tree in the open sunny paved court a few select Manchu princesses and Chinese ladies of high degree, in elegant and decorative attire, sat at polished tables, and with slender, dexterous fingers arranged their miniature ramparts of ivory and bamboo tallies for the fray.

Mah-jong requires an afternoon's leisure. I was due elsewhere before tea, so I did not sit down but wandered from table to table ; lingering to wish Mrs. Sung good luck, which she said she needed, as she was not a frequent player and she had fallen into a regular nest of mah-jong experts.

An elderly princess called me to stand by her side and bring her luck too. She put down her long cigarette-holder on the edge of the table, to tell me it was a sad pity for me that she had not taken in hand my education in mah-jong. We could have gone partners together and wiped the board with the other people.

We had sat next to each other at the tiffin preceding the mah-jong. She was a little older than on my last Peking visit, but full of verve. Our hostess had, at the moment, no other foreign guest present who could utter even the few words of Chinese which had clung to my brain during my years of absence from the beloved country. Moreover, the Princess had asked who else was coming when she accepted the tiffin invitation, and had been pleased to express approval of the renewal of her acquaintance with myself. Had we not sat, long ago, holding hands—not sentimentally, believe me, but so that she might emphasize her points better by tapping me with a finger—while she gave me her views on women's education ? She gave a short " Ha ! " when I appeared this time on her horizon. " I heard you were in our unworthy country again," she said, " and guessed you would presently be arriving in this neighbourhood."

At the table, she naturally sat in the place of honour at our hostess' right hand.

" Now then," she asked, " what is there to eat ? " She plucked the menu from the table and handed it me. I began to read it, and thought I had better explain some of its gallicisms. She took it from me and laid it down.

" Never mind, never mind," she stopped me : " I always enjoy my tiffin here,"—and truly our hostess was noted for her cuisine, and rightly so.

" Well, I thought——" I began.

She turned to me, clicked her tongue, folded her hands well under her abdomen, settled that comfortably for herself, told me without mincing her speech about an internal trouble, added that there was nothing to be done about it so she might as well pay it the least possible attention, and ended :

" I suppose they have put you next to me because they imagine you can talk Chinese ! " At this she guffawed : I politely and ruefully smiled. " However, I see there is nobody else who can, so I 'll have to make the best of you. But there, I am very glad to see you ! First, though, let me say, I am going to do all the talking. You just listen. See ? "

" Good ! Good ! " I began.

" Chut ! " she hissed. " I do all the talking, I tell you ! "

As one may guess, I was enchanted. Here was the fine-flavoured vintage of my youth, a China in which no younger woman ventured opinions when there was an older present to tell her what to think. The Princess talked, as she promised. Many of her remarks I did not understand, which caused her much amusement. I had to concentrate all my attention to follow her very rapid and colloquial speech, not to mention her unexpected turns of thought. I would not surrender, or say I did not understand. She would suddenly shoot a question at me. Sometimes I had not the faintest idea what she was asking me. For a fraction I would hesitate whether to ask her to repeat her phrases : but I had done this once or twice, and plainly she did not like it. She told me I had grown stupid in my absence from China and her tutelage. Several times I hedged, nodded my head and said with great and assumed energy, " Pu ts'o, pu ts'o—you are right, you are right ! " This is a polite phrase and, cunningly used, is excellent camouflage. It can mean anything or nothing. Presently, my attention for a second was distracted elsewhere, I was giving her half an ear : and she chose that instant to fire off something extra fast and furious. Then she awaited my response. The keen old eyes, the rather hooked nose—as far as Chinese noses go—were fixed on me. I felt like a lamb—or a silly bleating sheep—face to face with an eagle. She waited, with a ghost of a smile. " No, I don't think so," I plunged, about as senselessly as that sheep would blether : and hastily offered her some salted almonds.

She thumped the table with her wrinkled jewelled hand. She let out a great cackle of laughter. Then she pounced.

" No, I don't think so ! " she mimicked. " What sort of an answer, pray, is that, to all I have been saying ? You fraud ! " She shook her finger under my nose. " You did not understand a word of what I was saying, did you ? "

I laughed.

" You foreigners ! " she exclaimed. " My goodness ! You are a set of innocents. Fancy imagining you can deceive us ! "

This time I smiled within myself : for I had been marvelling that she had not found me out long before.

" But, there, I daresay you can beguile the fools we have now in the government," she went on. " Clever lot they think themselves ! Clever ! " She scorned them. " A set of jumped-up jacks-in-office ! "

As quickly, she hushed. " Oh now, what have I been and said ! K'o liao pu te ! There are one or two wives of those same people present. I 'd better be quiet."

She then muttered long and fast in my ear. She was not

going to be cheated out of finishing what she had to say in this particular.

"Not that any of the wives here would mind my remarks," she ended in gruff *sotto voce*, shooting out her lower lip. "They are decently bred women enough, though their fathers were not the sort we used to see as viceroys exactly. Reformers they called themselves, because they had not had much classical education! However, they were a very different set from the revolutionaries of to-day. These women, well, they have been abroad and learned foreign languages and know how to comport themselves. They rather value meeting us of the old social classes, you know."

She as near as winked an eye at me as possible: she nudged me.

"As for their husbands, every wife knows best what she has to put up with in that way. Best not to rub it in too much. I expect they don't find things easy. I should not like to have a husband a politician nowadays. Anyhow, with the Northerners after their blood on one side, and Communists on the other, life can't be dull. Why! There was one minister of state had to flee to Tientsin dressed in a woman's clothes, they told me."

"Some of the modern wives are happy, all right," I interjected, for Mrs. Sung's eye from the end of the table had caught mine. She raised her eyebrow saucily towards the Princess and then smiled knowingly at me. The Princess was famed for her conversational candour.

"What did I tell you?" asked the Princess vigorously. "No talking on your part. I do it all."

"Speak, I beg," I bleated.

"Do you remember when we met in Tientsin after the Revolution?" she resumed. Indeed I did. "It was the morning I had betrothed my third daughter. You called: and you were brought by the wife of Kung Ta Jen, who was so famous a scholar. Now, there is a fine woman for you—she was almost as pleased as myself over the business. And what manners! Young people nowadays simply don't know what manners are." She bent double to laugh, and settled herself easefully once more into her chair. "She called me her aunt, and I told her she must be my great-aunt. Now you may speak and tell me where she is and how she is."

Both Kung T'ai T'ai and the Princess had lost their husbands ; but, though I knew Aunt Kung would always feel the loss, I fear the Princess took hers philosophically. When I mumbled my sympathy, she replied with a click of her tongue and with equanimity, " Well ! Well ! These things have to happen ! "

" And is Third Princess-Daughter well and happy ? " I asked.

" It has been quite a success, that marriage," she confided. " She has two children : and that is plenty in these days. I had six—but I was a fool." She cackled again over this. " Most women are fools—and men, too," she added : " but, as a rule, I am not. Really, sometimes, looking round on my acquaintances, I think I am the only person I know who is not a fool."

I was convulsed. Most people are of this opinion at some period in their life : but few proclaim it.

I was sorry when tiffin ended and the real business of life, mah-jong, began. The Princess won the first game as I stood watching : which was pleasant. I was slipping away, but she beckoned me back, to say that my mother and I must go and see her. She was so deeply engaged, and so were we, that it ended in a fixture for me, without my mother, at half-past nine next morning ! However, as I reminded her, that was her favourite hour for receiving me.

" I shall have my hair done by then," she promised me. It was flattering that she should consider me a suitable person to be thus admitted to toilette intimacy. It was also a trifle crushing. In her eyes, I was of the younger generation and to be disposed of accordingly.

When I had last seen her, she was living in a small house in Tientsin, tucked behind an intricate maze of dwellings. The dear old woman—for so she is—had now discovered once more for herself a hidden-away cottage dwelling, in the Legation Quarter in Peking, this seclusion in cottages being her mania since the dynasty fell. It was one of what was originally a row of soldiers' houses. The officers' quarters were occupied by people of far less blue blood than herself.

" Compradores ! Bank compradores ! " she chuckled to

me, as she pointed the fact out. " They pay twice what I pay. Ha, ha ! "

I told her the smart thing in London amongst the New Poor was to live in a mews. I was almost sorry I said it : she at once began to look thoughtful. If I go back to Peking, I am certain to find her living in a coach-house. Is she very poor ? Is she at bottom well off ? I have no idea. Some say one thing : some another. The only way to know would be to ask her direct : and, even if I had had the impertinence, would any one suppose for a moment that she would tell me the truth ? Why should she ? And how delighted she would be to puzzle me !

The Princess came out to meet me next morning, which was polite on her part. Her hair was dressed : in the neat knot on the top affected by the Manchus—not unlike the Frenchwoman's fashion. She had a red flower in it.

" No time to rouge my cheeks," she began.

She was seventy-three, she told me soon. " Who would think it ? " I exclaimed. " Your hair is perfectly black ! You have not as many grey hairs as I have. My mother's hair is snow-white."

She snorted. " Huh ! And so would mine be if I did not put a little something on to disguise it. What do you think ? You don't suppose my hair is black at my age ? Of course not ! "

But she would say no more. She hitched her shoulders and giggled mockingly. The disguising was done very well. Every hair appeared as shining black as if in her youth, and to its roots. She pretended not to understand when I asked what her recipe was, and marched into her dwelling, laughing to herself.

It must have been the orderlies' room that she was using as her house-place. A very long room, parts of it were screened off by Japanese screens, some very cheap, others very magnificent. A sound of washing in an enamel basin came from behind one screen.

" That 's my daughter," she informed me ; " she has been dressing my hair for me. I expect she has done her own now." She whispered. " It is my eldest daughter. Most unfortunate business. Her husband was no use at all : a real bad lot. Life became unbearable for her. At last I told her she had better come back home to me and finish with him. I have enough for her to share. And she had no sons. I had my doubts about the marriage, after I had a glimpse at him : but there seemed nobody else at the time suitable, and with five daughters one can't afford to be too particular." She dug me in the ribs. " But you know all about that, eh ? You knew the Lo girls, I remember. Their mother was too soft-hearted for anything ; I always said she was stupid. Oh, she was a friend of yours, and so you won't hear anything against her ! Well, look at the nice mess those girls' lives have been. And there is one, the youngest, refuses to marry, they tell me. What is the world coming to ? She goes about doing good works, they say : teaching the poor. That is a nice state of things. Then take this son-in-law of mine. He is one of those men who look like prawns, you know : protruding eyes,"—she goggled her eyes at me in exhibition, and I smiled. " But, as my husband said at the time, you can't always judge a man by his looks. His younger sister's husband, he said, had just the same sort of face—like a prawn : protruding moustaches too, he had. For all that, he was able to govern a province and put down a rebellion."

" So she came back to you ? " I queried.

" Yes, and at the bottom a great comfort it is. Truly it is better to have your daughter living with you than your daughter-in-law, who is half terrified of you and laughs at the wrong places. I have packed mine off with her husband to live in the old house : and it is quite a relief. But about my daughter, I tell her, even if I had been married to a prawn, I would have managed him somehow."

" Made curry of him," I suggested, but found it impossible to translate my small joke.

" These modern girls," she said, " are too soft. That is the matter with them. I would not have stood half what she stood. I would have let him know what I thought of him and pretty well scared him out of his evil ways. But you will see her in a minute, and her daughter—my grand-daughter."

At that moment the grand-daughter came—with the Princess' cigarette. She fitted it into the long holder, put it into her grandmother's mouth and applied a match. I could hardly take my eyes off her : she was so pretty. There was such a bantering gaiety in her eyes. As the elder lady talked, the girl—who was perhaps fifteen—gave little spurts of laughter at her grandmother's outrageous persiflage, and shot sidelong mirthful glances at me. Her duty was to shake the ash off her grandmother's cigarette, take out the stump and replace it with a fresh cigarette when wanted : listen to her elders and betters, and profit by their remarks on life. She went out to see about the visitor's tea. The Princess bent towards me, shot out her lips, darted her hawk eye on me, and whispered : "You keep looking at her, I notice. Do you think she is passable in appearance ?"

"She is lovely : a fairy : bewitching," I replied, with whole-hearted fervour. The girl, with her oval face, round chin, clear complexion, the natural rose-leaf bloom on her cheeks, her gay eyes and laughing mouth, was a picture She carried herself well : was as slender as a willow wand : as sure and easy in her motions as a silver minnow. The fish simile came to my mind, for the Princess demanded :

"No trace of a prawn ancestry, eh ?"

"None," I agreed heartily. "But you know very well that everybody must think her lovely. Your daughters are renowned." This was true, for two or three of them were famous beauties. "Their children ought to have fair looks."

"Ah ! You are uttering 'good words, good words,' for politeness' sake !" quoth she, insincerely—as we both knew. She wrinkled her nose at me, her jaded palate tickled by my appreciation. "They are not too bad, perhaps—my girls and their daughters. I do not know if it is from their father or from me they inherit their appearance." I ought to have replied that it was she : but honesty compels me to admit that neither she nor their dead father had half their beauty—though possibly she had double their wits, which could not have been said about him, though he was a good enough man.

I asked if the young lady spoke any foreign language. Alack, she did not. She had had some sketchy teaching in Chinese : and that was the extent of her book education. I tried to argue the point with the Princess.

"What is the use ?" she asked. "She will have to be married in four or five years, and to a Manchu : and you know how stupid and unlearned our Manchu men are. She had much better learn from me how to manage people than to read books, English or Chinese."

The girl came back; also her mother, who had by now finished her toilette. We sat and talked of old times. The Princess said she scarcely ever went to the British Legation now, as she did in the days of Sir John and Lady Jordan. "I am invited to the big functions, of course," she said; "but you know how I used to go and sit with Sir John and tell him what I thought ought to be done in the country, and he would argue with me because he knew I was worth arguing with: and I would tell him what the Empress Dowager, Tzŭ Hsi, would have done about things. We should never have come to this pass if she had been alive. I told him much he was glad to know. That is the way to be a successful diplomat, I say: listen to the people who can tell you things. And every one admits women know more about other people than men do."

She drew her chair close to mine. She leaned forward and tapped my knee with her cigarette-holder. She ejected some undesired tobacco juice into a handy vase on the floor.

"Tell me," she peered into my face, "tell me what this Commission of yours is going to do about this Boxer money?" I was taken aback. Through the whole of China never one single woman had asked such a question or taken the least interest in it except Miss Wu of Nanking, the earnest fighter for women's education. Not one! And here was this keen old Princess out to pump me. And for no purpose except that, like my mother, every mortal thing on earth was of interest to her. *Humani nihil a me alienum puto* is a good working motto for a princess in Peking as well as for a poet in ancient Rome. Moreover, this woman had been used to talking with men who were administrators of big affairs under the dynasty, and she missed the beneficial friction of wit rubbing against wit.

"It is not decided yet," I said, truthfully. "Anyhow, the Commission has nothing to do with me--nothing at all."

She nodded her head half a dozen times: she pulled down those expressive lips. "You won't tell me," she sniffed. "Oh, highly cautious you are!"

"I speak the truth ; I vow it," I declared heatedly.

"Tell that to others, but not to me," she jeered. "Is not your father on the Commission ? Are you not his daughter ? Does not a daughter know what her father is thinking, whatever he says to the outside world—and even if he does not tell her ? Of course she knows. Come, now ! Tell me. What harm can it do for me to know ?"

I must give her a few crumbs of such discreet knowledge as I had—for sheer charity.

"You are aware," I said ponderously, "as is every one, that there are railways and schools needed in China, and farmers ought to be given scientific help. The difficulty is to decide which most needs help. My father and the others are seeking advice and opinion. Now how would you spend it ?"

She was mollified.

"I ! Do you really ask my opinion ?" She tapped herself on her nose, as do the Chinese to indicate themselves, instead of the chest, as we do. I assured her I should be much profited by garnering her ideas as to her country's needs : and would pass them on to the proper quarters.

"Let me think !" she said, leaning her elbow on the table and waving cigarette smoke out of her eyes.

"This takes some cogitation," she pondered. "However, you have come to one of the few Elders left with sense. Did I not tell you just now that nearly all the people with any brains are dead ? The old Empress would have thought out a fine scheme. I am capable of it too—but, eh, I suppose I am getting old. I don't know any other Chinese woman who could do it, though."

She ran her mind through her acquaintance and decided against them all with a shake of her head.

"I 'll tell you how I would use the money," she announced presently. "I would start large manufactures, and help existing ones. I would put every cash into keeping our poor people employed. Supposing I had not enough to eat, what would I do ? I would join the nearest army, of course ! If I did not receive pay, I would loot—just as they do. If still that was not sufficient, I would turn bandit. What else can happen ?"

"What about education ?" I ventured.

"Education!" she shrieked. "Not a cent for it! It is no earthly use."

"You did not talk like that to me twenty years ago," I charged her. "And I do not approve of your bringing up your clever grand-daughter an ignoramus either."

"Meaning my brain is softening, now I 'm becoming old, eh?" she riposted. "If the schools were good schools, it would be a different matter. I told the Regent, years before the Revolution, that it was a mistake suddenly opening dozens of schools. They could not possibly all be efficient. There were too few teachers trained in the new-fangled ways. 'Better two good schools than ten bad ones,' I warned him."

But gradually she allowed there might be some value in establishments which trained doctors and nurses: then she permitted a few for railway, mining and industrial engineering; and finally bridge and canal builders. Her most urgent point was that there should be some women to help take charge of so much money.

"Chinese women, I suppose?" I queried, my ears attuned to nationalistic slogans—though not from her lips.

"Certainly not!" she snapped. "Foreign women, of course. Foreign women are trained to use their intelligence. It is true that we women in China have always had charge of home finances, and very well we manage them on the whole. But now that the Empress is dead and I am old, I know no Chinese women capable of dealing with big masses of people and large sums of money. They could manage small sums: but the huge ones would frighten them. Foreign women have been trained to this sort of thing. Naturally any woman can make a dollar go twice as far as any man: so it must not all be left to men. We know their extravagant ways! A woman gets much more value for her money any day, does she not?"

When I informed this very practical and Oriental exponent of a feminism old as the first cave-dwelling, that there was a woman on the Commission—Dame Adelaide Anderson—she slapped first her own thigh, then mine, in her satisfaction. She insisted on a short biography of Dame Adelaide: how she had worked all her life for the betterment of conditions for women and young people in English factories. How, for instance, laundry women used sometimes to catch their hands in machinery, and lose them, till she thought out a way to prevent such accidents. And finally, how our King had given her a Name of Honour to show people that the whole country esteemed such service.

" Good ! Exceedingly good ! " ejaculated the Princess : and drank off her tea with enthusiastic suction.

This final drinking being a sign in Chinese manner that an interview may now be considered as drawing to its close, we parted, with mutual protestations of having enjoyed each other's company. I hope they were as genuine on her part as mine. She said that at any rate I had listened to her and laughed almost as discerningly as her daughter !

Once again we met. But it is true what she had said, that no longer the gambit of her old social circle coincides as closely as formerly with that of the modern foreigner in Peking. It is too easy to find interesting Chinese who speak English to make any Occidentals but the few seek out those who only speak their own tongue.

She came, unexpectedly, one evening, shortly before we left Peking. She brought presents which we were to take back to England for her, to her old friend, Lady Jordan—Chu T'ai T'ai. She had been delayed at a mah-jong party ; and she wished to goodness she had left earlier, for she had lost thirty-seven dollars and had had atrocious luck.

It happened that a number of other people had also chosen that afternoon to call on us, so that the drawing-room was full. The Princess delivered her parcels, then stood up suddenly, dramatically. She beckoned my mother and myself, waved to the others to stay where they were, and led us out, down the three steps of the brick parapet on which the single-storey house was built, to the court below with its beds of carefully tended nasturtiums. She pulled us close to her, dived into the front of her long satin gown, and brought out two little packages.

" That is for you," she whispered surreptitiously to my mother, " and this small worthless object is for my niece there,"—indicating me. Then she tried to slip back : but we caught her gown while we thanked her and opened the wrappings. To my mother she had given an agate ornament, translucent and fine, carved into a lucky figure and smooth with age. For me was a lump of green tourmaline with a small fastener of seed pearls : not very valuable, perhaps, but it has given me much pleasure. When we protested, she answered :

" The first, the agate, was my mother's, and the other piece I had when I was a girl." She gave a last guffaw. " So we have had them long enough in our house. It is time somebody else had a turn at them ! "

Of course, we sent her a present in return : the most elegant foreign bag we could lay our hands on : of a sort of black plush material, with an oxidized clasp, suitable, we hoped, for elderly princesses anywhere.

" For your mah-jong parties," we wrote on the cards accompanying it. From our hearts we wished her good luck. It is not every aristocrat who faces the new conditions with her spirit and intelligence.

ONE day Blossom's family invited us to accompany them to visit the Winter Palace, the erstwhile Forbidden City being now open to the public on payment of a small coin at the entrance.

Our party came unexpectedly on Mrs. Sung at the edge of the lake where, on hot summer days, empresses were rowed in their "flower-boats," with their ladies-in-waiting enjoying the fresh air beside them. Mrs. Sung and I left our respective parties and took a few steps towards each other. She was with the relatives-in-law at whose house she was staying in the metropolis. The lady of the party was the smart and sophisticated wife of a modern Chinese diplomat. A wealthy woman, she always wore, either as bracelet or pendant or ear-drop, some perfect, exquisite piece of jade, as translucent as an emerald and more costly. She had created for herself a distinctive dress which combined attractively and cleverly both Eastern and Western fashions. She had lived a cosmopolitan life, in New York, Paris, London, Brussels. Her husband had moved most of his days in similar surroundings. He was dressed that afternoon in the morning coat and striped trousers of the Occident. He wore white spats on his feet and an impeccable top-hat on his head, for they were going later to a garden party. Both he and his wife had far closer affinities with the American and European sojourners in Peking than with the ordinary Chinese folk rambling in the Palace grounds for an afternoon's festa. It was to their credit that they had returned to live in their Ancient Motherland, that they were trying to do their duty by her and working for her interests, as they conceived them.

He was of a school still Oriental enough, despite his outer appearance, to think of diplomacy as primarily the deceiving of other nations. This school is apt to try the patience of the older trained diplomats of the West who regard such methods as being of the world's childhood, beneath the notice of grown men and nations. The modern pro-consul, sighing over his typewriter, wonders how he can bring home the innate profitableness of candour without wounding very tender susceptibilities and engendering further suspicion. Nevertheless he usually ends with personal liking for these younger pupils in his profession.

" At bottom they mean well," he will comment. " It is true that they have much at stake—though no more than others, I suppose. But their responsibilities have come on them suddenly. They feel they have to watch very carefully every one else's step as well as their own."

Mrs. Sung's diplomatic friends sat on chairs near the lake edge, and waved to me. Blossom turned, saw my companion, and came back to greet her blithely.

" All Peking is taking pleasure to-day ! " she smiled.

" Look ! " I said. " And that is very real pleasure." I pointed to the scene in front of us.

Half the lake was covered with lotus in full pink flower, exceedingly lovely. The blooms stood up on strong stems from amongst their large floating leaves. No wonder that in Buddhist sutras the adored Buddha sits on a lotus throne while lotus flowers rain from the air. To our eyes, however, even more delightful was the spectacle of a number of rowing-boats on that once-forbidden imperial lake. In the boats sat modern Chinese young men and maidens. Blossom waved her hand at one boat where a girl was the rower.

" She came to our school for a time," she explained. " That is her brother with her. She is a medical student now. Oh, is it not good to see them out together like this ? "

The girl was not adept with the oars. The lifting of her hand in response to Blossom's upset her manipulations. She ran her craft into the half of the lake preserved for the lotus. Her bow and rudder-lines were entangled in the long stems. Her brother and she laughed, pushing away the leaves and tentacles with the boat-hook. Another boat with two other students, young men, went to their aid.

In the East India Company days in Canton, not much more than a century ago, one of the complaints of the Chinese gentry against the British young men of the time was that they rowed in boats against each other. Such proceedings were very undignified, vulgar, and intolerable in a civilized country like China. Physical prowess was not an attribute of the gentleman in the long gown, or the upper classes. To row and perspire in a public place was nauseating behaviour. This criticism held long after tennis had won its way amongst the younger men, for tennis is not often played where every and any coolie from the street can watch his betters running about in a dishevelled state.

On this lake were Chinese students not only rowing in public like common labourers, but giving their consent and aid to their sisters, conducting themselves in a like manner. A few years ago, and it would have been a disgrace, an impossibility, for brother and sister to have been seen out together. Sisters were confined to the Within Apartments and the adjacent courtyards. If they went out, they were accompanied by a hobbling old duenna, and certainly not by their menfolk.

The young men had their coats off. They had rolled up their sleeves and would soon be rowing as skilfully as any young men on earth. Chinese limbs can achieve much graceful action, and Chinese heart muscles have much staying power. When a Japanese girl can cross by the Siberian train alone, and win the world's long jump for women, Chinese women will be running her close shortly. These girls on the lake, in their fresh inexpensive tunics, with their free movements, with colour in their cheeks, were a sight to give thanks for—as far as we of an older generation than they were concerned. Their laughter came ringing across the water. Mrs. Sung and I looked at each other, and gaiety flooded our hearts.

" It is to women like you they owe this, Miss Lo," she said to Blossom, jerking her head at the rowing-boats.

" Little Cloud will be rowing with Strong-as-a-Rock like that some day," I enlarged.

" I hope it, I hope it ! " she breathed.

On this we had to part, to rejoin our different friends. Curious that she should be stepping off rapidly with the newest of New China : and I taking slow paces by the side of rather old-fashioned China.

By permission of T. Butler, Esq., F.R.G.S.

Summer Palace, Peking. The dragon and the phœnix in copper symbolize the Emperor and the Empress

Up the short steep hill in the centre of the Palace grounds we climbed. Chinese palace and temple steps are incredibly steep—like the steps of old castle keeps. Mid-way we stayed to sit at a high square Chinese table of redwood set in a pine grove, to drink tea and crack melon seeds between our teeth. Finally, Blossom's sister-in-law and I reached, before the others, the highest point of Peking. A shrine stands there, surrounded by a carved balustrading from which one looks out upon the marvellous square-cut precision of Peking at one's feet.

Soldiers were lounging around. One of them had brought his baby son, arrayed in a semi-foreign straw hat with orange-coloured pompons. Into the shrine I went, and he after me. There, within, a hideous clay image sat grinning, with terrible mouth : black of face, with anger depicted by red flushes, white eye-balls goggling, and many arms springing out from both sides his body, each arm more menacing than the last, hurling a thunderbolt, a lightning flash, a trident, a hammer. It was as if the whole figure yelled threateningly, " Beware ! The powers of ill can rush in and ruin you so easily ! "

His shrine was well tended. Fresh incense was burning. Each of the many pleasure-seekers who had mounted to that height had offered his or her tribute to keep the demons off the city and its inhabitants. The soldier bought a stick of incense from a hawker outside and put it into his son's hands : placed the tiny palms together with the incense-stick between them, helped the childish head to bow three times, and then stuck the sweet-smelling offering into the full incense-brazier. The babe, wearing his foreign straw hat, nodded seriously as directed, looked to its father for a smile of approbation and received it. " Come and see the view," called young Mrs. Lo from outside. Glad to forget this religion which dwells upon the propriation and fear of evil, I went into the bright clean sunlight.

Side by side young Mrs. Lo and I surveyed Peking, she, a slender lady of five feet, with painted cheeks, and wearing a turquoise-flowered satin gown to her feet. She was raised up another couple of inches on her Manchu pattens, the high soles of which had been whitened and were immaculate. We overlooked from our terraced hill the imperial buildings. Far away we looked—beyond the symmetrical yellow roofs of the crumbling and neglected palaces ; beyond the high stucco frontages of the neat and banal Legation Quarter ; beyond the grey encircling city wall with its red-and-blue painted bastions and towers ; beyond the homely dwellings of the Chinese suburb in the south. There, against the horizon stood the Temple of Prayer for the Year. It raises its coloured dome from amidst a cypress park, above its companion, the marble tricentric Altar of Heaven. The temple and the altar are rightly accounted as amongst the most wonderful creations of man : emanations of his spirit caught and interpreted and translated into the material by the skill of his eye and hand. The milk-white dais, lying glimmering to the skies like a pearl on the bosom of the earth, takes the breath with its purity. The conception, in such form, of a meeting-place for intercourse between the Seen and the Unseen is majestic.

No nation which dreamed such grandeur can be other than great.

And yet few Chinese speak of either temple or altar with a tithe of the awe or enthusiasm which bursts from the lips of an Occidental. To us, the night-blue dome of the Temple of Prayer for the Year almost prostrates the soul with its depth of colour. Crowned with a golden flambeau, mystic, symbolic of the elements, it might be striving to lift the element of earth, so shifting and unstable, out and up into the clean fire and steadfast law of the heavens.

After that horrific menacing figure of hate in the shrine behind, the gleam of the distant pure altar was a fanfare of silver ;

" Trumpeting man through beauty to God's side."

It was significant, too, that I stood on that topmost tower, looking over the Palace with one of the last of the daughters of an official Manchu family. She sighed, as she pointed out to me the various dwellings : where the Emperor's rooms were, and the Empress's, the library, and the garden of rare plants.

" Not that I had much to do with the Palace," she explained. " As you know, I was only nineteen when the Revolution took place, and it was few of our favoured families who had the entrée. We other Manchus kept very much to our own family circles. I never came within the grounds till they were thrown open to the whole populace. It is sad for us Manchus to come here, and know that our name is vanished from the annals of history. My father and brother used to come to pay their respects to the Throne sometimes. Now my father is dead, and there is no Throne."

"Have you ever been there?" I asked the little lady, pointing to the Altar. For the price of a cheap ticket, the Altar is also open to the public, like the palaces once sacrosanct to the Emperor, the Son of Heaven.

"N-n-no," she admitted reluctantly: then beamed on me. "But you—have you seen our city Waterworks?"

I shook my head. She pointed them out in the east.

"You should go," she admonished: "for they are excessively good to see. We have had them ten years and more now. One is permitted to inspect the machinery. It is wonderful."

She began talking to me with much detail about the machinery: how the water was sucked up here by pumps, and then poured elsewhere. She surprised me. For a moment, yet another new world for Chinese women in some not too distant future, with its own interests, flashed before my ken. If an occasional young Chinese man can find salvation, like his brothers on the western side of the land-mass which we have arbitrarily divided into Europe and Asia, in the intricacies of motor-bicycles, why should not a Chinese woman be redeemed from inanity by the same means?

I wondered, standing beside her, listening to her talk of machinery, if Mrs. Lo would not better understand Blossom's wish to teach rather than marry if she herself had a sewing-machine or a bicycle of her own. The times will not be ripe for her to drive a car for some years. In Peking it is still considered undignified for a Chinese gentleman to sit in the driving-seat. He would rather endure the mazes of string and the contraptions which a Chinese chauffeur attaches to the gadgets on the dashboard. It would do young Mr. Lo good to drive a motor-car, for he has nothing to rouse him to thought except the deficiencies of pawnbroking institutions in this era of turmoil. Sometimes a Western woman has an aptitude for mechanics: why not a Chinese? "God fulfils Himself in many ways." To some, the Way of Enlightenment is found in the hum and beat of a piston. The law of the Lord leaps to their eyes far more clearly through the accurate cogging of a wheel than in the strophe and antistrophe of a psalm or the versicles of a sutra. And truly the marriage of oil and steel is an amazing discovery of the mind of creation.

I could but dream such things for Mrs. Lo: not bring them to her. Each generation fancies that the next has better opportunities and advantages than its own, and meanwhile has to endure deficiencies.

The water-carriers of Peking disagree violently with Mrs. Lo's admiration of the Waterworks. Only that week they went on strike, complaining that the Company were taking the rice out of their bowls. Their union—an ancient Guild—passed a resolution, pledging its members to refuse to carry water to any street wherein a single offending householder was parleying with the Waterworks for the installation of hydrants, pipes, faucets, and such inhuman devices. After perceiving the willing labour of these coolies, one could regret the inevitable onmarch of the Waterworks. The water-bearers drip their cooling way through the streets, a bucket at each end of a swaying shoulder-pole, their muscles rippling under their naked gleaming copper skins. With healthy cheerful faces they earn their two copper-cash a bucket: and they delight the eye for nothing. Yet young Mrs. Lo is right in her enthusiasms. More pleasing to the eye than dripping buckets or muscular shoulders are the new beauty and the cleaner streets of many Chinese cities: not to mention better laundered clothes and more wholesome babies. Especially do the insidious disintegrating Waterworks entail results more pleasing to the nose.

Mrs. Lo went down the steep steps to do the honours of hostess to my parents: and Blossom joined me. She began to ask after the Kung family, with whom I had stayed during the Revolution; after Li Cheng and Flower and the others. Her father had been governor of the Shansi province, while Kung Ta Jen was Chief Judge: and the ladies of the family had met. We leaned over the balustrade and I spoke of them.

Far away, amongst the intricacies of the South City lanes, outside the grey city wall, lived Gentle Calm, as I told her;

my friend of twenty years' standing, the eldest living daughter of the house of Kung. Children have been born to her: and died: only two being left of the eight she has clasped to her arms. "Little Puss," my special playmate, grew to be sixteen years old: consumption then carried her off. I was glad I sent a gift to her by her uncle Li Cheng, when he came to England. She, in return, had worked me a cushion cover with the words in English, in cross-stitch, upon it: "With love from Susan Huang"—because I had named her "Black-eyed Susan" in her babyhood. Of Gentle Calm's two remaining, the little girl is shockingly bony with rickets. I doubt if she will live. Her husband is in no lucrative post. She is a wife in a thousand. Selfishness does not enter into her composition.

Sorrow has turned Gentle Calm into a strong Buddhist, as it did her father before her.

"There is a temple close at hand to us," she told me with content, when I found my way to her simple household in a series of rickshaws over miles of execrable lanes. "The priests in our temple are good and serious men: mostly old," she continued. "We go there, the women of our household and of the courtyards of two of our neighbours, every Saturday morning to pray. And Buddha hears us. I have persuaded my mother-in-law and my two sisters-in-law, living in the adjoining courtyards, and they are quite glad to come with me nowadays."

The ardent flame of the propagandist lit her face. The temple gong struck as she spoke. Her brother Li Cheng had hinted that it was a trouble to him that Gentle Calm should thus betake herself so vehemently to Buddhism.

"It is like looking back into the past all the time," he said: "and I am alone in the family to press forward. Persuade her otherwise if you can."

Perhaps Gentle Calm felt a touch of an opposing spirit within me, though I tried to sublimate it into a spirit of understanding and to go more than half-way to meet her in her religious fervours. For truly we have a vast heritage of spiritual experience in common.

"Do you remember sending me a Holy Book when my father returned to the heavens?" she added. It was a copy of St. Luke, bound in blue figured silk at my request by the publishers. When Kung Ta Jen had died, I was far away, in England. Not knowing how else to express my sympathy, I had sent each of his daughters an evangel : and had chosen for her St. Luke, who so well knew the woman's point of view.

" That Holy Book has done us much good," she now declared. I wondered.

" Yes," she assured me, " when Chang Tso Lin's aeroplanes came over Peking, dropping bombs, a number of houses near by us were hit. It was frightful—*li-hai* ! But our house received no injury. Then I knew it was because of the foreign Holy Book of yours. It kept off the harm devised by foreign aeroplanes ! "

There is never any end to the surprises Mother China springs upon one.

" Have you read the Book ? " I quavered, confounded by this reasoning.

" Well, no ! " she confessed. " But," she hastened to add, " all those books you sent the children we have kept, and my son is very fond of them."

The books were children's picture-books which I sent at the New Year for my various Chinese nephews and nieces.

The son, a boy of twelve or so, with a face of intelligence and sunshine, had his eyes fixed on me the whole time. He was attending a school where he learned some English and mathematics, and other modern phenomena. Perhaps he noted the dismay in my face.

" My mother has little time to read," he explained : " she is always sewing and cooking. My uncle Li Cheng tells her she works much too hard, and he scolds her for it. But nobody can stop her, I think. I will read the Holy Book, if you wish it, shall I ? "

" Do," I said, " if your mother permits : then you can tell her about it." If Li Cheng's womenfolk imagine that the foreigners' Holy Book breathes the same spirit as foreign aeroplanes and bombs, no wonder they try to hold him back from such an atmosphere of violence and will not accompany him one step ; so I thought to myself.

Gentle Calm's house was so far away in the South City that we could not often meet. We used to telephone to each other: about nothing. Personally, I find this kind of telephonic conversation difficult. My father would laugh in the next room. He said I filled in the gaps by mimicking realistically the thorough-going grunts of a Chinese woman. Chinese ladies, having lately discovered the telephone, use it incessantly and hold these lengthy conversations on the most trifling excuses. There is shrewdness, as well as pleasure in it. For in a manner of speaking, one is paying a call and strengthening the filaments of an acquaintance or friendship, without the trouble of changing one's dress, or the expense of hiring a rickshaw or buying extra dainties for tea.

Blossom was very interested in all I had to tell her of the Kung family, and Gentle Calm. I now asked her if she had ever visited the Altar of Heaven. Once, she said, in Yuan Shih Kai's day, before the soldiers became troublesome.

"The last time I was at the Altar," I told her, "Wu Pei Fu's soldiers were there. I asked two of them, who attached themselves to us, how it was that there were always foreigners beholding its beauties, but rarely any Chinese. One of them, the spokesman, looked scornfully at me: then said, 'You speak Chinese. One would imagine you knew something about Chinese ways, and yet you ask a foolish question like that. Don't you see that we have an encampment of soldiers here?' 'Well?' I queried. 'Well,' he mocked me, 'they are frightened of us, of course. I would not hurt any one myself: I am like my General in that. But most soldiers would certainly molest and rob unarmed citizens if they came into this lonely park!'"

A Chinese soldier has his pride and sense of honourable occupation, like any other: nor does he fall from grace as a rule till he has been treated with the harshest lack of consideration, such as no other armed man would tolerate. Our own British army has suffered much mismanagement in its day, but ever the officers have fought the battles of the men's welfare. Unfortunately for the Chinese soldier, his officers have been his worst enemies, stealing his pay and sending him into battle while remaining in safety themselves. So long as he receives, however, food, clothing and shelter—poor though these may be—he is a tractable creature, even minus pay. When these fail, he loses every sense of *li* or right feeling, and attacks the feeble and defenceless, finally robbing without the smallest mercy his own poorest countrymen. He tortures them to disclose their microscopic hoards. He laughs and devours their rice unconcernedly, while their agonized bodies are stretched and quivering about him in the middle of the tormenting. He pours kerosene into the bosoms of the women's tunics and threatens to set them afire if they frustrate him. He smashes the poor little doors and floors and rafters for firewood. He steals the solitary mule or plough-ox. He takes what he can carry of corn from their precious bins: then pulls out the bung and lets his stolen mules trample it into the dirt till all is destroyed. He kicks aside the women who kneel and cry to him and abase themselves to the ground for a shadow of clemency.

But before he reaches this, "the white wolf state," he has suffered months and years of cold-blooded neglect. Treated with the veriest modicum of consideration, he is as kindly and willing as his brother coolies, whom he thus maltreats. General Feng Yu Hsiang's soldiers have received this humane consideration: so that even the fierce Mohammedans in his new army, having mingled with his original brigades, wept when they relieved Hsianfu to see the Chinese population suffering starvation, and gave them out of their own meagre ration-bags.

It was not as easy as one might imagine to take snapshots of any of China's two millions of men under arms. A legend was current that whoever was photographed would be the first to be killed at the next battle. At sight of a camera, therefore, soldiers naturally walked quickly off. They hunched their shoulders into shapelessness. Their spirits would be taken away by the click, they said. We should not feel over-exhilarated ourselves by being snapshotted on any and every occasion by strange-looking Asiatic visitors to our shores. Yet there would be no harm in it: possibly good. Photographs of homely scenes might counteract the unfortunate ideas of our habits and modes which are reaching Asia through the cinema alone.

There was one ruthless and likeable fellow, however, a sergeant in Chang Tso Lin's army, who called to me during an entrainment on a North China railway station: "Take my photo ! I am brave, I am ! What do I care if I die ? I don't mind if I am the first to die. Somebody must be." He spat. " Cowards, these others—how shall we beat Feng Yu Hsiang, with such a feeble spirit ! " He struck an attitude with his rifle, and commanded me to take his likeness, and I obeyed. Then he betook himself and his equipment into his compartment, to the admiring looks of his company —of which he was very conscious.

At the Altar of Heaven, it had seemed so incongruous to find soldiers perambulating its park, that I had asked the soldier who attached himself to me if I might take a photograph of him against its white dragon newel-posts. " Certainly not ! " he replied at once : " not even for ten cents."

" I regret having troubled your heart," I apologized. "Am I worthy to take the Elder Born's likeness ? Yet, when I return to my home in the Great Brave Country, I should like to look upon remembrances of the brave soldiers of the Central Kingdom."

At this the soldier leaned against the altar stairway, posed his comrade beside himself and said :

" If you will promise faithfully to send me a print of the snapshot, I will consent." He insisted on my promising twice over. He would have liked to make me swear by all the dead emperors that ever reported there to Heaven and the Ancestors. I gave him the back of an envelope, and in his untutored peasant's writing he scrawled his name, the name of his regiment, and the address close by the Temple of Heaven. Our Chinese servant had trouble in deciphering it when I redeemed my word. I sent an uncovenanted print for his friend, who had been a dummy of silence.

" I should have liked to evade my promise," I ended my account to Blossom, " for they were not very good results. But how could I, having sworn on such an altar, eh ? "

Blossom's father had been to the night sacrifices in the imperial days, she added, when he was a young man.

" When my father was buried," she told me, " it was six years after he died. His body had been waiting in its splendid thick coffin in a temple near the North Gate. We had a very great funeral for him—he was nearly the last of the high Manchu officials. Sixty-four men carried the catafalque,

Some foreigners sent word to us beforehand asking if they might take photographs. That was very polite of them, so we gladly gave permission and they sent us copies which I will show you."

In time I saw these photographs, but the chief thing that took my attention in them was Blossom's own pure grave face looking out of the cart, with the white mourning bands around it.

We came down from our eyrie. It became time for us all to go home. We said our good-bye and thanks outside the turnstile—the turnstile of the Forbidden City! Young Mr. Lo was punctilious in seeing us into our motor-car, bowing ceremoniously and sedately as we parted, before he called for his own. His final words reached us. "You were my father's friend." He was speaking to my father. "I thank you for honouring us with your company to-day."

China has new beauties—for which one offers gratitude to Providence. Praise be, she has also retained a number of the old.

CHAPTER XXV DANGEROUS TIMES

LIFE pressed around us in Peking—dances, junketings; cosmopolitan gatherings, luxury on one side: history made far in the past and being refashioned again in the present, on another. Poverty, patience, injustice, agony of heart, death, jostled intellectual debatings, old-fashioned courtesy and occasional new-fangled abruptness. Peking presented the whole gamut of life and gave everything, except that slow quiet leisure wherein friendships comfortably grow. I saw Mrs. Sung less and less.

At the dinner-parties on the roof-garden of the well-ordered hotel, there gathered most of the chiefs of the diplomatic corps, together with the Chinese elegants. Outside the revolving glass doors of the hotel stood on guard two well-washed members of the Peking gendarmerie in grey cotton uniforms, trousers stuffed into Russian boots, their bayonets fixed on their rifles, their bandoliers filled with ammunition. At any time somebody might plan a wild coup, or soldiers mutiny and turn to looting. In the street, a motor-car, occupied by a Chinese general would flash by over the broad macadamized road, a large dinner-bell clanging from its roof to announce his coming. Two soldier-footmen, clutching their caps in the wild rush through the air, stood on the running-board, smiling boyishly at the speed. The general inside the lighted vehicle in full khaki uniform, flaunted gold lace and epaulettes of large size. His cocked hat, with its white feathers a-blowing, looked small on his round head with his fat cheeks. A Chinese student on the roadway would give a bitter glance at this swollen military glory, before the onslaught of which the population of the street scurried to the side—like leaves in autumn fleeing.

At the side of the road in the daytime, long camel-trains raised clouds of black dust. They were bringing coal from the mines in the north. Peking carts, of an ancient heavy type, rumbled and swayed on their iron-studded wheels, drawn by mules. At night innumerable rickshaws flickered like fire-flies.

On one large street a primitive makeshift mat-shelter stood: the dining-hall for the Salvation Army poor. On another, at some distance away, rose a roof among larger roofs: a hospital, the life-work of a Chinese doctor trained in England, and the only hospital of its kind in these parts. Nearly all the hospitals in China have been founded by various sections of the Church Ministrant, just as the hospices of Europe mostly bear the names of saints. This Chinese doctor, when he returned to his country, thought that he would like to take his share in helping his poor neighbours. He started private practice for his own sake, and a hospital for theirs. A brave fight he puts up for the latter. His face is lined and grey with care far too soon for his years. Honoured by his compatriots, he is like other scientists and philanthropists, obliged to be content with honour, and manage as best he can with very little money. His friends and admirers are as generous as they can afford, for they know the value of his work. But a hospital eats up a quantity of dollars.

To keep his hospital going, he has had recourse to the services of the Catholic sisters as nurses. Full of praise for them he was when he talked to me.

"They work for nothing but sheer love," he told me. "They will stay up for nights on end to save a patient or to soothe dying folk. They are wonderful women."

Most of the ladies being French, I told one of them of the hoot-hooting of motors in modern Paris, when she complained of the general's motor dinner-bells. A most engaging trait of these sisters was their attitude towards that other great branch of Redemptionists which also seeks out the wretched and forlorn; and which gives them dinner in the aforesaid mat-sheds. The plain British folk of the Salvation Army know the Peking poor as do none other, particularly the Manchu banner-men, who had their meat given them from the Throne, and who have now no helpers. Never shall I forget one worn-out septuagenarian in a back street pulling a rickshaw over its shocking rutted surface. He was *sans* teeth and very nearly *sans* eyes, for one of them was closed up. How he besought me to sit in his grimy decrepit conveyance ! He kept calling to me in a tone of despair, lowering with every breath his already too low price. I gave him a few coppers rather than run him to death. Indeed, he could not have run, only hobbled : as I saw him do later when a poor woman and her large heavy child of ten or eleven were persuaded to climb together into his man-carriage.

The Salvation Army has cared, with inadequate funds, for some of these unhappy creatures. Sometimes only one member of a house has enough clothing to go for the food provided in the shelter : so they take it in turn and the others go hungry. Brave these starving folk are, and often very courteous and unselfish. The rule of the Shelter has perforce to be that the thin gruel—which is all that can be supplied—should be consumed on the spot. One man of fifty or so tried very hard to take away his gruel, and when he comprehended that this was not permitted, he left it. He was away a short while and then the Army women saw a strange sight. He was returning with an old woman pick-a-back and she was clothed in nothing but a sack. Her feet, wrapped in rags, stuck out through holes at the bottom. She was his mother, and was seventy-three. He slid her gently off his back on to a bench. He fetched a bowl of gruel and fed her himself as a bird would its young, little by little with the chopsticks. Then he ate. They almost wept to see.

The sick, and the soldiers wounded in some battle but left untended, the Salvation Army take to the hospital over there in the West City. The Chinese surgeon operates or prescribes for them. And the French Catholic sisters nurse them to health, if it can be done by devotion. I do not say that either the Army or the sisters have a great store of scientific knowledge in their dealings with these social and medical problems. Certainly scientific training is desirable in a nurse. But I do know that a French sister, with huge flapping sails of a head-dress, said to me :

" The Armée de Salut—they are good people. They will certainly go to heaven finally : their stay in purgatory will be short ! "

And the Army man, with his spectacles and pale, tired, under-nourished face, asserts gravely :

" Those Catholic sisters are lovely Christians."

What a blessing that " the uncovenanted mercies of God " provide both of them with sound theological foundation for this fellowship of the saints which they undoubtedly enjoy !

Neither the sisters nor the Salvation Army know each other's national tongue. They converse in Chinese. " But we have not much time for talk," they briskly add.

The Chinese patients lie in their beds, sick and weak, often suffering from the results of heart-breaking neglect. With eyes of pure trust and affection, they follow the figures of these their friends walking down the wards in such strange clothing.

One evening my father and I had supper at the Central Park on the invitation of some members of the university, my mother being engaged elsewhere. We sat in a pavilion at a long dining-table spread with a white foreign tablecloth and had an excellent dinner, half Chinese and half foreign. The pavilion was at the end of the broad walk leading from the square Altar of the Land and Grain, where emperors sacrificed lest the sunshine should fail and crops die : for the Park was a part of the Palace grounds. A bowling-alley has been made near the altar, and the clatter of the wooden balls echoes within the walls of the once sacred enclosure.

Some of our hosts had been in England and America, and very hospitable and gracious they were. They asked my father questions about England's feelings towards China, and he spoke frankly of the West's friendly wishes for China's happiness and well-being. Long they talked together, and all was peace between us and pleasant understanding. They listened earnestly, eagerly, as he showed plainly his affection for their country and wove schemes for her future progress. As we came away, down the darkling avenue, to the gates where our rickshaws waited, he took my arm and said :

" More and more I see that what the East wants from the West is our affection. They are only waiting to be wooed. They want us to woo them."

I knew he was right. Unfortunately, there are not many

who have the leisure to spend in such courtship, though most would wish to do it. The Soviet, shortly afterwards, found time.

The next day, my mother and I went calling, and came to the house of an Englishwoman with grey hair, slightly and refreshingly Edwardian in her gentle ways. She had just begun to tell another caller something that had happened to her the preceding summer in a port on the Yangtsze. So we asked her not to stop. This was her tale.

She, this middle-aged lady, had been caught on the crest of a high wave of anti-foreign emotion. In that port a handful of white folk lived in a small concession. Although the port had long been declared open for the residence of foreign merchants, big trade had mostly passed it by. Only a small stream of riches was diverted into its gates. The city was in the neighbourhood of beautiful scenery and a mountain resort. In summer the port becomes very hot : and Western women and children grow blanched as lilies if they stay too long in its damp, steamy heat. When summer came, however, this grey-haired lady had remained in the concession ; for she was living with her unmarried son, and was unhappy to leave him to suffer the heat alone. English wives on the Indian plains will sympathize with her. In their house with the wide verandas, near the river front, with the French windows open to every breeze, she could tolerate it if he could. So she thought. Moreover, she was China-born and China-married, and knew how to manage a household in a Chinese summer.

Rumours of trouble up river reached them : but she stayed. Her son was more tied to his work when trouble approached. Then, one day, as they sat at tiffin, they were startled by a mighty smash. The pots of chrysanthemums, which stood in rows on the veranda being budded for their autumn glory, came hurtling through the windows. A crashing of glass announced that other rooms were suffering. There were two hundred such chrysanthemums in pots, for they had an indefatigable gardener and the lady loved the flowers : and the whole two hundred came flying in at the ground-floor windows, earth and pot and broken budded stem. At the same time, by their back door, came in the manager of a British merchant firm and his wife, pale but composed. Their house had been attacked, and they had left it to rioters. In an instant it was decided that the two men should run to the Japanese Consulate to seek the armed help which it had been arranged should come from that quarter, if need arose. The two ladies were alone.

" Something prompted me to go round, pull together and bolt down the outside green venetian doors," said the narrator of the story. " Yet it seemed impossible that we should be attacked. I had lived in China all my days : and my father and mother before me. I love the Chinese, as did they, and as does my son. We had forgotten that we were foreign to their common life. But I had also lived in China too long not to know that their mobs can do dreadful things—and repent too late afterwards."

My mother had been through a riot also : and signified consent.

" I went into the kitchen where the servants were standing frightened. I told them to go away from the house : to leave us : that we should prefer it. We did not want their blood on our heads. They could stay near at hand, but they were better out of our house. The Number Two Boy thanked us, and bowed so politely that I knew he thought never to see us alive again ; which gave me a shock. He went. He was a new Boy. He had a family, and he was right to go. The coolie also was a new servant : but he said he would think over it. We urged him to go at once, as there was no time to linger. The cook, however, and the head Boy were in terrible distress. For they were men from the North, whom we had brought with us from Peking. They said that in Canton, only shortly before, the Cantonese hot-heads, who were then engaged in a war with their neighbours from Yunnan province, had killed in the street every Chinese who did not speak with a Cantonese accent. Some from Northern provinces had lived in Canton for years. ' Thy speech betrayeth thee,' had been the answer to each plea for mercy, ' thy speech is not Cantonese.' It was useless to plead that neither were they Yunnanese : they had been killed. Lately, said the cook, when he had gone shopping, the base people of the port had followed him, jeering because

By permission of T. Butler, Esq., F.R.G.S.

Water-carriers. Their livelihood is being taken away by the new waterworks

of his Northern origin. ' They will certainly kill us directly we leave this house. We must stay with you,' he said."

Heavy of heart, the grey-haired Englishwoman went round locking up the house, at top speed : every room and every window. Marauders should be held off as long as possible. Hard for a woman suddenly to plan how to stand the siege of her house, and at a minute's notice. She cast quick eyes about, for she had three lives to consider beside her own, another Englishwoman and two Chinese. Rapidly she decided on making as her last stronghold the spare room, for it had the stoutest doors. No sooner settled than the mob, whose existence she had scarcely believed possible, broke in. The four sought their asylum, bolted the doors, pulled furniture across and then kept silence.

" The most dreadful part was the laughter. Such maniac laughter. As if these simple folk were possessed by demons. Screams of laughter. I could never have imagined it. My heart failed when I heard it. And then pandemonium was let loose, as they went smashing through the house : and soon a smell of burning came. We found afterwards that they had heaped the clothes from our wardrobes on to the beds, poured kerosene and set fire to the pile—except where a few of the more calculating had spied our best garments and trinkets and carried them off ; my furs, for instance. Our two servants were trembling and weeping. No wonder, poor souls, for they were not even of foreign blood, and it was hard for them to have to die like that because of having served in our household."

Soon the rioters found the closed room. They battered upon the doors : they wrenched at them. They yelled taunts : they smashed on the panels. Mercifully they had no battering rams ; but the doors shook. The Boy and the cook wept and wrung their hands. The other Englishwoman said, " I cannot believe God will let us die like this." " If we have to die, He will give us strength to go through with it," said the elder woman. Neither of them dared foreshadow the sort of death which might face them. They could only hope it would be quick. " But that was not what troubled us," she said. " I think by that time we hardly minded if we should die. It seemed so long, so very long since my son and her husband had gone for help. We both made sure our dear ones had fallen in with the crowd and been killed. We could think no other. That anguish was the worst pain of all."

In the room was a cupboard for hanging clothes. The two ladies, full of pity for the two Chinese retainers, bade them go into this, and shut the door : and in they went.

" When the mob breaks in, they will see only us, and perhaps thus they will escape," said the Englishwomen to each other.

So the two Chinese servants went into the cupboard, which was not very big. The fury was redoubled, and the yelling and laughter. The doors bent under the blows. They could hold but little longer. The Chinese in the cupboard—servants for years of the elder Englishwoman's —put out their hands. Weeping they were : but they said, " Mississy ! Both must come within cupboard too ! "

They would not accept their lives at the expense of others —women and foreigners. They insisted, and the two women were creeping in when there came a shout, a rush of feet : then silence, and her son's voice calling, " Mother ! "

Half fainting, they staggered out, and across the room, pulled away the shaking furniture : and lo, the handle of the door came off in their hands. One more feeble push and the door would have been down.

And what was the first sentence which came from the lips of that grey-haired Englishwoman, as she fell on her son's heart ?

" Oh ! " she cried. " Oh, I do hope that no Chinese has been killed for us ! "

He replied, " None. Not one drop of blood, Chinese or foreign, has been shed."

She answered, " Thank God."

He and his friend, it seems, had run hot-foot to the Japanese Consulate for help as arranged. But the Japanese were reluctant to call out armed forces, and thought the British were exaggerating matters. The two men had small time to argue ; so left, running. At the corner of the road they hesitated a second and looked back. In that short time the Japanese Consulate looked as if a whirlwind had struck it. They heard later that the consul escaped by the kitchen door. The Japanese bank, near by, was beginning to shoot up flames. Knowing that now the Japanese would perceive the urgency of the need, the two rushed down the Bund again. To their immense relief they ran into a small but efficient band of volunteers, the handful of foreigners who had formed themselves into a small defence corps. It was on its way to their own beleaguered house.

Who had brought about this dénouement ? The coolie, who had been in the household only a few months, but who had appreciated his just and considerate treatment, had hummed and hawed when his mistress bade him leave her house and seek safety elsewhere. He was a Yangtsze man, a native of the place. He stayed.

" I am but a stupid coolie, a man of no account ! " he murmured.

When the mob came, he was ironing dinner-napkins, and he continued to iron them. They shouted to him to tell where the foreigners were hidden, and where they kept their " gold "—this hoard always in demand by a Chinese mob, reminiscent of the days before banks.

" I pretended to be even more stupid than I am," he explained later—enjoying his narrative powers. " I pretended I could not understand what they wanted. They called me simpleton, blockhead, and they smote me with the mistress' own irons ! "—exhibiting faithfully the bruises. " But when I found how wicked were their thoughts, I slipped out when their backs were turned, and ran and fetched the foreigners who met to drill."

He made the volunteers understand that danger threatened her whom he respected.

" Come plenty quick ! " he implored. " Come velly plenty quick ! Velly bad men wantchee hurt my Mississy."

" And, can you imagine it ? " she ended. " The whole affair from the smashing of the windows with the chrysanthemum pots to our rescue from that dreadful room took exactly ten minutes. Ten minutes ! I could not believe it at first. I would have sworn that we were at the least two hours shut in, thinking our men were killed."

At the remembrance, her lip trembled. As for us, we sat

there and listened spellbound, horrified at the fearful danger she had passed through ; and then wrapt round with pride in her, this elderly woman of our stock. Indeed we smiled, for presently she spoke, and the only sense of injury she expressed was that the mob had torn down her country's flag, trampled on it and burnt it. Even that was modified by her next remarks. She and her son had lost everything ; their clothing, their pictures, books and bedding—not insignificant trifles. We supposed they would receive compensation.

"That is what I say to my son," she said. "I honestly think we ought to have our goods replaced. But he says he does not think he will apply ! He argues, how can we make the innocent Chinese—who are so poor and oppressed—pay for the misdemeanours of a few of their rascals ? But, you know, it is expensive starting out afresh from nothing. However, I daresay he will have his way."

When all was calm again—which was shortly—and the people smiling in the streets at them, there came to the port a resident, of another nation, usually amiable, who had been on leave during the frenzy. He kept declaring, in hot tones, that the mob had been let off too easily. They had fled at the approach of the volunteers and been allowed to flee.

"They ought to have had volleys fired into them," cried Boanerges. "I should have liked to see your veranda surrounded by corpses of the murdering rascals. There ought to have been two hundred dead laid there ! "

At last it was more than she could bear. She looked at him.

"I suppose," she said gently, "that I have as much right as anybody to speak on the subject. The first words I uttered when we were saved were to hope that no Chinese blood had been shed for us. And when my son said 'Not one drop !' out of the bottom of my heart I said 'Thank God': and I say it again now, with all my strength."

That very evening of our visit to her, a famous Chinese preacher came to dine with us. He and his wife had both been educated in America, had taken brilliant degrees, and done fine work. After dinner we sat out in the paved court. Around us were the four latticed one-storeyed buildings of the Peking house. Above, the moon glowed yellow as a lantern—one of the melon-shaped variety which one may buy in Lantern Street in the South City, where they also make other enchanting varieties at the due seasons : such as gold-fishes, which move their fins and tail, and roll their eyes as soon as the candle inside has nicely warmed the air.

The preacher's wife and I sat a little apart from the others. That day she had been outside the city wall, and had seen a rickshaw coolie impressed as a soldier. And she was sad.

" The unfortunate man," she was saying, " he was weeping. But little notice they took of that. They bound his hands and arms with a rope and dragged him off. He will either have to become a soldier or be forced to carry their knapsacks for them."

" What became of his rickshaw ? " I asked.

" There it was, left by the roadside : it looked so pitiable," she said. " I keep thinking how his wife and children will be waiting for him to come home. He was not a young man. It was dreadful."

Her eyes filled with tears. Then she became filled with fury. At that time, Marshal Chang Tso Lin of Manchuria and Marshal Wu Pei Fu of Loyang, after years of warfare and enmity, had agreed to unite and were to come the next day into Peking to swear blood brotherhood. It must have been a satellite of these Marshals who was responsible for that particular press-gang : but all China's armies have been guilty of his methods. Under the moonlight this educated Chinese woman leaned forward and whispered in English, with her American accent : " I wish I were a man ! "

" Why ? " I naturally asked, startled at the venom with which she said it.

" Then I would be brave. If I were a man, if I were brave, I would take bombs in my hand and go and throw them at those two generals who are eating up our country : and try to kill them," said the preacher's wife.

" Oh ! " I ejaculated. " That does not sound very Christian surely ! "

" Why not ? " she asked. " Does not the Bible say that it is expedient that one man should die, instead of a whole nation ? They are tigers, these two generals, who devour the blood of the proletariat. They deserve to die. Yet, alas, they are well guarded—their consciences are evil! Nobody can approach them."

She then told me various points of recent history which had been obscure. She praised General Feng Yu Hsiang. "The rumour goes that he betrayed General Hsü and had him murdered?" I suggested.

"Of course, he did!" she hurled back at me. "But General Hsü was doing his best to have General Feng murdered!"

"So General Feng got his blow in first, eh?" I queried; and she assented. I was translated centuries back; to the days of Sisera and Jael, of Judith and Holofernes.

While we talked, a shadow fell upon us. A Chinese girl in the white uniform of a nurse, a girl efficient in her service, came to tell us that a mutual Chinese friend in a nursing home in the next courtyard had safely given birth to a daughter. Would we like a peep? We went and saw the babe, with its crumpled rosy face, its tight shut eyes and puckered mouth, lying—a bundle on the bed.

Would she ever want to throw bombs, I wondered. I hoped not—even in a just cause. I thought of an elderly English gentlewoman who thanked God that no drop of Chinese blood had been shed on her account.

CHAPTER XXVI AT THE SUMMER PALACE

ONE day we begged Blossom and Miss Way to take a holiday. We wanted to visit the Summer Palace once more, a few miles out from Peking. We had hired a motor-car for the day, and there were two empty seats going waste as we told them, to satisfy their economical hearts. They would not have dared to go out so far from the city precincts by themselves, for fear of ruffianly soldiers. Since Yuan Shih-kai died—the same day as Kitchener—it had not been safe for Pekingese women to go pleasuring very far afield.

"Blossom must go! It would be good for her health," Miss Way decided, and Blossom mildly acquiesced. Miss Way was constantly planning some little kindness or fête for her, she whispered in an aside, with a glance of affection at her brisk tall companion.

"Besides, our drawing mistress has been away ten days for a funeral in the family, and Blossom has been doing her duty as well as her own. It was no use my trying: I have not Blossom's gifts! She draws almost as well as the mistress, whom we expect back to-morrow. If she does not come, and if I accompany you, the girls must learn an extra ode or two for me for once."

I began to quote: sheer braggadocio it was, for I only ever knew one ode, and that the first in the book!

Kuan, Kuan! The wild ducks
Are on the islet in the River.
A refined and modest maiden
Our prince desires as mate.

Tangled is the water-weed,
Floating to and fro.
A refined and modest maiden,
Waking and sleeping, he seeks.

"What a pity you are not in my school," declared Miss Way, helping me out when I stumbled. "I would soon teach you to recite more than one ode to me—at the top of your voice, and with your back to the teacher so that you could not catch sight of the words and cheat! We maintain the old way of reciting in our school."

Blossom ultimately coaxed Miss Way to allow herself this rare day off; the first for a long time: and the defaulting teacher helped matters by returning. To simplify matters, we all took our own lunch. Their baskets were models of daintiness and neatness: they included, besides food, tied-up packages of toilet requisites, comb and mirror and face-powder; also envelopes of aromatic seeds for the party to masticate during the trip.

"To keep off diseases," said Miss Way, nodding her head sagely. We were adventuring into strange air, amongst unwashed countryfolk and had better be prepared with preventives. My parents soon grew weary of chewing seeds, but I ruminated like a cow, till my mouth grew numb with the pungency.

The road to the Summer Palace was a model for other Peking roads in the days of the dynasty, having been macadamized when the Court frequented it, they naturally preferring as smooth a road surface as possible. But when war brought the soldiers of varying armies upon it with every variety of vehicle, and nobody repaired it, the road gradually became a pitiable thing. Our motor-car leaped pot-holes, and rattled, till I feared that it would come to pieces; also that my mother and Blossom would be prostrate with headache before they arrived. At last we reached the final avenue of acacias planted for the Empress' pleasure. Some of the trees had been cut down for firewood by prowling soldiers, and their gashed stumps looked reproachful. Others had been hacked about from sheer desire for destruction. But all this was forgotten when our bouncing and rattling came to an end. In front lay spaciousness, colour, beauty without stint.

The Palace was plotted out by an architect with a genius for great composition. Who was he? History never troubles about architects in China. No scenic artist of the Western stage could excel such a décor. It is not an old Palace, being built after the French and English allies in 1860 burnt the then Summer Palace—not far off. They decided that only in this way could they bring home to the Chinese Court the heinousness of their international offences. The Emperor and the Court fled, of course. The Forbidden City within Peking itself was spared, for it was the older and more beautiful, and to set it afire would have endangered the Chinese populace. The Summer Palace of those days was a mere century or so old. It was built in the eighteenth century, under the supervision of the Jesuit Fathers who were at that time in favour at Court. Till recently one could still trace the influence of the Grand Palais du Louvre in its architecture, in the carving, the balustrading, and the arched halls. Homesick priests of the Missions Etrangères had breathed their beloved France into the stones and pillars of a Chinese Emperor's palace. No wonder that Baron Gros, at the head of the French army of occupation, had refused to look on while it went up in flames. Every year, as time goes on, the ruins of the old Summer Palace grow smaller : the peasant carries it off, stone by stone, tile by tile, for his byres and his kilns. To-day it is America which is leaving its mark on Chinese architecture.

Oh, young Chinese of five hundred years hence, what has happened with regard to the impact of Europe and America on your buildings ? And have we been learning from you about line and outline ? I took tea yesterday with a Chinese friend who told me that the grey lace-work of Magdalen Tower against the grey Oxford sky was very lovely. When she looked at it, she felt it as beautiful as China's red walls, fretted parapets, and yellow spiked dragons : so she said.

The new Summer Palace—the Hill of Ten Thousand Years—is pure Chinese. It is piled up the side of a hill, and looks on to a large lake, with trees all about it. This is perfect *feng shui* in Chinese eyes : that is, no evil forces are roused in opposition to such a site of hill and lake and trees. A camel-back marble bridge in the distance is mirrored into an exact circle in the water. Through magnificent lofty gateways, across spacious paved courts, up flights of marble steps, immensely steep, immensely lofty, by temples and pavilions, we walked—the five of us, three English and Miss Way and Miss Lo. Infinitely small we were. At last we craned our necks backward to look up at a final gateway which crowns the summit ; the " Gate into Heaven." It presents massive brass-studded vermilion closed doors, and tosses the curving horns of its ochre roof into the azure empyrean.

The composition, simple, broad, majestic : the colouring, vermilion, lapis lazuli, bronze, gold ; the blazing white of the marble; the placid lake, with the delicate-fingered willows on its banks : and the twisted boles of the fir trees in the avenues ; all combined to make a picture to ravish the soul. And it did not grow during centuries, as our great architectural achievements have grown. It was planted down there in a few years. The brain and eye of its conceiver, or genius, saw it completed. Yet is his name never mentioned !

Above, shone the brilliant sky of North China. A few fragments of cloud were as pearls in its limpidity. It was early summer : which charmed our two Chinese ladies. The Chinese artist soul loves a few summer clouds. No woman forgets them in her embroideries. They mean rain, and fertile spring, and gentilesse.

We climbed to the summit by a way through pine groves. My father stepped out, and kept waving us on. Miss Way and Blossom were eager enough : but the day was warm, and the trees hindered the breeze. My mother flagged. She sat in a wayside arbour and thought she would go no further. My father came on fleet foot from the top. He took her by the arm, and helped her to climb. He stayed to let her have short rests. Miss Way and Blossom and I waited for them at the top.

" Look ! " I cried, pointing to the Palace below, " It is fairyland."

But they would not look. Their eyes were turned down the hill at my parents coming slowly up. To my dismay I saw Miss Way's fine lips quivering. I touched her arm and asked her what ailed. " I am looking at something much more beautiful than a palace," she said slowly. " Look at your father helping your mother up the path, holding her sunshade over her, waiting on her. Oh ! when will such a thing be possible to a Chinese man and his wife? To you it is nothing. You expect such conduct from any father to any mother."

"It is coming in China," I protested to her.

"Blossom and I will be dead by that time," she shook her head. "We have a saying in Peking that a man pays fifteen dollars for a donkey, and can buy a wife for five."

"And it is true, literally true," echoed Blossom Lo, her eyes striking fire.

I was silent: for I had heard the phrase before from a kindly American woman, whose husband was visiting China for a few months, and who had rented a house from an American mission. With it, he had taken on for charity's sake the amah who did the household sewing, for she was very poor. The woman did her darning and mending in the exquisite and perfect, but rather slow, way of Chinese amahs. She sat working in my friend's sitting-room, and was so quiet that sometimes they forgot she was there. Now, as a rule, few men kiss their wives before other folk either in China or elsewhere, and missionaries meticulously avoid giving the slightest caress before Chinese, for old-fashioned Chinese would have been horrified by such exhibitions. However, my friend's husband was only temporarily in China. One morning, going out for his work, he looked in on his wife in her sitting-room. Amah being so inconspicuous, he forgot her existence, stooped and kissed his wife au revoir.

When he had gone, my friend heard a little noise: and behold, amah, weeping. "Amah, dear amah!" she exclaimed, astonished, and moved across to her. "What is the matter? Let me help you, if I can."

The woman presently was able to speak. "Amah has been seeing these three months how your husband treats you, always loves you, always likes to talk with you. Amah never knew such happy things could be. In Peking we women say, 'A man can have a wife for five dollars, for a donkey he must give fifteen.'"

Standing upon that sunshiny hill of the Summer Palace, with heaven's translucence bathing us, Miss Way uttered such a diatribe against Chinese men in general as would have startled some of them. She used no soft speech.

" Surely the younger generation is better," I interposed at last.

" The younger men are worse than the old," she asserted. " The old stopped at two or three concubines : the younger stop at nothing. No sense of sacredness or respect for women is in them. How can a decent woman marry a Chinese man, when she knows how he will behave—his self-indulgence, his complete disregard of her ? "

" But it is not only in China that marriage is sometimes spoiled by selfishness," I protested. " Moreover, I know some very good Chinese men." I spoke of Li Cheng, of his father, of modern men I knew personally : of the railway director and of the professor. I told her that she, through the unusual social conditions of Peking, knew only Chinese society where such men as she detested prevailed. " I know good Chinese men," I ended.

" Then you know all there are," she rapped out.

Some few months later, I told my friend, the Professor, of that conversation.

" Do good Chinese women really speak of us like that ? " he asked me, dismayed.

" Some of them are apt to," I explained. " It is not fair, of course : but they consider their experiences justify their views."

On the crest of the hill above the Summer Palace, we talked thus. To Miss Way the beauty below was but a fair semblance compared with the reality of the invisible beauty of a life of respect for self and others, for which her soul longed above all things. Ahead, a pagoda stood pillared against the sky on a neighbouring hill, its yellow porcelain a shaft of gold. Presently Miss Way went apart from Blossom and myself, and stood quiet, looking out on the Palace below and the pagoda raised in Buddha's glory ahead—Old China. And her heart was torn with doubts about New China. Yet its owner has spent its strength freely in the service of China's new womanhood. Blossom put an arm through mine and we remained in the background. I was troubled.

" Sometimes even her heart shakes, and her courage grows small," Blossom tried to comfort me. " But do not fear : never for very long. When it happens, she walks away like that from every one, and waits. She says, you only have to wait quietly and always courage grows big again."

Miss Way was looking at a pagoda, symbol of Buddhism: but it was not Buddha she was calling to her aid: nor was it the Way of Tao. It was not Christianity either, for neither she nor Blossom know much of "the Doctrine." Chinese intellectuals of Christian upbringing have been too much occupied with political and international discussions to have much time left to guide the feet of their stumbling country-men and women into that way of peace. Is not the making or breaking of a treaty with a foreign Power more enthralling than speaking of the tender mercies of a Dayspring from on high for the encouragement of such gallant courage as Miss Way possesses? She and her compeers, male and female, have been left very much alone as far as religious propaganda of any sort is concerned. Once I was stung into speech on this subject when I met the famous Chinese theologian. I asked him how it was that I could leave his country for seven years, and when I came back find that my own friends, who were mostly bred in the stoicism of Confucius, had heard nothing more of the Way since I left them.

"Only the poor; the fishermen and the carpenters," I ended, "go forth speaking of that which is committed to the charge of you all. They can be trusted: nobly they play their part. But what of your students, to whom so many talents have been entrusted?" I was sorry I spoke: it was waste of breath. He thought me captious and unsympathetic with China's desires of freedom.

Miss Way believes in righteousness, that it matters supremely: and righteousness is indeed a sure staff. She waits upon Something, when her own heart fails her, and that Something restores her soul. The souls of the righteous, are they not in the hands of God? Here is confirmation from a troubled, but steadfast Chinese woman, a Confucianist.

What more do I want on her behalf? Fortitude, self-forgetfulness, courage: are they not of the very splendour of God? Ah, but there is His smile. Of the living honey of its sweetness, we in the West have been so often given full taste, despite our amazing unworthiness. Is it not written how St. Catherine of Siena, though prostrate in illness, could be " full of laughter in the Lord " ? If any woman deserves the grace of spiritual soaring, the south wind blowing upon her garden, the singing-birds lilting amongst her apple-boughs, surely it is this Chinese woman : my friend, Miss Way of Peking.

Is never a draught from the deepest wells of imperishable delight to be brought to her doors ? Is she never to find some day upon her earthly threshold One exceeding fair, who shall say : " Come, my labourer, my daughter ; my yoke is easy and light ; and the fruit of my spirit is Joy ? "

CHAPTER XXVII AN ACADEMY FOR YOUNG LADIES

DOWN the hill we all went. Gradually Miss Way's sombre mood wore off, and she was showing us with much appreciation the pavilion of black copper and the Empress' theatre with its famous drop-scene upper chamber. We came to the most exquisite corridor in the world. A covered walk, open at either side, raised on a built platform, it wends its way through white pines. Its roof, supported on myriad red-painted slim pillars, is encrusted with pictures of flowers and birds and butterflies, scenes of mountains and waterfalls. Long, long vistas of it loom ahead, straight as a die; a marvel of mathematically accurate construction. It is not superb, but enchanting: as if some one had said: "Let us make a pretty thing, and a very pretty thing: so that people can walk about, as on an enamelled cloisonné vase."

We ate our meal alfresco, on a marble fretted parapet which surrounded a locked pavilion. Through the lattices a cool empty space was to be seen, peopled only by the shadows of its lofty timbers. At our feet a square enclosed lotus-pond was spanned by a white marble bridge whereon cavorted stone dogs with carved curling manes and laughing jaws. I ate twice as much of our Chinese friends' provisioning as of our own, for they had come with ample and delicious repasts. Later Miss Way produced the powder and rouge and comb, and we titivated ourselves in the hand-mirror. All very feminine: and how Miss Way reached home without a wrinkle or stain upon her tunic of sheerest white gauze silk, hand-embroidered with tiny bouquets of yellow roses, I do not know, unless by her Chinese woman's talent for restrained and careful movement.

My father started off on a walk. We wrapped my mother round in a rug and propped cushions behind her back, and left her with the day's news on her knees. Then the two women sat on the parapet, threw crumbs to the fishes hiding under the lotus-leaves, and talked to me.

Blossom spoke of Miss Way, and the school. Miss Chi, an erudite Manchu woman, the founder, had begun at the Revolution to wonder if her methods were a little lacking for to-day. So she looked round for a young colleague who would combine a love of the Classics with a mind capable of assimilating modern ideas. Presently she heard of a girl who was the best classical scholar at a semi-foreign school near Tientsin. She took the railway journey and made an occasion to see her : and forthwith invited her to come as second-in-command to her school. For a year she tested Miss Way. Then she called her, and insisted on making her the head of the school, while she herself was to take second place and help only in the teaching of Chinese. Miss Chi was well over fifty : Miss Way was twenty. The school was entirely Miss Chi's making. Could there be people who take one's breath more by their magnanimity than some of these Chinese women ?

The school-house was originally Miss Chi's own family mansion. Its several one-storeyed blocks with their curving roofs are grouped round small secluded quadrangles ; for Chinese houses somewhat resemble colleges at Oxford or Cambridge in ground plan. Miss Chi, an only child, had few family ties. Her father was a Manchu general : and when she realized that there never would be a son, she, the daughter, had donned a boy's dress, sat by her father as his secretary and even ridden behind him at manœuvres—nobody penetrating her disguise. When he died, she had mourned for him and offered ceremonies as a son : and when the three appointed years of mourning were ended, had taken off her man's garments, put on a woman's and retired to the Inner Apartments. So she was not precisely an ordinary woman. She used the family mansion as a school, and had finally given it to the school by bequest.

Unfortunately as the years went by, her funds ran low. Chinese can be most generous people at an initial outlay. They sometimes fail to appreciate the difficulties of upkeep. This failure applies all the way through their public finance, and is one of the stumbling-blocks to civic and national progress. Miss Chi spent her capital on the school. After the Revolution, times were harassing. Scholars failed to pay their fees, and she would not turn them away. Then she became ill. I gathered that she was paralysed. Miss Way in those days lived in the school with her. Many times in the night she would rise to massage Miss Chi's limbs, which troubled her. In the daytime Miss Way would carry on the school, half dead for lack of sleep. Miss Chi, a proud woman, never said a word to her young Principal about money. That was still her affair.

" But now I know that she must often have been sorely anxious," said Miss Way, " and I am sad to remember it."

After six months of illness, and when Miss Way had nearly reached the end of even her splendid physical powers, Miss Chi died. A great sorrow, this.

" The day after her death, it was evidently my duty to see to her affairs. Was I not the only daughter she had ? Had she not died in my arms ? There was nobody who loved her as I did. I sought and sought. Oh, my sister, will you believe it, my honoured teacher had no money left ! There were just twelve tungtzŭ—twelve coppers—in her bag."

She stood up and walked about.

" That was not enough to bury her ! I sent round to her cousins, who are well off, to say that no doubt they would wish to have the privilege of burying, suitably to her rank as daughter of a Manchu general of high birth, their relative, and a somewhat famous woman who had accomplished so much for girls' education in Peking. Imagine ! They answered that they had never approved of her fads about girls' education, that if she had kept the money instead of hiring teachers to benefit the daughters of strangers, there would have been plenty not only to bury her but to leave to her uncle's children, as was proper. ' We will, of course, pay funeral expenses,' they ended. Then they enclosed a sum hardly more than would buy a pauper's coffin ! "

Her eyes flashed. The shame of that proffered sepulture still rankled. A funeral in China is as much a vindication of the character of those arranging it as of the character of the deceased.

"How could I permit such a thing? Yet what could I do? For I could not ask for money from my own family. At that time they wished me to marry, and were setting dowry aside for me. I had, however, gold bracelets and gold ear-rings, given me freely by my dear dead father. I did not wish to part with them: but I knew he would have honoured Miss Chi, for it was he who had sent me to a good school. I sold my bracelets and ear-rings, and have worn silver trinkets since. But I gave my teacher a worthy burial. Our girls attended, and many many parents. His Excellency Chao Erh Feng wrote the funeral oration. It was not a grand, costly funeral, but it was at least a scholar's and a gentlewoman's. Between us we also raised enough money to set up a stone memorial tablet in the school playground. The tale of her virtues upon it was written by the hand of His Excellency Chao Erh Feng himself." I had seen it.

More than this. Miss Chi had one family obligation which she observed strictly: to her dead father's concubine. A grumbling old harridan, I gathered she had become; yet entitled to proper housing and raiment for the sake of the old general's honour. But twelve coppers would not keep her now. So Miss Way had taken over her dead Teacher's responsibilities.

"Every moon Miss Chi had sent her money to live on from her small store, or from the school when it paid its way. Should not Miss Chi's adopted daughter, myself, take on her debts as well as accept her gifts?" she asked proudly. "So I also send her every moon her living. Nobody can say that our school is depriving people of their rights."

Twice after our day's outing to the Summer Palace, Miss Way and Blossom came to tea with us. The first time, Blossom brought my mother and myself two handbags made from the square embroideries which Chinese officials used to wear stitched on their brocade coats, their badges of office. One square was sewn in the middle of the breast, the other between the shoulders. They were to them as Urim and Thummim to the high priest, or as his gold and silver oak leaves to an English consul. We protested at her bringing gifts, knowing that she had no money to buy lovely articles, and for us.

" Oh, they have cost no money," she objected.

" But we can see they are valuable," we replied, thinking she was quibbling, as Chinese do : meaning that she had not spent what some people would call much money.

" They are new embroideries : yet old," she cried nervously. " Now I will tell you truly. The square for this bag, oh my Fu Yün—Happy Gardener," she turned to me, " came from a small pile of such embroideries, a dozen maybe, which my father kept for his various robes of office, and which he had never used. And the other, which is for you, my aunt "—looking at my mother—" was from my mother's similar official wardrobe, as is very suitable : for were you not her sister ? See, it has mauve stitching in it, this circular one. Only the Manchu wife of the highest Manchu official of the imperial blood was entitled to wear insignia of this pattern. I have seen foreign ladies in our streets carrying bags made of our official insignia, but none like these. They look very pretty. It is but fitting that you who are our own friends should be able to carry such bags too. With my love, please use them."

Blossom had sewn the embroideries, with neat fine Chinese stitching, to carved handles. She had lined the bags with remnants of figured black silk, left over from the very pleated skirt which she was wearing at the time. To us two women of an alien race she gave those treasures of hers—the badges of rank of her parents.

When she saw how we appreciated them, she proceeded to bring further personal gifts on her next visit, and we had to chide her.

" They are nothing—nothing ! " she affirmed. " See ! This tiny flower-pot : it is not very fine porcelain. It comes from Chintechen, the great porcelain centre. The Governor of Honan under the Ch'ing dynasty had the duty of inspecting the porcelain factories, and usually the manufacturers made a few special pieces for him. This is one of the small pieces they gave my father when he was governor of Honan and inspected the Chintechen factories."

Miss Way also had her ideas about gifts. She had been unhappy because both my parents had been slightly unwell during our Peking visit. The weather had become hot, for it was now June. She brought a circle—" a magic ring "—of brown flecked Han jade, polished very smooth.

" This is what Chinese gentlemen wear in their breast pockets to ward off disease," she informed my father, smiled maternally, and slipped it into his waistcoat pocket. She had strung for my mother a necklace of aromatic seeds, similar to a pendant of them she was wearing herself, to ward off infection. She presented us with further packages of seeds to browse upon. Her beautiful mouth was at work masticating all the time, lest these jaunts to unaccustomed points of the city should somehow cause her to breathe up harmful breaths. She showed two necklaces of carved seeds, refreshingly pungent in odour, shut in a lacquer box, and gave it and them to me, to put by me for the time when illness might approach. I come upon the box sometimes in our cabinet of curios here at home, and am swept with tides of tender memories. Were there ever kinder women than are found in China ?

I twisted my foot later in Tientsin, whereupon Li Cheng's wife gave me a scolding " for wearing high heels as all foreign women do "— a totally unjust attack on me. (This from a Chinese woman who had only been emancipated so short a while from bound feet !) She gently took off my stocking and said, " Now I have in my cupboard exactly the right medicine-water for this foot. I always put it on the boys' bumps and bruises. But I suppose you will scorn it because it is Chinese!"

" Oh, put it on, please," I begged.

" I will give you the few drops at the bottom of the bottle to take home with you," she appended after her ministrations: and I meekly accepted. To be sure, when I reached home and told my mother, we laughed as she put her nose to smell the " medicine-water."

" It is eucalyptus ! " she had exclaimed. Which it was.

Miss Way's final anxiety over us was caused by the sudden recollection on her part that we were going to the seaside—" to clamber about the rocks at Peitaiho," was her own picturesque version of our future movements.

" You have only leather shoes to wear, being foreigners," she bethought herself. " You will surely slip on those rocks —covered with seaweed they are, you know ! Leather shoes are most treacherous on slippery rocks."

The least harm that could happen, she became increasingly sure, was that we should break our legs : at the same time we should be wearing out the soles and toes of good expensive leather. A pair of leather shoes costs sixteen or seventeen dollars in China—a whole month's salary to a woman teacher.

She measured our feet, heeded no protest, and told us that her amah should be set to work immediately to fashion two pairs of plain ordinary Chinese shoes for us. Of black sateen they were to be, lined with fancy blue spotted calico : and the soles made of and padded thick with many layers of cotton cloth. The shoes, being an afterthought, were not finished till the very hour of departure. The two ladies brought them, together with cakes for our sustenance, to the station when my mother and I were leaving. My father was staying a fortnight longer, reluctant to quit Peking.

There the two friends stood, charmingly dressed, Miss Way towering above Blossom, and both of them looking at us regretfully. I walked up the platform with Miss Way.

" Surely Blossom will come to no harm with you near at hand," I said rather uneasily, for Blossom was pale that day.

" If the worst comes to the worst, and Sister-in-law scolds her too severely, she shall come and live altogether with us," she assured me. " My mother loves her like a daughter by now. I marvel how any one can help loving Blossom ! "

After the train had drawn out, I asked a Chinese gentleman of thirty-odd sitting opposite if I might draw down the window-blind behind him, as the sun was glaring in my mother's eyes. He was dressed in a superlatively elegant gown. Never have I beheld thick white silk of such superb quality. He was sitting delicately so as not to crease it, as I realized, having studied Miss Way's methods with best clothes. His servant came, when the train was well on its way, took his gown off him—to my relief—folded it, and supplied him with an everyday grey silk gown for the journey. He was courtesy itself over the blind, so much so that I felt I ought to make a trifle of conversation, and I admired a basket of curiously flat peaches which were on the floor beside him. In a trice, to my consternation, he brought them across and laid them at my feet—the whole basket, with its twenty or thirty peaches.

I would warn all who have dealings with Chinese people, whether of the old or the new fashion, that it is utterly dangerous to admire any object in their possession. They immediately wish to make a present of it to you! This is the normal generosity of their hearts: their idea of everyday good manners. Well may I warn you, for my own feet are constantly being entangled in their snares. Here I was, as usual, in a pretty pickle. Li Cheng would have laughed at my maladroitness: his wife, Shu Ying, would have deplored my stupidity. Mrs. Sung—I hope—would have had mercy and given me a wrinkle of etiquette as to how to extricate myself from the impasse.

I besought my young gentleman to accept back his own peaches: I commanded him to do so. Each time I carried the basket across the carriage and laid it at his feet, with the merest flicker of a movement he laid it again at mine. The carriage under the broiling sun became insufferably hot, and I grew hotter with the transits across the car. At this game, no other human being can cope with a Chinese. At last I sank back exhausted, the basket at my feet, and the Chinese gentleman bowing and smiling his satisfaction at having beaten me. But indeed I was no foeman worthy of his steel.

The basket remained where it was, and I inhaled the agreeable peach fragrance, while cogitating at intervals how to levitate it once more across the floor. Finally, at the end of our journey, I took out a couple of peaches, and thrust the basket into the hands of the servant who had come to gather up his master's belongings, bowing to the elegant gentleman and explaining that a whole basket of peaches would be beyond my capacity. And then—he took it as a matter of course, and went off with the basket: and it is probable that this was the proper course for me to have taken after all!

In the intervals of his sport he spoke of Miss Way and Blossom. Politely he bowed, and asked:

"Those ladies who saw you off, are they your friends?"

"Very dear friends," I answered. "Do you know them?"

"Indeed no," was his reply: "I could not presume to their acquaintance. But I know of them. They are the most respected and honoured ladies in our quarter of the metropolis. I had not realized that foreigners also knew of their virtues. But truly such ladies, who spend their lives as they do, deserve honour from all—as do their friends." He bowed: I bowed. I said we were unworthy.

"You know their school possibly," I queried.

"No. And unfortunately I have no small girl-child, or she should certainly seek instruction there. For the girls at that school are taught first of all the most important things: good principles and good manners."

Thus did the Real China speak its sentiments: and not out of a poor or a small heart.

Presently he touched on more vexed questions. "I hear that their schoolgirls do not walk in the students' processions. It must be the only school that has managed to avoid being dragged into politics. Processions are, of course, ruinous to good manners."

Miss Way had told us of these processions instituted by Chinese students, on any and every occasion. Begun originally in fine frenzies of protestation over various political questions, they had grown into an incubus on the body educational. By this time, small boys received ten cents for walking in such processions, youths twenty cents from the propagandists. The more sincere walked for nothing, and received what bullets happened to be flying.

Miss Way heartily detested such ways of coercing a government. She, a daughter of official traditions, found these goings-on very much against her grain.

"The student leaders come and waste our time. We have to give them tea and they talk unendingly, while we are longing to go on with our classes. We have been obliged to become one of the union of schools: but so far we have not paraded the streets. The parents know I am old-fashioned in this, and thank us for keeping their daughters at their studies instead of carrying banners and shouting slogans. Why, if we were that kind of school, they would not send their daughters to us!"

The last procession had been against the British, it happened. The student leaders became very urgent, and said that the school must join the parade, or it would be definitely branded as anti-patriotic. The parents would be forbidden to allow their daughters to attend it ; the school-lane would be picketed and scholars turned back.

" I thought I should have to shut up the school for a holiday," said Miss Way. " But I did not want to, for firstly, I dislike being ordered to do what I do not believe in : and secondly, we were approaching our examinations, and the girls needed more lessons, not fewer."

In passive obstruction a Chinese is past-master, and his women are cleverer at it than he. " You therefore adopted the famous Taoist method of *wu wei*—Do nothing," said I to her. She laughed.

" On the appointed day, our old gatekeeper took down the name-board of the school. When the student leaders came to fetch us for the procession, he pointed to its empty place and said, ' No school to-day ! ' Blossom and I and the other mistresses were just inside, in our guest room, and our hearts were beating rather fast. It was a great mercy nobody insisted on coming in. They would have found a hundred girls doing ' silent study.' After a few days we put up the board again, and went on as usual."

I do not know what the moral of that story is. A " name " means more to the Chinese than to us : it actually stands for the thing itself, so that this name-board business would not seem so much of a " lie direct " to them as to us. It is for the Recording Angel, who is accustomed to Chinese hearts and psychological processes, to judge : not for me, thank goodness.

But I cannot help agreeing with Miss Lo and Miss Way that they, rather than the processionists, were on the right track to " Save China "—the admonition imprinted upon the processional banners.

CHAPTER XXVIII MY FRIEND LI CHENG

ON our way up to Peking, I had met at Tientsin a very dear friend of mine. On our way back, we had more time to see something of each other. Li Cheng, the son of a family in whose home I had been a guest, a part of the household during the Revolution of 1911, has ever since those days been my close and constant correspondent. At least every few weeks I may count on receiving a letter from him. His opinion and comments are my guide to Chinese affairs. During the year of wrath, 1927, when the anti-foreign feeling was running high in his land, his letters were a source of much comfort to me. In them was sanity, clear vision, and unshakeable friendliness. However furiously certain of his countrymen raged, it was evident that their foaming rather offended the good sense of the more balanced members of the Republic of China. Once did Li Cheng state in a letter that foreigners were sometimes too proud; and that the modest amongst them were reaping the harvest of the loud voices and rough methods of the baser sort. I might have answered that the Chinese are a proud race also: but when a friend indicates a few failings, it is reasonable to imagine that one is not yet perfect, and one may be grateful for the mildness of his criticisms.

The pleasure of the Kung family in meeting my parents on our way through to Peking had been warming to the heart. Li Cheng's father having died since my parents had been in China, his mother was now head of the house in Chinese eyes. Li Cheng had been asked by the foreign firm, for which he was working, to move to their branch office in a small seaport on the Gulf of Chihli.

"I ought to go," he explained: "but it is so difficult."

"Why?" I asked. "It will be good for the children."

"Yes, and my wife is willing. But, you see, there is my

mother. She is used to the company of many friends and to the social gaieties of Tientsin"—which are not few. "Of course, too, this house is hers and the furniture. And my wife must always look after her, as a daughter-in-law should. Her duty to my mother comes before her duty to me or anybody else. So, unless my mother agrees, I must go alone and come back at intervals to see my family."

This arrangement actually held for a while. Then my dear Aunt Kung, who, after all, has the kindest heart in the world, saw its hardship for her son: and the family moved over *en bloc* to that east coast port. She has not found life too dull there either, for she is the *grande dame* of the Chinese community. Recently she celebrated her seventieth birthday: and in fine style. Theatricals, the club decorated in her honour, scrolls and embroideries hanging in homage: all very charmingly thought out by her family and friends. In fact, nearly the whole family was down, staying there for the occasion. Li Cheng wrote in great fettle over such a gathering.

When we came through Tientsin that first time, Li Cheng had arranged for us to have tiffin at his house; and his two sisters were also to be present. I longed to see Flower, my blood-sister, with whom I had shared confidences in the days before we both married. Small Six, his younger sister, was also married, lived in Tientsin, and had a small son of two. We would be a *partie carrée* of eight, the exact number for a Chinese high square table, sitting two on a side. The table is not very large: but a rice-bowl for each person and a pair of chopsticks and perhaps a small porcelain soup-spoon take much less space than our luncheon arrangements. The Chinese drink very little at their ordinary meals: sometimes wine, made hot, in porcelain cups as small as liqueur-glasses. They drink cups of tea after the rice, which finishes off a meal.

As we sat down at table, the telephone bell rang. Alack, Flower would not appear. She lived near: and Li Cheng was vexed and disappointed—and so was I.

"But you will forgive," he said. Flower had telephoned that it was raining, and her mother-in-law had therefore pronounced it an unfit day for a Chinese lady to be abroad.

In the old days Chinese ladies always kept within doors when it rained. They had a detestation of the wet. Flower is thirty-eight. She has had ten children. She has lost four. She herself fears not the rain : and, besides, her husband's family is wealthy and possesses a motor-car *de luxe*. But it would have been harsh and self-willed of her if she had disputed her mother-in-law's fiat.

Next day I went to see her : and a joyful meeting it was. Whereas in her youth she had none of the beauty of her elder sister, Gentle Calm, or the piquant attraction of her younger sister, Small Six, now that she has come to her full woman's estate, her face has moulded itself into very sweet and fine lines. At twenty she was a little lumpy in the figure : now she is erect and graceful and elegant. In short, she has been one of nature's late developers, and in her maturity she outshines the others. Her look was direct, kind, and honest as ever.

But the birth of ten children has made the difference to her which one might expect. She never forgets the anguish of losing the first two. In a way, she is not a born mother like Gentle Calm. It is one of the ironies of fate that she has six living, and Gentle Calm but two out of her eight. As also seems irony, her six, whose birth was a constant sort of surprise to her, are healthy skipping little people, while Gentle Calm can never feel too sure or at ease about the two left to her. Flower's children are occupied heart and soul with books, with each other, with pieces of sewing, with games. They were teasing each other behind my back, giving half-suppressed giggles at private childish jokes. They had small time for me, a foreign auntie who appeared from nowhere : and they were plainly relieved when allowed to go from the room—bless them. My heart yearned towards them, the children of my friend, had they but known it : but what child can take pleasure in being yearned over ? Later I went out on to the wide sunny balcony to watch them play, the girls preponderating in number. They wore gay chintz tight trousers and short white jackets. Their smooth pigtails were tied with neat red worsted at the nape of the neck. The elder children looked after the younger virtuously—exactly as Flower, their mother, had done in her time. And I fancied the boys were holding their own in the laughter and teasings, just as Flower's brother had done before them!

The home was an immense mansion, and housed fifty persons in patriarchal Chinese fashion. Flower is the wife of the eldest son, so has charge of the working of the establishment: not a small task. She takes precedence of the wife of her husband's younger brother and family—also under the same roof. Each child has his or her own amah, or servant woman, till ten or eleven years old. Then the family tutor takes the reins. There was a bathroom attached to most of the bedrooms. There were flowering shrubs in the gravelled and paved court. There were wonderful carved blackwood screens in a huge salon. Flower's husband—who is still so shy of me that we have never met—sends to London, Brussels and New York for illustrated magazines dealing with houses and gardens, and delights in planning architectural alterations to his home. What between children and housekeeping, mothers and sisters-in-law, there could be little peace for Flower. She looked tired. She said her only quiet was when she went out to mah-jong parties; and Chinese ladies stay up very late at these parties—till early dawn.

The true head of the house is not even Flower's mother-in-law, but that lady's own mother-in-law! A little old lady of eighty, with perfect manners, her rulings according to tradition ought to be obeyed first of all: and in that house they are. The father-in-law and the father-in-law's father are long since both dead. The two old ladies are devoted to each other, and spend most of their time together. Both of them are fond of Flower, and she reciprocates their affection, though sometimes she feels they are too careful of her, as witness the incident of the rain. Public opinion would not blame her these days if she occasionally rebelled. Young China, of both sexes, can now be found publishing repudiations of the betrothals made for them in their childhood by their parents. Does not the modern bride at her wedding display her face, or cover it only with a flimsy white foreign veil instead of shrouding it in modest impenetrable red silk? Do not bride and groom insist on seeing each other before marriage? Does not the bride wear a pink satin dress with a train instead of the traditional red tunic and green pleated skirt : and the bridegroom a flower in his foreign-cut coat ? The power of the mother-in-law is similarly in process of change.

It can readily be believed that a bride coming into an old-fashioned household like this, eating her meals, not with her husband but with her mother-in-law, finds her young dreams of love are not fulfilled quite as she expected. Whose, indeed, are ? However, it often happens to her, as to others, that the reality is in the end greater than her romancings. It is my belief that Li Cheng's wife, and Flower, and Mrs. Sung have all come to that happy conclusion : perhaps because their husbands had the same shy hopes of true love as themselves. I respected Flower the more for putting aside her own legitimate wishes so often for the sake of keeping intact those old ladies' trust in her deference and obedience.

One day I made their rather terrifying acquaintance, for they expressed their readiness to meet me. Flower coached me in my manners, so that I should be exceedingly polite. I took off my eyeglasses, as in the old style : I sat, or tried to sit, in the lowest chair : I stood to receive with both hands my cup of tea : I called myself their youngest sister, and kept my eyes down as a mark of respect. Having become forgetful of old manners through having mixed with modern Chinese, I was much afraid of making a *faux pas*. I asked Li Cheng afterwards if I might send them one of the bouquets favoured by younger China. He hushed away the idea at once.

" They will wonder what you want from them, if you do ! " he ejaculated.

" I want their blessing on my foreigner's friendship with Flower," I protested. He shook his head and quelled my ambitions. Flower, he said, was to come to a large tea-party which my family was giving, to celebrate our return to our Chinese friends. My father would be there and several Chinese gentlemen.

" The old ladies would not object overmuch to a foreign man or two : they understand that that is your custom. But if they once had an idea that Flower might meet Chinese gentlemen at your party, they would become so dreadfully distressed that Flower would not be able to leave them with any comfort. And I want Flower to come. She needs to be brought out more into modern life."

" Suppose they ask her afterwards," I suggested uneasily.

" She will tell the names of the ladies, and then, if they persist, she will say that your father was talking to two or three gentlemen. But it is best she should not know beforehand."

This is not an uncommon method of avoiding direct disobedience by the younger towards the older generation. In China, of course.

When we returned to Tientsin, he invited me to see his father's collection of *articles de vertu*, to which he has fallen heir. He told me of a friend of his whose mother had taken to playing mah-jong fast and furiously and disastrously, and whose debts of honour the son has to take on his own shoulders.

" He could pay them off if he sold his family heirlooms. But," said Li Cheng emphatically and flushing at the thought, " he will not do it ! His children shall have them after him, he vows. It means pinching and borrowing now : but the thought of parting with all his beautiful things is intolerable to him. And I do not blame him ! "

Li Cheng had spread them well out for inspection. A few other friends had come, and we passed from one distinctive piece to another. There was a rose-red Mongolian carpet on the floor which had been three hundred years in the family. There were old bronze Buddhas which his father, who loved Buddha, had collected. There were tiny sacrificial cups of jade. There were ink-slabs, some very ancient, some less ancient, but all done in exquisite relief. There were scrolls on the walls, some with poems, others with flowers or scenes or figures. One scroll dated back to the fourteenth century, and was perfect. There was a magnificent set of furniture : carved blackwood chairs set around a high square table of polished redwood, its top of one flawless piece.

Perhaps the most attractive object to my eyes was a long scroll depicting a day in the life of an empress. Gingerly Li Cheng unrolled it, foot by foot—in true connoisseur style. There she was in her morning déshabillé, with hair simply knotted on the top of her head. Here she came walking across the gentle fields to tend her silkworms, and place them for their food on the mulberry leaves. Next, her waiting-women were dressing her for a court function. Then came the full court and the emperor in all his state, while she and her ladies sat behind a latticed screen and listened and looked. Finally sunset, and the emperor arriving to take his evening meal while she served him with food on painted dishes. I could have looked at that one scroll for hours.

There was a slab of strangely-coloured brown-green jade, mottled and streaked, some six to eight inches long, lying in a padded box.

" Don't take it out," said his wife, Shu Ying. He looked up at her teasingly. " Do you know what her name means ? " he asked. " It means the Virtuous and Brave One ! and she is very much afraid." She made a *moue* at him.

" My father brought it home one day," Li Cheng said. " It was taken from some ancient grave and was given him by an old Chinese archæologist. Han jade, it is called, because it was jade buried in graves of the Han dynasty."

" What a curious colour," I remarked.

" Once it was green," so he told me. " It is a piece they used to put under a dead man's neck, if he was of a rich enough family to afford it, as a pillow. They say it is this colour because it has been soaked with his blood and brains and viscera. Some think it very lucky to have such a thing in the house." He put it into my hand with a mock shiver. I cannot say I felt drawn to it.

" Shu Ying won't touch it," he said mischievously.

" It is rather an unpleasant object," I said.

" It is not its unpleasantness she dislikes," he answered : " it is because she says, having been taken from a dead person, it may have evil qualities."

" Yes," she interpolated, " its owner might have been a bad man. His evil spirit might never have issued from the grave but become mixed into this jade. I am frightened of it. Put it back in its box," she urged, " or I shall leave the room : and if anything evil comes of it, you will have to bear it by yourself. Don't you agree ? " she turned to me.

" I don't see anything to be frightened of. It is rather

disgusting," I said slowly, choosing my words to reach her. " Yet no dead evil man can hurt the clean-and-bright soul. Don't you agree with that ? "

" I am not taking chances," she said : and left the room, nor would she return till assured that the horrid thing was safely in its box.

CHAPTER XXIX HOW THIRD PRECIOUS WROTE A LETTER

ONE of the guests was a young Chinese gentleman of twenty. He had been married two months earlier to a cousin of Shu Ying's, a girl of eighteen, who had chosen for herself the English name of Imogen after seeing a Shakespeare play acted by Chinese schoolgirls in Shanghai, where her home was. Never was there a being daintier than this slip of a bride who came up to my shoulder in height. She had put a dab of rouge in the centre of her lower lip to make " a petal lip." Her eyebrows were finely pencilled. But no doll was she. No artifice could disguise the intelligence sparkling in her eye or the mischievous tilt at the corner of her mouth. Correct it is for a bride to look a flower, and a flower she looked in her straight lavender silk gown embossed with branches of peony flower. From her shining black hair and the brilliant red on lip and cheek-bone, to her white silk stockings and embroidered black satin shoes edged with tiny balls round the instep, she was slim and young and desirable. She and Shu Ying disappeared into the latter's bedroom, while we looked at the antiques. Presently, after most of the other visitors had left, they came back smiling over some private jest.

" I do my best," complained Li Cheng pointedly to me, " to make Shu Ying remain in the salon while I have visitors. I particularly wish her to meet my men acquaintances. Then we share more of life together. But is she amenable, this contumacious wife of mine ? No : every time she can, she slips away ! "

Shu Ying looked at him with a quip in her eye, and a saucy smile on her lip : but, like a naughty child, said nothing. Suspicion assailed me.

" Perhaps your wife finds some of your acquaintances tedious," I hinted. She laughed, and addressed me.

"Precisely when I am longing to do some sewing for the children, Li Cheng's men friends come and sit talking—oh, how they talk: for hours! On politics, of course; and you know how unsatisfactory our Chinese politics are: they change every day—and always for the worse. I cannot be bothered to follow them. Flower declared last week to me she would read no more newspapers. There was nothing in them but battles impending, and bandits harrying the poor, and diatribes about the wickedness of the foreigners. Half the news is lies: and the editors have to admit it next day! Then why do grown men sit and discuss it seriously? It is better to sew."

However, she and Imogen sat down to drink tea with us at the polished table. In old days, we should not have been sitting thus, the sexes freely mixed. I was the first foreigner whom the young bridegroom had met. His father, a noted general, was often in the company of foreigners, of all nations. His mother had died long ago, and his father's first concubine had taken the place of legal wife, as sometimes happens. She was an agreeable and good stepmother to him. Lately, the father, whispered Li Cheng to me, had taken another concubine. The general spent most of his time in Peking, and the Number Two wife lived with him there. The family mansion was here in Tientsin, in a foreign concession, where his family and goods would be reasonably safe. In this abode lived Number One wife, her children and his family by his first wife—two sons and a daughter. Number One wife in Tientsin did not as yet know of Number Two's existence in Peking: or so it was hoped. But as his son had inklings, Li Cheng was not at all sure that Number One was wholly without suspicions. There would be trouble, weepings and wailings, when the dénouement came: but the general would be out of it. He would find business which took him temporarily elsewhere, and would leave the matter to the two wives to settle between them. When he came back, peace would probably be restored; at least on the surface.

In Peking, when foreign visitors called on the general, his Number Two wife received them as would a foreign lady. She gave them tea, showed them her rock-garden, chatted freely, and looked very charming, for she had been brought up in arts and graces. I met later one of the foreigners who had been received thus by her.

"The general is a very liberal-minded modern man," quoth my friend with satisfaction. "His wife showed us round, and he was chaffing and laughing with her."

"Then I will disillusion you," I said. "You shall know the general's true opinion of the foreigners. His legal wife is not allowed to know us. His son has been kept close studying Chinese classics. He speaks no word of any foreign language. He had never met a foreigner before he met me. His father considers that the foreigner's free and easy manners between the sexes indicate lewd minds, and he refuses to have his son's morals corrupted by intercourse with us. Number Two's morals being already shattered, she is fit to mix with foreigners!"

Mind you, as Li Cheng explained to me that afternoon, the general is a good man in his own way. "He is strict and just with his soldiers, and pays them their wages. Every city desires that his troops shall be quartered on them rather than other troops. He is a classical scholar too. His son has to work with his tutor many hours every day, and is now a really learned student."

The young man had an attractive face, and I liked him. But his eyelids were swollen with night-study, his eyes weak and inflamed, his cheek pale. He bore the signs of overwork and of too little physical recreation. "He is looking specially tired now," said Li Cheng, "because he had to finish extra work for his tutor before his marriage. But he is having a holiday from books now."

"Cannot you persuade him to join a tennis club?" I asked.

Li Cheng shrugged his shoulders.

"Do you not think I have tried?" he asked. "He would very much like to play, and to take walks as I do. But his father is afraid, if he plays tennis or becomes athletic, that he will meet foreigners and become like some of the other modern young Chinese he meets in Peking, loose of life and with bad manners. He thinks these are all due to foreign influence. You are truly the first foreigner this new young kinsman of mine has ever met. He has long wished to meet some, and to study new ideas. Now he is old enough to be married, I felt I could ask you together without betraying his father's principles."

Though this was personally flattering, the same could not be said of the general's views of foreigners. The young man partly followed our conversation, which was half Chinese, half English, and nodded assent spontaneously when he understood. We sat on, cracking salted melon-seeds, talking on many things : on divorce, for instance, which has come to the fore lately in China. In the past, if a rich husband lacerated his legal wife's feelings too sorely by attentions to a favourite concubine, she often lived in virtual separation from him, sometimes in another city, and this by mutual consent : but that was not divorce. In Modern China the usual reason is incompatibility of temper, and not only of the wife or the husband, but of the wife's "parents-in-law," very sacred beings in Chinese eyes. There is a woman in prison in Moukden to-day who has been there for twenty-five years because she once raised her hand and struck her father-in-law.

It was not my doing that the conversation turned on concubines, divorce, and similar unhappy intimate affairs. I hold, from personal observation, that in the East as in the West, there is more goodwill and wedded affection than not. Happiness has no publicity. But Li Cheng held us to such talk, and Shu Ying abetted him. Presently it dawned on me that they had a purpose. An Occidental could say to the young bridegroom that which, being Orientals, they could not say themselves. They led the talk determinedly to secondary wives. Li Cheng declared outright that he detested the system. Shu Ying spoke next, and similarly. "Of course you do not approve of it in England ?" he asked me point-blank. The catechism was going round the table apparently. "What do you think, oh Fu Yün ?" he persisted. "It is a bad custom," I responded at last. "Solomon took many wives and they turned his heart from the right. Thus says our Holy Book, very succinctly."

But that was not enough for Li Cheng. If he did not nudge me, he made a motion to it. Almost before I knew it I found myself asking the young bridegroom what he thought of secondary wives. What a personal question—of a man almost a stranger, and with such a family story ! I ran cold after I had asked it, and felt very indiscreet. Then I realized a watchfulness round the table. Li Cheng had a sidelong glance fixed on the young man's face. Shu Ying had her eyes fixed with such unusual demureness on her lap that I knew in a flash that she and Li Cheng had manœuvred me into this embarrassment. And the slim young bride? She sat, very very still, her eyes also down, waiting. Waiting for the answer which would mean so much for their future together. Would her husband go the way of his fathers? Or would he breathe in the fresher air of the new times and take the way of the best Young China which asks comradeship of a wife? The young man did not hasten to answer. He considered the matter. Then he spoke easily, frankly, as if it were an impersonal affair. "I think," he decided, "the new way is best. No concubines."

He certainly had experience of the old way. Of course, he may change his mind. He had been married but two months. If any one, however, could keep a Chinese husband loyal, it surely would be pretty Imogen, with her admirable mixture of sparkle and real worth—that nice balance between the charm of the unexpected and the rock of steady dependability. Li Cheng flickered an eye at me, satisfaction writ in it. Ah! Li Cheng is no fool.

In an instant the atmosphere eased, and we shifted in our seats. Imogen heaved a little sigh. She gave her husband a short quick glance: but there was trust in it and content, and even a touch of that maternal protectiveness which enters into all wifely love. I daresay she had already come to see that life was not entirely honeyed for him in his home circle, and wanted to make up to him for it. They were starting well.

Li Cheng began to talk of the visit he had paid to Europe the preceding year. A delightful time it had been, and vicariously I had enjoyed it as much as he. He had been secretary to a Commission of inquiry into Western methods, and had dined and lunched with the departmental heads of half a dozen European governments. He had won golden opinions by his straightforward honesty, his friendliness, and his sympathetic and discreet translations of speeches. He had visited aeroplane and submarine factories. He had gone over the Naval Dockyard at Portsmouth and called on subalterns in their rooms at Aldershot—and thought these latter superlatively well cared for! Chambers of Commerce had lunched his chief in full state, and he had interpreted for both sides.

One day I had taken him to the Zoo, and we had wandered like children in the fairyland of the fishes' tanks. Another day we went to the Tate Gallery, where he had listened with intelligence to a peripatetic lecturer on Turner's early style, and examined Epstein, whom he thought too alarming to suit Chinese tastes. We had shopped at a big store in Oxford Street to buy presents for his family. Two bedspreads there must be, one for his mother, the other for his wife: sailor suits for his boys: lengths of the new fancy artificial silk for his wife's tunics: toys for the children; and the latest thing in dazzling dressing-gowns for himself. Recklessly he bought, with myself trying to guide his outlay. Then he halted in front of a remnant counter—albeit a very superior one. Tossing in its maelstrom sea, pieces of gold and silver tissue floated on the surface.

"Here be presents for my sisters, my sisters-in-law, and all the wives of all my friends!" he exclaimed joyously. "They shall each have a piece of this beautiful tissue, out of which they will fashion elegant evening shoes for themselves!"

He pounced. The saleswoman, who had reached thirty-five, the age of sense, seeing that we meant business, aided our search. We bore forth enough gold and silver tissue and brocade to dance through all the halls of China's Foreign Office. There are more ways than one of promoting peace between the nations, and the efficient politeness of that shop-woman was one.

"English shopkeepers," said Li Cheng to the young bridegroom in Tientsin a year after her ministrations, "are the most polite, considerate, and best mannered of all the Europeans." A most unusual laudation.

"Oh, Li Cheng! *Hao shuo*—good words!—this is flattery!" I fluttered.

"Not so," he assured me. "Also: nobody pushes anybody else in the street. Nobody stared rudely at me when

I went out. Everybody went in orderly fashion about his own business. If I asked my way, people actually walked some distance with me to show it. Not one of your shopmen or women tried to give me bad money, or to cheat me. They tried to help me to buy usefully! They did not even raise their prices when they saw Chinese approaching."

It appears that some continentals occasionally practise this trick on the Oriental as well as the Anglo-Saxon, and it is more resented by the Oriental than by ourselves.

He spoke long of London: an admirably managed city, but he would dislike living in it. "Those high buildings on each side the street made me feel as if I were in a dark prison," he commented. What would he say of New York? He could imagine himself living very contentedly in one of the pretty country houses in the midlands, or a farmhouse on the borders of Sheffield, whose countryside he thought the loveliest he had seen in England. Indeed Sheffield took his imagination altogether. The most wonderful thing he had beheld in his life was the manufacture of steel there. The metal, pouring out white-hot, hissing, at a terrific temperature, spoke of man's triumphs in science.

"What did you enjoy most of all in England?" I asked him. He thought a moment, then he looked at me with great kindness.

"The time I spent in your father's house," he answered. "When my uncle put his head into my room in the morning, and said, 'Now, my boy, it is your turn for the bath,' my heart was quite full."

Lovely and pleasant indeed is such a thought.

"What struck me in my turn, Li Cheng," I told him, "was the strange fashion your thoughts took—or so it seemed to me—when you told your chief you must go back home to China. He was working you to death—keeping you up till three in the morning writing despatches and then waking you again at seven with more telegrams to put into code."

"Ah! what a tremendous worker he was, and as strong as a horse! He nearly killed three secretaries. He had heard that the American motto is 'Do it now!' and he adopted it. But at three in the morning it is an abominable phrase."

"You said at last to him, you will remember, that you

could not be killed by him, that you must return to China. If you stayed with him, you would soon be dead and then your mother would be left without a support."

"Well?" he queried, puzzled.

"Li Cheng, you have a wife: you have five small children. The eldest was twelve years of age. You never mentioned them to him. You mentioned your mother who is seventy!"

"Of course," he agreed. "That is Chinese way!"

Chinese way it may be: but he had written every day to his wife, and she to him during their separation, and only occasionally to his mother. When the Siberian mail was delayed, he was unhappy and grumbled to me about it. His children wrote regularly to him; and while we were one day sitting in the lounge of a Woman's Club, to which a friend had invited us, he showed me a letter from Third Precious, which also contained a specimen from the latest drawing lesson of an attractive large red radish with green leaves.

This was what Third Precious, aged seven, had written to his father in London. His father sat in the lounge and translated with smiling tender eyes behind his horn-rimmed spectacles.

"Your small son offers this below your knee, and hopes that your body is healthy. Fifth Precious has just come to join our classes. He does not behave very well, but the teacher says he will not be cross with him as he is only five years old. The cat has had four kittens, one is black and white. They are very pretty. There is no more news. Your small son, Third Precious, wishes you Golden Peace, and offers this letter up to you."

"Look, quite good writing, is it not?" Li Cheng had commented, showing me the ideographs. Done by little fingers, doubtless they appeared childishly brushed-in to a Chinese of mature age, as our children's handwriting is known to us for what it is. But they were so much better than anything I could have achieved that I lavished praise enviously. Strange, how race shows itself in handwriting! It is impossible, almost, for the member of one nation to make his handwriting exactly like that of another nation. Li Cheng gets nearer to it than any one else I know, when he writes English.

In the eighth century A.D. a great Chinese poet, Tu Fu,

was taken prisoner of war. From his exile, he wrote poems and letters to his small son. Mrs. Ayscough has translated them charmingly.

The poem written by Tu Fu,[1] when in captivity in Ch'ang Lu, runs :—

THINKING OF MY LITTLE BOY.

Chi Tzu ! it is spring, we are still apart !
The song of the bright oriole, the warm weather verily
but sharpen my distress.

Cut off, separated, I am startled by the change of season ;
With whom can I talk of your quick perception ?

Of the mountain torrent which pours its water
beside our pathway in the lonely hills ?
The rough branches which form our gateway in the hamlet
surrounded by old trees ?

I think of you, and in my sadness find no comfort
but in sleep ;
Leaning on the balustrade, I warm my back and doze
when the sun shines after rain.

And here is another poem set down by Tu Fu in his captivity :—

My Child Chi Tzu, the Thoroughbred Horse, is a dear
little man ;
Year before last was the time he learned to speak.

He knows how to inquire politely the surname of guests
and people whom we meet,
And already recites the poems of his revered old father.

The world is in disorder ; I grieve for his tender youth ;
In a household severed by poverty he can only look up
to a mother's love.

I cannot fulfil my desire to go hand in hand with wife and family
to Mount Lu Mên,
Nor in this time of difficulty can I bind a letter
to the leg of a wild goose.

---

[1] *Tu Fu : The Autobiography of a Chinese Poet.* By *Mrs. Ayscough.*

The feathered signals of armies overflow Heaven, Earth;
The horns of battle mourn through mountains,
down the streams.

Even supposing that I return home, can we avoid
missing each other on the road?
Dare I delay, postpone our day of meeting?

Li Cheng would have intoned these poems, each group of English words corresponding to one chanted Chinese ideograph.

THE next day being Sunday, Li Cheng and I went to the English Church together, for he likes a service in English : but he was aghast at the paucity of the congregation. He asked, in fact, whether this was perhaps a service only for children.

Afterwards he said he would see me home to my hotel, for he wanted a walk, and it was his turn for the Sunday holiday from his firm. We went down the wide dusty Tientsin roads, past the warehouses, past Chinese labourers carrying incredible weights on their back, mostly flour sacks. They toiled slowly with sweat pouring into their eyes : off to Chinese flour-mills. We spoke of them. We spoke of the coming of the modern mills. Li Cheng had lately been seeing some glass-works—glass being a new and acceptable adjunct to Chinese homes. Great sheets of plate-glass being made he had seen, and told me the wonder of their making. Then we spoke of mill conditions. I had the advantage over him because the Scotswoman, my father's colleague and an authority on factory and labour conditions, had allowed me to accompany and interpret for her.

She had taken our party at Hangchow to inspect the best factory in that city, a silk filature run on modern lines by Chinese anxious to do the best by their workpeople. Coming back, I had groaned to her that the smell of the boiling vats, the grind of the machinery was intolerable to me : and she had chidden me because these things, common to all factories, had occupied my attention to the exclusion of the comparatively good conditions prevailing in that filature.

The next day I had gone an errand of my own to the centre of the congested city, through the old narrow streets and over odorous stagnant canals. My rickshaw-puller was a young man of twenty, lean and healthy, with well-formed chest and shoulders. He seemed to make nothing of his grinding toil, and smiled with clear eyes in satisfaction when we reached my far destination. When I was ready to return, I found he had bought two small live turtles and had hung them, together with a wet piece of green weed, on the shaft of his carriage. On our way we came to a long lane, perhaps ten feet wide, on the left side of which towered a high blank wall, so that the lane was sunless. On our right was a row of small one-storeyed hovels, very mean and dreary, crazy with age. Their shutters, which constitute at night the front wall, were down for the day, as is the custom. Passers-by could thus see the whole interior at a glance. We came to a group of four such dwellings, of rotting blackened wood. The rickshawman put down the shafts and gave an ingratiating grin.

" Will the Lady permit that I leave these turtles here at this house? They are for our supper, and they can be cooking. I will run with them inside. The Lady will not be delayed one small morsel of time."

He was so nice a lad that I readily permitted. As I looked, my heart failed to think that such manly strength and courtesy should be housed like that. He added that his parents lived in the country, but he had come to better himself and earn more, and was living with his father's sister there.

By this time the small household was at the threshold, aware of an unusual occurrence: and so were the neighbours. " Will you allow me, oh mother, to visit your house a moment? " I asked the woman of the place, bowing. " This rickshaw-puller of mine, your kinsman, has been using his heart's strength well to pull me while I have been in your beautiful city."

They welcomed me in: they wished me to sit on the one bamboo cane chair—but it was very dusty; also unsafe. There were two rooms to the house: this one in front, in which all lived and worked: and a dark one behind where the cooking was done, and where the two daughters of the house slept on a board for a bed. One of the girls, aged twelve, was helping her mother to weave silk—the silk for which Hangchow is justly famed. The loom, with its large wooden beams, took up half the space of the front room. They sat, the mother and daughter, on a narrow long stool before the loom, and shot the shuttle to and fro to show me how they worked. The high wall, ten feet away, kept off light and air, and the two of them were round-shouldered with peering into their fine work. The elder girl, of fourteen, was making nail-brushes. These are new toilet necessities for China. With a species of crochet-hook, she pulled the fibre through the holes ready punched in the wooden back. For nothing on earth would I have used her nail-brushes. Her hands were covered with itch.

She was working hard ; her eyes were tired and she looked listless. She informed me, but with no feeling of indignation or rebellion, the horrifying number of brushes that had to be threaded before she received a few cents. The household were grateful for the extra pittance. The rickshaw-puller took them for her to the depot of the Chinese fibre company for whom she worked. It was as if a page of Kingsley's *Alton Locke* were being enacted before one's eyes. In the same way, the reports of Chinese prisons take one straight back to Charles Reade. Well, he quoted the proverb over English prisons of his day, " It is never too late to mend," so there seems no logic in despairing over Chinese conditions.

The young man who could take a rickshaw and run away from such a house was better off than his aunt and cousins, all of whom had bound feet. Yet the girls' feet were not excessively tightly bound, so I spoke as gently as I could, told their mother that it was no longer considered necessary to lame girls' feet since the Republic came into being. To my gratification, the young man, their cousin, agreed with me. He said that he had been struck how none of the young ladies from fashionable Shanghai who came to Hangchow for pleasure and health, and who sat in his rickshaw, bound their feet. He said their natural feet looked very pretty. He would prefer a wife, when he was betrothed, to walk with " heaven's feet," he would ! His aunt looked at him in bewilderment. She said it was a mercy, then, she had not bound her girls' feet very tightly because she had heard rumours of this new fashion, and foot-binding did hurt as she knew. Perhaps the girls' feet might be unbound, but it needed some thinking over first.

The neighbours were peeping round the wooden partition

wall which separated the households, and invited me in to see them. Two elderly toothless men and one young man were hammering and making nails on an anvil. The red sparks flew : they laughed to show me their skill. I tried to smile back. But how could I ? Each of those three men had terrible sore red eyes : trachoma, no doubt. One was half blind, the other was scarcely able to keep his eyes open, and the young man's lids were obviously very painful. They kept wiping them with the backs of their gritty hands or on a little filthy rag which lay about.

They spoke to me of their trouble, for every foreigner is supposed to know medicine.

"My eyes hurt me," said the eldest : "do you know a medicine, T'ai T'ai, to wash them right ?"

"Possibly there is one," I told them, and spoke of the fine mission hospital not so far away, which they could visit. "If you have no money, I believe they will help you for nothing. You must go soon : at once. If you wait, you will go quite blind, and then how will you fill your rice-bowls ? Meantime, you must each have a piece of clean cloth and wash it with boiling water daily, and allow no one else to use it."

Earnestly I spoke. I turned to the rickshawman for support, but this time he failed and could not explain. He had not been long enough in the city to know the hospital. I fear they thought I was laying traps to take out their eyes to use in foreign medicine. They smiled at me, but hopelessly, because I did not at once produce healing washes from my pocket, or white powder to dissolve.

"Yes, yes," they soothed me, as a child : and I had to go away.

They weighed on my mind, and the next afternoon I tried to find them. That particular coolie had unfortunately sought another beat, and I never found the little lane again. Once he rushed past me with another fare, waved and called, "T'ai ! T'ai !" to me to show his friendly remembrances : but was gone in a second, and was for ever lost.

I told our factory expert, Dame Adelaide of all this.

"There !" she triumphed. "Perhaps now you will understand why factories are a great improvement on the old ways. You personally may not like the clatter of machinery, the presence of so many workers together, the tedium of always doing one piece of mechanical work. But would you not prefer the well-lit airy factory we visited to the conditions which you have just seen ? "

" Infinitely," I concurred : and remembered the girl's itch.

" I assure you," she continued, " that the modern industrialization of China means Hope. The new conditions are far from ideal—often atrocious, disheartening. Many adjustments will have to be made : but, at their worst, they are better than what you saw to-day. Is it not true ? "

I told Li Cheng something of this as we walked in Tientsin. He said he agreed also, for he had known both sorts, mill and home crafts. I told him how I had been to visit a cotton factory in Tientsin with her, managed entirely by Chinese, with Chinese capital.

" I know it," said he, " the promoters wanted my father to put his savings into it, and he was tempted. He had not enough money, he finally decided, to take risks. It was as well, for the factory has had many ups and downs."

And no wonder. The managing director of the mill and son of the chairman of the company, is a young man of five-and-twenty perhaps. I met him at a Rotary lunch, and he invited me to go out at the same time as my expert friend. He drove me in his two-seater coupe. He had been educated in an American university. Therefore, his elders argued, he must know how to run a huge modern mill in North China. In him they put their trust. Such is the strain which may be put upon returned students. The marvel is that they ever stand it. This young man was setting his teeth and trying to take hold of things : admirably. Now he was seizing this chance of expert advice to learn how to improve conditions.

" It has touched me," said Dame Adelaide, " how desirous is every factory management out here—the innumerable Chinese or the few foreign which exist—to make any improvements I suggest, if at all within their power. No human being, after all, prefers to run his mill to the detriment and destruction of his staff."

The difficulty with that mill, as with others, is that in order to pay its way it must be kept running day and night : and that there are no limits to the number of hours which a

Chinese workman will allow himself for toil. To earn a few cents more, a man in China will nearly kill himself. Starvation stands, skeleton, so close at his hand.

Our small party of inspection came to the workmen's cottages : rows of two-roomed one-storey cots, stoutly and compactly built. They broke every rule of any modern sanitary inspector ; for there were no openings at the back, no ventilation, no sanitation. Yet they had been erected not long ago by earnest people as " model dwellings," with the best intentions. They formed a hamlet, enclosed by a thick and high wall. Necessary, this, for defence both against the bitter winds of winter which sweep ferociously across the dun bare Tientsin plain ; and against marauders whose tooth is almost as keen as those Siberian blasts.

The occupant of one cot, a man of forty, so he said he was, but who had the worn face of a man of sixty, sat on a narrow stool in front of his dwelling, resting. Inside it his wife, a youngish woman, had tidied up the room and made it gay by hanging a couple of scrolls with a dish of oranges in front for some pious occasion.

" Look at him ! " whispered the young director to me, his voice charged with feeling.

" What is the matter with him ? " I asked. The man seemed almost palsied.

" He is only used up—that is all ! " answered the young man bitterly. " Exhausted ! He has worked too hard. He is now nearly blind because he worked day and night for so long. That was before our company took over the mill from the last Chinese owners. We have stopped women and children from working night shifts. This will make it much harder for the mill to pay for some time : and the people complain and say it is harsh and mean of us to prevent women and children from earning. I could not endure to see this man about the mill. He would soon have fallen in his tracks and died. So we have given him the job of drawing water for the workmen's hamlet here. The men are away all day, and it is too hard work for the women, especially the bound-footed. We cannot persuade them to unbind their feet, you know, these working women. They are so conservative ! "

Camera Craft Co., Peking

A Labourer on the Railway. He carries a heavy sleeper on his back

There was one common pump for several rows of houses. It had been installed, as another piece of philanthropy, by the factory owners.

He led us to the apprentices' sleeping quarters : a long low shed in which twenty or thirty boys would sleep in a row on the one long brick bed, heated from underneath by a slow-burning fire, agreeably warm in the awful cold of North China. Trouble looked from the young man's eyes. The apprentices were evidently dear to his heart : and he would have liked to give them better quarters. He had begun classes for them, he said. His face lit up when we came to the small dispensary which had been installed at his wish, with the willing consent of his father, the Chairman. The two dressers had been trained in a mission hospital ; and in their spotless white jackets and with their rolls of bandages and few bottles of antiseptics, they were a source of communal pride to the two thousand operatives who passed by their Red Cross sign every day.

Presently we met the young man's father, a plump good-humoured quick-moving gentleman of the old punctilious type of solid merchant prince. He said frankly that he depended on his son for the new-fangled ways of mill management : and pride was in his tone. There might well be pride, thought I, and did not envy the son his life's burdens. The elder man knew sufficiently about safety devices to ask if theirs were in working order. He listened intently when our expert spoke of forced draughts and covering hoods to carry off the cotton fluff. And she was able to tell him that on the whole she was satisfied with the machine-rooms. Being of short stature, she made me read the thermometers for her, and nodded her head mostly with approval when I gave the figures. The machines had come originally from abroad, and were soundly made. The Chinese corporation had been advised by the selling firm to buy them with the devices attached which are used in the West for the safety of the workers, and they had agreed to the devices though it had meant a greater outlay. One workwoman, in blue cotton trousers and coat, was specially quick with eyes and fingers. She kept saying to me, " Look ! It is an English spindle ! " At last, I answered, " Yes, and I am English too ! " Then she enlarged, saying that English spindles were well made. They do not crack or break easily. It seems she had worked in other mills with inferior spindles, and that few things are more trying to a cotton operative than defective spindles. If you remember, Jane Eyre objected to being supplied with sewing-needles of poor quality, which broke.

As Li Cheng and I walked and talked, we came to the Tientsin Municipal Gardens. They looked inviting. The sun was shining pitilessly on the dry streets. I wanted to sit and talk longer, in the open air.

" Will they turn you out, if you go in with me, Li Cheng ? " I asked.

" I am sure I do not know," he answered : " the keeper ought to, but perhaps he will not—because I have on a silk gown ! We will try, if you like."

In we went, and there was nobody to say us nay. A few Chinese amahs with their foreign charges were sewing or gossiping. So it is not race which is the motive of the discriminatory notice announcing that the gardens are reserved for the use of foreigners.

In Shanghai there has been a great deal of heart-burning over this matter of late years. At first, when an evil-smelling mud-bank was presented to the community by the British Consulate to be transformed into a public garden, no Chinese took any interest. A park is an occidental institution. At Nanking the Viceroy would beg that he should not be annoyed by any business concerning these tiresome barbarians. Let them do what they like in the area set apart for their odious and odd use. As the years went by, it still remained hard to induce Chinese residents in the Shanghai Settlement to take any interest in its municipal administration or arrangements. Chinese expect a government to do its work and not trouble them to do more than pay reasonable taxes.

Then suddenly China woke to the fact that here was a mighty city sprung up at her threshold ; wealthy, well managed : and outside her range of government. At the same time, a legend circulated that a printed notice was to be seen at the gates of the Public Garden to the effect that

Chinese and dogs were not allowed within it. Here was a pretty insult. It was, of course, sheer legend, but it was believed whole-heartedly. I met a Mr. Lu, when later on we were returning to Europe via Siberia: a Bachelor of Science of Hong-Kong University, the nephew of the first member of the Hong-Kong legislature to receive the honour of knighthood. Mr. Lu was a theosophist and a reader of theosophical literature—which nobody can call simple reading. A modern man, too, for he enjoyed night-clubs and danced the Charleston for exercise in the corridors of the train, and showed me the photograph of his pretty and shingled wife. Mr. Lu assured me that he had seen the notice with his own eyes.

"In what month were you in Shanghai?" I asked.

"In April," he answered.

"In April I walked daily in the Park, for a fortnight," I told him; "and I studied every notice-board, and sought in vain. I could not believe that any municipality on earth would be so rude or stupid as to put up such words." Indeed the municipality has during succeeding years denied the notice so often that it has grown weary.

"I tell you I saw it," he asseverated violently.

It was no use pressing the point, but I think I shook his belief. "Was it I myself who saw it?" I hoped he was asking himself, "or was it that young friend of mine, Wang, who said it when he came in one evening?"

At any rate, Li Cheng and I found an arbour in the Tientsin municipal park, and sat down peaceably to finish our talk. It often pleases me how Li Cheng thinks conversation the finest way of entertaining friends.

"My friends came and we had conversation," he would report of some afternoon of high pleasure. His invitation to me always ran, "Please come to tea and we can then converse."

"In the Shanghai Gardens," I now told him, "there is a little fountain with a statue of two children in bronze holding an umbrella between them, and laughing as the water falls on it. Childish, but agreeable. When we were small, my amah used to say they were my brother and myself. She and we stood looking at it for minutes together in appreciation."

" I know it ! " he said. " I almost believe it is that statue which has made Chinese want to enter your garden. It is so innocent that it seems hard to be shut out."

" Does your own heart swell with rage, my brother, at not being allowed to enter municipal gardens or join foreign clubs ? " I asked.

He laughed.

" Not at all," he assured me. " To begin with, I have too much to do to stroll in gardens : and I prefer walking to sitting about on a bench. Then also I realize that we are such a preponderating mass of Chinese that, if we came in our thousands, there would soon be no room for you foreigners who made the gardens. Besides, do we Chinese not know only too well the habits of our uneducated classes ? What manners can you expect from poor coolies who have never had any of the decencies of life ; never possessed a handkerchief, for instance ? "

It was, however, somewhat pointed, I reflected aloud, to permit Japanese, Indians, and other Asiatics to frequent what was originally the white Resident's garden, and not invite the Chinese, simply because as hosts their numbers would be overwhelming. We talked of the suggestion that every one should pay a coin to enter : and agreed it was a bad solution. " The Russian refugees who go there to sit when starving, and die there without a copper in their pockets, where will they die now ? " I queried. I told him of the benevolent Chinese merchant in Hongkew who opened his kitchen doors, after his Chinese servants had eaten, and let starving Russians take away the food remaining.

" Yes, and it is the poor among our Chinese who need a park first," he said. " The others can make a garden of their own. I am ashamed that race consciousness should have degenerated into distinction between the moneyed and the poor. And nobody seems to mind this ! "

" You have well spoken, Li Cheng," said I.

" As for clubs," he said : " when I come to England, do you not invite me into a women's club ? " We laughed over this.

I bethought me of an experience of which the Railway Director told me. He, the Chinese head of the Railway, travelled in his own railway coach down another line to a city, on the Yangtsze, where was a foreign hotel. A European and his wife gained a precarious living as its proprietors. Tired of his many hours' confinement in his coach, the idea came to him to transfer himself into the hotel and stretch his legs.

"But they refused to have me!" he announced, with a twinkle in his eye at being able to tell us the story. "Oh, nothing personal! The hotel manager and his wife were in fact regretful, but they said they dared not risk having me for fear of offending their other clients. The amusing part was that they allowed my secretary to stay: my young clerk, a mere cub. Because the boy was wearing foreign clothes! Very bad clothes, too, they were. I had told him on the way down that if he wanted to wear foreign garments, he must really have them cut decently. They looked like a suit of pyjamas. I had worn foreign clothes for years: but that trip I happened to be in Chinese dress. So I went back to my coach, and he stayed. Not that I cared a rap—saved my money instead." I truly believe he did not mind: he could afford to smile. "Besides," he added, "it is only hitting back a little for all the barriers and prohibitions the foreigners have had to endure. It happened a few years back—it would be different to-day probably."

Freely, frankly, Li Cheng and I talked. He spoke of the old days, when the foreigners first came over the sea-way, of how his great-uncle in his Memoirs commented on them and discussed their treatment. I urged him to translate the most interesting parts so that foreigners might read and learn.

Only once have I felt acute discomfort in Li Cheng's presence at a conversation. A company of us, all foreigners except himself, were sitting on a veranda after dinner: and the subject of Chinese law courts rose. I wished it further. Li Cheng knows well enough—far better than we do—their horrors and possibilities. But before he came, one of the party had begun to tell a story and it was hard to break off, so it had been finished in his presence.

A girl in the South, of very poor family, had been betrothed in infancy. As often happens amongst the very poor, she was sent to her prospective mother-in-law's home when she was eleven or twelve. Thus the onus of her upkeep rested on the new family, and they had the use of her in return as a servant. Sometimes such children are kindly used : at other times they become sad little drudges. The actual marriage would not take place till the contracting parties were eighteen or nineteen. The son of the house was a peasant lad, labouring on his father's few plots. This girl was atrociously used by his mother. She was a healthy growing lassie : the older woman grudged her every morsel of food, and beat her mercilessly.

One day, when the girl was sixteen, being hungry, she took some extra rice beyond that apportioned to her by the woman. The latter, in evil fury, enticed her into an out-shed where a buffalo had once been kept ; fastened her feet with ropes and craned her, feet up, to a beam in the roof by a pulley, and left her there, hanging head downwards. For two nights and a day, the girl hung by her feet, off the ground. At first she cried, then moaned, and at last came silence. But the neighbours became uneasy, and said to each other that some wicked thing was being done, that this was going too far : that, by the new laws of the Republic, women and girls were to have justice, and a mother-in-law no longer held right of life or death. They went, they found her unconscious. They cut her down and took her to a mission hospital. Both her feet had gone gangrenous, and had to be amputated. Benevolent people sought out the magistrate, and he agreed that the girl should be loosed from her betrothal engagements. Her own folk were desperately poor ; so the hospital taught her to make lace. It also taught her the Christian faith. She was never very clever, but she was intensely earnest. Presently a poor farmer married her, and she bore him four sons. She cannot follow him into the fields, as the other women do : so she makes lace. She also started a church in the village, holding services in her own home at first. And she is the most beloved woman of her locality.

" But did not the magistrate put the mother-in-law into prison ? " asked Li Cheng hotly. " He must have been a very bad magistrate. Such stories make me sick."

Whereupon, at the mention of Chinese prisons, one of our party burst forth into the indignation which their mention raises in the Occidental mind. Chinese lawyers of acumen and great earnestness have succeeded in formulating a fresh and admirable code of laws. As yet the power to put these into working force is absent. The administration of justice cannot be established in a year or two. The talk went on, and very wretched did I feel; for Li Cheng was growing whiter and whiter, more and more silent.

Down the lane I walked with him after the evening was over.

"Oh, brother," I cried, "you must not be too hurt by the talk this evening. It is not fair to dwell on China's failures. She has made tremendous progress and has started prison reform. Rome was not built in a day."

He shook his head. He gave a heavy sigh.

"You mean to be kind, my sister," he said: "but you know very well that every word uttered to-night was true."

CHAPTER XXXI EAST AND WEST

OPPOSITE us as we talked loomed the empty bandstand. I told Li Cheng how my friend, the Professor of Logic, had confessed that he cared little about music, and on the whole, if he had to listen to it, preferred the foreign variety as perhaps less cacophonous to his ears after his life abroad than Chinese. Li Cheng contemplated the bandstand.

" We often wonder, you know," he ruminated, " we Chinese, what your king has to do with the finish of some band music, a theatre, or a cinema film. He would not even approve of some of the scenes, I think, for the whole world knows how honourable and good he is."

This view of our National Anthem had presented itself to me before, naturally, as it must to every member of the British Commonwealth : but it reduced me to incoherence from Li Cheng. He looked at me inquiringly.

" Perhaps that is the reason," I stammered. " The notes of our inadequate national anthem recall us after the film nonsense, and not always good nonsense, to duty and the recollection of some one who has a vast sense of duty. And then—well, I suppose the moral strikes home that our country expects the same of us. It certainly stirs our British hearts to hear it : as all our various national anthems stir our European and American hearts."

" But you play them so often," he persisted. " It is fatiguing for us Chinese to keep rising to our feet. For we are not British, or French or American. Do you think it would be considered impolite if we rose, say, once a month, and you could take it in turns which national anthem was played ? "

" Oh, do not ask me," I moaned.

" Moreover, this is China ! Would it not be very polite if foreign bands played our national anthem sometimes too ? " he suggested blandly.

" It would," I answered, " and desirable. Perhaps that would remind us of our foreigner's duty to China also, eh ? "

He smiled back at me, and nodded his head.

" Oho ! I see your innuendo ! You think it might make us Chinese think a little more of our duty to our own land too. We might even learn to know our own anthem if you played it often enough to us. I know it myself, but very few of my friends do."

I told him how once, at a big dinner in London, I sat beside the representative of his Government. Suddenly we were called to attention while the orchestra played a tune. " What tune is that ? " I whispered to him in the hush. He discreetly slid his programme into view.

" Oh, it is the Chinese National Anthem ! " he faltered in return, and we stood stiffly.

" They played it for me, I suppose," he said querulously as we sat down again. " One of our many Cabinets offered a prize for a national anthem. A Scandinavian musician was the judge, I believe. Copies of the particular melody he chose were sent to our legations abroad and distributed amongst the military bands of Europe and America. But I never heard a Chinese sing it yet. How can I possibly recognize it when a foreign band plays it, especially with those trimmings and harmonies ? "

He sighed. The West has laid it down that no self-respecting country should be without a national anthem. Europe, and America—for is it not peopled by the European overflow, or so says Sun Yat Sen ?—have hustled China into possessing a flag, or a series of flags. America, and Europe, have insisted on China feeling exceedingly nationalistic. China has courteously obliged these two continents, and added into the bargain many other symptoms of strong race consciousness for which they had not bargained.

After anthems, we discussed flags—Li Cheng and I. There is a good story in Tientsin of a British scoutmaster who, at an international rally, discovered that all his patrols were ready to march with their national flags displayed—except the Chinese. He ran into a Chinese shop forthwith to buy them. But his Chinese language was halting, and he asked for " wives," instead of flags," giving a breath too much, as though he had aspirated in the wrong place.

" I want seven wives," he fired at the astonished shopkeeper ; " seven Chinese wives ; and at once."

There were farcical scenes till his Chinese patrol leader came, seeking him, and eased the situation.

Li Cheng said it was a tale *bien trouvé* and he did not believe a word of it, and would I talk sense now ? So I told him of a letter which I had received perhaps three months ago, and which had lain heavily on my soul. The writer was an elderly Chinese gentleman, a Christian of long standing, a man looked up to by Chinese and foreigners, chairman of a dozen philanthropic committees. He was a director of one of the biggest modern Chinese business institutions run on modern lines. The employees had Sunday off, reasonable working hours, had pensions, and their women workers were specially cared for. Every industrial improvement which Chinese Christian directors could contrive they had put into practice. This did not prevent the employees from going on strike quite as frequently as in the other firms which provided no such benefits. Li Cheng's father had invested most of his money in this firm, so he had an interest in what I said of its Chairman.

This gentleman was much interested in my husband's map of China ; and I sent him a copy of a magazine containing an article of mine about China. Judge my dismay when I read, in a postscript to a pleasant typed formal letter of thanks, the words in English in his own handwriting, " Your article is unusually free from the superior complexity to which we Chinese are ordinarily treated by the foreigner."

The bitterness, the long-suppressed pain of such a sentence, the underlying injustice of it to his innumerable Western friends, burnt into my heart. I had shown it to one of his English friends, a man who sat under him in committees, and who had worked with him and tried always to put him in a higher seat of the synagogue than his own. He could hardly believe it, and dashed the letter down momentarily in despair. " What more can we do ? " he asked.

" Perhaps he thinks it is an effort you are making," I cogitated.

"But I like, I admire, I honestly respect him," he protested. Was it that the Chairman thought the foreigners on his committees were lauding his office and not thinking at bottom so highly of himself? I cannot say. I left the letter unanswered for many months. He had meant it as a compliment to me, but it was a very left-handed one.

Moreover, he was a man who had stood firmly as a Christian when it would have been much easier to let that religion drop. He had been tried in the faith as never I should be. He had done noble things with his life. It seemed impertinence for me to criticize him, however indirectly. Yet eventually I did reply, when that sentence had germinated in the soil of my subconsciousness a long time. "I suppose," I wrote him, "that St. Paul called the superiority complex of which the East accuses the West, probably with justification, plain Pride. But also he called the Inferiority Complex by the chill of Envy. And both sins can poison and destroy the soul."

I might equally have quoted Lao Tzu who said: "The greatest directors of men are those who yield place to others. This is being the compeer of heaven."

"Why should we hate the West?" Li Cheng now asked of me. "My distinguished grandfather, who was so long our Chinese Prime Minister, and who fell into disgrace because he was willing to learn from the foreigner, would have been ashamed at such talk. If you read his Diaries, you would know that he could never have been of such a narrow heart."

And, then, this modern Chinese gentleman in the thirties, scion of one of China's most ancient and learned families, secretary now to a foreign manufacturing firm, and father of five small boys, made one of the most magnanimous remarks I have heard in my life.

Simply he inquired.

"Tell me, do not you of Modern Europe and America owe much, very much, to Greece and Rome: yes, and to Judaea?"

"We do truly," I replied. "Only lately did our Prime Minister say when he was praising the classics, that it was not for nothing that Western Europe was forged on the anvil of Rome."

"You are not ashamed of your debt, are you? I scarcely take up a book by a Western author about your civilization without being struck by the fact that you glory in tracing your culture back to others."

"Of course we are proud of it," I assented.

"Very well then," he pursued his argument, "I can see no reason why we of the East should not now be glad and proud to accept lessons from the West. To me, it shows that we have a spirit willing to learn. Is not that a first essential in the renascence of a nation? Those of our people own small souls, who think it shameful that we should ask of the West to teach us of its science and culture. That is not true patriotism; it is conceit. But they are, of course, the young. So we must forgive such children. You are not ashamed to 'remember your roots' in Rome and Greece and Judaea. Let us be equally great and not be ashamed to own our indebtedness either!"

Do you wonder that I am happy to write to him as my brother, when he can speak thus?

"Then what is it ails between us, as East and West?" I asked him.

"Perhaps it is that you are too impatient with our slow progress," he said thoughtfully.

"When I contemplate the progress you have made during my short life, I am filled with amaze and admiration," I told him. "Yet you are right. It is so much easier to look at what lacks than at what has been accomplished."

"Perhaps you scold us too much also," he shook his head at me. "How can we help our misfortunes; the injustices we suffer? Can a poor farmer resist a military commander in his district who forces him to sow the poppy with a rifle at his head? If you would sometimes intimate that you also suffer from some injustices and imperfections, and be sorry with us instead of for us, it would be easier for us who know how good your hearts and intentions are when you scold!"

Thereupon we went into partnership together once more. I was to write an Open Letter for a Chinese daily newspaper whose editor we both knew, and dedicate it to "China, my Foster Mother." I was to try to write what we Occidental people at heart feel about her people, and Li Cheng was to put it into Chinese.

"Now write it in such English as will be easy for me to translate!" he adjured me: and I promised to do my best.

By the time it was printed, we were settled at Peitaiho. Feeling elated at having thus made a first feminine flight into Chinese journalism, I took the paper nonchalantly round to Mrs. Sung on her veranda. She seized it: she read it there and then, muttering the Chinese words aloud as is the Chinese habit of reading. Every now and again, she exclaimed:

"Good, good! Excellent!"

"Oh not so very good!" I modestly demurred.

"Very good, I tell you!" she assured me vehemently.

Who could have helped feeling a trifle of self-satisfaction? She gave me the paper back, and spoke. "That," she declared, "is the best piece of Chinese I have read for years. I thought every one was dead who could write Chinese like that. These phrases are admirably turned. Of course you did not write that yourself! Now who did? It is a most beautiful style!"

Not one word about the subject matter of the article. She asked if she might keep the paper—she wanted to send it to Mr. Sung, and he should show it to her father. This was the best Chinese the latter would have seen for many a long day and would please him.

Acquiescently I left the newspaper. Half-way home I was overtaken by a fit of mirth and sat down to contemplate the infinitude of the sea, to round off my lesson. Mrs. Sung's last words rang in my ears. "You are very lucky to have a scholar like young Mr. Kung to translate your article, I can tell you!"

Exactly so might any of my English friends and relatives have pricked conceit and put me in my place, for the good of my soul. It seems that Chinese have no more illusions about their friends than Western folk.

What had Li Cheng said of my precious article, which had been dug out of the very rock of my soul? His comments had been: "It took me two hours to translate your essay. There was one paragraph I approve of very much—the last, where you give the Buddhists a piece of your mind! It will do them good."

" Oh, I hardly meant it that way," I stammered.

Not for nothing was it written for our example of the man Moses, who led a people from slavery to freedom, that he was very meek, above all the men which were upon the face of the earth. The proud may attempt to drive : it is obviously the meek who successfully lead.

Li Cheng and I had many serious talks together, amongst all our jokings. One day, for instance, he proffered the remark in troubled tones, " I fear I can never become a baptized Christian, though indeed it seems to me I have long been a Christian in thought. You see, I can never give up ancestral reverence."

To him the two seemed incompatible : to me they have never seemed altogether so. Much controversy has raged over this in times past, both in the Catholic and Protestant churches in China. Yet it may be that his instinct is truer than my philosophy.

" One might imagine that you thought Christianity did not require us to revere our parents and elders," I remonstrated. " Do not forget that on the Cross one of the last words of the Saviour was about His mother."

" Yes, I remember," he said, troubled : " but would He have burnt incense to her if she had died first, as I have done for my dear father ? And I cannot and will not depart from this custom of ours."

" We put photographs of our dead in our rooms," I suggested, " and take flowers to their graves. Neither are we lacking in reverence. Do not think it of us." I felt his perplexity. " China must work out in her own soul that problem ; and who doubts that light will finally come to the sincere ? " I appended glibly.

" That 's an easy way out of it for you," he answered pertinaciously.

The whole structure of Chinese life and thought seems built on other foundations than ours in this particular, just as a Chinese house is different from ours. Yet, houses they both are ; warm dwellings for frail human beings. And what is life without variety ? What would be more soul-destroying than a world whose houses were each alike, where all the inhabitants had the same complexion, shape of head, spoke the same tongue and elaborated the same thoughts? What a shocking thing would be a world composed of Anglo-Saxons only, of Chinese or Indians! How deplorable and tasteless a society where all worshipped alike, a society composed entirely of Methodists or Mohammedans, Catholics or Parsees! The joy is to discover the ties between us, to build on the common factors in our philosophies and experiences, to perceive the likenesses in our dissimilarities, the unifying principle in our variability. If now and again we lift our eyes, we may catch a glimpse of the rainbow-hued pattern in the heavens of our interwoven humanity here below. We hold our breath, perceiving a glimmer of the great Artist's idea. Does He perchance, who painted the face of man in varying hues, just as He did the pigments of the leaves and the many-coloured soil, see a harmony of colour working out, where we can only as yet see a confused clash? Sure I am, at any rate, what is His desire for a woman's hands to do. When a hole has been torn in that Cloth of Gold by the ignorant and the rough, who more fitted than she to sit patiently and mend the rent? Into the intervening spaces she must weave—with that efficient instrument, because so small, her needle—threads of generous affection strong enough to stand a tug of occasional misunderstanding.

Yet try as I would, I never understood what exactly it was that had troubled Li Cheng in his defence of ancestral reverence: for troubled he was and is. Some touch of thought from Western sources prevents his being at ease in the matter as he would have been in the old days. He is far too modern to believe that his own spirit will rest any the easier for the incense his sons may offer, when he himself has to go forth into the spirit world. He comes of a family which for generations has been founded on the highest Confucian philosophy, mixed with the purest of the Buddhist doctrines with which China has been stayed in days of sorrow. His grandfathers and great-grandfathers have smiled pityingly on the superstitions, the incantations, the satyr-like idols, the abracadabra of the necromancers and the geomancers; which constitute religion for the unlettered. If sickness or financial loss afflicts his family, he does not think it is because his great-uncle is laid in his grave facing the wrong way, and is making the family uncomfortable till they have paid the geomancer a fee to tell them the right direction he ought to lie. If his little son has fever, he sends for a doctor. He does not call in half a dozen medicine-men, take their different prescriptions—often very unpleasant ones—before the gods, and shake the sticks till one falls out to indicate which prescription is right. Nor would he split open a cock and lay it, hardly dead, bleeding entrails and all, upon that little son in his bed, so that he might perchance absorb the life of the cock and be helped in the sickness. Neither would Mrs. Sung. Yet to both of them, the family or New Year gatherings at the ancestral tablets have a depth of meaning which cannot be measured by us. The tablets contain nothing but the names of the ancestors : but the Name still to them contains something of the soul of the Names. *Nomen est Numen.* As the family bows in remembrance, as the smoke goes up, and all the air a solemn stillness owns, there comes a sense of awe. Confucius, who refused to discuss the gods, and to whom Heaven's messages were a matter for the Emperor rather than for the people, once spoke of those ancestral ceremonies in a famous passage, with an unwonted vividness, unlike his usual reticence. " How abundantly," said the Master, " do spiritual beings display the powers that belong to them ! We look for them, but do not hear them ; yet they enter into all things, and there is nothing without them. They cause all the people in the empire to fast and purify themselves, and array themselves in their richest dresses, in order to attend the sacrifices. *Then, like overflowing water, they seem to be over the heads, and on the right and left of their worshipper.*"

Are the spirits present ? " How can we tell ? " asked Confucius, and still asks Li Cheng to-day.

" There comes a sense of presences—benign and great," said Li Cheng to me.

Or is it but the One Presence showing thus its Immanence to wistful Chinese hearts in the only way in which they have been able to understand its call during their many generations. Strange to think that Confucius in China was refusing to discuss the gods less than a century before Socrates in Athens was discussing them much too much, according to the notions of his fellow-citizens.

By permission of Rev. A. Shorrock

General Chang Chih Chiang. A Christian; a strong supporter of the Anti-Opium Crusade; for many years General Feng Yu Hsiang's second-in-command

new thoughts pouring like a flood upon him? The great

But why, then, is Li Cheng not at ease, for all his loyalty to his traditions ? Is it that ancestral reverence, though he experiences it at its highest and most spiritual and intellectual, has come to seem small to him in these days, when " the great wind has blown " upon the land-locked seas of Chinese thought ? Is it that the ancestral shrines seem but a paltry window to open upon the vast spaces of eternity ? Or is it that this clinging to the past plays a little too much for safety ; that it lacks a touch of steel, of a trumpet-call to subdue the unclean and dark things of this earth ?

So stood a Young Ruler, halting before the difficult narrow rocky way. A Chinese youth of to-day, whose foundation is laid on the old intellectual philosophies, reminds one even more of some young Roman stoic, imbued with the ethics of Marcus Aurelius. Fresh from his races, the laurels on his brow, the son of the governor of a province, he picks up the prison literature of an insistent little Jew. " You possess indeed virtue, your old Roman shield, to guard yourself from attack," runs the argument of that very gallant gentleman, and scholar. " It is no unworthy escutcheon. I, too, have kept clean ; I, too, have run races. But now—now," rings the urgent voice, " put on the whole armour of light and go forth in the daylight to battle with the powers of darkness, oh knightly heart ! True, I am here in chains because I took on that warfare : and likely to die a cruel death. Yet would I not be elsewhere, for dying, I can say, ' I have fought the good fight.' "

Can you perceive the young man, Roman or Chinese, flushing at the challenge, bewildered at the strangeness of the new thoughts pouring like a flood upon him ? " The great wind has blown." Shall he wrap his cloak the tighter round him, shut his windows and hug the chimney-corner ? Or shall he venture forth and brave its fangs ? For, indeed, there is a bite to that wind, a keenness that searches bone and marrow. Yet is it also a wind that blows away the chilly mists of past inhibitions and terrors, and lets in the sunshine on the earth. It is the wind that ushers in the spring, could he but believe that dauntless Jew, whose soul had bourgeoned and blossomed with its life-giving breath.

AND so we came to Peitaiho, north of the Tai River, the modern seaside resort which has grown up on the sunny breeze-laden Gulf of Chihli: a product of the foreigner. Chinese rarely used to take a change of air, and then mostly to the hills. It is becoming more and more the fashion for Chinese of wealth and social standing to send their families to the seaside in summer. Brown-limbed, cheery Chinese youngsters, the girls in becoming bathing-caps, swim like fish in the mornings, and in the afternoons play tennis exceedingly well. America and Hawaii add their quota of idea as to what is desirable to wear, or to leave off, in such surroundings: and as to what should be done in the way of sea-sports. French and Japanese, Germans and Russians also contribute their different notions as to the gaiety of nations by the sea. In four days running, you may be offered coffee by the French, tea by the English, beer by the Germans, and ice-cream by the Americans: and then go on to nibble sesamum-seed cakes on the veranda of a Chinese friend, and borrow her fan to cool your brow. Yet it is but twenty years since Peitaiho was mainly a resort for quiet missionary folk, the wives of Customs officials, and relays of Legation people rather less easily *ennuye* in those days than these. The gayest hospitality was dispensed by Russians of the grand old school, whose villas to-day are theirs, alas, no longer.

There are many new Chinese houses built up the hill-sides amidst groves of trees. To be sure, the wildness of Lotus Valley, where we used to gather scented tall white lilies, has been tamed. But although one may sigh at having to go further afield for Heaven's wild flowers, one is vastly entertained by the spectacle of man's flowers of the mind which have crystallized into architecture before one's eyes. The new Chinese houses are luxurious, and solidly built, too: but chiefly are they magnificent for the scope of their imagination. One might think that here was a touch of Northern Italy : but they are, I believe, of pure Chinese conception. These Chinese merchant-prince dwellings are immense houses: no cottages. Their owners have had imaginary vines painted climbing up the front wall, a group of trees pictured on the back, and a flock of birds life-size near the eaves on the side walls—all done in bold and impressionist lines and colours. It is as if the owner, seeing a large empty side of wall, felt his artistic temperament roused at once. "What a heaven-sent space for a good-sized painting: a picture of the vines and groves that may some day grow about my new house!" So it is done—and with a brush that may well compare with one of "comet's hair" for size.

Mrs. Sung had leased a pleasant villa with a very wide veranda. She was still not very well. I told her it was her late nights at Shanghai which had undermined her health : but I am not sure. I rather wish I were.

Perhaps the reader has begun to wonder if ever he was going to hear of Mrs. Sung again—the lady of my tale. Well, well, praise be there are plenty of excellent literary precedents for wandering about as I have done in company with a vast host of other people and leaving my heroine alone in peace. At least I have not killed her off at the outset as did one, William Shakespeare, with Julius Caesar, the namesake of a play of his. True, there might have been added to the title-page a codicil, in the manner of Thackeray, "A novel without a Heroine," but this book is not fiction. It is real, not imaginary : a drama of people alive to-day, a portrait of Chinese life going on this living minute. Mrs. Sung comes walking into it now and then, speaks her part, then goes off to attend to her family or enjoy her leisure in the way of all women. The last thing she wants, she says, is to be on the scene the whole time. She likes a little privacy.

For my part, here at Peitaiho, I was very glad to see her again—the darling! As she was not well, I was also glad to see one morning on her veranda a young doctor, a Cambridge graduate, who had walked the wards of a London hospital. He wore his college blazer, he lay in real graceless British style sprawling on a long cane-chair: he had a cooling drink on a table by his side: he wore shorts, and he was filling his pipe when I came up the steps. He was the Cambridge medical young man to the last hair, which was smoothed down with brilliantine. He spoke with the Cambridge accent; and, being a Cambridge woman myself, I was enchanted with him and his accent, his blazer, and his pipe. We understood each other at once. Without a word, we knew an infinite and common compassion for the multitudes who had not been granted our undeserved and supernal advantages. Mrs. Sung sat by, and looked at us with charmed eyes, proud as a mother hen of her young doctor. He had just become engaged to a relative of hers, a girl who had been educated in Hong-Kong.

"So she is distinctly English in her ways too, and they will suit each other," she asseverated.

"But not so English as Miss Mary Lee, eh?" I queried. Mrs. Sung and I had argued on the subject of Miss Mary Lee. The young lady in question had spent a portion of her young life in England: but I did not consider her typically English, and Mrs. Sung did. Miss Mary had unexpectedly arrived at Peitaiho with three other Chinese girls from the South of China, each girl more amiable than the last. Imagine it! These young women had quietly taken rooms for themselves at the hotel. No chaperon, no fussing with anybody.

"We did not want to miss the nice times you are having in Peitaiho," explained Miss Lee to us. "Our parents could not come. We did not want to foist ourselves on to our various friends and relatives here, though it is quite Chinese so to do. It is a bad custom, and we are determined to change it. We did as any American or English girl would have done: made up a party and took rooms together at the hotel."

The combined age of the four girls was perhaps eighty.

"My child," I said, "I do not honestly believe that English parents have reached such a stage of decontrol with their daughters of twenty as that. They would have put up a modicum of battle for authority."

"Our parents washed their hands of us," she replied, "and said that they supposed we should be safe enough at Peitaiho, with so many friends about." I did not like to remind them that the ship they came on to Tientsin had been pirated a year before.

Mrs. Sung extended her bright wing over the girls, daughters of her own friends or friends' friends. One day she brought Mary Lee over to see us. She herself travelled in a rickshaw, bumping over the uneven footpaths. Mary came riding on a donkey, which was my own preferred form of promenading at Peitaiho. It pained me beyond words that a man should stagger over those inclines and declivities, pulling me behind him in a rickshaw, when I might be trotting on the broad back of a low-statured furry friend with long upstanding ears. Still, donkey-riding is not considered an elegant method of progression by sophisticated Peitaiho society: it is dishevelling to afternoon garb. And these four girls being very elegant, the other three rode in rickshaws. But I liked to see Mary Lee riding her donkey in solitary light-heartedness: and she chose spirited steeds.

She rode astride. She wore a well-cut pair of khaki breeches, fitting at the knee, and her pink silk blouse was tucked into the top of her breeches. Her sombrero hat was caught under her round chin by a leather strap. She looked a slim and girlish cowboy. When she and Mrs. Sung left, she vaulted on to her donkey over its tail: she slapped her thigh with her whip, gathered the reins with her left hand, waved her right in farewell and galloped off.

New China: and the child-touch of melodrama was naïvely alluring. One had to smile, with sympathy at the gallantry underneath such assumption of gaiety and devil-may-care freedom. I fancy Mary Lee is like our other young people: very chivalrous to the under-dog, hating injustice, or the suspicion of it, to such an extent that she often runs with her head full-tilt against the brick wall of convention in the attempt to shatter it.

Mrs. Sung's comments, however, brought me to earth with a shock, as we watched Mary Lee canter away.

"How English!" she said to me, clambering into her rickshaw to toil far behind in Miss Lee's wake.

"English!" I exclaimed. "What makes you say that?"

"But look at Miss Lee, how very English she is," she persisted. "The other girls tell me she is even more English than appears on the surface. She walks on the beach after dinner, to see the stars and listen to the waves. Recently, you know, two Chinese village girls were carried off by bandits near the hotel. It is useless to speak to her of such danger, they say. She goes out bare-headed at night to the edge of the sea, all alone, without a fear. She is very English."

"What you say about the stars and walking in the moonlight may be English," I agreed. "But never in the whole of the United Kingdom did I see a young lady pay an afternoon call, even at the seaside, in a pink silk shirt tucked into khaki riding-breeches, and leap on to a donkey over its tail. I do not say it should not be done: in fact, I rather enjoy seeing it done. All I say is, I never saw an English girl do it."

She would not listen. "Mary Lee is typically English," she said stonily. "Every one says it."

The young doctor sitting on the veranda did not understand our allusion to Miss Lee. He began to talk of England. His cousin, also trained in England and older than himself, had occupied a responsible position in an English hospital during the War, while our doctors were at the Front: and had shown conspicuous ability.

"We often talk of our English posts and patients," said the young man. "I tell you, your slums are a problem."

"They are," I agreed. He turned to Mrs. Sung.

"How can a poor widow with five children live on a pound a week? It simply can't be done, you know. That is only ten dollars." He shook his head sorrowfully.

Mrs. Sung began puzzling away, turning that into New York values in money and food, which she knew better than English. I knew she was wishing that every poor widow in China with five children had ten Chinese dollars a week, but understood that this represented far less value in Europe.

"It is impossible," he went on, "when she has to pay ten shillings for rent. How is she to buy enough food, not to mention boots for the children? London is like Hankow in winter, not Tientsin: cold and wet. Good boots are a necessity. Of course in such circumstances there is always one of the family in hospital."

I had not expected to drop into a dissertation on London

slums and the problems of our English poor by a young Chinese doctor who had worked amongst them, on that shady Peitaiho veranda. Yet perhaps my husband was right when he declared that the world's economic questions were all bound together : that the key to their solution should be sought, not always under our own doorstep, but far away in another land.

I had heard of the young man before I met him. He and his cousin were in practice together in Tientsin. When the English doctor at the mission hospital went on furlough and there was nobody to take his place, the two young men had acted alternately three mornings a week in his place, with but a small fee from the Mission. They were Christians, as were their fathers before them : and had been brought up to believe that Christianity entailed service. Mrs. Sung thought better of "The Doctrine" because this Dr. Ma and his family practised it.

Not easy for a young man to show forth all the Christian virtues, when he is merely engaged in his daily avocations and beginning to earn his living. People expect him, also, to be a leader of the young Chinese Church. It would be simple to let The Doctrine drop, or keep it for very private moments. Mrs. Sung was looking at Dr. Ma as if she took it for granted that he would be different from other young men of her acquaintance. He was supposed to be possessed of a high standard in truth, kindness and cleanliness, from which he would not swerve, however tempted.

"How very hard it is to be a Christian!" exclaimed Browning. What would he have said if he had been a young Chinese medico fresh from England, with a practice to make, and most of his entourage hostile to the motive springs of his life? I said to Dr. Ma that I had been to a Chinese church when I was last in Tientsin and had heard a very helpful sermon by a Chinese Doctor Lei. This man, modest in manner, known to a handful of Europeans, is the remarkable house surgeon of a mission hospital. He was often up all night working over a patient, he shared the heavy strain of the dispensary and the wards, and he operated. Yet he contrived to find time to produce a sermon, and a fine one, nearly every Sunday morning—because the students loved best to hear him preach. He had a family: a wife and four small children. "Dr. Lei," said the young doctor on the veranda, "is a marvel."

He told us that Dr. Lei had received only what training could be given at a mission hospital, which is bound to consist of much practical work and very little book teaching.

"Yet none of us can touch him for certain diagnoses and operations. His instinct and his touch are so sure. And, then, he is so utterly good."

"I first heard of him in a strange way in Tientsin," said I.

"Oh!" cried Mrs. Sung. "My sister, Fu Yün, will tell us another tale of our people. She has not told me one for a long time. She has become lazy. Start away," she commanded, and drew a bamboo footstool under my feet, to settle me comfortable.

"There is not much about Dr. Lei in it," I hesitated: but she brooked no excuses.

So I told them how one day in Tientsin I broke my eye-glasses. Now in the South of China there are spectacle-shops in plenitude: too many by far, one hopes. Particularly the Southern townsfolk wear glasses, and one wonders if they are invariably necessary. The African of to-day, for instance, is very susceptible to the spectacle-lure: but with great good sense he wears them round the back of his neck or under his nose or chin, if they seriously incommode his sight. In the North of China, however, spectacles are rarer. The Northerner is a bigger, broader-made man than his Southern brother: is less of a townsman, and has glorious sunlight for seven months in the year.

However it comes about, instead of being lamentably multitudinous as in Shanghai, spectacle-shops in Tientsin have to be sought for diligently. On I trundled in my rick-shaw till at last, far in the heart of the Japanese Concession with its wide streets, its trams, and its hundreds of Chinese shops interspersed amidst the relatively few Japanese, I spied the window for which I sought full of spectacles of every variety of American device. The head of the establishment, a Chinese of seven-and-twenty, dressed in the long ash-grey gown then in the mode, and wearing a small round black satin cap with a button of red cord on the top, promised me my glasses the next day at the hotel.

The next day came, again the next; but no glasses. As I was visiting Li Cheng's family the following afternoon, I asked Li Cheng after tea if he would accompany me to upbraid the shopkeeper in good round Chinese about their non-arrival. We entered the neat shop. The young optician saw me; came across and said:

"You have come for your spectacles?"

"You promised me them yesterday," was my reproach.

He looked at me: then with simple dignity, he said, in his student's English:

"My wife is died yesterday."

Taken by surprise, I stammered some word of sympathy.

He hesitated, then added: "If you will wait five minutes, they can be ready, I think. The glasses have just come from the workshop."

Li Cheng and I sat down opposite him, at a table covered with green baize. Under a green-shaded lamp he began to manipulate with quick clever fingers the tiny screws. The Chinese shopkeeper of the big cities is proud to possess the modern appurtenances, and to keep up to date. Li Cheng sat clearing his throat nervously at intervals. I could feel his embarrassed sympathy with the man. For, while we sat and the spectacle-maker deftly used his pliers, his hands being in the full glare of the lamp, there in the shadow we could both see the tears falling slowly down his cheeks.

Silence: and that widower's slow tears.

What could I do? What can any one do, or say, in such case? But his sorrow, and his silence, came across the baize table and hit us like an electric shock.

Perhaps speech would be for his good.

"How old was your Within-One?" I asked.

"Twenty-two," he answered, "only that": and lifted troubled eyes for a minute.

Alas. Twenty-two.

"It was a baby?" I queried: for so often it is, in China.

"Our first," he replied: "a girl, well and healthy, so my mother-in-law says. But I—I cannot care."

" You did not think of calling a foreign doctor ? " I asked : " for that would be too dear, would it not ? "

" We called in Dr. Lei at the last, of the London Mission," he said. " He is a good man, besides being clever. He was very gentle with my sufferer, and spent much trouble. But he told me—he had to tell me, I had called him in too late. He was very kind when he told me."

Then silence once more ; and the tears flowed more freely for the speaking. Li Cheng cleared his throat.

Suddenly a thought struck me. I put my hand into my bag, and found what I wanted. An Englishman had invited me, when we were in Shanghai, to go with him one morning to the municipal gaol for Chinese prisoners. It is a model gaol, and its humane methods are beyond praise, as is also the reformatory for young offenders. A few English police are in charge, and their forbearance, justice and humanity made me a proud and thankful woman. The prisoners walk about the buildings and yards with the smallest amount of oversight possible. The heaviest punishment for a recalcitrant is to leave him for the day in his cell, which has open bars down the front, so that he has to watch his mates work, while he is compelled to endure idleness.

It was a terrible thing to pass the cells of the condemned men. How ordinary were their faces ! Yet each man had done murder—and usually for money. Most were by profession armed robbers, who had killed without respect for age or sex. Simple unafraid alert faces they had : a little sullen perhaps, like unimaginative children who had torn the wings off flies or stoned a bird and were being punished. What will their immature spirits do after their bodies have fallen to the firing squad ?

The prison had no central hall or chapel. But the Shanghai Municipal Council some time ago decided that good physical conditions were not enough for these prisoners of such a strangely different mental upbringing from their own ; that their spirits also needed help. They had asked my English friend to take some charge of these souls. He had gathered a band of his former students about him. Christians, they gave up their Sunday mornings to this piece of work. One of them was a clerk in the Maritime Customs : another, on the staff of a British firm which sells kerosene, oil and candles all over China for the desirable illumination of its dark corners. The third had opened a bicycle business.

I had been left with the illuminants' man, and provided with a small Chinese New Testament. A beautiful face had this Mr. Wu, who clerked in candles. It was as strikingly illuminated and sensitive as Dr. Wang, the leper Doctor's. I never heard a more applicable text than the one he chose : " They that are whole need not a physician ; but they that are sick." The convicts smiled like children when Mr. Wu asked if they had ever gone buying medicines at the medicine shops when they were feeling perfectly well : and their faces sobered like children's when he told them that they were there in prison because they were " sick."

In a few months Mr. Wu was to die of typhus. That summer the water in Chapei, the area adjacent to the Settlement, which is inhabited by the hundreds of thousands of Chinese who come daily for business into the Settlement, became badly impregnated with impurities and cholera bacilli. The Waterworks were under Chinese management which found civil war no aid to its administration : and Chinese died by thousands. " They that are whole need no physician." I think Mr. Wu would not die comfortless.

The small Testament had remained forgotten, in my hand-bag, ever since the Sunday morning in the Shanghai prison. Now I had a use for it in Tientsin. While my eye-glasses were being finished under the electric lamp, and while the widower's tears flowed and silence filled his shop, I passed Li Cheng the book, and in English bade him find the fifteenth chapter of First Corinthians. He, also, should help, if help could be given. There might possibly be comfort in that dithyramb of St. Paul's. You remember he cries out that of course Christ is risen from the dead and become the first-fruits of them that sleep ; or our faith is of no avail. Triumphantly he calls upon the whole creation, from the fish in the sea to the stars swinging their way through the heavens, to testify to the certainty and reasonableness of our resurrection with Christ, whatever the form it shall take : and joyously dubs fools those who quibble over matter and regard not spirit.

Soon Li Cheng handed me the little book, open. I hesitated, as any one may, to intrude. Yet what other stay is there for the broken heart? Diffidently I pushed it towards him and said:

"We people from over the sea read this chapter of our Holy Book, oh Elder Born, when our precious ones are recalled to Heaven. Can you read it?"—for I was not even sure that he could read.

He took the book, and began to read. Then he pushed it away again, and broke into a radiance which astonished me.

"Oh!" he cried, "then you are a disciple too!"

He put his hand below his desk and, from a shelf that was hidden to us, he brought out a Chinese volume. It was the Gospel of St. John—open at the fourteenth chapter. Aloud he began to read those words beloved, I suppose, above every other words in the world, "Let not your heart be troubled."

"I have been reading this all day long in the intervals of business," he said. "I cannot tell what I should have done without it. My dear wife was a Christian too. I do truly know that she is only in another of the Father's mansions, and that He will look after us both wherever we are, here or there. But it will be so long till I see her again. She was so sweet."

Again the tears stood in his eyes. He told me he was a member of the China Inland Mission Church. I was in amaze. A woman from a Samaritan town took her water-pot to fill it at a well and found, instead, a draught from the Water of Life. I had gone seeking for eye-glasses, and had been vouchsafed a vision of faith, hope and love.

Very true it is that to him that giveth it shall be given—full measure and running over. Some people in Western lands have taken upon themselves to send the Truth, as it has been given them, out to foreign lands. Troubled they are sometimes, and by many things—by doubts as to the power of the Master to help China: by perplexity as to whether China wants, or needs, the faith by which we feebly try to live. But, now and again, back its echo comes ringing, clearly, surely, to reinforce and confirm our hesitant souls. The voice of that Chinese widower in Tientsin as he singsongs, Chinese fashion, his way through the loved chapter, running his delicate pointed finger down the strangely printed columns of his gospel in Chinese, comes from round the other side of the globe, in the Master's words:

"Let not your heart be troubled . . . Ye believe in God . . ."

CHAPTER XXXIII A CHINESE ODYSSEUS

"IT is all very well telling us stories like these, to make our hearts big," said Mrs. Sung, the next time we were together on her veranda, Dr. Ma being down for the week-end again. "But just look what happens in our country! The very men who speak most furiously against corruption and bribery give way to these things themselves directly they get into office. Say what you like, but is that not true? It makes one despair!"

"The fact is," said Dr. Ma, "if any Chinese wants to preserve the least bit of his soul alive, he must keep off politics and avoid office. That means, then, that the worst of our people are running our government. And we grumble. It is true what Mrs. Sung affirms; the minute, the hour, one of those whom we thought honest and dependable takes office, his conscience seems to vanish, and he joins the band of sharpers!"

"What do you say to that now, sister?" she asked. "You can't deny it."

"I do not know enough of your governmental folk to judge," I said, "so I will take your word for it."

"Then you agree they are all scamps, eh?" she asked: and I knew how much she hoped I would contradict her What she said was very largely true. It has long been China's woe that too many of her officials consider office mainly as a purse from which they must help themselves while they can—for officials rise and fall with rapidity. In the old days across every yamen entrance, placed so that an official's eyes would fall upon it each time he went out, was a wall to avert demons: and painted upon it was a large tiger showing his teeth. This was supposed to remind the official that any money he made was the life-blood of the people; that he should not resemble the tiger who devours without mercy.

" I wonder if you ever met Dr. Ling," I said, " when you were in Shanghai. He told me the story of his life one evening, and I have just had permission from him to write it. Shall I practise it on you ? "

" Go on now and speak without more humming and hawing," said Mrs. Sung : then turned to Dr. Ma. " You will see she has some ulterior motive in telling it us ! "

I laughed, and began my tale.

With his pale face, his spectacles, his aggressive black moustache, he was as undecorative a Chinese as you could wish to see. Short of stature, too : and on the defensive. What in particular moved him during that half-hour to impart his biography, only the Providence knows that looks after such matters. He told his tale, ate his dinner, and went away up in the lift to his everlasting work.

The next day he finished his tale : and all night long his jerked-out sentences lay in my subconsciousness. When morning came, I sent up a note by the house-boy, for we were staying in the same hotel in Shanghai, to ask if I might write them down, so that others might learn by his experiences. " No, certainly not," came the answer scribbled on the envelope ; or very nearly as curtly as that.

A week passed—I took German measles and was confined to my room and balcony. The hotel people were good enough not to evict me, being only thankful it was not smallpox, which had been the disease inflicted on them by their last infectious clients. The smallpox, they thought, was due to carpets hand-made in uninspected hamlet homes. As the measles receded, the seed of desire to capture the man's story grew within me, and I sent a note begging him to reconsider. This in return for a huge basket of pink roses with streamers of smilax, fit for a bride, which he and his colleagues had sent me on hearing of my sickness—in the fashion of China's new politeness, and very charming. " Truly I was a very bad young boy," he scribbled on the back of my half sheet : " no fit subject to be written about. I dislike publicity exceedingly. I have not had a photograph taken for fifteen years. I cannot tolerate the way our modern claptrap Chinese militarists and politicians scatter abroad like summer rain their life-history and their photographs in self-advertisement."

One respects a man who writes that way. For three months more the seed grew, and disturbed my mentality with its roots. At any rate, he had enlarged his answers to me. From Peking I wrote again to him where he still was, in Shanghai, several hundred miles away. " There is only one nation on earth more dogged than the Chinese," I wrote. " The English and the Chinese have had many sparring matches in the past century. We know each other's staying power. I am English. Let me tell your tale." He gave way.

" But be kind to the poor Chinese boy who was struggling, like his nation, to his feet : and who made any number of mistakes. And you won't flatter me, will you ? That would be worst of all."

" The world shall know you to be as pernickety and annoying and prickly as the Scotsmen you lived amongst in Glasgow," I answered, marvelling at his grasp of our mother tongue.

This was the tale he told in the Shanghai hotel, between the courses, plying his knife and fork, enjoying his foreign dinner frankly in the way Chinese who have lived much abroad sometimes do—to the great pleasure of an English housewife.

He began with a bombshell; which he threw down on the little round hotel table with its white cloth where my father and I had invited him to have his dinner with us. He manifestly hoped it would explode with a loud thud and leave us stupefied. I had asked him the rightful question which any decent woman in my position would ask any decent Chinese man of his ; at least as a beginning of conversation.

" How many children have you in your home ? " and of course I meant sons, not necessarily daughters.

" None," said he. Then he looked me squarely in the face, pursed out his lips and his moustache like a hedgehog sticking out its quills, and added with great deliberation : " Thank goodness."

He knew, and he knew that we knew, that he was uttering blasphemy. In those two words he wished to tell us, once for all, that he was emancipated from the shackles of past

By permission of Professor Soothill

A wandering Buddhist Friar with begging-bowl and bell

tradition, that he held " enlightened " views as to ancestral reverence. He implied that he was an agnostic and was above such trifles as a hankering for an After-life, where his spirit would be soothed and served by the sons of his body, through the burning of incense and the homage of kotows. What would you say if an archdeacon looked across a dinner-table and jerked out, to begin a conversation the first time you met: " I don't believe in the Apostles' Creed "? It was almost as atrocious and uncalled for. It was so deplorably uncalled for that it smote me to the heart with compassion. If an archdeacon did such a thing, you would know that he was either mad or had gone through scorching fires. If ever a man carried in his heart the motto : " Truth, truth in the inward, and outward, parts ! " this short, inornate, firebrand Chinese did. The pity is that so far he has found Truth such a bitter cup, that he does not willingly believe in the exceeding sweetness which it may sometimes hold in Heaven's appointed ways.

" No children at all : no, not even a daughter to worry about. It is the greatest blessing. It leaves me quite free to do what I like in life." He piled it on, his sin ; daring us to fling his Chinese birthright or his ancestral traditions in his face. Then he waited, glaring at me behind his spectacles. My father looked up at him a moment, and then went on with his soup. Dinner is no time for argument with eccentrics, he as good as said. But I picked up the gage ; for here was a foeman worthy of good steel. Deep had called. Deep should answer.

" It is one of my regrets that my husband, when he died, left but one child in the world behind him," I answered deliberately. At once his face softened : his aggression fell from him ; his eyes—black, liquid, Chinese eyes—went a deeper black with gentleness. Smoothing his moustache, he put his elbows on the table and began his story, stopping off to eat his fish or his chicken, and explaining that he had been hard at work all day and had eaten little till now. Soon my father was listening, as spellbound as myself.

It was May : the weather had begun to grow hot. Dr. Ling had discarded the short, top waistcoat of ceremony which is high-necked, but without sleeves. He was sitting in his long, straight Chinese scholar's gown of dun grey silk. He would probably have preferred to wear foreign dress, finding it, as my friend Li Cheng told me when I reproached him for wearing it continuously, " so much more convenient—and also less expensive in the long run." Beneath the skirts of his long gown I caught the same glimpse of Western trousers and leather boots as wore the Railway Director and the Professor.

What with the clatter of dishes, the whirring of the electric fans overhead, the deep-chested conversation of the Germans at the next table, it was not too easy to hear. Mercifully we were late for dinner ; and the band, mainly consisting of Russian refugees from Bolshevik Russia, had gone off duty.

" When I was sixteen," he said, " I was a violent revolutionary. I persuaded my father to let me go to Tokyo to study foreign learning. I was convinced of the futility of any sort of Chinese learning. Almost as soon as I reached Tokyo, the Chinese students there held a meeting and declared that the first necessity of a revolutionary movement was a newspaper for the expression of views. Few of them in those days had grasped the radical nature of the changes needed for a New China."

Nobody else offering for the task, our friend took it upon himself. His name in English means " River of Learning," and he comes of learned descent. For six months he was editor of the first revolutionary Chinese journal in Tokyo University.

" And let me tell you : it really was a revolutionary paper," he interposed. Then, being blessed with some commonsense, even at the age of sixteen and a half, he realized two things. " Firstly, I realized that the paper was costing me a lot of money, more than I could afford : for it did not sell very well, though I slaved over the editorials. The results were not commensurate either with the efforts or the good hard cash which I was expending. Few people were reading my flaming sentences. Secondly, I had to spend so much time over it, for nobody else would, that I was missing the education I had gone to acquire."

So he resigned his editorship : and at the same time he decided that the civilization of Modern Japan was only veneer

—a phrase much in vogue at the beginning of the century. I smiled at him.

" Yes, I had any amount of assurance," he agreed, nodding at me.

" You still have a certain amount," thought I, remembering his bombshell. But who are we English to cast stones for this particular foible ?

" I only wish China had some of Japan's ' veneer,' " he added.

He talked the matter over with two other Chinese students at the university, aged seventeen and seventeen and a half. Very flatteringly to Britain, they decided that Japan had learned most from her, and therefore to Britain they would go.

" And particularly to Scotland," he interjected with a half-comic bow in our direction, lest as English folk we should become too vain.

" My husband was Scotch," said I sweetly.

" Ah," he accepted it. " A revolutionary friend, years older than any of us, wrote to me from Edinburgh at that juncture telling me to shake off the dust of Japan and her ' lacquer-work education ' from my feet, and saying that Edinburgh was undoubtedly the greatest brain centre in the world."

So to Edinburgh these three young Chinese in Tokyo decided to go. And at once. There was no time to be lost. Any delay in their education meant delay in China's rejuvenation. Four hundred million people, waiting to be freed from tyranny, expected them to do their duty and come back educated from Edinburgh at the earliest possible moment.

" But what about your families, your expenses ? " we queried. " Surely your father would object ! "

" No," said he, with a short laugh, " mine agreed at once. The other two fathers objected. But, you see, I had six brothers, so I should not have been an insuperable loss. Besides, I was the bad boy of the family—the exasperating one at any rate. Really, looking back, I can see what a trial to my family I must have been."

I did not dare to flatter him : but I mentally interjected, " I daresay you are their pride now." I discovered later that he is also a great support.

The three young adventurers reckoned up their funds. " We decided that we could, with extreme economy, manage by going steerage to reach Scotland and live the first year on £70 apiece. So I asked my father for 700 dollars : and he was so thankful to be rid of me that he sent me back by return 1000 dollars ! I tell you, I felt rich."

The second boy's father was a judge, or Taotai, in Hupeh province at the time. After some hesitation and writing to and fro, he agreed to his son going so far away, and promised him the 700 dollars. But just as they were preparing for departure, there came a political upset. The Taotai was dismissed. He had a large family, several wives, and a cluster of children. He visited his natural annoyance with the delinquent throne on his absent son. He told him he could not afford to send any more than he was already doing, for his wild-goose chase after foreign education. He would not forbid his going to England : but if he did, he must manage on what he had. The son, possessing at the time £30—300 dollars—decided to go to Scotland ! The third boy had no money : just a few dollars.

" However, that did not matter to us," said the " River of Learning," and smiled again with a tenderness worthy of fatherhood, " because of course we were Communists, and it was our privilege and duty to share all we had in common. So, between the three of us, you see, we had 1300 dollars—£130."

There were many lions in the way. When they reached Shanghai from Japan, the Russo-Japanese War had just broken out, and the Japanese navy had commandeered the steamship lines. The boys had paid their passage money : they received it back. There they were as far as Shanghai ; but the Japanese was the cheapest line to England, and now it was closed to them. Should they give up ?

" I am afraid I rather forced the hands of the others," said our historian, and put down the menu card he had taken up for a moment. " For when I found them hesitating, I walked out, took three tickets in the French Messageries Line, and paid the money. That settled the matter."

He cocked an eye over the top of his spectacles, and we

chuckled. " That is how he behaves in committees," said my father, in parenthesis.

They had a wretched passage down the coast to Singapore. The weather was bad, the boat rolled, they were unused to foreign food, and were overcome with sea-sickness. Their only comfort was another young Chinese who was travelling first class, but who came down most of the time and talked to them. He was lonely up in the first class, nobody troubled to make friends with him, and he could not speak French.

When I consider the way in which Chinese will start off for any and every foreign country knowing not a word of the tongue, I am amazed at their intrepidity. A girl of twenty and her brother of twenty-one came to call the day we were leaving Peking, while our luggage was being locked, to ask if French was a compulsory subject for entrance to Oxford University. " We leave for Oxford in a month," they said, " and we are quite well provided, for our father is giving us £200 a year each : he is a senator in Peking. Which college do you advise us to enter ? "

We contemplated these Innocents Abroad with dismay. We tried to tell them it was not easy to enter a college at Oxford in the present days of competition. They had been partly educated at an American school in China, and we asked why they did not go to America, for they had more likelihood of finding friends ready made to their hands there, acquaintances of their teachers in Peking.

" We are going to England," they said obstinately : " our passages are taken. America owes her language and institutions to England." Shade of George Washington !

" Do you know anybody in England ? " we asked.

After consultation, they said they knew one Chinese student. And meanwhile our baggage coolies were at the door. Hastily we gave them addresses of friends in London, and hoped the friends would not forswear our future friendship on that account.

But that is an aside. The " River of Learning " and his two young friends, all but dead with sea-sickness, arrived at Saigon and then Singapore. They could not afford the attentions of a steward, or any other minor consolations. In their ignorance, in Yokohama they had bought extra blankets, for they did not expect to be provided with bedding as is our foreign style; and pillows also—at the cheapest shop they could find. They had each had an outfit of foreign style clothes made by Japanese tailors: and in those days, Japanese tailors were cutting their milk teeth in the matter of foreign clothing, the cut of a suit being unknown to them. It is a different matter nowadays. If you travel from Dairen to Moukden on the South Manchuria Railway, you will sit in a Pullman second to none in the world for spotlessness and luxury. Opposite you will be faultlessly garbed Japanese gentlemen, whose silk ties match their socks and whose lounge suits fit them to perfection. But not so in 1903 or 1904, when they were still finding the European collar an unpleasantly stiff proposition—as it is: for this was before soft collars came to bless a world of men.

When the boat at last reached Singapore, the three Chinese boys staggered ashore, white of face, deplorably clad, and with precisely 30 dollars—£3—in the world between them. Their friend had an introduction to the Chinese Consul-General there, and boldly took them with him.

"And he, a charitable soul, despite our sorry pea-green complexions and our truly shocking garments, asked us to dinner. We were young; for days we had not eaten food fit for mankind, so we thought: and the blessed expectation of holding chopsticks in our hands again and sitting down to a bowl of good rice and well-cooked Chinese food was too much for us. We knew we were not reputable guests for a Consul-General: but we stayed. I don't know what he thought of our appetites. I expect he realized we were but boys, and therefore created to eat vastly. Anyhow, he listened without obvious amusement to our tremendous revolutionary tirades. He did not agree with us altogether, he admitted, for which we pitied him: but we could not reproach him, as we were eating his rice, and very good rice at that."

The story-teller had warmed to his tale. The hotel boy brought us dishes and he ate, but I doubt if he knew much what he was eating. Neither did we. "The Consul-General suggested that it would be only seemly, as fellow-revolutionaries, that we should pay a call on that great Progressive,

K'ang Yu Wei, when our ship touched Penang, for he was living there in exile."

" K'ang Yu Wei ! " exclaimed my father and myself simultaneously. It was K'ang Yu Wei who had led the Emperor Kuang Hsü in 1898 to desire a modern constitutional government in China. He had given the Emperor modern books to read. He had made great schemes for China's reform, and had been the Emperor's friend. But the Empress-Dowager, discovering that she was to be put out of the way when these reforms came into being, turned the unfortunate Emperor into a prisoner, while K'ang Yu Wei had to flee for his life. Indeed, like his successor, Sun Yat Sen, he had fled on board a British gunboat and, in exile, chosen British protection. Certainly the British can hardly be said to have been illiberal in their aid of China's reformers, or their salvaging of China's revolutionaries from the clutches of reactionary pursuers.

" Of course," went on the autobiographist, " K'ang Yu Wei seemed nothing of a revolutionary to us. Why, he still believed in a monarchy, even though it was constitutional ! We believed in nothing short of a Republic. Nowadays, I suppose, the revolutionaries of to-day do not even believe in that : they only believe in continuous and successive revolution which need not even necessarily be successful ! "

We chuckled.

" However, K'ang Yu Wei had undoubtedly spent his life in China's service and nearly lost it too, and had a great name. We boys murmured to each other that we must not be intolerant towards those older ones who could not possess our enlightenment."

Accordingly, at Penang, the three boys were pleased to call on the older gentleman.

" And K'ang Yu Wei was so kind, so courteous," went on the " River of Learning " gratefully. " He took us to his own study "—a mark of intimacy, for he might have kept them in the guests' hall. " He must have felt perplexed over us. There we were in our atrocious clothes : obviously poor, yet saying as a foregone thing that we were going to study in Great Britain. As we stood up to take our leave, he began to talk to us personally, and not only about China and her needs of reform—' or revolution, whichever you like to call it,' he said. He told us that it cost very much money to be educated in Britain : he feared we did not realize how much. Were we sure we had enough ? In our pride, we answered, ' Oh yes, thank you, sir ; plenty of money '—and all the time, our exact amount was less than £3, for we had spent a little on rickshaws and tipping the servants at the Consulate-General at Singapore, as is our Chinese way after a dinner, you know. We had been wondering exactly how we should reach Edinburgh from Southampton or London, wherever we landed. We had been calculating how long it would take us to walk to Edinburgh. But K'ang Yu Wei was very persistent, and finally he asked us outright exactly how much money we had. We replied that we had 5000 dollars."

" Oh, Dr. Ling ! " I could not help laughing. " And again oh ! "

His eyes twinkled. " We would have died rather than be so humiliated as to tell him the truth about the £3 ! You know how proud we Chinese are in such matters. To our astonishment, he became most uneasy. ' 5000 dollars—£500 for the three of you ! It is much too little,' he exclaimed. ' Why, I have to give my one nephew who is being educated in England 3000 dollars a year for himself, and he can only just manage on that. He ought to have more. You three can never do it on 5000 ! ' He was distressed. What would he have said if he had known the truth ? He went to his desk, unlocked it and took out a canvas bag. ' See,' said this kind good man, ' you know our Chinese habit of making a little gift for a journey. I have no time to buy you a present : so I want you to take this instead from me — from one old revolutionary to the young ones coming on. Inside this bag are ten golden sovereigns, which I have kept. But of course they are of no use in Penang.' "

His generosity bore down their pride, and the three boys accepted the gift with respect and gratitude.

" We went by train from Southampton to Edinburgh," said the story-teller, peeling his last section of pumelo.

" And now I must go and work," he pushed his chair back. " There is my secretary waiting." A young Chinese with a large portfolio was hovering near the door and looking in our direction.

"That is no end to your story," we cried.

"Oh you must be desperately bored," he smiled, bowed good-night and made towards the lift and his everlasting work.

Bored!

You see why I could safely promise him to let people know what an aggravating and annoying a man he is.

CHAPTER XXXIV THE CONSOLATIONS OF GEOLOGY

MRS. SUNG glared at me, as I came to the same dead halt as had Dr. Ling, striding off to the lift.

"You do not leave this veranda till you finish this tale," She rang a bell. "Amah! Bring more tea."

"Well, Dr. Ling came and had tea with us next day," I told her. He had no time as a rule for such a break, he said. He had just been made the Chief of a new administration in the city and area round about Shanghai: the real Shanghai, with its million and a quarter Chinese inhabitants—not the Settlement which is its fringe, and in which the foreign traders are supposed to have their residences. The "fringe" has somewhat over-weighted the garment: the guest has outshone the host. Hence these tears and recent misunderstandings. And as Chinese have sought the amenities of the Settlement and bought out the foreign householders, so these latter have gradually overflowed into the true and original Chinese-ordered area of Shanghai itself and its outer suburbs. Some foreigners, seeking homes, have had to find them miles away from the concentrated areas to which they are supposed to be restricted by treaty; and must be till China throws open her hinterland to their residence. Just as three-quarters of a million Chinese have flowed, so to speak, into the Settlement leased to the foreigners in the middle of last century, where they might dwell undisturbed, so the displaced foreigners have been sucked by the backwash into various localities hitherto sacred to the original citizens of China. When one considers the small numbers of the foreigners compared with the two million Chinese in the two territories of indigenous China and the foreign Settlement, it is all the more astonishing that foreign influence is so great in effect. My father says: "Shanghai is a window for China to look through upon the world."

For the first time in history this purely Chinese area was in 1926 made into a municipality. A Chief was appointed to administer it according to modern ideas in the matter of sanitation, education, police, lighting ; doing the work of a clerk to a city council in England, but with the executive power also in his hands. Greater Shanghai is the name of the area, for it includes not only the large teeming city which once was behind walls and whose narrow foetid streets still appal the passing foreign visitor, but also the surrounding district. Till recently it was an agricultural countryside, rather desolate, as alluvial land is apt to be at a river-mouth, but now covered with factories and workmen's dwellings. Not unlike the growth of London in the last twenty years has been the growth of Shanghai. The mere thought of beginning sanitation in the citadel of the old city would cause a brave man's heart to falter. Our health boards in the Occident have after all been the product of a generation of modern medicine and, at root, have the approval of the people. But in the Orient the task is Herculean in every respect. And sanitation is but one of the problems.

Our " River of Learning " came a little late for the cup of tea which we had urged on him : and sank wearily into a chair.

" You have a stupendous burden," said some one : " all power to you ! "

" I have," he said, " but I do not despair. I am experiencing less opposition, for instance, than I feared. I find our Chinese populace wistful for a change from past conditions, and more reasonable than I could have hoped. If I can but lay foundations for my successors to build upon, I shall feel something has been accomplished. For now we have begun, it is certain that there will be successors."

We asked him how he had begun : what had been his plan. How should we ourselves have faced such a labour, such an Augean stable ? We knew without his saying that he would have vampires of corruption, nepotism and bribery to contend with, as well as the more material foes of dirt and disease. Not least of his difficulties would be ingrained superstition. It has been fixed in Chinese women's minds for centuries, for instance, that if they provide a dead infant with a good burial, the spirit of that child will come and whisper to the living child left in the family of the honour done him. This child will then die, too, in order to obtain a similar privilege. So dead babies are cast out: not buried. That is why a philanthropic Chinese society in Shanghai gains merit by paying coolies to retrieve the bodies of infants and give them sepulture. Thousands of the little corpses, put out on the streets, are buried by this Society every year—when they have funds. The "River of Learning" wanted the babies buried whether the Society had funds or not.

He said, "You will be surprised: but I am discovering that the first thing I have to do is to persuade our people to register births and deaths." He explained that, in whatever direction he turned, he constantly came up against the need for statistics of some sort. "I have nothing to go upon: I must ascertain facts and numbers first." He smiled. "You remember that Saul realized the first thing he needed was to take a census of the people. And the Roman Emperors also. I know now they were right, though I never thought so before."

In less than a year he fell from office, for political reasons; so did his successor and a number of successors very quickly after him, some good men striving truly to serve, some bad and only desirous of growing rich in office. It has been a commentary on this basic method of his that, soon after each of the good men and true take up the reins, he is found once more trying to persuade the city folk to register births and deaths. Indeed, lately—and I am sure Dr. Ling, a political outcast at present, must have smiled with satisfaction—there has even been a rough census taken. The foundations which he dug—he had no time for more—were sound. The sanitary service which he began has been functioning, however shakily, ever since he gathered a staff of earnest young doctors fresh from their studies in Europe and America who were eating out their hearts in the very exiguous beginnings of private practice.

"Now tell us the rest of your life-story," we demanded presently. "You arrived at Edinburgh at the age of seventeen and a half with two companions about the same age: and you were determined to obtain an education there, on about twopence a year. Did you do it?"

"I did," he answered. "We arrived in Edinburgh one wet evening and made our way—bedding and all—to the Chinese student who had first written to me to come to Edinburgh to study. He lived in a poor quarter, for he was not well off."

"I suppose he knew you were coming," I asked.

"No," he said, "he did not."

"Do you mean to say that you and your two young companions, strangers to him, arrived without a word of notice at his lodgings, and he welcomed you ?"

"He did !" said Dr. Ling. "At about half-past eight of a rainy Saturday night too !"

Such are Chinese ideas of hospitality and friendship. They made shakedown beds on his floor, ate his supper and talked.

"How we talked ! Mostly revolution, of course : but I must tell you that after our trial of communism on board ship, we all three gave it up for ever—especially myself. You see, I was keeper of our common purse, and the others were young and wanted to expend our microscopic store. Small temptations constantly came our way. It is so easy for youth to spend its all. But education at Edinburgh was my single aim ; I would not let them have the money, and they were angry with me. I should hate to be in charge of the Treasury in a Communist State. I am sorry to say that I lost the friendship of one of them, the son of the Taotai, altogether. He was unused to being without small change. We parted soon after our arrival at Edinburgh, and have never met since."

The day after their arrival, Sunday, they held a council of ways and means with their new mentor, their senior in the struggle. To begin with, they spoke almost no English, and their smattering of Japanese learned in Tokyo, and of French learned on board the Messageries Maritimes boat, was of little use in Edinburgh. The older Chinese went to the window and looked out on to the Sabbath calm of the Edinburgh street, and then tapped hastily at the pane. He ran down the stair and led up a tall Scot of middle years : a missionary doctor on leave from South China, who had already proved himself friendly in the strange land of Scotland. To him were introduced three very young men from the East, with their mixture of wisdom and unwisdom, and he was confidently asked to show them the way of education. The trust which the East showers upon the West is a compliment we have not yet fully appreciated. Yet I daresay we could send young people of that age to China in similar circumstances and find they had been well enough treated. Which is a testimony to human nature.

Having had more than once the same situation to face as that doctor, we listened eagerly. Once three young Chinese arrived at our door on a Saturday afternoon, newly come from China, and asked for lodging and learning instanter. We poured out fresh tea for Dr. Ling, and gave a humorous glance at each other. But in those earlier days, twenty and more years ago, the problem was new, and we could imagine the doctor's perplexity as he faced it. There is nothing to do but take each such case separately : and, Heaven be praised, Providence often takes a hand in the game too. " Something turns up " in an astonishing way to seeking China, as it never did to Micawber.

" The doctor was on his way to church, but he sat and talked with us all morning instead, and we told him our money affairs. I remember he laughed a bit," went on the voice of the Chief Executive of Greater Shanghai. No wonder his heart had not failed him when he tackled municipal problems. He had not been daunted by his own " The doctor arranged with our older friend's landlady to let us stay with him till we could make other arrangements. Our friend agreed, and agreed heartily. He, too, had been helped in his turn, he said. Besides, he was a real violent revolutionary and befriended any with leanings that way."

" I suppose he is rather more of a conservative nowadays, eh ? " I asked.

" Curiously, he is not," answered Dr. Ling. " He is old in years, but very young at heart. He is always in the forefront of the most advanced thought. He is, in fact, so advanced that he dare not live here in China, but lives abroad. I do not agree with his views at all, but I love the man. We correspond : and he always hopes to convert me. He is full of hope, though he is about seventy, and he never ceases to plan how to upset present conditions. I suppose we need such people to keep us from stagnation."

"What did the doctor arrange for the three of you?" We brought him back to his story.

"The Taotai's son was bent on engineering. His father, in spite of his temporary annoyance with the Throne, would not eventually let him be moneyless, he said. He would write to his father and say he could not manage in a strange land on the little he had. The doctor persuaded some one to advance him a small sum, and he was duly apprenticed to an engineering firm. Alas, we parted more in anger than grief, he and I. The other boy, who had no money at all, but was a good lad, the doctor managed to persuade a philanthropic lady at his church to take charge of: and she paid his school fees."

"Then there was yourself."

"I was a hard nut." We believed him.

"To begin with, I refused to write to my father and ask for more. I had said I could manage on £70 a year, and I would keep to it. I was too proud to say I had made a mistake. The doctor urged, but I would not change. Neither would I be helped by any charitable person, even if he could find another so disposed, which was doubtful: and especially not by a Christian. I wished to owe nothing to religion. At last, in desperation, the doctor said, 'Your funds will never maintain you here, even in Edinburgh. You cannot at your age go into our public elementary schools, supposing they would admit you. You say you must and will learn Latin for entrance to Cambridge University (it was then compulsory), and it is not taught in elementary schools. The only solution I can think of is that you go to the grammar school in the English county town which I myself attended as a boy. The fees are low, the school standard fairly high. You will learn your English from the son of the local doctor, banker and successful draper, and might do worse. If I write to the headmaster, for my sake I think he will take you and give an eye to you."

So the erstwhile youthful editor of a Chinese revolutionary journal in a Japanese university went meekly at seventeen to a grammar school in Lincolnshire. His English was poor, his Latin non-existent, his income some £70 a year. For the sum of 15s. a week he boarded with a widow woman known to the headmaster.

"Was she kind?" we asked, for he fell silent.

"Very kind," he answered, "though unlettered. The worst was those dreadful wet English winters. I liked to play football in the school playground with the other boys. I would wear holes in my one pair of boots. Then they had to be mended, or my socks became wet. I had but two pairs of socks, one pair on my feet and the other at the wash. So I would sit at my mid-day dinner with my feet bare, while my socks were drying over my chair-back at the fire."

"Brave lad," I said. He was no longer the Chief Executive of Shanghai Municipality, struggling to make a new city out of an old one: but a courageous boy in an English grammar school, liking to play football and determined to master the *Aeneid*. He continued. "At the end of two years, I, the Chinese boy, was head of the school! What was more, my headmaster, thinking too well of my accomplishments, sent me in for an open scholarship to Cambridge, whither I had next decided to go. Heigh-ho! I missed the scholarship. By just two places," he added reminiscently, "although I passed the entrance examination." He, who knew no Latin or Greek, mathematics or English history, two years earlier, took a second class.

"I took a second class also: I, who had had years of English education," I told him. And, imagine it, the self-same year of grace as he did! My soul paid him homage. I remembered then how rumours had come to me of there being another Chinese student resident in college beside the one I had discovered and invited once or twice to a tea-party.

"But what became of you?" I asked, for in Cambridge I had never been able to trace that other elusive student.

"I had no scholarship," he said. "I had but my £70 a year. I could live on it in a Lincolnshire market town: it was not enough for Cambridge University."

He was defeated. The head of his college in his large-heartedness gave him opportunities for earning more by writing articles for magazines. "But in one term I found,

By permission of T. Butler, Esq., F.R.G.S.

The Rev. John Li, B.A. Pastor of a church in the wilds of Yunnan Province.

even with economy, that I had spent nearly the whole of my year's income."

So, without crying over the impossible, he went to Belgium where, at that time, the Chinese Government were paying for the education of a certain number of Chinese students. He hammered at the doors of the Chinese official in charge of the funds till he recommended him for a scholarship. He had become deeply interested in science at the grammar school. He passed his Belgian examinations in biology so brilliantly that he felt justified after two or three years in returning to his first love, Edinburgh, for research work. There he eked out his income by coaching the budding young medicos, English and Scottish, who had failed their zoology preliminaries. His constant friend, Sir Arthur Shipley, the master of his college at Cambridge, sent him more literary work. "I wrote an article for the *Nineteenth Century*," he said with pride, "Sir Arthur correcting the English of it for me, and they gave me £20. £20! That kept me for months and months. In fact, on the strength of it, I went to Glasgow and took a course in geology."

"What was your article about?" we asked.

"Chinese politics, of course," he said, "and I knew plenty about them."

He did not tell us all his achievements, and it was from some one else that I learned how he won the gold medal for geology at Glasgow.

Then things began to stir educationally in China, and word came to him that a Bureau of Geology was being formed in Peking, and he was offered a post in it. So, not staying to take the doctorate examination, to the disappointment of his professors, he joined the first boat back—steerage, of course—rejoicing that at last he could begin his service for his country. True to his habit of facing the worst, he realized that since the science of geology was new to China, there could be but little known of China's geology, apart from what a few learned foreign travellers like Richthofen had discovered. He determined to make his own contribution as a tribute to his motherland from her son.

"I left the boat at Bangkok, and went geologizing through Siam for practice, and thence over the Chinese border, through Yunnan up to the Yangtsze. I was on foot most of the way, and had a pack-mule for my instruments and personal goods," he ended simply.

We sat up electrified, hardly able to believe our ears. "To the Yangtsze from Bangkok!" we exclaimed. "You cannot mean it!"

The distance from Bangkok in Siam to the Yangtsze at Hankow, where he came out, is a thousand miles, through steamy unknown jungles and over stern mountain passes. Moreover, the wild Shan tribes who dwell on the first part of the road are hardly less lawless than the Miao clansmen of Yunnan on the second half.

"I am glad to know something of what your travellers endure for the sake of exploration," he rejoined, "and I quite enjoyed some of those weeks and months wandering with my mule over the Yunnan mountains—till it became too cold. How awfully cold it can be in Yunnan! The bandits, when I reached the province of Kueichow, were the worst nuisance. They would never have had any pity or understanding for a poor Chinese scientist like myself. At last I made for the Yangtsze and civilization, because I grew tired of packing up my precious instruments at the sight of prowling bands of mountaineers. It was not good for my work. I was not sorry when I saw the wide waters of the Yangtsze."

We stared at him, frankly, this gold medallist of Glasgow. Surely he was the first Chinese who had done that hard dangerous journey for the sake of an idea: a not unworthy successor of General Chang Ch'ien, of the second century B.C., who reached the waters of the Oxus, or of the monk Fa Hsien, who in the fourth century A.D. sought India through the grim gorges of the Tibetan borders to bring back to his people a deeper knowledge of Buddhism.

At the Yangtsze he joined a river steamer, enjoyed its comforts, and reached Shanghai again after many years and varying experiences. He took up his new post in Peking, and worked hard at Chinese geology, till once more political changes upset China, and her scientists were left unpaid for many months at a time. It was not the money that troubled him, for the lack of it seemed no insuperable obstacle to him: but that a condition of things should exist whereby government geologists could be left penniless. Therefore he started out into politics again.

"My idea is to make China a safe place for Chinese scientists," he said firmly, "so that they can pursue their highly technical and important work. It is waste of good life to suffer the fate of the great Archimedes. It is stupid to be killed during some siege in one of our spasms of civil war; or be knocked on the head by an ignorant bandit in Yunnan. Moreover, consider our political confusion; half of it is nothing but sheer muddle-mindedness. Our politicians have not learned to think accurately: they jump to conclusions without having sufficient facts and foundations. That sort of inaccuracy is what science abhors. I say, deliberately, that what China needs most of all, to my mind, is the scientific mind. I weary of this *ch'a pu to*—'near-enough' method."

Then he started on to his favourite subject. He yearns for a central research institution in China with many ramifications, where Chinese scientists can carry on their work: agricultural, geological, medical. "Our students abroad do some good work, you know," he ventured. "When they come back from abroad, for instance, we often find they have taken fine degrees and are members of learned societies."

"Even in Scotland, one of them became a gold medallist!" we added.

"Chinese make fine scientists, when they have the chance—and peace. That is all I want to say," he ended wistfully.

We had listened to the Railway man on his iron and steam way to progress. The Professor, we knew, desired the means of education for the masses as well as the student classes. Before this autobiography, however, we had been inclined to think the scientist a little tiresome with his perpetual harking on science as the main need of Modern China. Now we looked at him differently. A pernickety man he will always be, and his Scotch training confirmed him in his ways. You could never persuade him against his reason, and he would hold with aggravated tenacity to his premises. But once let him be persuaded that you mean no harm to his principles, and he will give his mind to practical compromise; also his affection generously to new friends.

We left him at his gigantic task in Shanghai. The last I saw of him he was once more being elevated in the hotel lift to his private study with his secretary beside him, a sheaf of papers in the young man's arms. He is out of office now. The pendulum swung too far towards radicalism for his taste. Educated in Britain, he has that cautious habit of mind which we value and which hesitates at violent change. Moreover, science looks before it leaps. He is as profoundly nationalistic in his ambitions for China as any one. He wrote to me in one long letter his views on concessions and settlements, and they would have suited the most extreme radical. He wrote how it was outrageous that defaulting politicians, and generals absconding with the funds due rightfully to their armies, should be able to run for refuge into foreign concessions and live blatantly on their ill-gotten gains. So it is, as I agreed. Only, such complainings do not help the foreign business man for whom these areas originally existed to find another resting-place for his feet ; where he can feel his family is safe and where he can trade without fear of molestation and oppression.

But there is a gentler sequel to his story than talk of even science, much less of treaties and concessions. When we were staying in Tientsin, about ten o'clock one evening I came upon the Professor of Logic dashing down the hotel steps looking for a rickshaw.

" Whither away ? " I queried.

" I am going to say ' bon voyage ' to Madame Ling, the wife of our friend in Shanghai," he called, stopping his rickshaw-puller. " She has come from Peking this afternoon, and sails this evening to join her husband."

" Then we shall not meet her ! " I exclaimed. " How disappointing ! " I felt I should like to meet the wife of this man who had done such wonderful things.

" Come with me to the ship : it is close at hand, tied up to the Bund," he called back.

" Oh, she can't possibly want a strange Englishwoman calling on her at ten o'clock just when she goes on board a ship," I objected.

It is an astonishing country, China. The Professor returned, and ran back up the steps to me.

" On the contrary," he urged me ; " it will show great politeness on your part, if you thus snatch at the barest chance of paying your respects to your father's colleague's wife. Come ! Besides, I should like you to see what a charming woman she is. When I was passing through troubled times in Peking, she made me welcome in her home. My friend is very fortunate in his wife. Come ! We must not delay."

I flung a cloak about me. Down the quiet wide street of the Concession we rode, the oil lanterns of the two rickshaws dancing yellow light. It was a warm delicious night ; very black and velvety the sky hung above us. We came to the wharf. The river, in daylight a muddy stream, was also black velvet. Our men put down their shafts and prepared to squat by their rickshaws till we returned. Down the gangway walked the Professor in his long Chinese gown and with his felt foreign hat on his head ; into the ship's saloon, with its mahogany and electric-light and long tables. We sent our cards by the Boy, and soon Mrs. Ling came out of a cabin.

" Ah ! " I sighed.

It was exasperating to think I should have so short an acquaintance with this lady. Intelligence and a sort of restrained vivacity lit her up. Her features were more finely cut than Mrs. Sung's. The Chinese have a greater variety of feature than the West always realizes ; just as Europeans have many more differences in facial formations than are apparent to the Chinese. They dub us all " outside kingdom people " without seeing the difference between an Italian and an Englishman. Sometimes a Chinese woman strikes the foreigner as beautiful. A Chinese will understand why, but will say, " You admire her because she is not typically Chinese " ; and will explain that she is more of the Aryan type. From certain provinces, notably perhaps Anhui and round about the centre of China, come a number of Chinese, men and women, with shapely bridged noses, Aryan cheek-bones, oval faces, sparkling jet eyes and vivid manners ; evidently the descendants of some nationality absorbed by the more strictly Mongol. Gentlewomen of those provinces might be sprightly, well-bred Frenchwomen.

My uncle Kung, father of Li Cheng, had something of the same look, and of such was Mrs. Ling. I should have enjoyed knowing her as much as Mrs. Sung and Flower, Miss Lo and Blossom. Ah well, it shows that Mrs. Sung and Flower and Mrs. Ling also, are but a few in a garden full of pleasant women. One can but gather a posy from amongst them in one's short life.

We sat, Mrs. Ling and myself, on the red plush settee of the saloon sofas and made a little conversation, she speaking no English. I never saw the Professor, before or since, so beaming with innocent pleasure. He was totally unselfconscious, his only wish to put the lady he admired in the centre of our attention. He brought two boys, of sixteen and seventeen, out from a corner where they were shyly retired from view, and introduced them as nephews of Dr. Ling's.

" Yes," said the lady, " they are going to Shanghai with me, partly to look after me and partly to go to school there."

We talked a little longer, then said good-bye, so that they might settle down in their berths before the ship started. As we went down the gangway, the Professor said to me, " Dr. Ling is such a good uncle to his nephews : and these two he has practically adopted, paying for their education."

Oh, oh, Dr. Ling ! I smiled within myself. You are a fraud. You have no children of your own ! " Thank goodness," I believe it was, you said, when you thumped the table and glared so fiercely at my innocent query about your family that night in the hotel at Shanghai. But it is not beneath you to take other people's under your wing : precisely as your fathers did before you. Yes, I daresay it is not that you believe in the efficacy of ancestor worship when you are dead, or that you want them to offer incense before your tablet at the New Year when you have left the body. Still, you said it was a mercy you need not bother about children. Here you are, clustered about with other people's ! Oh, Dr. Ling, I promised not to flatter you. I said you were as pernickety and tiresome as one of those argufying Scotch with whom you lived so long. Then you are like them in another matter : you have just as soft a heart as they have, though they do choose to pretend that theirs is of Aberdeen granite for hardness. Did I not tell you that my husband was Scotch?

Dr. Ling, you are a fraud, and in my turn I say "thank goodness" for it!

Still, Science must end his chapter. There came a letter to me from him a little time ago. He wrote: "For the last six months I have been travelling in South-western China, principally in Kwangsi, from which province I brought back nearly a ton of fossils, collected in a trip extending over 1500 miles. I intend to stay in Peking to work out the scientific results of my journey."

Fifteen hundred miles for a ton of fossils! A mere bagatelle, he would doubtless say, with a shrug, twisting his moustache.

CHAPTER XXXV APPLES OF GOLD

LI CHENG came over to see us one day from his new place of business, which was not far away from Peitaiho. After tiffin, I wondered what we should do.

" Why not take me to call on Mrs. Sung ? " he suggested. " Mercifully, that is perfectly correct procedure these days. What a change from old times : and a good one, too ! "

" Come along," I said, and we soon arrived at her house. Little Cloud and Strong-as-a-Rock were playing on the veranda, while Amah sewed. While Mrs. Sung titivated—" to receive gentlemen callers," as I told Li Cheng—we were happily employed. Li Cheng called the children to his knee.

" Have I not five small urchins of my own ? " he asked me. He spoke to them sagely ; about learning to read and write, as is the decorous Chinese way with children, and they listened to him with equal sagacity. I fear they did not expect, or receive such wise dealing from me and, foreign fashion, they had to go a-riding on my knee.

" Just as your sons have done, Li Cheng," quoth I. Yet his baby, Fifth Precious, the little ingrate, would desert me when his father came in sight. He would flee and lean on Li Cheng's knee, and gaze at me from that safe harbourage as if we had been no nearer acquaintances. Once Shu Ying lifted him on to Li Cheng's lap to make him show me how much he loved his father. The tiny fellow's eyes remained fixed on me, and he heeded no command to " love ah-pa." Gently, gently, Li Cheng won him, putting his cheek to his and whispering loving words : till at last his eyes wavered from me. Then his little arms went round his father's neck and he put his cheek up in his turn—and forgot me. His mother turned upon me a smile infused with such fullness of content that I forgave her smallest son for his desertion of myself.

Mrs. Sung soon came to us on the veranda, and with peculiar pleasure I introduced Li Cheng. Never before had I had the opportunity of introducing Li Cheng to any of my Chinese women friends. Mrs. Sung was a little shy, for it is still something of a novelty for a strange Chinese gentleman to pay a call like this. But Li Cheng felt a positive joy at meeting a Chinese lady who had yielded thus to new ideas in social life, and he began at once chatting away of mutual friends in Shanghai : even relatives-in-law. Truly, Chinese family ramifications are prodigious. Soon they broke into their own Soochow speech, long unused by Li Cheng, but familiarly used by Mrs. Sung. It is a very pretty speech, reckoned the most melodious in China.

" Do you excuse us ? " asked Li Cheng presently, and Mrs. Sung turned abashed to apologize.

" Ah, I forgot you did not understand ! " she said.

I begged them to take no heed to me, and said I was very content to lean back in my chair and rest, now that my two friends at last met. So they talked, and thoughts drifted in and out, mostly out, of my mind. I had run into a missionary friend that morning. He was saying how thankful he was to have his family in a peaceful spot. He told me how, in Shantung, where he lived far away from the railway, a band of Chinese soldiers walked into his house when he was out one day that spring, and took possession of it. He came back from his walk abroad amongst his parishioners to find his wife with set face offering tea to the soldiers and doing her best to keep them from wandering upstairs, where their two small children were playing.

" We are so anxious that our children should receive no undue frights while they are young," he interpolated, having read modern psychology.

The officer was not unreasonable, except that he demanded money and stores for his men. " Such stores as we have, you shall share," said the Englishman : " but we do not keep money here. It is in a bank in Tientsin." He then found himself in the difficult position of explaining the workings of our banking system to a sharp-witted and suspicious man who could neither read nor write, officer though he was. For two hours the interview lasted. The white man thrust his hands instinctively into his trouser-pockets to keep calm. As all seemed going well, unconsciously he sighed relief and began to take them out. Immediately he was looking down the barrels of a pair of revolvers held by the officer. Staggered, dismayed, he cast a wild thought towards his wife and children.

"Where is your little gun?" demanded the officer.

Then my friend understood what was the matter. The officer had told him of a march on Tientsin, and an evening spent in a cinema there. Doubtless the villain of the piece had brought out a revolver from his pocket to shoot the hero: and the officer suspected the Englishman of a similar trick. Wearily he smiled.

"I have no little gun," he said. But the officer reiterated, still covering him with the revolvers—an unpleasant sensation: "Oh yes! That little gun which your king gives each of you foreigners before you leave your country!"

It took another hour of talk to refute the legend.

How different were these friends of mine, Li Cheng and Mrs. Sung, as they laughed over some joke and talked their soft Soochow speech! It was hard to think that compatriots of mine in bungalows near by had gone through troublous times because of compatriots of theirs. But China is a vast country. We should not like to have to answer for what goes on in the whole of Europe. It would be as fair to lay on French or English shoulders the deeds that happened during the 1918 Terror in Moscow as to blame all China for the crudities and cruelties of some amongst the Chinese. Besides, if we impute the sins of some members of a nation to the whole of that nation, we must in justice also credit the extraordinary fortitude and generosity of others to them all. Is this not equitable?

Mrs. Sung and Li Cheng soon tried politely to bring me into the conversation, and we gossiped for a time on various themes. Then Mrs. Sung said to Li Cheng: "The English sister was telling me a story of Dr. Ling, a scientist, last time she visited me. Does she tell you tales too?"

"No," he said, "it is too bad of her."

"He provides them for me," I protested.

"I shall have few more chances," she said, "tell me another to make our courage great, as you did before."

So, as they would not let me off, I told her a final tale. It was in my mind that if I stayed long enough in China I might at last understand St. Paul's reasoning when he says that if by one man sin comes into the world, by another may come salvation—which doctrine the Soviet has labelled " solidarity." I told her a tale of Yunnan, the province farthest away in the south-west, high on its tableland behind its rampart of mountains—the Switzerland of China.

I had heard the story in a drawing-room in England. With water-colours on the walls, chintz-covered chairs, flowers in bowls, a polished silver coffee-service—it was after dinner—the story seemed as unreal as here on this calm and hospitable veranda. I had been recommending a book by an American doctor who had been captured in Manchuria, to a young man well under thirty, a fellow-guest from China.

" Banditry is an over-rated business, according to the doctor," I said. " The men suffer horribly from every disease, specially trachoma and other eye diseases. They never have their gunshot wounds dressed. They only endure life and the memories of their hideous crimes by smoking opium."

I spoke of one chapter which particularly affected me. After many false alarms, the doctor was suddenly face to face with immediate death. They proposed to stand him against a wall and shoot at once : and for a moment his heart seemed to stop with overpowering fear. His mouth went dry. This breakdown of his self-control was more horrible to him than anything else. His spirit cried from the depths, God, help me not to die a coward ! In a flash, so he said, help came somehow, from somewhere outside himself. He was never overwhelmed by terror again.

" His mouth went dry ! " exclaimed my young man in the drawing-room. " That was just like mine when I was captured by the bandits ! "

" You captured by bandits ! " I cried. " Will you tell me ? " And the other guests stayed their talk to listen.

It was when " his years were in the young green leaf," as China puts it. He was the only Westerner working in a parish the size of Wales, keeping track of and encouraging some ten thousand tribespeople who had during the last twenty years sought Christianity. He visited about sixty places of worship as best he could in the year. Like the Celtic races, these tribespeople of the South-west have been pushed, by the Chinese oncoming civilization with its insinuating force, into China's mountain areas. On all the Chinese borders are such races—" barbarous tribes " they have been truthfully called during the centuries by civilized China. Warfare constantly breaks out between them and their Chinese suzerains, much as between the Welsh and the English in mediæval times. Raids are carried out by either side, usually to the benefit of the tribesmen who cross the mountain torrents, break down the flimsy bamboo bridges, and dare the less hardy Chinese to follow them to their fastnesses. They make slaves of the Chinese agriculturists whom they capture, such unfortunates disappearing for ever into the maw of the hills. These particular tribespeople had no written language, till a cheerful little man called Pollard lived amongst them and set it down. Chinese is a foreign tongue to them.

Not only were the Miaos unlettered raiders, ignorant, dirty and infinitely poor, but they indulged in tribal orgies of appalling drunkenness and immorality to make up for the wretchedness of their lives : and then, of course, felt rather the worse afterwards. The Chinese despised them and their goings-on—except when they feared their barbarities. The little man Pollard learnt to know them when two of them came trading to his city on the plain. Somehow they sought hospitality, which he freely gave, never twitting them with the fact that they were wild tribesmen, not civilized Chinese —a thing which had not happened to a Miao before. Thus Pollard won them. He fought their orgies, and they responded to his devotion and gave him great love. Finally, Pollard died in their midst, of typhus, their dread enemy. They buried him and still go to weep over the grave of their " little father." And now this young man whom I met in the English drawing-room, had taken up Pollard's fallen torch.

At the time of his adventure he lived alone, in the mountains. About once a month he journeyed on his pony a day's ride along the mountain goat-tracks, down to the Chinese city on the plain where lived the superintendent of his mission. It was only a provincial city, and set in the midst of farmlands, very much out of the way of travellers, foreign or Chinese—except to inveterate explorers like my husband who had visited it. It was a fortnight's journey by pony and sedan-chair from Yunnanfu, the capital of the province, where ends the railway line from the coast: for the French have built a wonderful railway through the mountains from Indo-China, across the most insalubrious gorges in the world. A million Yunnanese labourers, it is said, died of fever for the making of that steel road to the coast.

The young man felt almost in the world when he took his monthly trip to the provincial city, to fetch supplies and money, and, above all, to use English speech again. However, being naturally a cheerful soul, and having great business in hand, he was not unhappy in his mountains. An enormous task is in itself a spur to noble minds. "Young men in the War had as huge jobs to tackle," he said philosophically, "and they did it without much fuss. I was born just too late for that. All the same, I could have wished for a helper or two." He looked at us with clear blue eyes: he took out a pipe unconsciously and began to stuff it. He lit it perhaps six times and let it go out again during his recital.

"One morning," he began, "I started off from Shih Men for the plain. I had plenty to consult my chief about. We had had a terrible famine, and I reckoned that ten thousand of the tribespeople had died of it. He and I were discussing means of combating its recurrence. It was after that famine that he began to build stone granaries and buy up the millet in good years, to sell at cost price to the people in poor years: like Joseph in Egypt. After the famine we had the usual typhus. He had troubles too. His own city had been besieged twice in six weeks by large bands of bandits, who had only been driven off with difficulty. And I arrived in time for the harvest festival!

"Oh, there was plenty to discuss: and I stayed the week-end unloading my problems on to him and gathering precious advice. The two Miao men who accompanied me kept saying they hoped we should not run into bandits on the way home.

"The country is very beautiful: for which I never cease to be grateful. It is also very lonely. We met a few Chinese pedlars, and they said the way was clear. As we approached a wood, however, I remember thinking it would make a good ambush. In a trice, a man was standing pointing a rifle at me, and shouting 'Stand!' in a very objectionable manner. In fact, he annoyed me excessively by the way he bellowed at me. I have a touch of red in my hair, you know."

He looked at us ruefully. He grinned. We looked up at his shining head. Gold; yes with a touch of copper. We smiled as the six feet of lean manhood sheepishly stroked copper-gold hair, inclined to curl but duly frustrated.

"I was furious," he said frankly. "I asked him who was he, pray, to point rifles at inoffensive travellers and shout rudely at them like that. Did he own the earth? But another ruffian joined him, and they both pointed rifles at me, and I thought the rifles might go off. So I stood.

"And then my mouth went dry. I saw they were considering whether to shoot me out of hand, at once."

He stopped again. "I was engaged to a girl in England. She is my wife now, and we have often gone past the place since." He stopped again: then he said that, like the doctor in the book, for a moment he was at the end of his resources and afraid, especially afraid lest he die a coward.

"Instinctively I thrust my hands into my jacket-pockets, to clench them, ready for the shot. Can you think what I found in them? An apple, a rosy English apple in each! My chief had given them me the last minute, off his trees. He had learned fruit-grafting during his furlough home and had brought back English slips to graft on to the wild Miao crab-stocks, hoping to give the people uplift by way of the orchard and reverse Adam's experiences. Very successful he has been, too.

"Well, his apples lifted me up. I was back in a flash in Gloucestershire, my own country, in its lanes and orchards. England came to me: and courage flowed back somehow—from somewhere quite outside myself. I never had that awful fear again, though there was plenty to frighten me. I took out an apple, and bit into it: and my mouth was no longer dry. I think I must have smiled : for the men lowered their rifles."

He would have stopped at this : but we insisted on hearing more, and how he escaped from the brigands' hands. He gave us a queer look. " If you want to know," he said, " I 'll tell you. It is something I do not forget."

The two armed men forced him to hold his hands above his head.

" They pawed in my pockets and stole everything. They drove off my two Miao helpers, beating them. I was thankful for this, as they might have killed them. I realized that I should probably be held for ransom. The bandits, who wear short jackets to distinguish them from soldiers, next tied my arms, and marched me roughly along paths in the wood. My temper rose again when they snatched off my wrist-watch and emptied my handbag and divided its contents. I kept stopping and arguing with them, hoping somehow not to be led to headquarters, for their Chief had a terrible name for torturing captives. He had captured some schoolboys and held them over fires, in order to terrify people into paying up ransoms quick : and some died, poor lads.

" But other bandits joined my two : and soon scores were streaming along, sneering and jeering at me so viciously that I thought it might be best after all to be taken to some sort of leader, and accordingly I demanded this. The brigands are organized as military units, and their leaders assume military rank. When we reached headquarters, I heard that Ma Hsien, the ' general,' and the worst criminal of them, was not back from a raid. I could not altogether regret it : and forthwith demanded to be taken to the second-in-command. This was a ' Major ' Yang. Now Yang was formerly an officer in the Yunnan army, but for lack of pay had joined the bandits."

" That is what is called ' economic pressure ' in other parts of the globe, eh ? " I interrupted.

" At any rate, he was not altogether dehumanized. As a captive, he treated me well. I modestly asked to be allowed to continue my journey, which made them all laugh immoderately. He pressed me to stay with him four or five days—a polite way of preparing me for a captivity of some length. I was alarmed, for I knew this meant they would ask a huge ransom for me. For some hours I was kept in suspense. Each time I asked to be released, they roared with laughter. I talked long with Yang, who asked questions about our work. In the course of conversation, I tried to persuade him to give up his bandit life, and this amused him greatly. I told him I might yet be useful in arranging a pardon for him. When he heard, however, that my horse and goods had been stolen by his men, he shouted and cursed them right and left, and made them bring me back all my property.

" And then, suddenly, in the middle of the afternoon, he began to relent : and to my astonishment he finally said he thought I might go, and told off two men to lead me back to the road ! "

Hardly daring to think it true, the young man mounted his pony without delay and started for Shih Men. In the distance he saw a group coming towards him. There were his two Miao helpers, and two of their finest Miao preachers. There was also Mr. Heo, a Chinese—a *Chinese*, mark you ! And where were these men going ? In grief, weeping as they walked, but without hesitation or delay, they were going into the bandits' camp, putting their heads into the wolf's mouth ; to beg that they might stay with him while the ransom was being arranged.

" You, oh teacher," they said, " are but young. You have been only two years in our land, so that you cannot yet speak freely as can those who have dwelt many years amongst us. You are as a son who came to serve us. We decided we must remain with you in your captivity, if allowed, and comfort and interpret for you."

If the brigand chief had refused to let them remain, they were going to ask that the English boy be allowed to go free, and that they might take his place ! And one of them was a Chinese, unused to the rough mountains, as were the others. " You know what it might have meant for them, being in the brigands' hands," said the young man, nodding at me. " Torture. They came prepared for all that—in my stead."

We held our breaths at such a tale.

" I could not keep my eyes off them as we journeyed to Shih Men : I was so filled with gratitude and admiration.

Photo by Lady Hosie

Mother and Small Daughter

For it was not a flash-in-the-pan courage theirs, but steady resolution.

"We reached the top of the hill looking down on our small township in that wild land: and I was startled. A crowd filled the level space in its centre: all the clan was there, three or four hundred people. They seemed to be in a ferment, in distress. Whatever had happened? Were the brigands next descending on them? I was greatly troubled. I stepped out ahead of the others, and marched quickly down the hill. Then they looked up and saw me. I shall never forget the rest of what happened."

He struck a match, and let it out again.

"They called my name in a great shout. They came running to meet me."

We could see it: the crowd of Miao villagers; the hill women with their plaited hair and coarse homespun pleated skirts, so different from more delicately nurtured Chinese women, grouped together weeping: their first glimpse of the English lad as he came striding like an eager young god down the hill, with the glinting gold of his hair, and his step swift as he hastened to know what ailed them.

They ran up the hill to meet him: they took him into their famine-shrunken arms: they snowed him under with their love. They told him how the two helpers had arrived, sobbing, to say the Young Teacher had been taken by bandits. The people at once rang the church bell. The folk poured in from the fields, from the houses. And they had spent the whole five hours of their Teacher's captivity praying there in their town-space, in front of his simple church, that he might be released and restored to them.

"Five hours they prayed for me—all of them: loudly and ceaselessly. They cried over me," he said. "One old woman had her arms round me. She had no teeth to speak of, her hair was wild, the tears had washed tracks down her withered cheeks with their marks of smallpox. She said to me, 'I prayed and prayed to the Lord and told Him: If our Young Teacher suffers, we shall know You are no good, but if he comes back to us, we shall love You all the more!' Her theology was primitive, but what is theology compared with love?"

" I should have wept too," I said, for he seemed to have come to an end. The young man pushed a chair for himself, and sat down, for he had stood to talk.

" The fact is," he said, " I did."

This time his pipe lit.

" Are you going back again ? " asked our host..

" I am," he responded, and then added in his usual joyous voice, " and my wife and baby with me. The Miao love white babies ! "

Did I not remark that we could not tar a whole nation with the cruelties and cowardice of only a percentage of her people ? If we do that, we must also credit them with the heroism and fidelity of others. That is how we ourselves would wish to be judged, is it not ?

" I wonder what made that Major Yang release you in the end so unexpectedly," murmured some one.

" I know," said the hero of the story : and, as a matter of fact, so did we all.

Mrs. Sung looked at Li Cheng as I ended this last " tale of her own people." " I wish I could think all Chinese were as brave as those tribespeople," she said. " And I wish I could think also that all the people of the West would be as brave," I responded, " in defence of friends of a different race and colour who visited their shores."

CHAPTER XXXVI A PICTURE OF SILVER

ALAS, that summer vanishes. My father had long since set out for England, home and duty. My mother and I began to make preparations to follow him. Up to Moukden and Harbin, thence across Siberia to Berlin, Brussels and London was to be our route, as it had been his.

Li Cheng came over one last afternoon : and, of course, it poured with rain. We had promised ourselves a walk.

" Never mind," he said, " let us be very English and go out in the rain. We will put on our waterproofs."

So we walked along the deserted beach, he and I. He showed me how to collect smooth oval pebbles, matching their colours and size. He had gathered pebbles better than those on the Mongolian desert, when he had gone a famous trip to Urga, capital of Mongolia. Five days in motor-cars his party had travelled across Gobi, which grows beautiful pebbles if nothing else. He had found Mongolian ways very outlandish, and told me how inexpressibly dirty and smoky were the insides of the yurts—the camel-hair tents.

" When you reach England," he said, " in the winter when there are few flowers you will put these pebbles, as you saw in my study, in a wide shallow bowl and cover them with clear water, and see how pretty and refreshing they are. You will think of us, of your Chinese friends, and you will know that it is time you wrote a letter to me ! "

There was half a gale on. The rain was blowing our speech from our mouths. We turned back. We never argue, Li Cheng and I. Arguing does not seem good manners to him. This is very restful. " Very well," I said obediently : " I listen to your words."

Reluctantly I said good-bye to him : reluctantly also to Mrs. Sung. Should we ever meet again ? In a few days she would be off back with the children to Shanghai. Mr. Sung wrote that life was dreary without them, and he would be glad when they returned, but they were not to curtail their holiday, and he hoped she was better. She was still suffering from headaches ; and that is another trial—leaving one's Chinese friends while not feeling altogether easy in mind about them. The thorns and pricks that accompany our daily life are also their portion. She came to our house to say farewell to my mother and myself. Amongst a crowd of visitors we parted: a melancholy business, which we contrived to cover with a semblance of cheerfulness.

But that evening—our last in Peitaiho—I was to dine with some friends at their bungalow about a mile away. I took the quickest route, which was also the least frequented. Over wild grass, within sound of the sea, down and over small chasms which, when the rains fall, are full of rushing streamlets, I pursued my way. I reached the final long sandy lane which dropped to my friend's house. On the right were the shady deserted lawns of the club ; the last tennis player had gone. On the left was an unfenced stretch of big millet, rustling its heavy ears with a metallic whisper in the softly stirring air. The stars had begun to show. A letter had reached me that morning from a friend which she had written in mid-Pacific. In it she marvelled at the stars hanging overhead there.

" So many of them—like seed tossed into a harrowed field," she wrote.

Is our earth, perhaps, a living grain : wheat flung into the fields of the sky ? Will it shoot out and sprout one day : and what sort of heavenly plant will bud from such a germ ? My mind wandered. What an infinite variety this world holds ! Take this heavy headed millet, copper-red in daylight : how different its deep colouring from the yellow of wheat or the honey-tints of rice !

A spasm of gratitude seized me towards Providence, which has poured out such a plethora within the filmy covering of our atmosphere. What a world !—which goes tossing and spinning along its appointed ellipse, hiding under its cloud-shell things as different as a snow-crystal and a peony, a volcano and a cedar, a rhinoceros and the convolutions of man's brain. Amazing : interesting : from a great irrigation scheme for a desert planned by puny man, to the last microscopic cross-section of a snail's tongue. What artistry: what stupendous craft! Awe takes the soul.

The millet rustled uncannily. Heavens! Was there a kidnapper lurking within it? My thoughts fled the universe and returned to earth. I quickened my steps. Scarcely a sound they made in the soft loose sandy loess. I tried to make them softer still. What was that story of Mrs. Sung's about the two village wenches being gagged and bound and carried off by pirates and held to ransom—not half a mile from where I was walking? For the first time I realized that I had no single weapon of defence. Not a pin, not a brooch; not even a scarf to obfuscate them—those imaginary attackers. I was wearing a dress of white Manila lace: my sleeves were short, my only ornament a chain of cut Japanese crystals. Not even a hairpin. I was as soft as putty, muscularly. There would be nothing but flight for me—and that would not be of long duration.

As my heart began to thump in my ears, and I to look over my shoulder, the noise which had startled me resolved itself into the tug of wheels over lumpy ground ahead, the rattle of iron, and the heavy laboured breathing of a man. A rickshaw came in sight, and somebody sitting in it. Two forms, a woman and a child: sleepy head was bent to sleepy head. The woman looked up as we approached each other. It was Mrs. Sung.

Little Cloud was on her lap, nearly asleep. She sat up for a moment, gave me a blinking childish smile, then sank back on her mother's heart, too tired for more.

"Stop!" cried Mrs. Sung to her man. She put her hand over the edge of the carriage and took mine. I put my other out and held her hand in both mine. She had been paying a last visit to her relatives: there had been a big tea-party, and she had been pressed to stay on afterwards. And now she really must go home, for Yün-Yün was too sleepy for words. But she lingered: and so did I. My friends would forgive my being two minutes late for dinner: they would think it was packing which had kept me. She laughed. "It is funny how easily we women find excuses, isn't it?" said she. "And how foolish of you to be here all alone, on this quiet road—not even in a rickshaw! Did I not say this was English? Now perhaps you will believe me about Mary Lee!"

"Never have you seen me vault over a donkey's hindquarters. I only wish I could do it!" I began, and then gave up the argument. Who could argue at such an hour? For now it was finally good-bye, the millet was rustling in the starlight, the frogs had begun their chatting, and in our ears was the kiss of the sea on the bosom of the beach.

The rickshawman took out his little towel and proceeded, after the manner of his kind, to mop his wet brow and neck. Glad of a respite, he looked kindly at me standing there, talking in the silver dusk to this lady of his land.

"Little Cloud has been so good all afternoon," said her mother, and pressed her closer. Then she looked at me, her face quivering with the depth of her emotion.

"Sometimes," she went on slowly, "when I think of her, Little Cloud, my baby daughter, I am frightened. What will become of her later? What sort of life will she have? How different is my life from my mother's! Hers will certainly be different from mine. Suppose when she marries, if she is unhappy—I could not help her then as I do now, or comfort her."

I held her warm slender hand: it clung to mine, and mine to it. How many mothers have taken this same fright over their children? I reflected.

"She is in God's hand now as well as yours. She will be in His then," said I.

"Do you truly believe that?" she asked me.

I reflected again. "Yes," I said.

She nodded. "I think I believe it myself. After all, it is so wonderful in itself to have a child. Of course when she becomes ill, I take terrible fright and forget everything, lest I should lose her." She paused.

"Sometimes, when I look at her—my daughter—I think I love her best of all at the bottom of my heart: better than husband or son or anybody!"

Over Yün-Yün's head she glared at me, as ferociously as a ewe over her lamb.

"Nonsense!" I ejaculated after another second's meditation. " Sheer nonsense ! What, better than precious little Strong-as-a-Rock ? "

She leaned back. " You are right," she agreed. " My small son. Yes, I suppose I love them equally. But there is a different sort of tie between a mother and daughter, isn't there ? "

" There is," I agreed. " As a proper Chinese woman you are supposed to think twice as much of your son as your daughter, as you know very well. You ought to put her under the bed and let her play with tiles and be suitably submissive, and nobody can say that of Little Cloud, eh ? "

She snorted. " In these days, thank goodness, I can say that I love my Yün-Yün as much as my son, and that she is a very important person to me."

" And to Mr. Sung, too," I interposed, and she assented. " You are a lucky woman," I added.

" I am, I am," she admitted, " my happiness almost frightens me sometimes. Why should I be happy, when others are unhappy ? "

In her vehemence she squeezed the small lassie on her lap a trifle too vigorously. Yün-Yün whimpered protestation. She half awoke. She put her hand up to her mother's cheek.

" Do let us go home, mamma," she begged. " I want to sleep."

Her mother put her lips into the warm small palm and kissed it. In silence she and I pressed hands again, and smiled speechlessly at each other.

" Walk away slowly ! Walk away slowly ! " she whispered at last. China's own farewell, which speaks of unwillingness to see the last of a friend.

" Ching an—Golden Peace, to you and yours," I whispered back.

The rickshawman started off again : I swung on my way in the starlight.

CHAPTER XXXVII EPILOGUE

"A GOOD play needs no epilogue," says Rosalind, and proceeds forthwith to speak one.

If there is one side of Schumann more delightful than another, it is when he comes to the end of his poems of music and announces, Der Dichter spricht. "Let me take one glance back on the scenes and emotions I have waked for you out of the impalpable air," he says in effect. "I will make a bouquet of them all for you in a Coda. You shall have a concentrated breath, a full and joyous remembrance, of the flowers in my garden."

An architect may surely be permitted to stand back a moment and contemplate the whole effect of the habitation he has fashioned out of stones and bricks, wood and glass: and even add a balcony, if he wishes, that shall look out towards a distant river. A sculptor, too, may certainly chisel a final hand's-breadth of bas-relief on the pedestal of his full-grown statue, if so inclined. Did not the Creator break off on the Seventh day to contemplate His achievements. In the same way, the Fate which shapes our lives, seemed bent upon placing a coping stone at Moukden on our Chinese experiences. Our last days in China, spent in Manchuria, gathered themselves into one spear-head of significance.

We had many adventures before we left China for good at its jumping-off place, the town of Manchouli, on the border between Siberia and Manchuria. A very dishevelled-looking town it is, where Soviet Russia and China meet. Pardoned criminals and political refugees of both nations maintain their own peculiar standards of life amidst its dust in summer and its menacing blizzards in winter. A sort of Chinese-Russian equivalent of Lone Man's Gulch, its corrugated-iron roofs and broken plank-walks make a shabby exit from either land.

The historic exit, however, from China proper is long

before that : at Shanhaikuan, the entrance to the new lands of Manchuria. There one passes through the last gate of the Great Wall. There that Wall looks forth upon the Pacific, after its three-thousand-mile journey from Tibet. In the waters of the China Sea, the Old Dragon's Head is stooped to drink.

The very first time I saw the Wall at Shanhaikuan, it was sundown. My ear was caught by the rising and falling of a voice in a strange tongue. On the broad grass-grown platform, where it ends in a tumble of broken masonry washed by the tides, was a dark-skinned Baluchi soldier. With a praying-mat and a worn vellum portion of the Koran before him, he alternately squatted and prostrated himself, and continuously chanted. Near at hand a Chinese peasant in blue cotton hoed a last few rows between his fields and took no notice of either the Baluchi or myself, equally strange though we must have been to him.

The Baluchi belonged to a small British force in camp near-by for the summer. At the other side of the Wall were a few tents, and English soldiers might be glimpsed washing in buckets after fatigue duty. The peasant was certainly not alarmed by the sight of such soldiers, as he would have been had they been his own. There was an old American missionary once whose friendship for England was tepid. "I will admit," he said to me, "that if my parishioners here in North China heard that the British army was going to be quartered on them, they would welcome them. They still tell me how in 1860, the time of the Second China War, when the Summer Palace was burnt, the British paid for every grain of rice or millet, every animal they took! That is some while ago: but they remember it."

It was not primarily the Baluchi, the English soldier whistling his sentimental airs, the American missionary or the Chinese peasant who spelled the charm of Shanhaikuan to me. Not even the Great Wall, or the Temple of the Winds which, set on a pinnacle, hangs its crazy wooden balconies over a precipice near one of its bastions. It was a tall Chinese, who intercepted myself and a friend the time I went journeying to see closer the Wall's coils and grand serpenting over lofty mountain crests and down sharp ridges. I was perhaps twenty-three, and my friend, an American girl, a year older. We were both riding donkeys, going a picnic to the Wall, and were well ahead of a little party of holiday-makers.

The tall Chinese came upon us when we had slipped down from our donkeys at a bridge to await the others. He bowed: he smiled : he said that this was a fortunate day. He then invited us to come to " li pai," or so I understood. Now " li pai " pronounced in one way means worship, and is the word normally in use by Chinese Christians for their services. The day was Tuesday : it was ten in the morning. In spite of dalliance, the other young picnickers would soon be on our heels. My friend and I had no objection to attending service at ten on a Tuesday morning, but there was only just time in the day to visit the Wall, that most laborious work of man. On the other hand, we did not wish to damp the Christian ardour of a young church.

" We have friends who will arive in a short space," I said bowing. " Our intention is to pay respects to the Old Dragon. To-day is the Second Day after Worship. Pray convey our greetings to those in the Worship Hall and our regrets."

He looked at me with a pitying eye. He quietly took the donkeys' leading-strings in his large hand and walked with them off down the lane. Perforce we followed.

" It seems he intends us to do some praying," said my friend, when I explained to her, for she spoke no Chinese.

" You have not understood," the tall Chinese enlarged : " not *li pai*, but *li pai*,"— he gave a twist to his voice, which still conveyed nothing to me.

In a minute we arrived at a blank white wall and a shut gate. He opened it, tied up the donkeys outside to an iron ring, and ushered us into a courtyard. Up some steps we went, as if to the usual guest-chamber of a Chinese house. He opened the door, and beckoned us to look in. It was a Mohammedan mosque ! Then he smiled quietly at our surprise. " I am the keeper of this hall," he explained.

The floor was covered with spotless matting, the walls were white-washed and immaculate. At the altar end was no altar : but high above hung the sacred hierogylphic of Islam. The curved Arabic word, like a scimitar splashed with sea-foam, stood out, the only object in the building which indicated its religious purpose. Not a table or chair, not a candle or incense-burner, not a picture, a kneeling-pad or a book: only clean matting and that sacred word.

It was beautiful, austere as the barns into which Clarendon drove the Puritans after Cromwell died.

The tall man was a student of human nature. His eyes were on my face. I gave a sigh of satisfaction at that severity of adoration. Clean as a sword it was—perhaps as lacking in the quality of mercy. He nodded at our tribute of appreciation, and drew nearer. " You and I," he said, his eyes fixed on mine, " are of the same religion."

Astonished, I stammered some sort of polite phrase.

" Yes," he assured me, speaking as to a child, " you and I are the same religion. We are not idolaters ! " Scorn came into his tone. " All round us, as we stand here, are temples with heathen idols in them ; and silly ignorant people go and bow to them, which is very displeasing to God. We Mohammedans are but a handful in this countryside. You and I, we know there is One God, and that idols are dirt and painted clay. Therefore are we kinsfolk—*hsiung ti* ! "

The sun streamed on the matting through the papered lattices and open door of the brave mosque.

" What does the man say ? " asked my friend, and I told her : and she too nodded approval.

She was a Unitarian : she is still. When she visits England, she pays pilgrimages to the quiet chapels whence the old Unitarians set out for America under the spur of persecution, to affirm there that God is One. Which of course He is. Does not even Athanasius sing this in triumph ? Next her stood myself, who humbly bless His infinite variations, and adore Him in that He breathes into us, poor human imperfect creatures, His Godhead and calls us sons and daughters.

The two of us stood at the mosque door and looked from it to the Mohammedan. He would cry aloud so many times a day the Verity of Verities, that there is but One God. We all understood each other. There was no need for speech. She and I raised our hands clasped and bowed ceremoniously, to thank him for showing us thus his Holy of Holies.

A trifle fierce, possibly, that light of faith of Islam : a naked flare that burns and blazes. The Mohammedan population of Northern China have passed through many vicissitudes. They have massacred fearfully in their lust for dominance, and their outbursts have been followed by equally fearful holocausts in their repression by the Chinese. In Shantung, after centuries of cohabitation, the non-Moslem Chinese stand in justifiable fear of their Islamic neighbours. In Kansu last year the Moslems suddenly rose, and were responsible for the deaths of nearly a quarter of a million people. I never came across another Mohammedan who welcomed me to his mosque in that fashion or said we were kinsfolk in religion. But I never sought.

Years after, another Chinese spoke to me similarly unbidden, in the same strain. I was in a train, coming up from Hankow way with my husband. We had been into the mountains and were untidy and weary, conscious that we had not bathed for ten days and hardly taken off our clothing. A very young Chinese officer walked through the coach, an armoury of weapons disposed about his khaki-clad person. He bristled with two revolvers, a stuffed cartridge-belt, a sheathed dagger at his hip, and a sword at his side. He was eighteen : so he told an older Chinese who tapped his weapons and smiled paternally at him, yet in a sort of dismay.

" Eighteen ! " he ejaculated : " and so many deadly weapons—how many will you have by the time you are thirty and full grown ? "

The boy flushed hotly and stalked away, huffed. Another Chinese of middle years, a stranger, sat next to me.

" A pity, a pity," he murmured to me, watching the boy pass out of the car. I agreed, but was fatigued and would have dropped the conversation. Then he, too, that fellow-passenger, in a comfortable wadded silk garment, an old-fashioned round black satin cap on his head, leaned to me and said : " You and I, we are of the same religion."

I sat up. I turned my head to regard him. A kind, round sober face he had. He must have been a merchant, of easy means. His feet were squarely placed, his hands set one on each knee, in the fashion of the older generation of gentlemen. No crossed ankles or sprawling legs for him. Does not the

Book of Rites bid one sit as grave and reverend as though representing a dead man? "You and I are of the same religion," he reiterated: "you are a Christian." Courteously he smiled into my eyes.

Now why should he think I must be a Christian? Because I was a foreigner? Christianity, it seems, is the religion expected of foreigners, whether they like it or no. Obviously a person must have some sort of a religion, and what else is there for a foreigner to have? So reasons the Orient. Moreover, it is the only name they have heard in connection with us.

"You are a Believer in the Way?" I faltered.

"Yes," he replied, "of the Lord of Heaven Church." The Catholics chose this name for the Faith in the days of K'ang Hsi, when he and the Pope disputed in a famous controversy as to the rightful term to be used for God. "A Believer in the Way—then you are a Protestant," said he: "but that is but a small difference between us. You and I, we believe in the same religion. We are brethren—*hsiung ti*. Is that not so? I am a deacon of the church in our city. I have here with me in my portmanteau the Evangel of St. Matthew. How delightful a book it is!"

My heart warmed to him. Never before or since, has a Roman Catholic sought to hold communion with me like this. But a Chinese merchant in the Pullman of the Peking-Hankow express did it. Is that not illuminating: also an allegory and hope for the future? Two sober middle-aged Chinese men, a Mohammedan and a Catholic, have deliberately gone out of their way to assure me, a woman and a Protestant, that we are kinsfolk in religion—*hsiung ti*?

It was these two men who came to my memory as, this time accompanying my mother, we passed through Shanhaikuan. The Gate between Sea and Hill, its name means. Through the last gate of the Great Wall the train rushed, and out into Manchuria, that country which is as Canada to China in all its newness of economic discovery, its coldness, its sparse population, its sunshine and enormous unfenced plains. I wondered if my two "brothers in religion" were as tolerant of their fellow-compatriots of another sect as they were of me. How much easier is it for us to speak fraternally of Buddhists and Hindus, of Latin Catholics and Orthodox Greeks, than of our immediate neighbour who holds a different view of ecclesiastical polity from ourselves !

We came to Moukden, that astounding city, the capital of the Three Provinces which constitute Manchuria. In one suburb, ten thousand workmen had been employed for more than ten years in making munitions of war for Chang Tso Lin, in an arsenal run on modern lines. Within its wall —a low parapet of hardened mud—is the huge building of the governor's palace, surrounded by an immense brick wall like a prison. Chang resided there, guarded by many armed men against assassination. To-day his son, not yet thirty, accustomed to luxury and indulgence, with an inadequate education, has had suddenly to grapple with even larger problems than his father. They say he is growing lean in the attempt. Electric standards carry light for the streets at night : trams rush by on their parallel iron tracks. Yet, at the same time, in every by-way and alley are the little old huts of the ancient craftsmen : beaters and smiths in brass and gold, copper and iron. A sound of hammers, the glow of a furnace ; and a passer-by catches a glimpse, through the open front of a one-roomed hut, of a man plying the tools and using the methods of the fourteenth century.

To be sure, Russia has had her share, and still has, along with Japan, in shaping the ways of Manchurian life. Thus droshkies take largely the place of rickshaws. My droshky, pulled by its tall raw-boned Siberian horse, turned me neatly over into its hood at the gate of our friends' abode on our arrival from the station. Horse, Chinese driver and myself, we lay at our ease, heads in the gutter. Having heaved myself about and disentangled my small impedimenta from about my neck, I was speechless with laughter. " Oh Mother China ! " I thought, " a last shake-up from you—I might have expected it. Fie upon me for forgetting your happy way of upsetting every Occidental's self-assurance sooner or later ! You thought I was becoming solemn and earnest, did you, and forgetting to laugh ? So you are sending me off by standing me on my head."

My mother, in a vehicle behind, was so perturbed at my silence that she thought I was killed, and I could hardly speak to disabuse her. Also speechless, but with gratitude, was the driver when I deducted nothing from the agreed fare because of the accident. I could have retained him to do it to me again, I felt, if only to remind me of China's many whimsicalities. " You would never do for a rickshaw coolie in Shanghai," I reproached him, however ; " they have to use their brains there."

" You 're right, you 're right ! " he assented, bobbing his silly head. He scrambled hastily to his high seat, flicked his animal with his ancient lashless whip, and drove off lest my woman's tongue lash him worse.

Moukden is an orderly place : the symbol in China's frozen North of her sovereignty. Yet not far off, bandits range. Only gradually is the law of the agriculturist displacing the law of the hunter. A year or two ago, a friend, a middle-aged American lady, a pacifist, coming down the Amur on a river steamer, just missed the bandits. The ship ahead was looted, and the passengers were marched off for ransom to the cruel wilderness. The captain of her steamer cut off every light and moored in an inlet till morning, or they might have suffered the same fate. At first my friend thought she ought to submit to any marauder and give up her modest possessions, not returning evil for evil. Then annoyance and indignation took her.

" The wicked shall not have it all their own way," she said. She fetched back her purse which she had left, a mute appeal for mercy, with her shoes put to be cleaned at her cabin-door. She hid it under some lily bulbs which she was taking back to Peking. She lay down to rest. Then she became more annoyed. " I have the right to protect myself," she thought, and took the enamel wash-basin which is an indispensable item in every traveller's baggage in those regions and, covering her heart with it upside down, lay down once more. Again indignation swept her. She fetched her umbrella, for it had a hard knobbly handle. " I 'll give any bandit one good bang with this knob," she thought. " One knock would not be wrong, I think. Nobody calls an umbrella an instrument of militarism."

She is an intrepid woman. I disagree with nearly everything she thinks or says, but I admire without stint everything she does.

The glory of Moukden is the tomb of the first Manchu conqueror of China. Away from the city it stands. We drove thither in droshkies which crawled gingerly one minute through liquid mud up to the axle, and the next swayed and bumped over ruts and boulders. What matter? We arrived at the magnificence of the Tomb. With unwonted piety, Chang Tso Lin had had it freshly painted the vermilion which is the colour symbolical of supreme emotion in China, whether joy or solemnity. The heavy yellow tiles rested their glorious gold on top of the red walls. Around lay a forest of green trees. The sky glowed overhead. Colour filled the eye and soul.

Past the stone replicas of the dead monarch's horses and dogs; past the stone elephants which tradition sets sentinel for an emperor, as we might place a lion; through small gates set in mighty thick walls; under towering bastions, we walked. On one rampart we came upon the only other visitor to the Tomb that day: a short young man who eyed us shyly. He hardly seemed Chinese, yet his native-cut suit of rough blue serge betokened decent Oriental poverty. We spoke together: and lo, he was Japanese! He answered us in Chinese worse than our own. "I am a government student," he said, bowing and sucking his breath as Japanese politeness enjoins. He vouchsafed more.

"I am a student at the government architectural school in Tokyo," he said and bowed again. We bowed also. "And I won a scholarship to come and study the ancient architecture of China."

How excellent a thought! "We hope you admire it?" we queried. He turned to east and to west: he looked down the length of the paved and tiled central court: he gazed at the yellow porcelain bulls' heads on the curving roofs.

"How can I not admire it?" he returned simply. "Is it not very beautiful?"

We bought picture postcards at a small pavilion off the side of the main massif, kept by a guardian appointed for the purpose. We looked at a notice probably, alas, unique in China, which said that this was a burial-place of kings, therefore conduct should be seemly. We sat to eat our picnic lunch at

By permission of T. Butler, Esq., F.R.G.S.

Great Wall of China

the foot of a large stone slab reared on the back of a stone tortoise. Three of us were there, our hostess and my mother and myself. As we were finishing, there came steps and, through a white-painted archway in one of the vermilion walls, walked a Chinese soldier. A sergeant he was, and followed by his corporal : come to inspect the guard. He was walking at his ease. He saw us : he stopped. Then he came swiftly on towards us, as we sat.

" Ah ! " he cried, and shook us each one warmly by the hand, to our surprise. " Ah ! " he cried again, and turned to his corporal. " Now that is the way to greet foreigners. It is a good thing I know. When we were in Tientsin last winter, chasing Wu Pei Fu, I saw a number of them there : and that was always how they greeted each other."

He then shook hands with us again, raising us to our feet in his access of friendship. He beamed at us. His teeth were perfect. He carried himself well, shoulders back. His uniform was clean, his buttons polished. He told us later that, if he was to be a soldier at all, he intended to be as good a one as he could—" like the soldiers of the Outside Kingdoms over the sea," he put it.

Who could have withstood his charm ? None of us there that day.

" We have been eating a little convenient food," explained our hostess presently. " How sorry I am that we have almost none left, or wc would have invited the Elder Born and the Young Brother to share with us."

He was interested at once, and looked at the remains of our feast. " What a pity ! " he agreed. " I have never tasted foreign food."

" Then please at least try it ! " said she. " See, this is a piece of what we call cake : it is made from hen's eggs, wheat-flour, and dried grapes. And this drink is made from lemons, which are like oranges but more sharp in flavour.

He took the cake doubtfully into his hand. He broke a piece off and handed it to his corporal. He squared his shoulders, and then cried gaily : " See ! I eat it ! I have no fear."

After munching a moment, he sipped a mouthful of

lemonade from the cup of the thermos flask : then passed it on to his corporal. He decided that cake and lemonade were fit foods, and he finished them off, sharing faithfully with his subordinate.

Friendliness radiated from him. It seemed to fill the silent vermilion courtyard, where once the body of a dead emperor had passed. As he ate the morsel of our food and sipped of our cup, the Presence brooded upon us, more Real than reality—lucid, living, warm as the clear pure sky above. It seemed very fitting that our friend should produce from her basket two coloured cards for them, one of which was a picture of the Good Samaritan raising the flask to the lips of the wounded man. Seriously the sergeant took it from her. She explained it simply, with the short legend below. " Ah! " he said, " I have heard of this. It is what foreign soldiers do for each other, and even for the enemy, when wounded in battle. It is very good."

He put the card in his breast pocket, handed the other to his man, clicked his heels, saluted, and was just going off.

" Ah yah ! I nearly forgot your honourable customs," he said, returning : and shook hands long and steadily with each of us, beginning at the oldest.

" The Sage wears coarse garments, but carries a jewel in his bosom," said Lao Tzŭ.

" *Man man tsou*—walk away slowly ! " we gave him good-bye.

A last flashing smile, and he and his follower had marched across the sunlit flagged court, and were gone.

" The best soldiers are not warlike," said Lao Tzŭ : " the best fighters do not lose their tempers."

" Good men are a fence," says one of the odes of classical China.

But there is in Moukden a glory of to-day which vies with that of the Tomb of yesterday, though in a different way. One morning I journeyed to the other side of the city to visit three medical women from the West, and stayed to tiffin. Their work was beyond praise, their hospital a model of thoughtful skill and economy. But no less lovely than their toil among sick Chinese women, was a scene which is daily enacted in their drawing-room after tiffin. As they come and go, get married or go on leave—or fall sick—these medical women fall heirs to a small family of Chinese children: girls, of course.

"Allow me to introduce our daughters," said one slender Scotch girl laughing. At that moment, two small Chinese children made for her with shrieks of joy. She fell into a chair. They scrambled over her while she showed them pictures in tattered fragments of *Punch*. Six others squatted on the floor or attached themselves to the other ladies and myself. I bethought me of my introduction on the river steamer to Little Cloud and Strong-as-a-Rock.

Girls they were, who had been found half-dead, thrown away into the millet; children born to people terribly poor. Till they learn to unbind their feet, girls can do little to earn their way in life. They are purely burdens. Ah, Miss Wu, you are going to alter that, are you not: and Miss Lo and Blossom too? A wail from a patch of tall grain, and how can a Scotch or any other Occidental woman leave a baby to die? Sometimes the foundlings were in a shocking condition, their eyes, their noses and ears full of flies or grubs; even their mouths. One child had rubbed its shoulders sore almost to the bone with its helpless fight for life, pleading with astonishing strength in its voice for some one to pick it up from the hard ground. Some had been deposited on the hospital doorstep. Whenever possible parents are traced. Such disposal of infants is discouraged. But always there is a residue who must perish unless adopted. Some of the foundlings have grown into noble women. They have chosen nursing, or teaching; and they often marry well, for they have had schooling. None of them has ever made her benefactresses wish they had not stooped to lift her hapless unwanted head from the grave which gaped for her.

"Ahma brings them in like this every day," explained one of the older women doctors. "Then we can keep an eye on their health." Out of their modest stipends, they paid a woman between them to see to the children. They have given up one of their precious studies as a nursery. But her eyes twinkled as a fat infant, whose rosy cheeks and sturdy legs spoke of health, drew attention to its new shoes by putting its foot on her knee. Another sang a song in her ear.

"Mostly she brings them because you enjoy their engaging company!" I taxed her; and she did not deny it. I told her of a certain Buddhist nun in Hangchow to whom Buddha in his mercy had sent a daughter.

I recalled three Graces I had met in Nanking—American girls. I bethought me of Catholic sisters of many European nations, scattered over China. I sat back, and considered these three women of my own blood, one young, two older. Fine and keen of face they were, because of lives wholesomely and scrupulously lived: three Graces, if ever women were, despite the lines of self-discipline about their mouths. Now here were eight Chinese maidens, with ages ranging from two to five, burrowing into their Scotch knees and shoulders like bees into honey-cells. The neat old-maidish room, its furniture handed down from one generation of women doctors to another, was now a litter of children, picture-books and building-bricks. A thin high soprano prattle trembled through the air, as of the four-and-twenty baked blackbirds joyously twittering because their pie was opened. "Mrs. Sung would have liked this sight," I thought. "I wish she were here. She would have liked these women. And they would have liked her."

In praise of one of the princesses of China long ago it was written: "She served her mother-in-law as if she had been her mother; her husband as if he had been a guest. She acted with such beautiful gentleness to all that even her sisters-in-law were harmonious. And she treated with considerate kindness the young, the timid, and the lowly."

A vision rose before my mind of the last time I had seen Mrs. Sung: in the silver dusk, on the sandy lane. Her rickshawman was mopping his neck. She was brushing with her lips the crumpled palm of sleepy Little Cloud, bending her face down to that other softer face.

Here in Manchuria three Scotch women were laying tender cheeks on the round black heads of Chinese babes. Not so very unlike, are they all?

Ecce ancilla Domini—Behold, the handmaid of the Lord!

Reverence and courtesy—that is, *li*—neither fall from Heaven, nor spring out of Earth, but are born of human relationships: so runs a line in a Chinese classic.